THEMES AND VARIATIONS
A College Reader

THEMES AND VARIATIONS
A College Reader

W. Ross Winterowd
University of Southern California

Charlotte Preston
University of Southern California

HBJ

HARCOURT BRACE JOVANOVICH, PUBLISHERS
San Diego   New York   Chicago   Atlanta   Washington, D.C.
London   Sydney   Toronto

Contents

CHAPTER THREE
Expository Writing
141

CHAPTER FOUR

Argument and Persuasion

313

CHAPTER FIVE
Focus on Style
381

Alternate Table of Contents

Description

Explaining

Evidence

First Person Perspective

Introduction

The selections in this anthology were chosen because, in our opinion, they have much to say to students in the last half of the 1980s. Some of the pieces were written during the present decade, and others were written as much as two centuries ago, but all speak to us here and now.

Readers can use this book for a variety of purposes, the first of which is extremely important though not immediately "practical." At its best, reading immerses a person in *someone else's* world of ideas, forms, images, and metaphors. The act of reading is perhaps the most effective way to sense an "otherness"—to experience another mind, another realm of values, another human goal. But for such an experience to come about, the writing that readers become involved with must go beyond merely giving information. It must have its distinctive style; it must speak with a personal voice. There is considerable difference between *The World Almanac*, that useful collection of "the facts and nothing but the facts," and, for instance, John McPhee's fact-filled essay about New Jersey's Pine Barrens (pp. 182–89). Regardless of their ultimate purpose, the selections in this anthology do "speak" with human "voices," exhibiting the craftsmanship that integrates content and form into a unified, satisfying whole.

As its second purpose, *The Contemporary Reader* provides models for writers. As you know, writing develops from reading: people who read effectively and widely will either write well already or be *able to learn* to write well.

For just a moment, it might be worthwhile to think about writing as a game with a set of rules. The most obvious analogy is chess. The possible moves of chess pieces are narrowly defined, but the possible number of moves is astronomically large. By combining individual moves, the chess master develops a strategy and tactics, adjusting both as the game progresses, so that each game is a unique event.

Like the chess game, each piece of writing is a unique event that results from a writer's use of what might be called the "rules" of the writing game. The rules for chess are strictly and precisely defined, whereas most of the "rules" for writing are more like "rules of thumb" than rigid "laws." Nonetheless, writers create strategies or techniques that result in highly individual "voices," in personal styles.

Using the "rules" of the game, Ernest Hemingway wrote like this:

> It was a pleasant cafe, warm and clean and friendly, and I hung up my old waterproof on the coat rack and put my worn and weathered felt hat on the rack above the bench and ordered *café au lait*.
>
> —A *Moveable Feast*

And also using the "rules" of the game, William Faulkner wrote like this:

> This was the American dream: a sanctuary on the earth for individual man: a condition in which he could be free not only of the old established closed-corporation hierarchies of arbitrary power which had oppressed him as a mass, but free of that mass into which the hierarchies of church and state had compressed and held him individually thralled and impotent.   —*On Privacy: The American Dream,*
> —*What Happened to It?*

Each of these passages speaks with its own distinctive voice.

Writers use the available rules to develop their own ways of choosing words, forming sentences, organizing compositions, creating emphasis, and employing metaphor, irony, image, and allusion—all of which makes for their individual styles and enables them to communicate through writing.

From the selections included in this book, you can learn methods to use in your own writing. The selections in *The Contemporary Reader* are, then, models for imitation in just this sense: through working with them, through conscious analysis of their several qualities, you will increase your possibilities as a writer, that is, you will gain the ability to express yourself fully and effectively.

In this book, the universe of writing is divided into three large areas: *personal*, *informative*, and *persuasive*. This division is a convenient way of classifying pieces of writing, but it is not airtight, nor could it be. It may seem to you and others, for instance, that a selection classified as informative might well fit into the persuasive category, and so on. Nevertheless, the present organization allows for a systematic approach to some of the important techniques and concepts of writing.

What, you may ask, is the basis for classifying the selections in this book as *personal*, *informative*, and *persuasive*? Why do we consider one piece of writing informative and another persuasive? We base this distinction on what we think the *purpose* of the writing is. For instance, if we assume that a piece of writing is intended to give us knowledge about a subject, we classify the writing as informative. (Textbooks are examples of informative writing, as are sets of instructions and directions; newspapers and most magazines contain largely informative writing; scientific and business reports are usually informative writing.) Persuasive writing, on the other hand, is intended to change opinions and bring about action. (Advertisements always have persuasive ends, as do political speeches and many editorials.) Personal writing—as in journals and diaries—is the writer's attempt to discover his or her self; it is often a means of "getting something off the writer's chest."

A typical reaction to successful informative writing might be, "I didn't know that before. I've certainly learned something from this piece." And to persuasive writing: "You've certainly changed my mind about that, and I'll take appropriate action." Finally, to personal writing: "Through this piece I've gotten to know the author much better."

Another way of viewing the categories is to think of relationships. All writing presumes a relationship between a writer, subject matter, and a reader. In personal writing, the dominant relationship is *writer to self*. In informative writing, it is *writer to subject matter*. In persuasive writing, it is *writer to reader*. It is important to recognize that these relationships are not rigidly separated in practice. Most writers are simultaneously concerned to satisfy themselves, to deal honestly with their subject matter, and to reach their readers, better known as their audience. For example, the persuasive writer is not only interested in convincing an audience, he or she is also concerned to treat his or her subject adequately and to achieve a satisfying level of self-expression.

Self-expression in writing involves *technique*: the ability to use effective sentences, appropriate diction, acceptable grammar, and so on. But it also—and more importantly—involves *rhetoric*: the ability to adjust to intended readers, to argue convincingly (with adequate evidence and "good reasons"), and to adopt an appropriate "tone." The questions that follow each selection in this book will help you gain both technical and rhetorical skill.

But we would like to end where we began, with the idea that reading is both instructive and pleasurable not only because of the information you gain from books and other print media, but also because through reading you can achieve that sense of otherness, a vision of the thoughts, values, and motives of another human being.

CHAPTER ONE

On the Writing Process

$\mathbf{A}$s you know, the writing process
is usually intense, demanding all of one's mental energy and attention. It is also messy and unpredictable.

One of the editors of this book has written,

> After intensive work, massive reading, and unsystematic mulling, I get
> the sense that I have come to a conclusion, that I have arrived at an
> insight. The point, then, is to develop a strategy that will give that
> insight meaning for someone other than myself. I agree with Kenneth
> Burke[1] and Morris Raphael Cohen,[2] among others, that we reach our
> conclusions by nonlogical processes and then use "logic" afterward to
> explain or justify them. In my own case, that logic takes place only
> after I begin to write; after I've sorted categories, arranged hierarchies,
> and developed arguments. There is no way that I could make sense
> without the tedium of "illogical" drafts that spill ideas out almost as
> they occur to me. . . .
>
> When I am clattering away on my IBM-PC . . . my wife asks me,
> "Are you typing or writing?" The import is something like this: "Do
> you know pretty much what you want to say so that I can interrupt
> you?" or "Are you conceptualizing as you type?" This distinction is
> important to me. . . .
>
> The difference, I think, can be traced to what might be called a
> sort of appropriation. I need somehow to make the subject mine, not
> in the intellectual sense, but in a much more personal way. I need to
> contextualize my work and make it relate to my world, to the people,
> quiddities, activities, scenes, smells, sounds, customs, textures . . . of
> what I take to be me.

---

[1] Kenneth Burke is an American thinker, literary critic, and philosopher of language.
[2] Morris Raphael Cohen was a professor of philosophy at the City College of New York. He is the author of
the influential book *A Preface to Logic*.

You see, I know for a fact that I cannot intellectualize until I have lived through my thoughts.

That, I think, is one of the main points about writing. Writing is the most human of actions; it forces the writer to live through his or her ideas and experiences, and to realize that the two are not strictly separable.

The essays in this section portray the frustrations and triumphs of writing, and they also demystify the writing process, for, as these professionals indicate, the ability to write is not a gift of the gods or simply a native talent embedded in someone's genetic codes; it is the result of hard work and motivation.

As you read the essays, you will begin to sense the multiplicity and complexity of reasons for writing. For example, Eldridge Cleaver says that he wrote to save himself. On the other hand, George Bernard Shaw confesses that he wrote "to earn his daily bread." And George Orwell lists four "great motives" for writing: sheer egoism, aesthetic enthusiasm, historical impulse, and political purpose; but in the essay he tells us also about discovering "the joy of mere words, i.e., the sounds and associations of words."

As you read the essays in this section, keep asking yourself the following questions: What insight regarding the writing process does this selection give me? How can this selection help me improve my own writing?

John Kenneth Galbraith

Writing, Typing, and Economics

A supremely skilled essayist, John Kenneth Galbraith has for years been one of America's leading intellectuals. Born in Canada in 1908, he completed his education in the United States, where he has since worked and lived. After a stint, as a young man, teaching economics at Harvard and Princeton, he worked a while for a U.S. government agency during World War II and then as an editor on Fortune *magazine. In 1949 he returned to Harvard as a professor of economics, from whence he was called to serve as adviser to President John F. Kennedy and later as U.S. ambassador to India. Galbraith has published extensively on a wide variety of topics, although he is still best known for his book on economic and social policy.* The Affluent Society.*

Features of the present essay that you might notice are its tone—that is, the attitude of the author to his subject matter (e.g., ironic, detached, concerned, or solemn)—and its style (sentence structure, choice of words, and use of figurative language, such as metaphor). If you have seen Galbraith on television, you might feel that this essay is typical of the way he handles a serious topic with wit and grace. You should also think carefully about the advice that he gives writers.

Six or seven years ago, when I was spending a couple of terms at Trinity College, Cambridge, I received a proposal of more than usual interest from the University of California. It was that I resign from Harvard and accept a chair there in English. More precisely, it was to be the chair in rhetoric; they assured me that rhetoric was a traditional and not, as one would naturally suppose, a pejorative title. My task would be to hold seminars with the young on what I had learned about writing in general and on technical matters in particular.

I was attracted by the idea. I had spent several decades attempting to teach the young about economics. And the practical consequences were not reassuring. When I entered the field in the early 1930s, it was generally known that the modern economy could suffer a serious depression, and that it could have a serious inflation. In the ensuing forty years my teaching had principally advanced to the point of telling that it was possible to have both at once. This was soon to be associated with the belief of William Simon and Alan Greenspan, the gifts of Richard Nixon and Gerald Ford to our science, that progress in this subject is measured by the speed of the return to the ideas of the eighteenth century. A subject where it can be believed that you go ahead by going back has many problems for a teacher. Things are better now. Mr. Carter's economists do not believe in going back. But they are caught in a delicate balance between their fear of inflation and unemployment and their fear of doing anything about them.

It is hard to conclude that economics is a productive intellectual and pedagogical investment.

Then I began to consider what I could tell about writing. My experience was certainly ample. I had been initiated by two inspired professors in Canada, O. J. Stevenson and E. C. McLean. They were men who deeply loved their craft and who were willing to spend endless hours with a student, however obscure his talent. I had been an editor of *Fortune*, which in my day meant mostly being a writer. Editor was thought a more distinguished title and justified more pay. Both as an editor proper and as a writer, I had had the close attention of Henry Robinson Luce. Harry Luce is in danger of being remembered for his political judgments, which left much to be desired; he found unblemished merit in John Foster Dulles, Robert A. Taft, and Chiang Kai-shek.[1] But more important, he was an acute businessman and a truly brilliant editor. One proof is that while Time, Inc. publications have become politically more predictable since he departed, they have become infinitely less amusing.

Finally, as I reflected, among my qualifications was the amount of my life that I have spent at a typewriter. Nominally I have been a teacher. In practice I have been a writer—as generations of Harvard students have suspected. Faced with the choice of spending time on the unpublished scholarship of a graduate student or the unpublished work of Galbraith, I have rarely hesitated. Superficially, at least, I was well qualified for that California chair.

There was, however, a major difficulty. It was that I could tell everything I knew about writing in approximately half an hour. For the rest of the term I would have nothing to say except as I could invite discussion, this being the last resort of the empty academic mind. I could use up a few hours telling how a writer should deal with publishers. This is a field of study in which I especially rejoice. All authors should seek to establish a relationship of warmth, affection, and mutual mistrust with their publishers. This is in the hope that the uncertainty will add, however marginally, to compensation. But instruction on how to deal with publishers and how to bear up under the inevitable defeat would be for a very advanced course. It is not the sort of thing that the average beginning writer at Berkeley would find immediately practical.

So I returned to the few things that I could teach. The first lesson would have to do with the all-important issue of inspiration. All writers know that on some golden mornings they are touched by the wand—are on intimate terms with poetry and cosmic truth. I have experienced those

---

[1]John Foster Dulles was Secretary of State under President Eisenhower. Robert A. Taft was U.S. Senator from Ohio and son of President Willam Howard Taft. Chiang Kai-shek was the leader of anticommunist forces in China. Each of these men was considered an archconservative.

moments myself. Their lesson is simple: It's a total illusion. And the danger in the illusion is that you will wait for those moments. Such is the horror of having to face the typewriter that you will spend all your time waiting. I am persuaded that most writers, like most shoemakers, are about as good one day as the next (a point which Trollope[2] made), hangovers apart. The difference is the result of euphoria, alcohol, or imagination. The meaning is that one had better go to his or her typewriter every morning and stay there regardless of the seeming result. It will be much the same.

All professions have their own ways of justifying laziness. Harvard professors are deeply impressed by the jeweled fragility of their minds. More than the thinnest metal, these are subject terribly to fatigue. More than six hours teaching a week is fatal—and an impairment of academic freedom. So, at any given moment, they are resting their minds in preparation for the next orgiastic act of insight or revelation. Writers, in contrast, do nothing because they are waiting for inspiration.

In my own case there are days when the result is so bad that no fewer than five revisions are required. However, when I'm greatly inspired, only four revisions are needed before, as I've often said, I put in that note of spontaneity which even my meanest critics concede. My advice to those eager students in California would be, "Do not wait for the golden moment. It may well be worse." I would also warn against the flocking tendency of writers and its use as a cover for idleness. It helps greatly in the avoidance of work to be in the company of others who are also waiting for the golden moment. The best place to write is by yourself, because writing becomes an escape from the terrible boredom of your own personality. It's the reason that for years I've favored Switzerland, where I look at the telephone and yearn to hear it ring.

The question of revision is closely allied with that of inspiration. There may be inspired writers for whom the first draft is just right. But anyone who is not certifiably a Milton had better assume that the first draft is a very primitive thing. The reason is simple: Writing is difficult work. Ralph Paine, who managed *Fortune* in my time, used to say that anyone who said writing was easy was either a bad writer or an unregenerate liar. Thinking, as Voltaire[3] avowed, is also a very tedious thing which men—or women—will do anything to avoid. So all first drafts are deeply flawed by the need to combine composition with thought. Each later draft is less demanding in this regard. Hence the writing can be better. There does come a time when revision is for the sake of change—when one has

---

[2]Anthony Trollope was a popular nineteenth-century English author; several of his novels made up the TV series called *The Pallisers*.
[3]Voltaire was a French satirist of the eighteenth century; author of *Candide*.

become so bored with the words that anything that is different looks better. But even then it may be better.

For months in 1955–1956, when I was working on *The Affluent Society,* my title was "The Opulent Society." Eventually I could stand it no longer: the word opulent had a nasty, greasy sound. One day, before starting work, I looked up the synonyms in the dictionary. First to meet my eye was the word "affluent." I had only one worry; that was whether I could possibly sell it to the publisher. All publishers wish to have books called *The Crisis in American Democracy.* My title, to my surprise, was acceptable. Mark Twain once said that the difference between the right adjective and the next-best adjective is the difference between lightning and a lightning bug.

Next, I would stress a rather old-fashioned idea to those students. It was above all the lesson of Harry Luce. No one who worked for him ever again escaped the feeling that he was there looking over one's shoulder. In his hand was a pencil; down on each page one could expect, any moment, a long swishing wiggle accompanied by the comment: "This can go." Invariably it could. It was written to please the author and not the reader. Or to fill in the space. The gains from brevity are obvious; in most efforts to achieve brevity, it is the worst and dullest that goes. It is the worst and dullest that spoils the rest.

I know that brevity is now out of favor. The *New York Review of Books*[4] prides itself on giving its authors as much space as they want and sometimes twice as much as they need. Even those who have read only Joyce[5] must find their thoughts wandering before the end of the fortnightly article. Writing for television, I've learned in the last year or two, is an exercise in relentless condensation. It has left me with the feeling that even brevity can be carried to extremes. But the danger, as I look at some of the newer fashions in writing, is not great.

The next of my injunctions, which I would impart with even less hope of success, would concern alcohol. Nothing is so pleasant. Nothing is so important for giving the writer a sense of confidence in himself. And nothing so impairs the product. Again there are exceptions: I remember a brilliant writer at *Fortune* for whom I was responsible, who could work only with his hat on and after consuming a bottle of Scotch. There were major crises in the years immediately after World War II, when Scotch was difficult to find. But it is, quite literally, very sobering to reflect upon how many good American writers have been destroyed by this solace—by the sauce. Scott Fitzgerald, Sinclair Lewis, Thomas Wolfe, Ernest Heming-

---

[4]*New York Review of Books* is a prestigious literary journal.
[5]James Joyce is considered one of the great writers of the twentieth century and extremely difficult to read.

way, William Faulkner[6]—the list goes on and on. Hamish Hamilton, once my English publisher, put the question to James Thurber:[7] "Jim, why is it so many of your great writers have ruined themselves with drink?" Thurber thought long and carefully and finally replied: "It's this way, Jamie. They wrote these novels, and they sold very well. They made a lot of money and so they could buy whiskey by the case."

Their reputation was universal. A few years before his death, John Steinbeck, an appreciative but not a compulsive drinker, went to Moscow. It was a triumphal tour; and in a letter that he sent me about his hosts, he said: "I found I enjoyed the Soviet hustlers pretty much. There was a kind of youthful honesty about their illicit intentions that was not without charm. And their lives are difficult under their four-party system [a reference that escapes me]. It takes a fairly deft or very lucky man to make his way upward in the worker's paradise." I later heard that one night, after a particularly effusive celebration, he decided to make his way back to the hotel on foot. On the way he was overcome by fatigue and the hospitality he had received and sat down on a bench in a small park to rest. A policeman, called a militiaman in Moscow, came along and informed John, who was now asleep, and his companion, who spoke Russian, that the benches could not be occupied at that hour. His companion explained, rightly, that John was a very great American writer and that an exception should be made. The militiaman insisted. The companion explained again, insisted more strongly. Presently a transcendental light came over the policeman's face. He looked at Steinbeck asleep on the bench, inspected his condition more closely, recoiled slightly from the fumes, and said, "Oh, oh, Gemingway." Then he took off his cap and tiptoed carefully away.

We are all desperately afraid of sounding like Carry Nation. I must take the risk. Any writer who wants to do his best against a deadline should stick to Coca-Cola. If he doesn't have a deadline, he can risk Seven-Up.

Next, I would want to tell my students of a point strongly pressed, if my memory serves, by Shaw. He once said that as he grew older, he became less and less interested in theory, more and more interested in information. The temptation in writing is just the reverse. Nothing is so hard to come by as a new and interesting fact. Nothing is so easy on the feet as a generalization. I now pick up magazines and leaf through them looking for articles that are rich with facts; I do not care much what they are. Richly evocative and deeply percipient theory I avoid. It leaves me cold unless I am the author of it. My advice to all young writers is to stick

---

[6] F. Scott Fitzgerald, Sinclair Lewis, Thomas Wolfe, Ernest Hemingway, William Faulkner are all considered major American writers of the twentieth century.
[7] James Thurber was a great American humorist.

to research and reporting with only a minimum of interpretation. And especially this is my advice to all older writers, particularly to columnists. As the feet give out, they seek to have the mind take their place.

Reluctantly, but from a long and terrible experience, I would urge my young writers to avoid all attempts at humor. It does greatly lighten one's task. I've often wondered who made it impolite to laugh at one's own jokes; it is one of the major enjoyments of life. And that is the point. Humor is an intensely personal, largely internal thing. What pleases some, including the source, does not please others. One laughs; another says, "Well, I certainly see nothing funny about that." And the second opinion has just as much standing as the first, maybe more. Where humor is concerned, there are no standards—no one can say what is good or bad, although you can be sure that everyone will. Only a very foolish man will use a form of language that is wholly uncertain in its effect. That is the nature of humor.

There are other reasons for avoiding humor. In our society the solemn person inspires far more trust than the one who laughs. The politician allows himself one joke at the beginning of his speech. A ritual. Then he changes his expression, affects an aspect of morbid solemnity signaling that, after all, he is a totally serious man. Nothing so undermines a point as its association with a wisecrack—the very word is pejorative.

Also, as Art Buchwald has pointed out, we live in an age when it is hard to invent anything that is as funny as everyday life. How could one improve, for example, on the efforts of the great men of television to attribute cosmic significance to the offhand and hilarious way Bert Lance[8] combined professed fiscal conservatism with an unparalleled personal commitment to the deficit financing of John Maynard Keynes?[9] And because the real world is so funny, there is almost nothing you can do, short of labeling a joke a joke, to keep people from taking it seriously. A few years ago in *Harper's* I invented the theory that socialism in our time was the result of our dangerous addiction to team sports. The ethic of the team is all wrong for free enterprise. The code words are cooperation; team spirit; accept leadership; the coach is always right. Authoritarianism is sanctified; the individualist is a poor team player, a menace. All this our vulnerable adolescents learn. I announced the formation of an organization to combat this deadly trend and to promote boxing and track instead. I called it the C.I.A.—Congress for Individualist Athletics. Hundreds wrote in to *Harper's* asking to join. Or demanding that baseball be exempted. A batter is on his own. I presented the letters to the Kennedy Library.

Finally, I would come to a matter of much personal interest, intensely

---

[8]Bert Lance was Director of Office of Management and the Budget under President Jimmy Carter.
[9]John Maynard Keynes was a highly influential English economist of the first half of the twentieth century.

self-serving. It concerns the peculiar pitfalls of the writer who is dealing with presumptively difficult or technical matters. Economics is an example, and within the field of economics the subject of money, with the history of which I have been much concerned, is an especially good case. Any specialist who ventures to write on money with a view to making himself intelligible works under a grave moral hazard. He will be accused of oversimplification. The charge will be made by his fellow professionals, however obtuse or incompetent. They will have a sympathetic hearing from the layman. That is because no layman really expects to understand about money, inflation, or the International Monetary Fund. If he does, he suspects that he is being fooled. One can have respect only for someone who is decently confusing.

In the case of economics there are no important propositions that cannot be stated in plain language. Qualifications and refinements are numerous and of great technical complexity. These are important for separating the good students from the dolts. But in economics the refinements rarely, if ever, modify the essential and practical point. The writer who seeks to be intelligible needs to be right; he must be challenged if his argument leads to an erroneous conclusion and especially if it leads to the wrong action. But he can safely dismiss the charge that he has made the subject too easy. The truth is not difficult.

Complexity and obscurity have professional value—they are the academic equivalents of apprenticeship rules in the building trades. They exclude the outsiders, keep down the competition, preserve the image of a privileged or priestly class. The man who makes things clear is a scab. He is criticized less for his clarity than for his treachery.

Additionally, and especially in the social sciences, much unclear writing is based on unclear or incomplete thought. It is possible with safety to be technically obscure about something you haven't thought out. It is impossible to be wholly clear on something you do not understand. Clarity thus exposes flaws in the thought. The person who undertakes to make difficult matters clear is infringing on the sovereign right of numerous economists, sociologists, and political scientists to make bad writing the disguise for sloppy, imprecise, or incomplete thought. One can understand the resulting anger. Adam Smith, John Stuart Mill,[10] John Maynard Keynes were writers of crystalline clarity most of the time. Marx had great moments, as in *The Communist Manifesto*. Economics owes very little, if anything, to the practitioners of scholarly obscurity. If any of my California students should come to me from the learned professions, I would counsel

---

[10]Adam Smith was an English economist of the eighteenth century; John Stuart Mill was an English philosopher of the nineteenth century.

them in all their writing to keep the confidence of their colleagues. This they should do by being always complex, always obscure, invariably a trifle vague.

You might say that all this constitutes a meager yield for a lifetime of writing. Or that writing on economics, as someone once said of Kerouac's prose, is not writing but typing. True.

QUESTIONS

1. Did you find the essay easy or difficult to read? Explain. (Think of the length or complexity of the sentences, your familiarity with the vocabulary and the references that Galbraith includes, and the clarity with which the author explains concepts.)
2. Galbraith presents eight pieces of advise for writers. The first two might be stated as "Don't wait for inspiration" and "Isolate yourself." What are the other six?
3. Is the author completely serious about all eight? Explain.
4. In the last paragraph, Galbraith says that writing on economics is not writing, but typing. Explain what he means?
5. What myths or misconceptions about writing does Galbraith hope to counter with his advice?
6. Characterize the author's attitude in this essay—its tone. Is it deadly serious? Tongue-in-cheek? Playful? Ironic? Sarcastic? Cite specific passages or sections of the essay that illustrate and support your characterization.
7. Explain why you think the tone is appropriate for readers of the *Atlantic*, the magazine in which the essay was first published. (If you are unfamiliar with the *Atlantic*, spend a few minutes thumbing through a recent copy in the reading room of your public or college library.)

GEORGE ORWELL
Why I Write

George Orwell (the pseudonym of Eric Blair) had a varied career. He is best known, of course, as the author of 1984, *that frighteningly anti-utopian novel that projected what came to be regarded as the classic image of big government—Big Brother— and, in fact, the term "Big Brother" comes from the novel. Orwell's essays are generally regarded as superb, and three of them—"A Hanging," "Shooting an Elephant," and "Politics and the English Language"—have been reprinted again and again.*

Born in India in 1903, Orwell attended Eton and upon graduation served five years in Burma as an officer in the Indian Imperial Police. "Shooting an Elephant" and "A Hanging" derive from that experience. In 1927 he returned to Europe and lived first in Paris and then in London, a period that he recorded in Down and Out in Paris and London *(1933). During this period and subsequently he wrote mainly for socialist journals. In 1936, he joined the socialist forces fighting on the Republican side in the Spanish Civil War and was seriously wounded. After his recovery he continued writing and in 1946 published* Animal Farm, *a novel-length fable satirizing authoritarian, especially Communist, government. He died in 1950, shortly after completing* 1984.

In the essay reprinted here, Orwell explores both his personal and his public motives for writing. Writing satisfied his ego, but it also gave him a way to affect the politics of his time—and as we just saw in the above paragraph, he was an intensely political being.

Widely admired as a clear, graceful writer, Orwell is, in fact, considered one of the great prose stylists of the English language, and his idea of what makes for good writing clearly emerges from this essay. As you read, you might keep this question in mind: What are Orwell's standards for good writing?

From a very early age, perhaps the age of five or six, I knew that when I grew up I should be a writer. Between the ages of about seventeen and twenty-four I tried to abandon this idea, but I did so with the consciousness that I was outraging my true nature and that sooner or later I should have to settle down and write books.

I was the middle child of three, but there was a gap of five years on either side, and I barely saw my father before I was eight. For this and other reasons I was somewhat lonely, and I soon developed disagreeable manner-isms which made me unpopular throughout my schooldays. I had the lonely child's habit of making up stories and holding conversations with imaginary persons, and I think from the very start my literary ambitions were mixed up with the feeling of being isolated and undervalued. I knew that I had a facility with words and a power of facing unpleasant facts, and I felt that this created a sort of private world in which I could get my own

back for my failure in everyday life. Nevertheless the volume of serious—
i.e. seriously intended—writing which I produced all through my childhood and boyhood would not amount to half a dozen pages. I wrote my
first poem at the age of four or five, my mother taking it down to dictation.
I cannot remember anything about it except that it was about a tiger and
the tiger had "chair-like teeth"—a good enough phrase, but I fancy the
poem was a plagiarism of Blake's "Tiger, Tiger". At eleven, when the war
of 1914–18 broke out, I wrote a patriotic poem which was printed in the
local newspaper, as was another, two years later, on the death of Kitchener.
From time to time, when I was a bit older, I wrote bad and usually
unfinished "nature poems" in the Georgian style.[1] I also, about twice,
attempted a short story which was a ghastly failure. That was the total of
the would-be serious work that I actually set down on paper during all
those years.

However, throughout this time I did in a sense engage in literary
activities. To begin with there was the made-to-order stuff which I produced quickly, easily and without much pleasure to myself. Apart from
school work, I wrote *vers d'occasion*, semi-comic poems which I could turn
out at what now seems to me astonishing speed—at fourteen I wrote a
whole rhyming play, in imitation of Aristophanes, in about a week—and
helped to edit school magazines, both printed and in manuscript. These
magazines were the most pitiful burlesque stuff that you could imagine,
and I took far less trouble with them than I now would with the cheapest
journalism. But side by side with all this, for fifteen years or more, I was
carrying out a literary exercise of a quite different kind: this was the making
up of a continuous "story" about myself, a sort of diary existing only in the
mind. I believe this is a common habit of children and adolescents. As a
very small child I used to imagine that I was, say, Robin Hood, and picture
myself as the hero of thrilling adventures, but quite soon my "story" ceased
to be narcissistic in a crude way and became more and more a mere
description of what I was doing and the things I saw. For minutes at a time
this kind of thing would be running through my head: "He pushed the
door open and entered the room. A yellow beam of sunlight, filtering
through the muslin curtains, slanted on to the table, where a matchbox,
half open, lay beside the inkpot. With his right hand in his pocket he
moved across to the window. Down in the street a tortoiseshell cat was
chasing a dead leaf," etc etc. This habit continued till I was about twenty-
five, right through my non-literary years. Although I had to search, and
did search, for the right words, I seemed to be making this descriptive effort

---

[1] "Georgian" here refers to a group of poets who were published during the early years of King George V's reign (1910–1936).

almost against my will, under a kind of compulsion from outside. The "story" must, I suppose, have reflected the styles of the various writers I admired at different ages, but so far as I remember it always had the same meticulous descriptive quality.

When I was about sixteen I suddenly discovered the joy of mere words, i.e. the sounds and associations of words. The lines from *Paradise Lost*,

> So hee with difficulty and labour hard
> Moved on: with difficulty and labour hee,

which do not now seem to me so very wonderful, sent shivers down my backbone; and the spelling "hee" for "he" was an added pleasure. As for the need to describe things, I knew all about it already. So it is clear what kind of books I wanted to write, in so far as I could be said to want to write books at that time. I wanted to write enormous naturalistic novels with unhappy endings, full of detailed descriptions and arresting similes, and also full of purple passages in which words were used partly for the sake of their sound. And in fact my first completed novel, *Burmese Days*, which I wrote when I was thirty but projected much earlier, is rather that kind of book.

I give all this background information because I do not think one can assess a writer's motives without knowing something of his early development. His subject matter will be determined by the age he lives in—at least this is true in tumultuous, revolutionary ages like our own—but before he ever begins to write he will have acquired an emotional attitude from which he will never completely escape. It is his job, no doubt, to discipline his temperament and avoid getting stuck at some immature stage, or in some perverse mood: but if he escapes from his early influences altogether, he will have killed his impulse to write. Putting aside the need to earn a living, I think there are four great motives for writing, at any rate for writing prose. They exist in different degrees in every writer, and in any one writer the proportions will vary from time to time, according to the atmosphere in which he is living. They are:

1. Sheer egoism. Desire to seem clever, to be talked about, to be remembered after death, to get your own back on grown-ups who snubbed you in childhood, etc etc. It is humbug to pretend that this is not a motive, and a strong one. Writers share this characteristic with scientists, artists, politicians, lawyers, soldiers, successful businessmen—in short, with the whole top crust of humanity. The great mass of human beings are not acutely selfish. After the age of about thirty they abandon individual ambition—in many cases, indeed, they almost abandon the sense of being individuals at all—and live chiefly for others, or are simply smothered under drudgery. But there is also the minority of gifted, willful people who

are determined to live their own lives to the end, and writers belong in this class. Serious writers, I should say, are on the whole more vain and self-centered than journalists, though less interested in money.

2. Aesthetic enthusiasm. Perception of beauty in the external world, or, on the other hand, in words and their right arrangement. Pleasure in the impact of one sound on another, in the firmness of good prose or the rhythm of a good story. Desire to share an experience which one feels is valuable and ought not to be missed. The aesthetic motive is very feeble in a lot of writers, but even a pamphleteer or a writer of textbooks will have pet words and phrases which appeal to him for non-utilitarian reasons; or he may feel strongly about typography, width of margins, etc. Above the level of a railway guide, no book is quite free from aesthetic considerations.

3. Historical impulse. Desire to see things as they are, to find out true facts and store them up for the use of posterity.

4. Political purpose—using the word "political" in the widest possible sense. Desire to push the world in a certain direction, to alter other people's idea of the kind of society that they should strive after. Once again, no book is genuinely free from political bias. The opinion that art should have nothing to do with politics is itself a political attitude.

It can be seen how these various impulses must war against one another, and how they must fluctuate from person to person and from time to time. By nature—taking your "nature" to be the state you have attained when you are first adult—I am a person in whom the first three motives would outweigh the fourth. In a peaceful age I might have written ornate or merely descriptive books, and might have remained almost unaware of my political loyalties. As it is I have been forced into becoming a sort of pamphleteer. First I spent five years in an unsuitable profession (the Indian Imperial Police, in Burma), and then I underwent poverty and the sense of failure. This increased my natural hatred of authority and made me for the first time fully aware of the existence of the working classes, and the job in Burma had given me some understanding of the nature of imperialism: but these experiences were not enough to give me an accurate political orientation. Then came Hitler, the Spanish civil war, etc. By the end of 1935 I had still failed to reach a firm decision. I remember a little poem that I wrote at that date, expressing my dilemma:

> A happy vicar I might have been
> Two hundred years ago,
> To preach upon eternal doom
> And watch my walnuts grow;
>
> But born, alas, in an evil time,
> I missed that pleasant haven,
> For the hair has grown on my upper lip
> And the clergy are all clean-shaven.

And later still the times were good,
We were so easy to please,
We rocked our troubled thoughts to sleep
On the bosoms of the trees.

All ignorant we dared to own
The joys we now dissemble;
The greenfinch on the apple bough
Could make my enemies tremble.

But girls' bellies and apricots,
Roach[2] in a shaded stream,
Horses, ducks in flight at dawn,
All these are a dream.

It is forbidden to dream again;
We maim our joys or hide them;
Horses are made of chromium steel
And little fat men shall ride them.

I am the worm who never turned,
The eunuch without a harem;
Between the priest and the commissar
I walk like Eugene Aram;[3]

And the commissar is telling my fortune
While the radio plays,
But the priest has promised an Austin Seven,
For Duggie[4] always pays.

I dreamed I dwelt in marble halls,
And woke to find it true;
I wasn't born for an age like this;
Was Smith? Was Jones? Were you?

The Spanish war and other events in 1936–37 turned the scale and thereafter I knew where I stood. Every line of serious work that I have written since 1936 has been written, directly or indirectly, *against* totalitarianism and *for* democratic Socialism, as I understand it. It seems to me nonsense, in a period like our own, to think that one can avoid writing of such subjects. Everyone writes of them in one guise or another. It is simply a question of which side one takes and what approach one follows. And the more one is conscious of one's political bias, the more chance one has of acting politically without sacrificing one's aesthetic and intellectual integrity.

---

[2]A roach is a fresh-water fish.
[3]Eugene Aram (1704–1759) was an English philologist (student of language) and murderer.
[4]The Austin Seven was a small, inexpensive auto, first introduced in 1922. "Duggie" is apparently a private reference. The meaning of the last two lines of the stanza is obscure.

What I have most wanted to do throughout the past ten years is to make political writing into an art. My starting point is always a feeling of partisanship, a sense of injustice. When I sit down to write a book, I do not say to myself, "I am going to produce a work of art." I write it because there is some lie that I want to expose, some fact to which I want to draw attention, and my initial concern is to get a hearing. But I could not do the work of writing a book, or even a long magazine article, if it were not also an aesthetic experience. Anyone who cares to examine my work will see that even when it is downright propaganda it contains much that a full-time politician would consider irrelevant. I am not able, and I do not want, completely to abandon the world-view that I acquired in childhood. So long as I remain alive and well I shall continue to feel strongly about prose style, to love the surface of the earth, and to take pleasure in solid objects and scraps of useless information. It is no use trying to suppress that side of myself. The job is to reconcile my ingrained likes and dislikes with the essentially public, non-individual activities that this age forces on all of us.

It is not easy. It raises problems of construction and of language, and it raises in a new way the problem of truthfulness. Let me give just one example of the cruder kind of difficulty that arises. My book about the Spanish civil war, *Homage to Catalonia*, is, of course, a frankly political book, but in the main it is written with a certain detachment and regard for form. I did try very hard in it to tell the whole truth without violating my literary instincts. But among other things it contains a long chapter, full of newspaper quotations and the like, defending the Trotskyists who were accused of plotting with Franco.[5] Clearly such a chapter, which after a year or two would lose its interest for any ordinary reader, must ruin the book. A critic whom I respect read me a lecture about it. "Why did you put in all that stuff?" he said. "You've turned what might have been a good book into journalism." What he said was true, but I could not have done otherwise. I happened to know, what very few people in England had been allowed to know, that innocent men were being falsely accused. If I had not been angry about that I should never have written the book.

In one form or another this problem comes up again. The problem of language is subtler and would take too long to discuss. I will only say that of late years I have tried to write less picturesquely and more exactly. In any case I find that by the time you have perfected any style of writing, you have always outgrown it. *Animal Farm* was the first book in which I tried, with full consciousness of what I was doing, to fuse political purpose and artistic purpose into one whole. I have not written a novel for seven years, but I hope to write another fairly soon. It is bound to be a failure, every

---

[5] The Trotskyists were followers of the Russian Marxist leader Leon Trotsky who were accused by the followers of the Soviet dictator, Joseph Stalin, of aiding and abetting the fascist forces under Generalissimo Francisco Franco in their attempt to conquer the city of Barcelona.

book is a failure, but I know with some clarity what kind of book I want to write.

Looking back through the last page or two, I see that I have made it appear as though my motives in writing were wholly public-spirited. I don't want to leave that as the final impression. All writers are vain, selfish and lazy, and at the very bottom of their motives there lies a mystery. Writing a book is a horrible, exhausting struggle, like a long bout of some painful illness. One would never undertake such a thing if one were not driven on by some demon whom one can neither resist nor understand. For all one knows that demon is simply the same instinct that makes a baby squall for attention. And yet it is also true that one can write nothing readable unless one constantly struggles to efface one's own personality. Good prose is like a window pane. I cannot say with certainty which of my motives are the strongest, but I know which of them deserve to be followed. And looking back through my work, I see that it is invariably where I lacked a *political* purpose that I wrote lifeless books and was betrayed into purple passages, sentences without meaning, decorative adjectives and humbug generally.

QUESTIONS

1. In your own words, but referring to the text, explain why Orwell became a writer.
2. Why does Orwell describe his early experiences with writing? What does he gain by this description?
3. In your opinion, what was Orwell's purpose in writing this essay?
4. In "Writing, Typing, and Economics," John Kenneth Galbraith presented direct advice about writing. Orwell's essay contains indirect advice. Summarize that advice. What can we learn about writing from "Why I Write"?
5. Orwell is known for his clear, readable prose. Did you find this essay easy to read? Why, or why not? As with Galbraith, think of the allusions as well as the language.
6. On page 20, Orwell says:

   So long as I remain alive and well I shall continue to feel strongly about prose style, to love the surface of the earth, and to take a pleasure in solid objects and scraps of useless information. It is no use trying to suppress that side of myself. The job is to reconcile my ingrained likes and dislikes with the essentially public, nonindividual activities that this age forces on all of us.

   In the next two paragraphs, he goes on to deal with this idea. In your own words, explain the attitude toward writing that Orwell discusses here. What writing problem does his attitude create?

JOAN DIDION

Why I Write

Joan Didion is a highly respected essayist whose work has been collected in
Slouching Towards Bethlehem *and* The White Album. *She is also a successful
novelist, author of* A Book of Common Prayer, Play It as It Lays, *and* River Run.

*She was born in Sacramento, California, in 1934. The year of her graduation
from the University of California at Berkeley, she married John Gregory Dunne,
himself now a successful novelist whose* True Confessions *was made into a popular
motion picture. Didion was associate feature editor for* Vogue *magazine from 1956
to 1963 and was a contributing editor to* National Review *for several years. With
her husband, she now lives in Malibu, California.*

*In the following essay, Joan Didion introduces a theme that we find again and
again in writers' accounts of their motives: "I write entirely to find out what I'm
thinking, what I'm looking at, what I see and what it means." For her, then, writing
is not only an aid to thinking and understanding; it is thinking and understanding.
In this opinion, Miss Didion echoes the work of modern philosophers such as Jacques
Derrida, who believe that there are no ideas prior to expression. Didion, then, is
quite different in belief from George Orwell, who thinks of writing primarily as a
means of conveying ideas, not of creating them.*

Of course I stole the title for this talk from George Orwell. One reason
I stole it was that I like the sound of the words: *Why I Write.* There you
have three short unambiguous words that share a sound, and the sound
they share is this:

I

I

I

In many ways writing is the act of saying *I,* of imposing oneself upon
other people, of saying *listen to me, see it my way, change your mind.* It's
an aggressive, even a hostile act. You can disguise its aggressiveness all you
want with veils of subordinate clauses and qualifiers and tentative subjunc-
tives, with ellipses and evasions—with the whole manner of intimating
rather than claiming, of alluding rather than stating—but there's no
getting around the fact that setting words on paper is the tactic of a secret
bully, an invasion, an imposition of the writer's sensibility on the reader's
most private space.

I stole the title not only because the words sounded right but because
they seemed to sum up, in a no-nonsense way, all I have to tell you. Like
many writers I have only this one "subject," this one "area": the act of

writing. I can bring you no reports from any other front. I may have other interests: I am "interested," for example, in marine biology, but I don't flatter myself that you would come out to hear me talk about it. I am not a scholar. I am not in the least an intellectual, which is not to say that when I hear the word "intellectual" I reach for my gun, but only to say that I do not think in abstracts. During the years when I was an undergraduate at Berkeley I tried, with a kind of hopeless late-adolescent energy, to buy some temporary visa into the world of ideas, to forge for myself a mind that could deal with the abstract.

In short I tried to think. I failed. My attention veered inexorably back to the specific, to the tangible, to what was generally considered, by everyone I knew then and for that matter have known since, the peripheral. I would try to contemplate the Hegelian dialectic[1] and would find myself concentrating instead on a flowering pear tree outside my window and the particular way the petals fell on my floor. I would try to read linguistic theory and would find myself wondering instead if the lights were on in the bevatron up the hill. When I say that I was wondering if the lights were on in the bevatron you might immediately suspect, if you deal in ideas at all, that I was registering the bevatron as a political symbol, thinking in shorthand about the military-industrial complex and its role in the university community, but you would be wrong. I was only wondering if the lights were on in the bevatron, and how they looked. A physical fact.

I had trouble graduating from Berkeley, not because of this inability to deal with ideas—I was majoring in English, and I could locate the house-and-garden imagery in *The Portrait of a Lady*[2] as well as the next person, "imagery" being by definition the kind of specific that got my attention—but simply because I had neglected to take a course in Milton. For reasons which now sound baroque I needed a degree by the end of that summer, and the English department finally agreed, if I would come down from Sacramento every Friday and talk about the cosmology of *Paradise Lost*, to certify me proficient in Milton. I did this. Some Fridays I took the Greyhound bus, other Fridays I caught the Southern Pacific's City of San Francisco on the last leg of its transcontinental trip. I can no longer tell you whether Milton put the sun or the earth at the center of his universe in *Paradise Lost*, the central question of at least one century and a topic about which I wrote 10,000 words that summer, but I can still recall the exact rancidity of the butter in the City of San Francisco's dining car, and the way the tinted windows on the Greyhound bus cast the oil refineries around Carquinez Straits into a grayed and obscurely sinister light. In short my attention was always on the periphery, on what I would see and taste

---

[1] A difficult concept of the nineteenth-century German philosopher, Georg Wilhem Friedrich Hegel.
[2] A novel by the American writer Henry James.

and touch, on the butter, and the Greyhound bus. During those years I was traveling on what I knew to be a very shaky passport, forged papers: I knew that I was no legitimate resident in any world of ideas. I knew I couldn't think. All I knew then was what I couldn't do. All I knew then was what I wasn't, and it took me some years to discover what I was.

Which was a writer.

By which I mean not a "good" writer or a "bad" writer but simply a writer, a person whose most absorbed and passionate hours are spent arranging words on pieces of paper. Had my credentials been in order I would never have become a writer. Had I been blessed with even limited access to my own mind there would have been no reason to write. I write entirely to find out what I'm thinking, what I'm looking at, what I see and what it means. What I want and what I fear. Why did the oil refineries around Carquinez Straits seem sinister to me in the summer of 1956? Why have the night lights in the bevatron burned in my mind for twenty years? *What is going on in these pictures in my mind?*

When I talk about pictures in my mind I am talking, quite specifically, about images that shimmer around the edges. There used to be an illustration in every elementary psychology book showing a cat drawn by a patient in varying stages of schizophrenia. This cat had a shimmer around it. You could see the molecular structure breaking down at the very edges of the cat: the cat became the background and the background the cat, everything interacting, exchanging ions. People on hallucinogens describe the same perception of objects. I'm not a schizophrenic, nor do I take hallucinogens, but certain images do shimmer for me. Look hard enough, and you can't miss the shimmer. It's there. You can't think too much about these pictures that shimmer. You just lie low and let them develop. You stay quiet. You don't talk to many people and you keep your nervous system from shorting out and you try to locate the cat in the shimmer, the grammar in the picture.

Just as I meant "shimmer" literally I mean "grammar" literally. Grammar is a piano I play by ear, since I seem to have been out of school the year the rules were mentioned. All I know about grammar is its infinite power. To shift the structure of a sentence alters the meaning of that sentence, as definitely and inflexibly as the position of a camera alters the meaning of the object photographed. Many people know about camera angles now, but not so many know about sentences. The arrangement of the words matters, and the arrangement you want can be found in the picture in your mind. The picture dictates the arrangement. The picture dictates whether this will be a sentence with or without clauses, a sentence that ends hard or a dying-fall sentence, long or short, active or passive. The picture tells you how to arrange the words and the arrangement of the words tells you, or tells me, what's going on in the picture. *Nota bene:*

It tells you.

You don't tell it.

Let me show you what I mean by pictures in the mind. I began *Play It as It Lays* just as I have begun each of my novels, with no notion of "character" or "plot" or even "incident." I had only two pictures in my mind, more about which later, and a technical intention, which was to write a novel so elliptical and fast that it would be over before you noticed it, a novel so fast that it would scarcely exist on the page at all. About the pictures: the first was of white space. Empty space. This was clearly the picture that dictated the narrative intention of the book—a book in which anything that happened would happen off the page, a "white" book to which the reader would have to bring his or her own bad dreams—and yet this picture told me no "story," suggested no situation. The second picture did. This second picture was of something actually witnessed. A young woman with long hair and a short white halter dress walks through the casino at the Riviera in Las Vegas at one in the morning. She crosses the casino alone and picks up a house telephone. I watch her because I have heard her paged, and recognize her name: she is a minor actress I see around Los Angeles from time to time, in places like Jax and once in a gynecologist's office in the Beverly Hills Clinic, but have never met. I know nothing about her. Who is paging her? Why is she here to be paged? How exactly did she come to this? It was precisely this moment in Las Vegas that made *Play It as It Lays* begin to tell itself to me, but the moment appears in the novel only obliquely, in the chapter which begins:

> Maria made a list of things she would never do. She would never: walk through the Sands or Caesar's alone after midnight. She would never: ball at a party, do S-M unless she wanted to, borrow furs from Abe Lipsey, deal. She would never: carry a Yorkshire in Beverly Hills.

That is the beginning of the chapter and that is also the end of the chapter, which may suggest what I meant by "white space."

I recall having a number of pictures in my mind when I began the novel I just finished, *A Book of Common Prayer*. As a matter of fact one of these pictures was of that bevatron I mentioned, although I would be hard put to tell you a story in which nuclear energy figured. Another was a newspaper photograph of a hijacked 707 burning on the desert in the Middle East. Another was the night view from a room in which I once spent a week with paratyphoid, a hotel room on the Colombian coast. My husband and I seemed to be on the Colombian coast representing the United States of America at a film festival (I recall invoking the name "Jack Valenti" a lot, as if its reiteration could make me well), and it was a bad place to have fever, not only because my indisposition offended our hosts but because every night in this hotel the generator failed. The lights went out. The elevator stopped. My husband would go to the event of the evening and make excuses for me and I would stay alone in this hotel room, in the dark. I remember standing at the window trying to call Bogotá (the telephone seemed to work on the same principle as the generator) and watching the night wind come up and wondering what I was doing eleven degrees off the equator with a fever of 103. The view from that window definitely figures in *A Book of Common Prayer,* as does the burning 707, and yet none of these pictures told me the story I needed.

The picture that did, the picture that shimmered and made these other images coalesce, was the Panama airport at 6 A.M. I was in this airport only once, on a plane to Bogotá that stopped for an hour to refuel, but the way it looked that morning remained superimposed on everything I saw until the day I finished *A Book of Common Prayer.* I lived in that airport for several years. I can still feel the hot air when I step off the plane, can see the heat already rising off the tarmac at 6 A.M. I can feel my skirt damp and wrinkled on my legs. I can feel the asphalt stick to my sandals. I remember the big tail of a Pan American plane floating motionless down at the end of the tarmac. I remember the sound of a slot machine in the waiting room. I could tell you that I remember a particular woman in the airport, an American woman, a *norteamericana,* a thin *norteamericana* about 40 who wore a big square emerald in lieu of a wedding ring, but there was no such woman there.

I put this woman in the airport later. I made this woman up, just as I later made up a country to put the airport in, and a family to run the country. This woman in the airport is neither catching a plane nor meeting one. She is ordering tea in the airport coffee shop. In fact she is not simply "ordering" tea but insisting that the water be boiled, in front of her, for twenty minutes. Why is this woman in this airport? Why is she going nowhere, where has she been? Where did she get that big emerald? What derangement, or disassociation, makes her believe that her will to see the water boiled can possibly prevail?

She had been going to one airport or another for four months, one could see it, looking at the visas on her passport. All those airports where Charlotte Douglas's passport had been stamped would have looked alike. Sometimes the sign on the tower would say "Bienvenidos" and sometimes the sign on the tower would say "Bienvenue," some places were wet and hot and others dry and hot, but at each of these airports the pastel concrete walls would rust and stain and the swamp off the runway would be littered with the fuselages of cannibalized Fairchild F-227's and the water would need boiling.

"I knew why Charlotte went to the airport even if Victor did not.

"I knew about airports."

These lines appear about halfway through A *Book of Common Prayer*, but I wrote them during the second week I worked on the book, long before I had any idea where Charlotte Douglas had been or why she went to airports. Until I wrote these lines I had no character called "Victor" in mind: the necessity for mentioning a name, and the name "Victor," occurred to me as I wrote the sentence. *I knew why Charlotte went to the airport* sounded incomplete. *I knew why Charlotte went to the airport even if Victor did not* carried a little more narrative drive. Most important of all, until I wrote these lines I did not know who "I" was, who was telling the story. I had intended until that moment that the "I" be no more than the voice of the author, a 19th-century omniscient narrator. But there it was:

> "I knew why Charlotte went to the airport even if Victor did not.
> "I knew about airports."

This "I" was the voice of no author in my house. This "I" was someone who not only knew why Charlotte went to the airport but also knew someone called "Victor." Who was Victor? Who was this narrator? Why was this narrator telling me this story? Let me tell you one thing about why writers write: had I known the answer to any of these questions I would never have needed to write a novel.

QUESTIONS

1. In your own words, but referring to the text, explain Joan Didion's reasons for writing.
2. Compare and contrast Joan Didion's motives for writing with those of George Orwell.
3. What does Didion mean when she says that she does not think in abstracts? (What is abstract thinking? Can you give some common examples of such thought?)
4. The author talks about *grammar*. What does she mean by this term? In what sense does she "know" grammar? What does she mean when she says she doesn't know grammar?
5. The author tells us that it took her years to discover that she was a writer. What does she mean, in her own case, by the term "writer"? (See especially pages 24–25.)
6. Why does Didion devote so much space to discussing the "shimmer around the edges" of the pictures in her mind?
7. Didion says, "To shift the structure of a sentence alters the meaning of that sentence, as definitely and inflexibly as the position of a camera

alters the meaning of the object photographed." Thus, Didion would say, the following sentences do not have exactly the same meaning:

a. The child slurped the popsicle.
b. The popsicle was slurped by the child.
c. What the child slurped was the popsicle.
d. The popsicle, that was what the child slurped.
e. The child, that was who slurped the popsicle.

In what ways do the five sentences have the same meaning, and in what ways do they differ? What do your conclusions reveal about the relationship between language and ideas?

ELDRIDGE CLEAVER
On Becoming

*Born in Wabbaseka, Arkansas, in 1935, the son of a dining car waiter and a
janitress, Eldridge Cleaver attended junior college, but he obtained most of his
education in California prisons: San Quentin, Folsom, and Soledad. When he was
serving time in Folsom, after being convicted for assault with a deadly weapon,
Cleaver began the thinking that led to his book* Soul on Ice, *excerpted here.*

*After his parole from Folsom, Cleaver became involved with the Black Panther
Party and was again arrested after a gun battle in 1968. He was freed on the
grounds that he had been held as a political prisoner, but a higher court overturned
the decision and Cleaver fled the country. He returned and gave himself up in 1975
and was required to complete his sentence.*

*For George Orwell, writing was a means of changing society; one of his primary
motives for writing was political. Joan Didion views writing as a way of thinking, of
understanding the world "out there." In the following selection, Eldridge Cleaver
tells us that he used writing as a means of sorting out his own problems and
understanding his own rage; he used writing, as he put it, to save himself.*

Folsom Prison
June 25, 1965

Nineteen fifty-four, when I was eighteen years old, is held to be a
crucial turning point in the history of the Afro-American—for the U.S.A.
as a whole—the year segregation was outlawed by the U.S. Supreme
Court. It was also a crucial year for me because on June 18, 1954, I began
serving a sentence in state prison for possession of marijuana.

. . . .

In Soledad state prison, I fell in with a group of young blacks who, like
myself, were in vociferous rebellion against what we perceived as a con-
tinuation of slavery on a higher plane. We cursed everything American—
including baseball and hot dogs. All respect we may have had for politicians, preachers, lawyers, governors, Presidents, senators, congressmen
was utterly destroyed as we watched them temporizing and compromising
over right and wrong, over legality and illegality, over constitutionality and
unconstitutionality. We knew that in the end what they were clashing over
was us, what to do with the blacks, and whether or not to start treating us as
human beings. I despised all of them.

. . . .

Through reading I was amazed to discover how confused people were.
I had thought that, out there beyond the horizon of my own ignorance,
unanimity existed, that even though I myself didn't know what was

happening in the universe, other people certainly did. Yet here I was discovering that the whole U.S.A. was in a chaos of disagreement over segregation/integration. In these circumstances I decided that the only safe thing for me to do was go for myself. It became clear that it was possible for me to take the initiative: instead of simply *reacting* I could *act*. I could unilaterally—whether anyone agreed with me or not—repudiate all allegiances, morals, values—even while continuing to exist within this society. My mind would be free and no power in the universe could force me to accept something if I didn't want to. But I would take my own sweet time. That, too, was a part of my new freedom. I would accept nothing until it was proved that it was good—for me. I became an extreme iconoclast. Any affirmative assertion made by anyone around me became a target for tirades of criticism and denunciation.

This little game got good to me and I got good at it. I attacked all forms of piety, loyalty, and sentiment: marriage, love, God, patriotism, the Constitution, the founding fathers, law, concepts of right-wrong-good-evil, all forms of ritualized and conventional behavior. As I pranced about, club in hand, seeking new idols to smash, I encountered really for the first time in my life, with any seriousness, The Ogre, rising up before me in a mist. I discovered, with alarm, that The Ogre possessed a tremendous and dreadful power over me, and I didn't understand this power or why I was at its mercy. I tried to repudiate The Ogre, root it out of my heart as I had done God, Constitution, principles, morals, and values—but The Ogre had its claws buried in the core of my being and refused to let go. I fought frantically to be free, but The Ogre only mocked me and sank its claws deeper into my soul. I knew then that I had found an important key, that if I conquered The Ogre and broke its power over me I would be free. But I also knew that it was a race against time and that if I did not win I would certainly be broken and destroyed. I, a black man, confronted The Ogre— the white woman.

In prison, those things withheld from and denied to the prisoner became precisely what he wants most of all, of course. Because we were locked up in our cells before darkness fell, I used to lie awake at night racked by painful craving to take a leisurely stroll under the stars, or to go to the beach, to drive a car on a freeway, to grow a beard, or to make love to a woman.

Since I was not married conjugal visits would not have solved my problem. I therefore denounced the idea of conjugal visits as inherently unfair; single prisoners needed and deserved *action* just as married prisoners did. I advocated establishing a system under Civil Service whereby salaried women would minister to the needs of those prisoners who maintained a record of good behavior. If a married prisoner preferred his own wife, that would be his right. Since California was not about to inaugurate either conjugal visits or the Civil Service, one could advocate either with equal enthusiasm and with the same result: nothing.

This may appear ridiculous to some people. But it was very real to me and as urgent as the need to breathe, because I was in my bull stage and lack of access to females was absolutely a form of torture. I suffered. My mistress at the time of my arrest, the beautiful and lonely wife of a serviceman stationed overseas, died unexpectedly three weeks after I entered prison; and the rigid, dehumanized rules governing correspondence between prisoners and free people prevented me from corresponding with other young ladies I knew. It left me without any contact with females except those in my family.

In the process of enduring my confinement, I decided to get myself a pin-up girl to paste on the wall of my cell. I would fall in love with her and lavish my affections upon her. She, a symbolic representative of the forbidden tribe of women, would sustain me until I was free. Out of the center of *Esquire*, I married a voluptuous bride. Our marriage went along swell for a time: no quarrels, no complaints. And then, one evening when I came in from school, I was shocked and enraged to find that the guard had entered my cell, ripped my sugar from the wall, torn her into little pieces, and left the pieces floating in the commode: it was like seeing a dead body floating in a lake. Giving her a proper burial, I flushed the commode. As the saying goes, I sent her to Long Beach. But I was genuinely beside myself with anger: almost every cell, excepting those of the homosexuals, had a pin-up girl on the wall and the guards didn't bother them. Why, I asked the guard the next day, had he singled me out for special treatment?

"Don't you know we have a rule against pasting up pictures on the walls?" he asked me.

"Later for the rules," I said. "You know as well as I do that the rule is not enforced."

"Tell you what," he said, smiling at me (the smile put me on my guard), "I'll compromise with you: get yourself a colored girl for a pinup—no white women—and I'll let it stay up. Is that a deal?"

I was more embarrassed than shocked. He was laughing in my face. I called him two or three dirty names and walked away. I can still recall his big moon-face, grinning at me over yellow teeth. The disturbing part about the whole incident was that a terrible feeling of guilt came over me as I realized that I had chosen a picture of the white girl over the available pictures of black girls. I tried to rationalize it away, but I was fascinated by the truth involved. Why hadn't I thought about it in this light before? So I took hold of the question and began to inquire into my feelings. Was it true, did I really prefer white girls over black? The conclusion was clear and inescapable: I did. I decided to check out my friends on this point and it was easy to determine, from listening to their general conversation, that the white woman occupied a peculiarly prominent place in all of our frames of reference. With what I have learned since then, this all seems terribly elementary now. But at the time, it was a tremendously intriguing adventure of discovery.

One afternoon, when a large group of Negroes was on the prison yard shooting the breeze, I grabbed the floor and posed the question: which did they prefer, white women or black? Some said Japanese women were their favorite, others said Chinese, some said European women, others said Mexican women—they all stated a preference, and they generally freely admitted their dislike for black women.

"I don't want nothing black but a Cadillac," said one.

"If money was black I wouldn't want none of it," put in another.

A short little stud, who was a very good lightweight boxer with a little man's complex that made him love to box heavyweights, jumped to his feet. He had a yellowish complexion and we called him Butterfly.

"All you niggers are sick!" Butterfly spat out. "I don't like no stinking white woman. My grandma is a white woman and I don't even like her!"

But it just so happened that Butterfly's crime partner was in the crowd, and after Butterfly had his say, his crime partner said, "Aw, sit on down and quit that lying, lil o'chump. What about that gray girl in San Jose who had your nose wide open? Did you like her, or were you just running after her with your tongue hanging out of your head because you hated her?"

Partly because he was embarrassed and partly because his crime partner was a heavyweight, Butterfly flew into him. And before we could separate them and disperse, so the guard would not know who had been fighting, Butterfly bloodied his crime partner's nose. Butterfly got away but, because of the blood, his crime partner got caught. I ate dinner with Butterfly that evening and questioned him sharply about his attitude toward white women. And after an initial evasiveness he admitted that the white woman bugged him too. "It's a sickness," he said. "All our lives we've had the white woman dangled before our eyes like a carrot on a stick before a donkey: look but don't touch."

. . . .

From our discussion, which began that evening and has never yet ended, we went on to notice how thoroughly, as a matter of course, a black growing up in America is indoctrinated with the white races's standard of beauty. Not that the whites made a conscious, calculated effort to do this, we thought, but since they constituted the majority the whites brainwashed the blacks by the very processes the whites employed to indoctrinate themselves with their own group standards. It intensified my frustrations to know that I was indoctrinated to see the white woman as more beautiful and desirable than my own black woman. It drove me into books seeking light on the subject. In Richard Wright's *Native Son*, I found Bigger Thomas and a keen insight into the problem.

My interest in this area persisted undiminished and then, in 1955, an event took place in Mississippi which turned me inside out: Emmett Till, a young Negro down from Chicago on a visit, was murdered, allegedly for flirting with a white woman. He had been shot, his head crushed from repeated blows with a blunt instrument, and his badly decomposed body was recovered from the river with a heavy weight on it. I was, of course, angry over the whole bit, but one day I saw in a magazine a picture of the white woman with whom Emmett Till was said to have flirted. While looking at the picture, I felt that little tension in the center of my chest I experience when a woman appeals to me. I was disgusted and angry with myself. Here was a woman who had caused the death of a black, possibly because, when he looked at her, he also felt the same tensions of lust and desire in his chest—and probably for the same general reasons that I felt them. It was all unacceptable to me. I looked at the picture again and again, and in spite of everything and against my will and the hate I felt for the woman and all that she represented, she appealed to me. I flew into a rage at myself, at America, at white women, at the history that had placed those tensions of lust and desire in my chest.

Two days later, I had a "nervous breakdown." For several days I ranted and raved against the white race, against white women in particular, against white America in general. When I came to myself, I was locked in a padded cell with not even the vaguest memory of how I got there. All I could recall was an eternity of pacing back and forth in the cell, preaching to the unhearing walls.

I had several sessions with a psychiatrist. His conclusion was that I hated my mother. How he arrived at this conclusion I'll never know, because he knew nothing about my mother; and when he'd ask me questions I would answer him with absurd lies. What revolted me about him was that he had heard me denouncing the whites, yet each time he interviewed me he deliberately guided the conversation back to my family life, to my childhood. That in itself was all right, but he deliberately blocked all my attempts to bring out the racial question, and he made it clear that he was not interested in my attitude toward whites. This was a Pandora's Box he did not care to open. After I ceased my diatribes against the whites, I was let out of the hospital, back into the general inmate population just as if nothing had happened. I continued to brood over these events and over the dynamics of race relations in America.

. . . .

Somehow I arrived at the conclusion that, as a matter of principle, it was of paramount importance for me to have an antagonistic, ruthless attitude toward white women. The term *outlaw* appealed to me and at the time my parole date was drawing near, I considered myself to be mentally free—I was an "outlaw." I had stepped outside of the white man's law, which I repudiated with scorn and self-satisfaction. I became a law unto myself—my own legislature, my own supreme court, my own executive. At the moment I walked out of the prison gate, my feelings toward white women in general could be summed up in the following lines:

TO A WHITE GIRL

I love you
Because you're white,
Not because you're charming
Or bright.
Your whiteness
Is a silky thread
Snaking through my thoughts
In redhot patterns
Of lust and desire.

I hate you
Because you're white.
Your white meat
Is nightmare food.
White is
The skin of Evil.
You're my Moby Dick,
White Witch,
Symbol of the rope and hanging tree,
Of the burning cross.

Loving you thus
And hating you so,
My heart is torn in two.
Crucified.

I became a rapist. To refine my technique and *modus operandi*, I started out by practicing on black girls in the ghetto—in the black ghetto where dark and vicious deeds appear not as aberrations or deviations from the norm, but as part of the sufficiency of the Evil of the day—and when I considered myself smooth enough, I crossed the tracks and sought out white prey. I did this consciously, deliberately, willfully, methodically—though looking back I see that I was in a frantic, wild, and completely abondoned frame of mind.

Rape was an insurrectionary act. It delighted me that I was defying and trampling upon the white man's law, upon his system of values, and that I was defiling his women—and this point, I believe, was the most satisfying to me because I was very resentful over the historical fact of how the white man has used the black woman. I felt I was getting revenge. From the site of the act of rape, consternation spreads outwardly in concentric circles. I wanted to send waves of consternation throughout the white race. Recently, I came upon a quotation from one of LeRoi Jones' poems, taken from his book *The Dead Lecturer*:

> A cult of death need of the simple striking arm under the street lamp. The cutters from under their rented earth. Come up, black dada nihilismus. Rape the white girls. Rape their father. Cut the mothers' throats.

I have lived those lines and I know that if I had not been apprehended I would have slit some white throats. There are, of course, many young blacks out there right now who are slitting white throats and raping the white girl. They are not doing this because they read LeRoi Jones' poetry, as some of his critics seem to believe. Rather, LeRoi is expressing the funky facts of life.

After I returned to prison, I took a long look at myself and, for the first time in my life, admitted that I was wrong, that I had gone astray—astray not so much from the white man's law as from being human, civilized— for I could not approve the act of rape. Even though I had some insight into my own motivations, I did not feel justified. I lost my self-respect. My pride as a man dissolved and my whole fragile moral structure seemed to collapse, completely shattered.

That is why I started to write. To save myself.

I realized that no one could save me but myself. The prison authorities were both uninterested and unable to help me. I had to seek out the truth and unravel the snarled web of my motivations. I had to find out who I am and what I want to be, what type of man I should be, and what I could do to become the best of which I was capable. I understood that what had happened to me had also happened to countless other blacks and it would happen to many, many more.

I learned that I had been taking the easy way out, running away from problems. I also learned that it is easier to do evil than it is to do good. And I have been terribly impressed by the youth of America, black and white. I am proud of them because they have reaffirmed my faith in humanity. I have come to feel what must be love for the young people of America and I want to be part of the good and greatness that they want for all people. From my prison cell, I have watched America slowly coming awake. It is not fully awake yet, but there is soul in the air and everywhere I see beauty. I have watched the sit-ins, the freedom raids, the Mississippi Blood Summers, demonstrations all over the country, the FSM movement, the teach-ins, and the mounting protest over Lyndon Strangelove's foreign policy—all of this, the thousands of little details, show me it is time to straighten up and fly right. That is why I decided to concentrate on my writings and efforts in this area. We are a very sick country—I, perhaps, am sicker than most. But I accept that. I told you in the beginning that I am extremist by nature—so it is only right that I should be extremely sick.

I was very familiar with the Eldridge who came to prison, but that Eldridge no longer exists. And the one I am now is in some ways a stranger to me. You may find this difficult to understand but it is very easy for one in prison to lose his sense of self. And if he has been undergoing all kinds of extreme, involved, and unregulated changes, then he ends up not knowing who he is. Take the point of being attractive to women. You can easily see how a man can lose his arrogance or certainty on that point while in prison! When he's in the free world, he gets constant feedback on how he looks from the number of female heads he turns when he walks down the street. In prison he gets only hate-stares and sour frowns. Years and years of bitter looks. Individuality is not nourished in prison, neither by the officials nor by the convicts. It is a deep hole out of which to climb.

What must be done, I believe, is that all these problems—particularly the sickness between the white woman and the black man—must be brought out into the open, dealt with and resolved. I know that the black man's sick attitude toward the white woman is a revolutionary sickness: it keeps him perpetually out of harmony with the system that is oppressing him. Many whites flatter themselves with the idea that the Negro male's lust and desire for the white dream girl is purely an esthetic attraction, but nothing could be farther from the truth. His motivation is often of such a bloody, hateful, bitter, and malignant nature that whites would really be hard pressed to find it flattering. I have discussed these points with prisoners who were convicted of rape, and their motivations are very plain. But they are very reluctant to discuss these things with white men who, by and large, make up the prison staffs. I believe that in the experience of these men lies the knowledge and wisdom that must be utilized to help other youngsters who are heading in the same direction. I think all of us, the entire nation, will be better off if we bring it all out front. A lot of people's feelings will be hurt, but that is the price that must be paid.

It may be that I can harm myself by speaking frankly and directly, but I do not care about that at all. Of course I want to get out of prison, badly, but I shall get out some day. I am more concerned with what I am going to be after I get out. I know that by following the course which I have charted I will find my salvation. If I had followed the path laid down for me by the officials, I'd undoubtedly have long since been out of prison—but I'd be less of a man. I'd be weaker and less certain of where I want to go, what I want to do, and how to go about it.

The price of hating other human beings is loving oneself less.

QUESTIONS

1. In your own words, explain what Cleaver means when he says toward the beginning of the excerpt, ". . . I decided that the only safe thing for me to do was go for myself."

2. On page 31, Cleaver uses a metaphor that means something like this: "I cut a pinup out of *Esquire* and fantasized that she was my bride. My fantasy was satisfying for a time." What is the metaphor? What advantages does the metaphor have over the literal statement above?

3. How did Cleaver come to recognize what he calls "The Ogre"?

4. Explain why Cleaver thought that writing would save him.

5. Discuss the following questions: Is writing an indispensable aid to complex thought? What advantages does writing have over speech? Would technology and philosophy be possible without writing?

6. What is Cleaver's attitude toward his subject matter and his readers? (That is, what is the *tone* of the selection?) Is he playful, serious, ironic, mournful, solemn? Refer to the selection to back up and illustrate your conclusions.

7. Compare and contrast Cleaver's tone with that of John Kenneth Galbraith in "Writing, Typing, and Economics," pages 7–14.

8. What sort of readers does Cleaver seem to have in mind? Explain, citing the text for support.

9. Explain why you did or did not find the selection to be worthwhile. In answering this question, you might think about *content*: Did you learn anything? *Style*: Did you find the piece exceptionally well written? *Effect*: Did the piece have emotional impact? Refer to specific parts of the text to support your explanation.

Henry Miller
Reflections on Writing

*A writer who, in his later years, turned to watercolors, Henry Miller was a leader in
the battle against censorship and for outspoken freedom in art. Born in 1891, Miller
spent the 1930s as an "exile" in Paris, where he wrote* Tropic of Cancer *and* Tropic
of Capricorn, *neither of which was allowed to be published in the United States
until the early 1960s. When Miller returned to the United States, he settled in Big
Sur, California, and continued to be a prolific writer with a growing reputation and
an ever larger public who took him seriously. He died in 1983.*

*Henry Miller's reflections may, at first, seem puzzling, but, after all, he is
voicing ideas that John Kenneth Galbraith, Joan Didion, and Eldridge Cleaver also
expressed. Like Didion, Miller tells us that he wrote to find out what he thought:
"Writing, like life itself, is a voyage of discovery." He was deeply concerned, like
Orwell, with the style, the "how," of writing: "I began assiduously examining the
style and technique of those whom I once admired and worshipped. . . . I imitated
every style in the hope of finding the clue to the gnawing secret of how to write." And,
finally, Miller realized that understanding is not permanent, forever, but that one
grows and in the process changes: "I haven't the slightest idea what my future books
will be like, even the one immediately to follow." Writing for Miller is, then, a
means of discovery, but discovery, though always intriguing, is perilous, for the new
sometimes contradicts the old and accepted. Writing seen this way is necessarily
revolutionary and always adventurous.*

Knut Hamsun[1] once said, in response to a questionnaire, that he wrote
to kill time. I think that even if he were sincere in stating it thus he was
deluding himself. Writing, like life itself, is a voyage of discovery. The
adventure is a metaphysical one: it is a way of approaching life indirectly, of
acquiring a total rather than a partial view of the universe. The writer lives
between the upper and lower worlds: he takes the path in order eventually
to become that path himself.

I began in absolute chaos and darkness, in a bog or swamp of ideas and
emotions and experiences. Even now I do not consider myself a writer, in
the ordinary sense of the word. I am a man telling the story of his life, a
process which appears more and more inexhaustible as I go on. Like the
world-evolution, it is endless. It is a turning inside out, a voyaging through
X dimensions, with the result that somewhere along the way one discovers
that what one has to tell is not nearly so important as the telling itself. It is
this quality about all art which gives it a metaphysical hue, which lifts it
out of time and space and centres or integrates it to the whole cosmic

---

[1]Knut Hamsun is the pseudonym of the Norwegian novelist Knut Pedersen (1859–1952). In 1920 he was
awarded the Nobel Prize in literature for his novel *The Growth of the Soil.*

process. It is this about art which is "therapeutic": significance, purposelessness, infinitude.

From the very beginning almost I was deeply aware that there is no goal. I never hope to embrace the whole, but merely to give in each separate fragment, each work, the feeling of the whole as I go on, because I am digging deeper and deeper into life, digging deeper and deeper into past and future. With the endless burrowing a certitude develops which is greater than faith or belief. I become more and more indifferent to my fate, as writer, and more and more certain of my destiny as man.

I began assiduously examining the style and technique of those whom I once admired and worshipped: Nietzsche, Dostoievski, Hamsun, even Thomas Mann,[2] brick-maker, an inspired jackass or draught-horse. I imitated every style in the hope of finding the clue to the gnawing secret of how to write. Finally I came to a dead end, to a despair and desperation which few men have known, because there was no divorce between myself as writer and myself as man: to fail as a writer meant to fail as a man. And I failed. I realized that I was nothing—less than nothing—a minus quantity. It was at this point, in the midst of the dead Sargasso Sea, so to speak, that I really began to write. I began from scratch, throwing everything overboard, even those whom I most loved. Immediately I heard my own voice I was enchanted: the fact that it was a separate, distinct, unique voice sustained me. It didn't matter to me if what I wrote should be considered bad. Good and bad dropped out of my vocabulary. I jumped with two feet into the realm of æsthetics, the non-moral, non-ethical, nonutilitarian realm of art. My life itself became a work of art. I had found a voice, I was whole again. The experience was very much like what we read of in connection with the lives of Zen initiates. My huge failure was like the recapitulation of the experience of the race: I had to grow foul with knowledge, realize the futility of everything; smash everything, grow desperate, then humble, then sponge myself off the slate, as it were, in order to recover my authenticity. I had to arrive at the brink and then take a leap in the dark.

I talk now about Reality, but I know there is no getting at it, leastwise by writing. I learn less and realize more: I learn in some different, more subterranean way. I acquire more and more the gift of immediacy. I am developing the ability to perceive, apprehend, analyze, synthesize, categorize, inform, articulate—all at once. The structural element of things reveals itself more readily to my eye. I eschew all clear cut interpretations: with increasing simplification the mystery heightens. What I know tends to

---

[2]Friedrich Wilhelm Nietzsche (1844–1900) was a German philosopher whose best-known work is *Thus Spake Zarathustra*. Fyodor Mikhailovitch Dostoievski (1821–1881) was a Russian writer and author of, among other masterpieces of world literature, *The Brothers Karamazov*. Thomas Mann (1875–1955), a German novelist and author of *The Magic Mountain*, *Buddenbrooks*, and other masterpieces of world literature, received the Nobel prize for literature in 1929.

become more and more unstatable. I live in certitude, a certitude which is not dependent upon proofs or faith. I live completely for myself, without the least egotism or selfishness. I am living out my share of life and thus abetting the scheme of things. I further the development, the enrichment, the evolution and the devolution of the cosmos, every day in every way. I give all I have to give, voluntarily, and take as much as I can possibly ingest. I am a prince and a pirate at the same time. I am the equals sign, the spiritual counterpart of the sign Libra which was wedged into the original Zodiac by separating Virgo from Scorpio. I find that there is plenty of room in the world for everybody—great interspatial depths, great ego universes, great islands of repair, for whoever attains to individuality. On the surface, where the historical battles rage, where everything is interpreted in terms of money and power, there may be crowding, but life only begins when one drops below the surface, when one gives up the struggle, sinks and disappears from sight. Now I can as easily not write as write: there is no longer any compulsion, no longer any therapeutic aspect to it. Whatever I do is done out of sheer joy: I drop my fruits like a ripe tree. What the general reader or the critic makes of it is not my concern. I am not establishing values: I defæcate and nourish. There is nothing more to it.

This condition of sublime indifference is a logical development of the egocentric life. I lived out the social problem by dying: the real problem is not one of getting on with one's neighbour or of contributing to the development of one's country, but of discovering one's destiny, of making a life in accord with the deep-centred rhythm of the cosmos. To be able to use the word cosmos boldly, to use the word soul, to deal in things "spiritual"—and to shun definitions, alibis, proofs, duties. Paradise is everywhere and every road, if one continues along it far enough, leads to it. One can only go forward by going backward and then sideways and then up and then down. There is no progress: there is perpetual movement, displacement, which is circular, spiral, endless. Every man has his own destiny: the only imperative is to follow it, to accept it, no matter where it lead him.

I haven't the slightest idea what my future books will be like, even the one immediately to follow. My charts and plans are the slenderest sort of guides: I scrap them at will, I invent, distort, deform, lie, inflate, exaggerate, confound and confuse as the mood seizes me. I obey only my own instincts and intuitions. I know nothing in advance. Often I put down things which I do not understand myself, secure in the knowledge that later they will become clear and meaningful to me. I have faith in the man who is writing, who is myself, the writer. I do not believe in words, no matter if strung together by the most skilful man: I believe in language, which is something beyond words, something which words give only an inadequate illusion of. Words do not exist separately, except in the minds of scholars, etymologists, philologists, etc. Words divorced from language are dead things, and yield no secrets. A man is revealed in his style, the language which he has created for himself. To the man who is pure at heart I believe that everything is as clear as a bell, even the most esoteric scripts. For such a man there is always mystery, but the mystery is not mysterious, it is logical, natural, ordained, and implicitly accepted. Understanding is not a piercing of the mystery, but an acceptance of it, a living blissfully with it, in it, through and by it. I would like my words to flow along in the same way that the world flows along, a serpentine movement through incalculable dimensions, axes, latitudes, climates, conditions. I accept *a priori* my inability to realize such an ideal. It does not bother me in the least. In the ultimate sense, the world itself is pregnant with failure, is the perfect manifestation of imperfection, of the consciousness of failure. In the realization of this, failure is itself eliminated. Like the primal spirit of the universe, like the unshakable Absolute, the One, the All, the creator, i.e., the artist, expresses himself by and through imperfection. It is the stuff of life, the very sign of livingness. One gets nearer to the heart of truth, which I suppose is the ultimate aim of the writer, in the measure that he ceases to struggle, in the measure that he abandons the will. The great writer is the very symbol of life, of the non-perfect. He moves effortlessly, giving the illusion of perfection, from some unknown centre which is certainly not the brain centre, but which is definitely a centre, a centre connected with the rhythm of the whole universe and consequently as sound, solid, unshakable, as durable, defiant, anarchic, purposeless, as the universe itself. Art teaches nothing, except the significance of life. The great work must inevitably be obscure, except to the very few, to those who like the author himself are initiated into the mysteries. Communication then is secondary: it is perpetuation which is important. For this only one good reader is necessary.

If I am a revolutionary, as has been said, it is unconsciously. I am not in revolt against the world order. "I revolutionize," as Blaise Cendrars[3] said of himself. There is a difference. I can as well live on the minus side of the fence as on the plus side. Actually I believe myself to be just above these two signs, providing a ratio between them which expresses itself plastically, non-ethically, in writing. I believe that one has to pass beyond the sphere and influence of art. Art is only a means to life, to the life more abundant. It is not in itself the life more abundant. It merely points the way, something which is overlooked not only by the public, but very often by the artist himself. In becoming an end it defeats itself. Most artists are defeating life by their very attempt to grapple with it. They have split the

---

[3]Blaise Cendrars (1887–1961) was a French avant-garde writer.

egg in two. All art, I firmly believe, will one day disappear. But the artist will remain, and life itself will become not "an art," but *art*, i.e., will definitely and for all time usurp the field. In any true sense we are certainly not yet alive. We are no longer animals, but we are certainly not yet *men*. Since the dawn of art every great artist has been dinning that into us, but few are they who have understood it. Once art is really accepted it will cease to be. It is only a substitute, a symbol-language, for something which can be seized directly. But for that to become possible man must become thoroughly religious, not a believer, but a prime mover, a god in fact and deed. He will become that inevitably. And of all the detours along this path art is the most glorious, the most fecund, the most instructive. The artist who becomes thoroughly aware consequently ceases to be one. And the trend is towards awareness, towards that blinding consciousness in which no present form of life can possibly flourish, not even art.

To some this will sound like mystification, but it is an honest statement of my present convictions. It should be borne in mind, of course, that there is an inevitable discrepancy between the truth of the matter and what one thinks, even about himself: but it should also be borne in mind that there exists an equal discrepancy between the judgment of another and this same truth. Between subjective and objective there is no vital difference. Everything is illusive and more or less transparent. All phenomena, including man and his thought about himself, are nothing more than a movable, changeable alphabet. There are no solid facts to get hold of. Thus, in writing, even if my distortions and deformations be deliberate, they are not necessarily less near to the truth of things. One can be absolutely truthful, and sincere even though admittedly the most outrageous liar. Fiction and invention are of the very fabric of life. The truth is no way disturbed by the violent perturbations of the spirit.

Thus, whatever effects I may obtain by technical device are never the mere results of technique, but the very accurate registering by my seismographic needle of the tumultuous, manifold, mysterious and incomprehensible experiences which I have lived through and which, in the process of writing, are lived through again, differently, perhaps even more tumultuously, more mysteriously, more incomprehensibly. The so-called core of solid fact, which forms the point of departure as well as repair, is deeply embedded in me: I could not possibly lose it, alter it, disguise it, try as I may. And yet it *is* altered, just as the face of the world is altered, with each moment that we breathe. To record it then, one must give a double illusion—one of arrestation and one of flow. It is this dual trick, so to speak, which gives the illusion of falsity: it is this lie, this fleeting, metamorphic mask, which is of the very essence of art. One anchors oneself in the flow: one adopts the lying mask in order to reveal the truth.

I have often thought that I should like one day to write a book explaining how I wrote certain passages in my books, or perhaps just one passage. I believe I could write a good-sized book on just one small paragraph selected at random from my work. A book about its inception, its genesis, its metamorphosis, its accouchement, of the time which elapsed between the birth of the idea and its recording, the time it took to write it, the thoughts I had between times while writing it, the day of the week, the state of my health, the condition of my nerves, the interruptions that occurred, those of my own volition and those which were forced upon me, the multifarious varieties of expression which occurred to me in the process of writing, the alterations, the point where I left off and in returning, completely altered the original trend, or the point where I skillfully left off, like a surgeon making the best of a bad job, intending to return and resume some time later, but never doing so, or else returning and continuing the trend unconsciously some few books later when the memory of it had completely vanished. Or I might take one passage against another, passages which the cold eye of the critic seizes on as examples of this or that, and utterly confound them, the analytical-minded critics, by demonstrating how a seemingly effortless piece of writing was achieved under great duress whereas another difficult, labyrinthian passage was written like a breeze, like a geyser erupting. Or I could show how a passage originally shaped itself when in bed, how it became transformed upon arising, and again transformed at the moment of sitting down to record it. Or I could produce my scratch pad to show how the most remote, the most artificial stimulus produced a warm, life-like human flower. I could produce certain words discovered by hazard while ruffling the pages of a book, show how they set me off—but who on earth could ever guess how, in what manner, they were to set me off? All that the critics write about a work of art, even at the best, even when most sound, convincing, plausible, even when done with love, which is seldom, is as nothing compared to the actual mechanics, the real genetics of a work of art. I remember my work, not word for word, to be sure, but in some more accurate, trustworthy way; my whole work has come to resemble a terrain of which I have made a thorough, geodetic survey, not from a desk, with pen and ruler, but by touch, by getting down on all fours, on my stomach, and crawling over the ground inch by inch, and this over an endless period of time in all conditions of weather. In short, I am as close to the work now as when I was in the act of executing it—closer perhaps. The conclusion of a book was never anything more than a shift of bodily position. It might have ended in a thousand different ways. No single part of it finished off: I could resume the narrative at any point, carry on, lay canals, tunnels, bridges, houses, factories, stud it with other inhabitants, other fauna and flora, all equally true to fact. I have no beginning and no ending, actually. Just as life begins at any moment, through an act of realization, so the work. But each beginning, whether of book, page, paragraph, sentence or phrase, marks a vital connection, and it is in the vitality, the durability, the timelessness and changelessness of the thoughts and events that I plunge anew each time. Every line and word is vitally connected with my life, my life only, be it in the form of deed, event, fact, thought, emotion, desire, evasion, frustration, dream, revery, vagary, even the unfinished nothings which float listlessly in the brain like the snapped filaments of a spider's web. There is nothing really vague or tenuous—even the nothingnesses are sharp, tough, definite, durable. Like the spider, I return again and again to the task, conscious that the web I am spinning is made of my own substance, that it will never fail me, never run dry.

In the beginning I had dreams of rivaling Dostoievski. I hoped to give to the world huge, labyrinthian soul struggles which would devastate the world. But before very far along I realized that we had evolved to a point beyond that of Dostoievski—*beyond* in the sense of degeneration. With us the soul problem has disappeared, or rather presents itself in some strangely distorted chemical guise. We are dealing with crystalline elements of the dispersed and shattered soul. The modern painters express this state or condition perhaps even more forcibly than the writer: Picasso[4] is the perfect example of what I mean. It was quite impossible for me, therefore, to think of writing novels; equally unthinkable to follow the various blind alleys represented by the various literary movements in England, France and America. I felt compelled, in all honesty, to take the disparate and dispersed elements of our life—the *soul* life, not the cultural life—and manipulate them through my own personal mode, using my own shattered and dispersed ego as heartlessly and recklessly as I would the flotsam and jetsam of the surrounding phenomenal world. I have never felt any antagonism for or anxiety over the anarchy represented by the prevailing forms of art; on the contrary, I have always welcomed the dissolving influences. In an age marked by dissolution, liquidation seems to me a virtue, nay a moral imperative. Not only have I never felt the least desire to conserve, bolster up or buttress anything, but I might say that I have always looked upon decay as being just as wonderful and rich in expression of life as growth.

I think I should also confess that I was driven to write because it proved to be the only outlet open to me, the only task worthy of my powers. I had honestly tried all the other roads to freedom. I was a self-willed failure in the so-called world of reality, not a failure because of lack of ability. Writing was not an "escape," a means of evading the everyday reality; on the contrary, it meant a still deeper plunge into the brackish pool—a

---

[4]Pablo Picasso (1881–1973) was an avant-garde Spanish artist working in France.

plunge to the source where the waters were constantly being renewed, where there was perpetual movement and stir. Looking back upon my career, I see myself as a person capable of undertaking almost any task, any vocation. It was the monotony and sterility of the other outlets which drove me to desperation. I demanded a realm in which I should be both master and slave at the same time: the world of art is the only such realm. I entered it without any apparent talent, a thorough novice, incapable, awkward, tongue-tied, almost paralyzed by fear and apprehensiveness. I had to lay one brick on another, set millions of words to paper before writing one real, authentic word dragged up from my own guts. The facility of speech which I possessed was a handicap; I had all the vices of the educated man. I had to learn to think, feel and see in totally new fashion, in an uneducated way, *in my own way*, which is the hardest thing in the world. I had to throw myself into the current, knowing that I would probably sink. The great majority of artists are throwing themselves in with life-preservers around their necks, and more often than not it is the life-preserver which sinks them. Nobody can drown in the ocean of reality who voluntarily gives himself up to the experience. Whatever there be of progress in life comes not through adaptation but through daring, through obeying the blind urge. "No daring is fatal," said René Crevel,[5] a phrase which I shall never forget. The whole logic of the universe is contained in daring, i.e., in creating from the flimsiest, slenderest support. In the beginning, this daring is mistaken for will, but with time the will drops away and the automatic process takes its place, which again has to be broken or dropped and a new certitude established which has nothing to do with knowledge, skill, technique or faith. By daring one arrives at this mysterious X position of the artist, and it is this anchorage which no one can describe in words but yet subsists and exudes from every line that is written.

QUESTIONS

1. Eldridge Cleaver titled his essay "On Becoming." Would Henry Miller have been justified in using the same title? By comparing the ideas in "On Becoming" with those in "Reflections on Writing," explain your answer.

2. What does Miller mean when he says that "even now I do not consider myself a writer"?

3. For Miller, what is the ultimate aim of a writer?

---

[5]René Crevel (1900–1935) was a French surrealist writer.

4. According to Miller, there is no such thing as a final, ultimate truth for a writer. By referring to specific passages in the text, explain his reasoning.

5. Explain what Miller means when he says, on pages 40–41, that "Words do not exist separately, except in the minds of scholars, etymologists, philologists, etc. Words divorced from language are dead things, and yield no secrets."

6. Miller varies the length of his sentences, some of them being very short. Find a passage in which several short sentences follow one another and read the passage aloud. What is the effect of the series of short sentences? Why do you think Miller wrote them as he did?

7. In the first two paragraphs of the essay, a great deal of the meaning is carried by metaphor, as in "Writing, like life, is a voyage of discovery," comparing writing with the sort of journey that brought Columbus to the New World. Literally, then, the writer bravely sets out, not knowing exactly where he or she is going, but hoping to discover something new and worthwhile. What are other important metaphors in the paragraph? What ideas do they convey?

8. Compare your response to this essay with your response to the Orwell essay. Did you find one more satisfactory than the other? Explain, using the text to support your reasoning.

BERTRAND RUSSELL

How I Write

Bertrand Russell (1872–1970)—philosopher, mathematician, social reformer—early in his career published two supremely important works: The Principles of Mathematics *(1903) and, with Alfred North Whitehead,* Principia Mathematica *(3 vols., 1910–13). In 1938, Russell, now an earl (having inherited the family title), came to the United States, where he taught at the University of Chicago and then at UCLA. In 1950 he received the Nobel Prize in literature.*

During his long life, Russell was the champion of many causes, including nuclear disarmament, gay rights, women's rights, and pacifism.

In his autobiography, Russell wrote, "Three passions, simple but overwhelmingly strong, have governed my life: the longing for love, the search for knowledge, and unbearable pity for the suffering of mankind."

In his brief essay, Russell gives a straightforward account of his writing techniques—and in the process contradicts some conventional wisdom about writing. For instance, he states that revision was a waste of time for him.

According to his own account, Bertrand Russell, unlike Joan Didion and Henry Miller, did not write to discover ideas, but worked his ideas out fully before recording them in prose. Thus, we have two contrasting views of the relationship between writing and thinking.

I cannot pretend to know how writing ought to be done, or what a wise critic would advise me to do with a view to improving my own writing. The most that I can do is to relate some things about my own attempts.

Until I was twenty-one, I wished to write more or less in the style of John Stuart Mill.[1] I liked the structure of his sentences and his manner of developing a subject. I had, however, already a different ideal, derived, I suppose, from mathematics. I wished to say everything in the smallest number of words in which it could be said clearly. Perhaps, I thought, one should imitate Baedeker[2] rather than any more literary model. I would spend hours trying to find the shortest way of saying something without ambiguity, and to this aim I was willing to sacrifice all attempts at aesthetic excellence.

At the age of twenty-one, however, I came under a new influence, that of my future brother-in-law, Logan Pearsall Smith.[3] He was at that time exclusively interested in style as opposed to matter. His gods were

---

[1]John Stuart Mill (1806–1873), English philosopher and economist and author of the classic essay "On Liberty."

[2]Baedeker was a publisher of guide books for tourists.

[3]Logan Pearsall Smith (1865–1946) was born in Millville, New Jersey, but in 1888 moved to England, where he studied at Oxford and ultimately became an influential essayist and man of letters.

Flaubert and Walter Pater,[4] and I was quite ready to believe that the way to learn how to write was to copy their technique. He gave me various simple rules, of which I remember only two: "Put a comma every four words," and "never use 'and' except at the beginning of a sentence." His most emphatic advice was that one must always rewrite. I conscientiously tried this, but found that my first draft was almost always better than my second. This discovery has saved me an immense amount of time. I do not, of course, apply it to the substance, but only to the form. When I discover an error of an important kind, I rewrite the whole. What I do not find is that I can improve a sentence when I am satisfied with what it means.

Very gradually I have discovered ways of writing with a minimum of worry and anxiety. When I was young each fresh piece of serious work used to seem to me for a time—perhaps a long time—to be beyond my powers. I would fret myself into a nervous state from fear that it was never going to come right. I would make one unsatisfying attempt after another, and in the end have to discard them all. At last I found that such fumbling attempts were a waste of time. It appeared that after first contemplating a book on some subject, and after giving serious preliminary attention to it, I needed a period of subconscious incubation which could not be hurried and was if anything impeded by deliberate thinking. Sometimes I would find, after a time, that I had made a mistake, and that I could not write the book I had had in mind. But often I was more fortunate. Having, by a time of very intense concentration, planted the problem in my subconsciousness, it would germinate underground until, suddenly, the solution emerged with blinding clarity, so that it only remained to write down what had appeared as if in a revelation.

The most curious example of this process, and the one which led me subsequently to rely upon it, occurred at the beginning of 1914. I had undertaken to give the Lowell Lectures at Boston, and had chosen as my subject "Our Knowledge of the External World." Throughout 1913 I thought about this topic. In term time in my rooms at Cambridge, in vacations in a quiet inn on the upper reaches of the Thames, I concentrated with such intensity that I sometimes forgot to breathe and emerged panting as from a trance. But all to no avail. To every theory that I could think of I could perceive fatal objections. At last, in despair, I went off to Rome for Christmas, hoping that a holiday would revive my flagging energy. I got back to Cambridge on the last day of 1913, and although my difficulties were still completely unresolved I arranged, because the remaining time was short, to dictate as best as I could to a stenographer. Next

---

[4]Gustave Flaubert (1821–1880) was a French novelist, best known for *Madame Bovary*. Walter Horatio Pater (1839–1894) was an English essayist and critic, much admired for his refined style.

morning, as she came in at the door, I suddenly saw exactly what I had to say, and proceeded to dictate the whole book without a moment's hesitation.

I do not want to convey an exaggerated impression. The book was very imperfect, and I now think that it contains serious errors. But it was the best that I could have done at that time, and a more leisurely method (within the time at my disposal) would almost certainly have produced something worse. Whatever may be true of other people, this is the right method for me. Flaubert and Pater, I have found, are best forgotten so far as I am concerned.

Although what I now think about how to write is not so very different from what I thought at the age of eighteen, my development has not been by any means rectilinear. There was a time, in the first years of this century, when I had more florid and rhetorical ambitions. This was the time when I wrote *A Free Man's Worship*, a work of which I do not now think well. At that time I was steeped in Milton's prose, and his rolling periods reverberated through the caverns of my mind. I cannot say that I no longer admire them, but for me to imitate them involves a certain insincerity. In fact, all imitation is dangerous. Nothing could be better in style than the Prayer Book and the Authorized Version of the Bible, but they express a way of thinking and feeling which is different from that of our time. A style is not good unless it is an intimate and almost involuntary expression of the personality of the writer, and then only if the writer's personality is worth expressing. But although direct imitation is always to be deprecated, there is much to be gained by familiarity with good prose, especially in cultivating a sense for prose rhythm.

QUESTIONS

1. What kinds of experiences shaped Russell's writing style?
2. Russell mentions several times that his experiences with writing changed over time. In what ways have your experiences with writing changed since you began high school? How have these changes affected your attitude toward writing?
3. What Russell says about rewriting may contradict what you have been told by your teachers about the importance of revision. How might these positions be reconciled?
4. At one point in the essay, Russell pokes fun at the silly advice some people give writers. Find that place in the essay, and explain why the advice cited there is ridiculous.
5. Russell says, "What I do not find is that I can improve a sentence when I am satisfied with what it means," implying that meaning and style, the

way words are put together, are inseparable. Explain why you agree or disagree with Russell. (You might want to think about Joan Didion's opinion regarding style and meaning. You will recall that she said, "To shift the structure of a sentence alters the meaning of that sentence, as definitely and inflexibly as the position of a camera alters the meaning of the object photographed.")

6. Summarize the point that Russell makes in the fourth and fifth paragraphs of the essay. Why might this be good advice for writers?

7. Explain Russell's point about imitating other writers. What is to be gained by it? Why is he opposed to it?

WILLIAM HOWARTH

From "Introduction" to *The John McPhee Reader*

John McPhee is widely regarded as one of the best contemporary writers. (A selection by McPhee is on pages 182–89 of this book.) In the excerpt that follows, William Howarth discusses McPhee's methods of gathering information and ideas and of putting them together in essays.

Howarth is a professor of English at Princeton University.

One question [readers] do ask is *how* does he work, and on that subject McPhee freely converses. He often talks to writing classes in schools, and since 1975 he has taught a seminar at Princeton as Ferris Professor of Journalism. Although limited in enrollment, his course ("The Literature of Fact") is popular because he devotes so much time and attention to students. In teaching "the application of creative writing techniques to journalism and other forms of non-fiction," as the catalogue statement declares, McPhee often refers to his own books. Yet he also has the students interview visitors, research set pieces, and submit ten compositions, which he discusses in private conferences. The course does not prescribe his working procedures, since he does not believe one writer's method should be a recipe for another.

The New Yorker encourages this tolerance, for as its staff writer McPhee holds one of the most liberated jobs in modern journalism. At the magazine there is an office he rarely uses, a cell flanked by those of two staff writers he has never met. Staff writers are not required to be in residence. They do not cover "story assignments" or write for "Special Issues," since *The New Yorker* does not work those familiar beats. Any staff writer may submit a brief sketch for "The Talk of the Town," the regular opening feature, and certainly McPhee has contributed his share of those breezy, unsigned reports. But mainly he works at his Princeton office on longer projects, developed with the editorial counsel of Shawn and others, chiefly Robert Bingham.[1] *The New Yorker* has a first option on all of McPhee's work. He is free to choose a subject and estimate its length; the editors are equally free to criticize, accept, or reject his proposal. If rejected, he may still write the piece and sell it elsewhere. The magazine pays him quarterly advances, plus most expenses he incurs for travel.

---

[1]William Shawn is editor of *The New Yorker* and Robert Bingham is one of his associates.

Travel occupies a large portion of McPhee's early work on a project. Not overly fond of junketing, however, he has logged only whatever mileage his stories have required. He prefers trains or cars over planes; a car with canoe strapped on top is his ideal vehicle. In the car he often takes along a tape player and several cassettes of his favorite Mozart or Brahms. When he arrives at a wilderness site, his ears and spirit are well massaged. Work has confined him largely to the eastern United States, north and south, although books on David Brower and Ted Taylor[2] entailed journeys to the far West, as did "Ruidoso," a short piece on the world's richest horse race, held annually in New Mexico. Across the Atlantic he has concentrated on England and Scotland, but "Templex," a profile of the travel writer Temple Fielding, required a trip to Fielding's home in the Balearic Islands east of Spain.

When McPhee conducts an interview he tries to be as blank as his notebook pages, totally devoid of preconceptions, equipped with only the most elementary knowledge. He has found that imagining he knows a subject is a disadvantage, for that prejudice will limit his freedom to ask, to learn, to be surprised by unfolding evidence. Since most stories are full of unsuspected complexity, an interviewer hardly needs to *feign* ignorance; the stronger temptation is to bluff with a show of knowledge or to trick the informant into providing simple, easily digestible answers. Neither course is to McPhee's liking; he would rather risk seeming ignorant to get a solid, knotty answer. . . .

McPhee's stories often develop from interviews with a principal informant, a strong personality who provides skeletal framing for the work. Finding this character may be an act of serendipity: in *The Pine Barrens* he accidentally met the indispensable Fred Brown, who knew all the people and nameless sandy roads of his region. Profiles built around a single character, like Frank Boyden or Thomas Hoving, are inevitably more planned from the outset; but in the cases of Ted Taylor and Henri Vaillancourt,[3] McPhee was led to his central figure on the advice of informants, who play minor roles in the stories. He never uses tape recorders when interviewing, for they inhibit some people and are too subverbal for his purposes. The writing process must begin with *words*—a scrap of talk, bits of description, odd facts and inferences—and only a pencil and notebook will answer these needs with literacy and economy.

---

[2]David Brower, a conservationist, founded Friends of the Earth. Theodore Brewster Taylor is an American physicist and professor at Princeton University.
[3]Frank Boyden was founder and, from 1902 to 1968, headmaster of Deerfield Academy in Deerfield, Massachusetts; after graduating from high school, McPhee attended the academy for a year to "brush up" for college. Thomas Hoving was director of the Metropolitan Museum of Art in New York. Howarth writes in a headnote, "Henri Vaillancourt had proved a superb craftsman, but he was a perfect 'bummer' (his favorite expression) of a voyageur: inexperienced in the use of canoes yet a master of their repair."

In some interviews he may play mental chess, anticipating answers or plotting questions, but usually he builds on what he has already seen and heard. Although he writes in a clear, left-handed script, the notes are unintelligible to anyone but himself. Yet they are not indiscriminate jottings; items entered in a notebook are likely to get into his final text as well. McPhee has a passion for details, for they convince readers that he deals in actualities. Added to his journalist's reverence for facts is a novelist's propensity for symbols. His task is to burnish objects until they become reflectors of character and theme. Instead of sermonizing on thrift or prodigality, he notes that Donald Gibbie's[4] teapot is plugged with fourteen wood screws, or that the light in Lt. Arthur Ashe's closet at West Point is always burning. . . .

When he starts to hear the same stories a third time, McPhee stops interviewing, returns to Princeton, and begins the tortuous process for composition. His working methods vary according to a project, but some steps are fairly constant. He first transcribes the notebooks, typing entries in order, occasionally adding other details or current thoughts as he goes. He likens this process to a magnet's attraction of iron filings; as the notes take shape, they draw from him new ideas about placement, phrasing, or possible analogies. When finished, he may have a hundred typed sheets of notes, enough to fill a large spring binder. He makes a photocopy of the original set and shelves it for later use. He then reads and rereads the binder set, looking for areas he needs to flesh out with research and reading at Firestone Library. The reading produces more notes, the notes more typed pages for his binder. Finally, he reads the binder and makes notes on possible structures, describing patterns the story might assume.

While its structure is forming, or when he senses how the story may end, McPhee often writes out a first draft of "the lead," a term journalists use to describe openings. In newspaper writing the lead is usually a single-sentence paragraph, designed to impart the classic who-what-where particulars of a story. In McPhee's work the lead is longer (fifteen hundred to two thousand words), more dramatic, yet rather more oblique. It establishes a mood, a setting, and perhaps some main characters or events, but not in order to put the story in a nutshell or even to hint at its full dimensions. One of his best leads is in "Travels in Georgia," where he manages to convey tone, style, characters, and theme in a few dramatic actions. Three people are riding in a Chevrolet across Georgia's back roads. They share some "gorp," exchange good-humored insults, and halt to eviscerate a turtle lying dead on the road. The action begins *in medias res* and continues without flashbacks or helpful exposition for several pages. When readers finally hit a backward loop, they already have a subliminal

---

[4]Donald Gibbie, a Scottish farmer and lobster fisherman, is the subject of one of McPhee's essays.

sense of who-what-where, and fulfilling this expectancy becomes McPhee's primary challenge in planning the rest of his story.

Having read the lead via telephone to an editor at *The New Yorker,* he goes back to the binder and begins to code it with structural notes, using titles like "Voyageurs," "Loons," or acronyms—"GLAT," "LASLE." These are his topics, the formal segments of narrative, which he next writes on a series of index cards. After assembling a stack, he fans them out and begins to play a sort of writer's solitaire, studying the possibilities of order. Decisions don't come easily; a story has many potential sequences, and each chain produces a calculus of desired and undesired effects, depending on factors like character and theme. When he has the cards in a satisfactory arrangement, he thumbtacks them to a large bulletin board. The shade of Mrs. Olive McKee, his high-school English teacher, smiles upon this array. McPhee defines the outline that finally emerges, in deference to her training, as "logical," but its logic is of no ordinary, abecedarian variety, A to Z or 1 to 10.

Cards on the board, committed to their structure, he next codes the duplicate set of notes and then scissors its sheets apart, cutting large blocks of paragraphs and two or three-line ribbons. In a few hours he has reduced the sheets to thousands of scraps, which he sorts into file folders, one folder for each topical index card on the bulletin board. These folders are pre-compositional skeletons of the narrative segments he will refine when writing a first draft. With the folders squared away in a vertical file, he is ready to write. A large steel dart on the bulletin board marks his progress. He stabs the dart under an index card, opens a folder, further sorts scraps and ribbons until this segment also has a "logical" structure. Then, without invoking the muse, he begins to type his first draft, picking up where the lead ends. When he finishes a folder, he moves the dart, gets the next folder, sorts it out, and continues to type.

Outlined in this fashion, McPhee's writing methods may seem excessively mechanical, almost programmatic in his sorting and retrieval of data bits. But the main purpose of this routine is at once practical and aesthetic: it runs a line of order through the chaos of his notes and files, leaving him free to write on a given parcel of work at a given time. The other sections cannot come crowding in to clutter his desk and mind; he is spared that confusion by the structure of his work, by an ordained plan that cannot come tumbling down. The strategy locks him in, gives him no easy exits from the materials at hand, which he must confront with that humorless partner, the typewriter. . . .

McPhee is a craftsman; he understands that his work must always have inherent form. A potter knows that, and so do carpenters; it was Aristotle who said writers should have a similar goal. But writers have infinite options for order, and McPhee delights in playing any that do not violate his story's "logic." A book on tennis can imitate the game's back-and-forth, contrapuntal action; but it could also resemble a mountain climb, with an ascent, climax, and descent arranged in pyramidal form. The choice is McPhee's: either find an idea for order *in* the material or impose one *upon* it, selecting what Coleridge called the "organic" or "mechanic" principles of structure. McPhee has experimented with both: *Oranges* follows the life cycle of citrus fruit, while *Encounters with the Archdruid* was planned *a priori*, as a matrix into which he poured the molten confrontations of Brower and company. He has a certain preference for mechanic form, since it arises from human logic, but he trusts the organic principle enough not to condone formal manipulation for its own sake. Too much shuffling of those cards leads to fussy and baroque patterns, reflecting the self-indulgent mind of their maker. Yet he is also wary of simple organicism, where subject matter dictates a work's form. The story of a horse race need not run in an oval, nor must a canoe trip curve at its ends—those limited formal objectives are dull and pious, like the "shaped" verse of seven-teenth-century poets.

McPhee wants to create a form that is logical but so unobtrusive that judgments of its content will seem to arise only in the reader's mind. And he also wants to stay loose himself, free to encounter surprises within the pattern he has formed. He is quite willing to manipulate contexts; in recounting Thomas Hoving's discovery of an ivory cross, McPhee cuts and reshapes time as though he, too, were a carver in ivory. In *The Deltoid Pumpkin Seed* he repeatedly digresses from the story's forward motion; his aim is to suggest an experiment in progress, lurching ahead ten yards and then around in circles. The pattern makes readers oscillate, too, between serious and satiric estimates of the experiment's probable fate. Despite his attraction to making these forms, he never trims evidence to fit a narrative pattern. When trouble begins on a canoe trip, "it comes from the inside, from fast-growing hatreds among the friends who started." That pattern an artist cannot control; McPhee accepts it with the "logic" of an athlete who respects the impartial rules of his game.

Writing a first draft is painful work for any writer, whether it moves like lightning or like glue. McPhee spends twelve-hour stints at his office, not writing constantly, but "concentrating" and distilling his research into prose. Some authors overwrite and later boil down; he culls before ever typing a phrase. He likens this method to the sport of curling, where great effort is spent sweeping the ice clean to advance each shot. With writing comes the need for endless decisions, mostly on what *not* to say, what to eliminate. The process is nerve-racking and lonely. His family sees less of him, he also cuts off most visitors and phone calls. Sometimes he talks to editors or friends about problems, but then generally follows his own counsel. Facing the typewriter for long stretches, he generates excess energy like a breeder reactor. A fly buzzing at sun-struck windows is not more manic, and often hard physical exercise is a welcome distraction. Tennis, squash, and basketball are favorite outlets; he professes to play at a level that "attracts ample company and no attention." In fact, he is capable of great intensity on the court, but he dislikes opponents who are arrogant or childish. Arthur Ashe plays in McPhee's preferred style, unpredictably full of contours and strata. Writing is the same sort of game: he has spent a long time learning to move *against* a habitual thought or phrase, which is always the easiest, oldest rut to follow.

QUESTIONS

1. What does McPhee believe about writers' methods?
2. Describe the techniques McPhee uses for interviewing.
3. Howarth tells us that "Instead of sermonizing on thrift or prodigality, [McPhee] notes that Donald Gibbie's teapot is plugged with fourteen wood screws, or that the light in Lt. Arthur Ashe's closet at West Point is always burning." How does this relate to the point that Joan Didion stresses in her essay?
4. In your own words, describe the methods McPhee uses for composition.
5. How does McPhee begin, or "lead" into, his stories? Why are such beginnings effective? In what way do they differ from the usual newspaper lead?
6. Explain how McPhee organizes his materials. What is the difference between "organic" and "mechanical" form?
7. How does McPhee go about completing a first draft?
8. What does McPhee mean when he calls a style "busy"?

A Change of Pace

In the following selections, three poets deal with their own writing methods: W. B. Yeats (1865–1939), Langston Hughes (1902–1967), and Dylan Thomas (1914–1953).

You might find it interesting to discuss the differences between poetic and prose statements. For instance, do poets seem to have different motives from prose writers? Why do poets usually state their meanings less directly than do writers in prose?

Prose and poetry represent different aspects of language and mind; therefore, the three poems included here—and others in this book—are intended to give a rounded view of what it means to be a writer.

W. B. YEATS

The Circus Animals' Desertion

I

I sought a theme and sought for it in vain,
I sought it daily for six weeks or so.
Maybe at last, being but a broken man,
I must be satisfied with my heart, although
Winter and summer till old age began   5
My circus animals were all on show,
Those stilted boys, that burnished chariot,
Lion and woman[1] and the Lord knows what.

II

What can I but enumerate old themes?
First that sea-rider Oisin[2] led by the nose   10
Through three enchanted islands, allegorical dreams,

---

[1]**The circus animals** were from Yeats' earlier poetry: **stilted boys,** Irish heroes that he wrote about; **that burnished chariot,** a carriage from his play *The Unicorn from the Stars*; the **lion** appears in several of his poems. The **woman** is possibly Maude Gonne, the great love of Yeats' life.
[2]In "The Wanderings of Oisin," a poem by Yeats, a fairy leads Oisin by the nose to the Islands of Delight, of Many Fears, and of Forgetfulness.

Vain gaiety, vain battle, vain repose,
Themes of the embittered heart, or so it seems,
That might adorn old songs or courtly shows;
But what cared I that set him on to ride,   15
I, starved for the bosom of his faery bride?

And then a counter-truth filled out its play,
The Countess Cathleen was the name I gave it;
She, pity-crazed, had given her soul away,
But masterful Heaven had intervened to save it.   20
I thought my dear must her own soul destroy,
So did fanaticism and hate enslave it,
And this brought forth a dream and soon enough
This dream itself had all my thought and love.

And when the Fool and Blind Man stole the bread   25
Cuchulain[3] fought the ungovernable sea;
Heart-mysteries there, and yet when all is said
It was the dream itself enchanted me:
Character isolated by a deed
To engross the present and dominate memory.   30
Players and painted stage took all my love,
And not those things that they were emblems of.

III

Those masterful images because complete
Grew in pure mind, but out of what began?
A mound of refuse or the sweepings of a street,   35
Old kettles, old bottles, and a broken can,
Old iron, old bones, old rags, that raving slut
Who keeps the till. Now that my ladder's gone,
I must lie down where all the ladders start,
In the foul rag-and-bone shop of the heart.   40

---

[3]In Yeats' play *On Baile's Strand*, Cuchulain, driven insane by the discovery that he has killed his son, does battle with the sea.

Langston Hughes
Theme for English B

The instructor said,

> *Go home and write*
> *a page tonight.*
> *And let that page come out of you—*
> *Then, it will be true.*   5

I wonder if it's that simple?
I am twenty-two, colored, born in Winston-Salem.
I went to school there, then Durham, then here
to this college on the hill above Harlem.[1]
I am the only colored student in my class.   10
The steps from the hill lead down into Harlem,
through a park, then I cross St. Nicholas,
Eighth Avenue, Seventh, and I come to the Y,
the Harlem Branch Y, where I take the elevator
up to my room, sit down, and write this page: 15

It's not easy to know what is true for you or me
at twenty-two, my age. But I guess I'm what
I feel and see and hear, Harlem, I hear you:
hear you, hear me—we two—you, me, talk on this page.
(I hear New York, too.) Me—who?   20

Well, I like to eat, sleep, drink, and be in love.
I like to work, read, learn, and understand life.
I like a pipe for a Christmas present,
or records—Bessie, bop, or Bach.[2]
I guess being colored doesn't make me *not* like   25
the same things other folks like who are other races.
So will my page be colored that I write?

---

[1] The college on the hill above Harlem is Columbia University. The references that follow are to places in New York City.
[2] Bessie Smith (1898?–1937) was a leading blues singer, working with such artists as Louis Armstrong. She was known as "Empress of the Blues." Bop is a form of jazz characterized by accent on the upbeat and unusual chord structures. Johann Sebastian Bach (1685–1750) was a German composer of mainly sacred music.

Being me, it will not be white.
But it will be
a part of you, instructor.   30
You are white—
yet a part of me, as I am a part of you.
That's American.
Sometimes perhaps you don't want to be a part of me.
Nor do I often want to be a part of you.   35
But we are, that's true!
As I learn from you,
I guess you learn from me—
although you're older—and white—
and somewhat more free.   40

This is my page for English B.

DYLAN THOMAS
In My Craft or Sullen Art

In my craft or sullen art
Exercised in the still night
When only the moon rages
And the lovers lie abed
With all their griefs in their arms,　　　　　5
I labour by singing light
Not for ambition or bread
Or the strut and trade of charms
On the ivory stages
But for the common wages　　　　　10
Of their most secret heart.

Not for the proud man apart
From the raging moon I write
On these spindrift pages
Nor for the towering dead　　　　　15
With their nightingales and psalms
But for the lovers, their arms
Round the griefs of the ages,
Who pay no praise or wages
Nor heed my craft or art.　　　　　20

SUGGESTIONS FOR WRITING

1. In a short paper, discuss your own composing process. How do you write? As you begin to answer this question, you can take three perspectives on the subject:

   a. *The camera view.* What would a sound camera record if it were focused on you as you compose? In what place do you write? What implements do you use? What props (such as munchies or coffee)? Do you make sounds (such as muttering or reading aloud to yourself)? What about tics? rituals? compulsions? movements (such as pacing)? What other factors would the camera record?

   b. *The rational view.* What conscious decisions do you make? Do you prepare an outline? Do you start with a jazzy beginning? with a thesis statement? or do you write the beginning last? Do you use notes? Do you write to find out what you want to say? Or do you write only after you know exactly what you want to say? Do you use humor? irony? When writing, are you conscious of tone or point of view? Do you use gimmicks (such as quotations)? the five-paragraph essay? What other conscious decisions do you make?

c. *The intuitive leap.* What hunches do you have about your composing process? Do you think that your personality influences the way in which you write? Do you have hidden goals?

Adopting different perspectives, supplied by the following sets of questions, might also help you with your project:

a. *The process itself.* What are your methods? Can you divide your writing process into parts or phases? What are they? Do you swoop from beginning to end and then come back to revise? Or do you inch from first sentence to last, revising as you write? Do you cut and paste, deleting, adding, rearranging, and substituting? What other questions are pertinent to your writing process?

b. *You.* How do your likes and dislikes influence your writing? Do you have any particular skills? Do you lack any skills? How does your past training help or hinder you? Do your career or personal goals influence your writing? Do your work habits help or hinder you? What other personal factors are important to your writing?

c. *Purpose.* What influence does audience have on your writing? Generally, what are your reasons for writing?

d. *Means.* How does your language ability influence your writing? Do you enjoy playing with words? Do you have any problems with language? If you write for publication, how does the medium of publication influence your writing?

2. Write an essay discussing how you first learned to read and write. Did you learn primarily in school or at home? How did you feel as you gained this new ability?

3. Think back to a school paper that you are especially proud of. It may not have earned a high grade, but you thought it was your best work. As you remember that paper, write about one, two, or all three of the following questions:

a. How did you decide what to write about? Explain your interest in the subject.

b. What particular difficulties did you encounter in writing the paper?

c. What was the reaction of others to your paper? Why did they react in this way?

4. Discuss the writing instruction that you received in high school. What kinds of help did your teachers give you? What sorts of writing were you asked to do? Did you enjoy writing, or did you find it unpleasant? Why?

5. Analyze the motives for writing that George Orwell, Joan Didion, and Eldridge Cleaver develop in their essays. Why did they become writers? What do these motives have in common? How do they differ?

CHAPTER TWO

Personal Writing

Most writing implies a desire to commmunicate to a reader, and this desire has certain implications that are worth thinking about. For instance, if you scribble a note for the sole purpose of reminding yourself to do something, the way you scribble is irrelevant so long as you can decipher the squiggles when you need to. But if you intend the note to be read by someone else, your penmanship must be at least moderately legible. The same can be said about the *mechanics* of writing: grammar, punctuation, and spelling. If you don't intend to have anyone read what you write, you can ignore the mechanics. But if you mean to be read, you need to watch your language. Many people have strong feelings about correctness and simply will not accept writing that is riddled with "mechanical" errors, no matter how brilliant the ideas might be; to avoid this sort of elementary rejection, we need to be meticulous about those "mechanics."

Some personal writing is, of course, extremely private. People keep diaries that they want no one else to read. On the other hand, many people, especially writers, keep notes and journals that no one else *could* read with understanding, but these materials eventually find their way into public writing as parts of larger projects. The personal writing in this collection is, of course, not private; the journal entries and autobiographical sketches reprinted here were written to be read by an intelligent public.

From the writer's point of view, their personal jottings are not intended to be read by others, but only to serve their larger purposes, whatever those might be. From the reader's point of view, however, personal writing reveals the writer—opens up his or her personality, character, and concerns to view.

When we read expository prose (the sort represented in Chapter Three of this book), our attention is on the information we gain, not on the writer. When we read personal writing, we are primarily interested in the writer, though we may also gain information about any number of other topics. Think of the difference between auto-biography and biography. We call autobiography "personal" because its focus is on the unique human being who is doing the writing. With biography, our focus is not on the biographer, but on his or her subject.

For interesting perspectives on personal writing, you might refer back to the essays by Eldridge Cleaver, Joan Didion, and Henry Miller in the first chapter of this book. For all three of them, writing is primarily personal, a means of self-discovery.

The Journal

The journal is a day-by-day account of a writer's experiences, impressions, and thoughts. Entries are usually quite brief and often contain the seeds of undeveloped ideas that will grow and bear fruit in longer writings. That is, many writers keep journals as repositories for ideas.

The journal is less personal, less private, than the diary, and often journals—such as the ones in this section—have been intended ultimately for publication.

One of the most famous (and delightful) journals in the English language is that by James Boswell, the friend and biographer of Dr. Samuel Johnson, who, among other achievements, authored the first real dictionary in English.

The last entry in Boswell's *London Journal* indicates the two-way nature of journal writing. On the one hand, Boswell is obviously writing for his own satisfaction and probably as a means of recording his experiences. On the other hand, he just as obviously has readers in mind.

Thursday 4 August, 1763. This is now my last day in London before I set out upon my travels, and makes a very important period in my journal. Let me recollect my life since this journal began [in 1762]. Has it not passed like a dream? Yes, but I have been attaining a knowledge of the world. I came to town to go into the Guards. How different is my scheme now! I am now upon a less pleasurable but a more rational and lasting plan [to go into the law]. Let me pursue it with steadiness and I may be a man of dignity. My mind is strangely agitated. I am happy to think of going upon my travels and seeing the diversity of foreign parts; and yet my feeble mind shrinks somewhat at the idea of leaving Britain in so very short a time from the moment in which I now make this remark. How strange must I feel myself in foreign parts. My mind too is gloomy and dejected at the thoughts of leaving London, where I am so comfortably situated and where I have enjoyed most happiness. However, I shall be happier for being abroad, as long as I live. Let me be manly. Let me commit myself to the care of my merciful Creator.

JOAN DIDION
On Keeping a Notebook

For information on Joan Didion, see "Why I Write," pages 22–28.

In her essay, Joan Didion talks about an extremely private kind of journal, writing that is not intended for others. She is totally consistent, collecting in her journal the same kind of concrete images that, in "Why I Write," she says are so meaningful to her. And in her dedication to the specific image, Didion is in the tradition of the great American transcendental essayist Ralph Waldo Emerson, who said, "Put the argument into a concrete shape, into an image,—some hard phrase, sound and solid as a ball, which they can see and handle and carry home with them—and the course is half won."

"'That woman Estelle,'" the note reads, "'is partly the reason why George Sharp and I are separated today.' *Dirty crepe-de-Chine wrapper, hotel bar, Wilmington RR, 9:45 a.m. August Monday morning.*"

Since the note is in my notebook it presumably has some meaning to me. I study it for a long while. At first I have only the most general notion of what I was doing on an August Monday morning in the bar of the hotel across from the Pennsylvania Railroad station in Wilmington, Delaware (waiting for a train? missing one? 1960? 1961? why Wilmington?), but I do remember being there. The woman in the dirty crepe-de-Chine wrapper had come down from her room for a beer, and the bartender had heard before the reason why George Sharp and she were separated today. "Sure," he said, and went on mopping the floor. "You told me." At the other end of the bar is a girl. She is talking, pointedly, not to the man beside her but to a cat lying in the triangle of sunlight cast through the open door. She is wearing a plaid silk dress from Peck & Peck, and the hem is coming down.

Here is what it is: the girl has been on the Eastern Shore, and now she is going back to the city, leaving the man beside her, and all she can see ahead are the viscous summer sidewalks and the 3 a.m. long-distance calls that will make her lie awake and then sleep drugged through all the steaming mornings left in August (1960? 1961?). Because she must go directly from the train to lunch in New York, she wishes that she had a safety pin for the hem of the plaid silk dress, and she also wishes that she could forget about the hem and the lunch and stay in the cool bar that smells of disinfectant and malt and make friends with the woman in the crepe-de-Chine wrapper. She is afflicted by a little self-pity, and she wants to compare Estelles. That is what that was all about.

Why did I write it down? In order to remember, of course, but exactly what was it I wanted to remember? How much of it actually happened?

Did any of it? Why do I keep a notebook at all? It is easy to deceive oneself on all those scores. The impulse to write things down is a peculiarly compulsive one, inexplicable to those who do not share it, useful only accidentally, only secondarily, in the way that any compulsion tries to justify itself. I suppose that it begins or does not begin in the cradle. Although I have felt compelled to write things down since I was five years old, I doubt that my daughter ever will, for she is a singularly blessed and accepting child, delighted with life exactly as life presents itself to her, unafraid to go to sleep and unafraid to wake up. Keepers of private notebooks are a different breed altogether, lonely and resistant rearrangers of things, anxious malcontents, children afflicted apparently at birth with some presentiment of loss.

My first notebook was a Big Five tablet, given to me by my mother with a sensible suggestion that I stop whining and learn to amuse myself by writing down my thoughts. She returned the tablet to me a few years ago; the first entry is an account of a woman who believed herself to be freezing to death in the Arctic night, only to find, when day broke, that she had stumbled onto the Sahara Desert, where she would die of the heat before lunch. I have no idea what turn of a five-year-old's mind could have prompted so insistently "ironic" and exotic a story, but it does reveal a certain predilection for the extreme which has dogged me into adult life; perhaps if I were analytically inclined I would find it a truer story than any I might have told about Donald Johnson's birthday party or the day my cousin Brenda put Kitty Litter in the aquarium.

So the point of my keeping a notebook has never been, nor is it now, to have an accurate factual record of what I have been doing or thinking. That would be a different impulse entirely, an instinct for reality which I sometimes envy but do not possess. At no point have I ever been able successfully to keep a diary; my approach to daily life ranges from the grossly negligent to the merely absent, and on those few occasions when I have tried dutifully to record a day's events, boredom has so overcome me that the results are mysterious at best. What is this business about "shopping, typing piece, dinner with E, depressed"? Shopping for what? Typing what piece? Who is E? Was this "E" depressed, or was I depressed? Who cares?

In fact I have abandoned altogether that kind of pointless entry; instead I tell what some would call lies. "That's simply not true," the members of my family frequently tell me when they come up against my memory of a shared event. "The party was *not* for you, the spider was *not* a black widow, *it wasn't that way at all.*" Very likely they are right, for not only have I always had trouble distinguishing between what happened and what merely might have happened, but I remain unconvinced that the distinction, for my purposes, matters. The cracked crab that I recall having for lunch the day my father came home from Detroit in 1945 must certainly be embroidery, worked into the day's pattern to lend verisimilitude; I was ten years old and would not now remember the cracked crab. The day's events did not turn on cracked crab. And yet it is precisely that fictitious crab that makes me see the afternoon all over again, a home movie run all too often, the father bearing gifts, the child weeping, an exercise in family love and guilt. Or that is what it was to me. Similarly, perhaps it never did snow that August in Vermont; perhaps there never were flurries in the night wind, and maybe no one else felt the ground hardening and summer already dead even as we pretended to bask in it, but that was how it felt to me, and it might as well have snowed, could have snowed, did snow.

How it felt to me: that is getting closer to the truth about a notebook. I sometimes delude myself about why I keep a notebook, imagine that some thrifty virtue derives from preserving everything observed. See enough and write it down, I tell myself, and then some morning when the world seems drained of wonder, some day when I am only going through the motions of doing what I am supposed to do, which is write—on that bankrupt morning I will simply open my notebook and there it will all be, a forgotten account with accumulated interest, paid passage back to the world out there: dialogue overheard in hotels and elevators and at the hatcheck counter in Pavillon (one middle-aged man shows his hat check to another and says, "That's my old football number"); impressions of Bettina Aptheker and Benjamin Sonnenberg and Teddy ("Mr. Acapulco") Stauffer; careful *aperçus* about tennis bums and failed fashion models and Greek shipping heiresses, one of whom taught me a significant lesson (a lesson I could have learned from F. Scott Fitzgerald, but perhaps we all must meet the very rich for ourselves) by asking, when I arrived to interview her in her orchid-filled sitting room on the second day of a paralyzing New York blizzard, whether it was snowing outside.

I imagine, in other words, that the notebook is about other people. But of course it is not. I have no real business with what one stranger said to another at the hatcheck counter in Pavillon; in fact I suspect that the line "That's my old football number" touched not my own imagination at all, but merely some memory of something once read, probably "The Eighty-Yard Run." Nor is my concern with a woman in a dirty crepe-de-Chine wrapper in a Wilmington bar. My stake is always, of course, in the unmentioned girl in the plaid silk dress. *Remember what it was to be me*: that is always the point.

It is a difficult point to admit. We are brought up in the ethic that others, any others, all others, are by definition more interesting than ourselves; taught to be diffident, just this side of self-effacing. ("You're the least important person in the room and don't forget it," Jessica Mitford's governess would hiss in her ear on the advent of any social occasion; I copied that into my notebook because it is only recently that I have been able to enter a room without hearing some such phrase in my inner ear.)

Only the very young and the very old may recount their dreams at breakfast, dwell upon self, interrupt with memories of beach picnics and favorite Liberty lawn dresses and the rainbow trout in a creek near Colorado Springs. The rest of us are expected, rightly, to affect absorption in other people's favorite dresses, other people's trout.

And so we do. But our notebooks give us away, for however dutifully we record what we see around us, the common denominator of all we see is always, transparently, shamelessly, the implacable "I." We are not talking here about the kind of notebook that is patently for public consumption, a structural conceit for binding together a series of graceful *pensées*; we are talking about something private, about bits of the mind's string too short to use, an indiscriminate and erratic assemblage with meaning only for its maker.

And sometimes even the maker has difficulty with the meaning. There does not seem to be, for example, any point in my knowing for the rest of my life that, during 1964, 720 tons of soot fell on every square mile of New York City, yet there it is in my notebook, labeled "FACT." Nor do I really need to remember that Ambrose Bierce liked to spell Leland Stanford's name "£eland $tanford" or that "smart women almost always wear black in Cuba," a fashion hint without much potential for practical application. And does not the relevance of these notes seem marginal at best?:

> In the basement museum of the Inyo County Courthouse in Independence, California, sign pinned to a mandarin coat: "This MANDARIN COAT was often worn by Mrs. Minnie S. Brooks when giving lectures on her TEAPOT COLLECTION."

> Redhead getting out of car in front of Beverly Wilshire Hotel, chinchilla stole, Vuitton bags with tags reading:

> MRS LOU FOX
> HOTEL SAHARA
> VEGAS

Well, perhaps not entirely marginal. As a matter of fact, Mrs. Minnie S. Brooks and her MANDARIN COAT pull me back into my own childhood, for although I never knew Mrs. Brooks and did not visit Inyo County until I was thirty, I grew up in just such a world, in houses cluttered with Indian relics and bits of gold ore and ambegris and the souvenirs my Aunt Mercy Farnsworth brought back from the Orient. It is a long way from that world to Mrs. Lou Fox's world, where we all live now, and is it not just as well to remember that? Might not Mrs. Minnie S. Brooks help me to remember what I am? Might not Mrs. Lou Fox help me to remember what I am not?

But sometimes the point is harder to discern. What exactly did I have in mind when I noted down that it cost the father of someone I know $650 a month to light the place on the Hudson in which he lived before the Crash? What use was I planning to make of this line by Jimmy Hoffa: "I may have my faults, but being wrong ain't one of them"? And although I think it interesting to know where the girls who travel with the Syndicate have their hair done when they find themselves on the West Coast, will I ever make suitable use of it? Might I not be better off just passing it on to John O'Hara? What is a recipe for sauerkraut doing in my notebook? What kind of magpie keeps this notebook? "He was born in the night the Titanic went down." That seems a nice enough line, and I even recall who said it, but is it not really a better line in life than it could ever be in fiction?

But of course that is exactly it: not that I should ever use the line, but that I should remember the woman who said it and the afternoon I heard it. We were on her terrace by the sea, and we were finishing the wine left from lunch, trying to get what sun there was, a California winter sun. The woman whose husband was born the night the Titanic went down wanted to rent her house, wanted to go back to her children in Paris. I remember wishing that I could afford the house, which cost $1,000 a month. "Someday you will," she said lazily. "Someday it all comes." There in the sun on her terrace it seemed easy to believe in someday, but later I had a low-grade afternoon hangover and ran over a black snake on the way to the supermarket and was flooded with inexplicable fear when I heard the checkout clerk explaining to the man ahead of me why she was finally divorcing her husband. "He left me no choice," she said over and over as she punched the register. "He has a little seven-month-old baby by her, he left me no choice." I would like to believe that my dread then was for the human condition, but of course it was for me, because I wanted a baby and did not then have one and because I wanted to own the house that cost $1,000 a month to rent and because I had a hangover.

It all comes back. Perhaps it is difficult to see the value in having one's self back in that kind of mood, but I do see it; I think we are well advised to keep on nodding terms with the people we used to be, whether we find them attractive company or not. Otherwise they turn up unannounced and surprise us, come hammering on the mind's door at 4 a.m. of a bad night and demand to know who deserted them, who betrayed them, who is going to make amends. We forget all too soon the things we thought we could never forget. We forget the loves and the betrayals alike, forget what we whispered and what we screamed, forget who we were. I have already lost touch with a couple of people I used to be; one of them, a seventeen-year-old, presents little threat, although it would be of some interest to me to know again what it feels like to sit on a river levee drinking vodka-and-orange-juice and listen to Les Paul and Mary Ford and their echoes sing "How High the Moon" on the car radio. (You see I still have the scenes, but I no longer perceive myself among those present, no longer could even improvise the dialogue.) The other one, a twenty-three-year-old, bothers me more. She was always a good deal of trouble, and I suspect she will reappear when I least want to see her, skirts too long, shy to the point of aggravation, always the injured party, full of recriminations and little hurts and stories I do not want to hear again, at once saddening me and angering me with her vulnerability and ignorance, an apparition all the more insistent for being so long banished.

It is a good idea, then, to keep in touch, and I suppose that keeping in touch is what notebooks are all about. And we are all on our own when it comes to keeping those lines open to ourselves: your notebook will never help me, nor mine you. *"So what's new in the whiskey business?"* What could that possibly mean to you? To me it means a blonde in a Pucci bathing suit sitting with a couple of fat men by the pool at the Beverly Hills Hotel. Another man approaches, and they all regard one another in silence for a while. "So what's new in the whiskey business?" one of the fat men finally says by way of welcome, and the blonde stands up, arches one foot and dips it in the pool, looking all the while at the cabaña where Baby Pignatari is talking on the telephone. That is all there is to that, except that several years later I saw the blonde coming out of Saks Fifth Avenue in New York with her California complexion and a voluminous mink coat. In the harsh wind that day she looked old and irrevocably tired to me, and even the skins in the mink coat were not worked the way they were doing them that year, not the way she would have wanted them done, and there is the point of the story. For a while after that I did not like to look in the mirror, and my eyes would skim the newspapers and pick out only the deaths, the cancer victims, the premature coronaries, the suicides, and I stopped riding the Lexington Avenue IRT because I noticed for the first time that all the strangers I had seen for years—the man with the seeing-eye dog, the spinster who read the classified pages every day, the fat girl who always got off with me at Grand Central—looked older than they once had.

It all came back. Even the recipe for sauerkraut: even that brings it back. I was on Fire Island when I first made that sauerkraut, and it was raining, and we drank a lot of bourbon and ate the sauerkraut and went to bed at ten, and I listened to the rain and the Atlantic and felt safe. I made the sauerkraut again last night and it did not make me feel any safer, but that is, as they say, another story.

QUESTIONS

1. Explain why Joan Didion keeps a notebook.
2. Explain what Didion means when she says, "I tell what some would call lies."

3. The entries in the notebook might seem strange: a recipe for sauerkraut, the fact that during 1964 720 tons of soot fell on every square mile of New York City, the impression of a "Redhead getting out of car in front of Beverly Wilshire Hotel, chinchilla stole. Vuitton bags with tags reading: Mrs Lou Fox, Hotel Sahara, Vegas." Why such entries? Of what use might they be to their author? Most important: what do they tell you about Didion?

4. How does this essay relate to "Why I Write" on pages 22–28? Are the two pieces mutually illuminating? Explain.

5. On the basis of the two essays by Joan Didion, write a brief character sketch of the author. What sort of person does she seem to be?

6. In your opinion, did Joan Didion intend to make her journals public when she was writing them? Explain.

NATHANIEL HAWTHORNE
A Murder on Shipboard

Most college students have read—or at least heard of— The Scarlet Letter, *the classic American novel about Puritan concepts of guilt and innocence. But few people today know the other works of Nathaniel Hawthorne. At one time, not too long ago, most young people were familiar with at least some of Hawthorne's short fiction, collected in* Twice-Told Tales, *and many had read* The Marble Faun *and* The House of the Seven Gables.

Hawthorne was born in Salem Massachusetts in 1804. He came from an old Puritan family and his father was a sea captain. In 1842 he married Sophia Peabody, friend of Ralph Waldo Emerson, the poet, and Henry David Thoreau, the author of Walden. *While attempting to establish himself as a writer, Hawthorne worked in the Boston customhouse. As "payment" for having written a campaign biography, President Franklin Pierce gave Hawthorne the post of United States consul in Liverpool. Hawthorne died in 1864. He is remembered primarily for his fiction, but his notebooks, which he kept with special care from 1853 to 1857, are also important.*

September 22nd [1853]—Nothing very important has happened lately. Some days ago, an American captain came to the office, and told how he had shot one of his crew, shortly after sailing from New Orleans, and while the ship was still in the river.[1] As he described the event, he was in peril of his life from this man, who was an Irishman; and he only fired his pistol, when the man was coming upon him with a knife in one hand, and some other weapon of offence in the other;—the captain, at the same time, struggling with one or two more of the crew. At the time, he was weak, having just recovered from the yellow fever. The shot struck him in the pit of the stomach, and he only lived about a quarter of an hour.

No magistrate in England has a right to arrest or examine the captain, unless by a warrant from the Secretary of State on the charge of murder. After his statement to me, the mother of the slain man went to the police-officer, and accused him of killing her son. Two or three days since, moreover, two of the sailors came before me, and gave their account of the matter; and it looked very different from that of the captain. According to them, the man had no idea of attacking the captain, and was so drunk that he could not keep himself upright, without assistance. One of these two men was actually holding him up, when the captain fired two barrels of his pistol, one immediately after the other, and lodged two balls in the pit of

---

[1]Since Hawthorne was American consul in Liverpool, the captain would naturally have reported the killing to him.

his stomach. The man immediately sank down, saying, "Jack, I'm killed," —and died very shortly. Meanwhile, the captain drove this man away, under the threat of shooting him likewise. Both the seamen described the captain's conduct, both then and during the whole voyage, as outrageous; and I do not much doubt that it was so. They gave their evidence (under oath) like men who wished to tell the truth, and were moved by no more than a natural indignation at the captain's wrong.

I did not much like the captain, from the first; a hard, rough man, with little education—nothing of the gentleman about him; a red face, a loud voice. He seemed a good deal excited, and talked fast and much about the event, but yet not as if it had sunk deeply into him. He observed that he would not have had it happen for a "thousand dollars"—that being the amount of detriment which he conceives himself to suffer by the ineffaceable blood-stain on his hand. In my opinion, it is little short of murder, if at all; but then what would be murder, on shore, is almost a natural occurrence, when done in such a hell on earth as one of these ships, in the first hours of her voyage. The men are then all drunk, some of them often in delirium tremens; and the captain feels no safety for his life, except in making himself as terrible as a fiend. It is the universal testimony, that there is no worse a set of sailors in these short voyages between Liverpool and America, than in any other trade whatever.

There is no probability that the captain will ever be called to account for this deed. He gave, at the time, his own version of the affair in his log-book; and this was signed by the entire crew, with the exception of one man, who had hidden himself in the hold in terror of the captain. His mates will sustain his side of the question; and none of the sailors would be within reach of the American courts, even should they be sought for.

QUESTIONS

1. In your opinion, did Nathaniel Hawthorne intend to make his journals public? Explain your answer, citing the text where relevant.

2. In this brief journal entry, Hawthorne draws a vivid sketch of the American captain. What sort of man is the captain? What are the details on which you base your opinion?

3. What is Hawthorne's attitude toward the event? Is he outraged, matter-of-fact, mildly interested, fascinated? Support your opinion by citing details in the text.

4. In what way does Hawthorne's journal resemble Joan Didion's description of her notebook? In what way does the Hawthorne journal differ from the Didion notebook?

THOMAS MERTON
From *The Secular Journal*

Thomas Merton (1915–1968) was something of a paradox: a Trappist monk living with the vow of silence, yet longing desperately to "speak" of his concerns, which he accomplished through his Secular Journal *(from which the following selection is taken), his autobiography,* The Seven Storey Mountain, *and his poetry. He grew up in France, England, and the United States, studied at Cambridge, and took his bachelor's and master's degrees at Columbia.*

The Secular Journal *entry for May 23, 1941, is somber. World War II has begun its devastation, and yet the Americans will not rouse themselves to action. Merton is talking about complacency before doom. In that respect, what he says is just as pertinent today as it was four decades ago.*

Even if I wanted to write history in this journal I don't know how I could. There is supposed to be a war going on.[1] But you don't know what is happening, what is important, what is unimportant; what is true, what is not; what means your life or death and what doesn't. Even those who think they know what matters are confused about it, and confuse everybody else by their own caution.

Roosevelt and his government all seem to want to help England with everything,[2] navy, army, airplanes and people like me, everything. If they know that is important, however, they feel that they can't convince people of that importance without playing some kind of trick on them.

Washington is full of weak tricks.

They make speeches on the radio. Maybe a lot of people listen. I haven't listened to any of them, or talked about any of them, so I wouldn't know. But apparently they make speeches on the radio, and each speech is supposed to be a little candy-coated pill. The people swallow the pill, and then the government watches them to see if they liked it or didn't like it.

But the government has been watching too close, and the people haven't been reacting right, and maybe too many haven't been listening to the speeches, which is probably the most disappointing thing of all.

All I know is, that if these politicians know what matters, if they know what is important, they ought to be able to say so sincerely and convinc-

---

[1]The war that was "going on" was World War II. In May of 1941, the Battle of Britain was being fought primarily in the air with the RAF attempting to stop devastating German raids on the British Isles. Hitler's disastrous invasion of Russia was only a month away. But America had not yet entered World War II; the Pearl Harbor attack was not to take place until December 7.

[2]President Franklin D. Roosevelt and his administration were trying to help the English survive the Nazi onslaught by "transferring, lending, or leasing" American war supplies to the embattled British.

ingly, without getting scared, hysterical, cagey, obscure, or in some strange complex way of their own, diplomatic about it.

If they know what is vital, what is necessary to save the world, they should be able to say it with some show of conviction. At least with enough show of conviction to scare the people who disagree with them, or to start some kind of real reaction. But all that is happening is a series of crazy, futile, artificial movements across the surface of the country. The land is being lightly stirred by wind, and everybody more or less refuses to pay too much attention. It may be a good thing, and it may be a bad thing, I'm sure I don't know which.

I was never so convinced of anything as that I haven't any idea what this is all about, what people are doing. I think a lot of people are crazy, and a lot of people just refuse to have anything happen to them, and have become, instinctively, stubborn, in a fairly good, animal sort of a way. They won't be moved.

That is another thing that nobody had expected.

The common rationalization that everybody was handing around before was: "The bands will play and flags wave and you will fall out of the window of your office, you poor sap, in your haste to go and save the world." Well, first, the bands were slow in getting started, and even now the band-playing is pretty timid and disorganised, and the bands are not making such a terrific racket, or a racket that is in the least exciting. The noise of the bands by now is still slightly annoying because of its timidity and its monotony and its confusion.

The other part of the rationalisation is that it had become everybody's property. Everybody knew that the bands would play, everybody knew that everybody else was going to fall for propaganda, everybody was, at the same time, thoroughly unwilling to go to war.

Now they are all sitting around waiting for the propaganda to start, and waiting to not listen to it.

If that is so, that would be the best aspect of the situation. Only that isn't so.

I came across some people in New York who were a lot more keyed up than they were when I last saw them. Girls. Their lipstick was brighter, their dresses fancier, they had hundreds of friends who were in the Army, and they were pretty free with the terms "fifth columnist"[3] and "lousy Nazi," and they used these words with quite a bit of feeling.

But on the other hand, their attitude was just as confused as anybody else's, because another of their phrases, and one that they also used with a

---

[3]The fifth column is a group of traitorously secret supporters of or sympathizers with an enemy nation. On the eve of World War II, the fifth column consisted of sympathizers with Nazi Germany.

lot of strong feeling was that "of course America wouldn't get into it—do you think?"

What these people are is: scared. They are the ones who have been reading all the papers and listening to all the radio reports, and they are excited. Their excitement is not caused by propaganda, exactly, because there has been no exciting propaganda. All the propaganda has been clumsy and equivocal and cautious.

So these people are really living on self-generated excitement of their own, built up from biting their nails in front of the radio. And the thing that makes them most nervous about the radio is not the abundance of scaring news that comes over it, but the fact that the same meager news is all they get five times a day, over and over, on all the successive news broadcasts.

Another weakness in the propaganda, as far as I know, is that it is all built up on completely equivocal guesses about the future or else self-contradictory and incomprehensible statements about the present that nobody can quite grasp.

The big weakness of the propaganda is that it is entirely abstract, and that the people who are uttering it have no firm grasp of abstraction anyway.

There has been no tendency whatever to play up the physically exciting propaganda, horror stuff, blood, cruelty, violence. All the propaganda has been abstract. What is physically violent about the propaganda is all left over from before the war: stories about concentration camps, stormtroopers, brutality, sadism, priests and pastors whipped and clubbed, and so forth.

The bombing of Rotterdam is the most horrible thing that has so far happened, from what I know.[4] There has not been much emphasis on it. It is one of the things that makes me sickest. But all we know about it, aside from wild stories, is the extent of the *physical* destruction. We are told that probably so many millions of dollars worth of property damage has been done. But who cares about a million dollars worth of property? That damage is completely abstract anyway.

We are told a little about the people killed. The stories are terrible. The people were probably killed in thousands and very painfully. Some of the stories of general carnage are so picturesque that they sound false. But Rotterdam has a frightful story, the frightfulness of which is only diminished by the unnecessary picturesqueness of some of the stories that are so gruesome that they sound like lies.

---

[4]Rotterdam, Holland, was bombed in 1940, about one year before this entry was written by Merton. At the time of writing, London had been blasted by Nazi bombing raids for some little while. It is interesting that Merton seems unaware of this and chooses to focus instead on a similar event more distant in time.

The general attitude of the people is to refuse to hear anything of this kind at all. They refuse to listen. They say it is propaganda before you start.

Catholics in this country don't particularly care what has happened to the church in Poland. They don't want to hear anything about it. But the information about the church in Poland is probably completely reliable, since it comes from the Vatican. Nevertheless, people are just as willing not to hear that news on the grounds that it is "British propaganda." That is their answer to it. The real reason why they won't listen is simply that they don't want to hear anything about suffering. They don't want to hear about the horrors of the war. They don't want to listen.

QUESTIONS

1. Do you think that, in his journal, Merton is "talking" only to himself or that he has other readers in mind? In other words, does he seem to want to "share" his meditations on the impending war with others? Support your answer by referring to the text.

2. What are Merton's attitudes toward war? Toward propaganda? Are they like those of your classmates or yours? Explain.

3. In your opinion, is Merton's writing easy or difficult to read? Support your opinion by referring to the text.

4. How did you react to the selection? Did you find it interesting or dull? Meaningful or irrelevant? Support your evaluation by referring to the text.

EDMUND WILSON
From *The Twenties*

One of America's great intellectuals, Edmund Wilson (1895–1972) edited the prestigious magazine Vanity Fair *in 1920 and 1921 and was on the staffs of* The New Republic *(1926–1931) and* The New Yorker *(1944–1948); he was the author of influential works of literary criticism (*Axel's Castle, The Wound and the Bow, *and* The Triple Thinkers*) and history (*To the Finland Station*); he wrote fiction (*Memoirs of Hecate County*) and plays. In short, he was amazingly versatile and enormously influential in American intellectual and literary life.*

The journal excerpts that follow are vignettes, images, impressions; they capture moments in the author's life and show his keen interest in the texture of experience: sights and sounds, smells, movements. In his fascination with the concrete and specific, Wilson is very much like Joan Didion.

The sea scrolling silver on the kelp-mottled beach—or the silver mirrors of the ebb, and, beyond, the deep wonderful blue and the brownleaf of the kelp, and, beyond, the brown blue-washed mountains answering to the blue brown-streaked sea—or at late afternoon with a purple carpet of loam, and, beyond it, blues and purples of the sea.

Hope Ranch—the cleft sand-aisled rock—mussel clusters petaling black rocks—little pearly and pink sand crabs that bury themselves backside foremost in the sand—a tramp fishing for sea perch—"Think of what a great life they really must lead simply living along the beach like that— once I found one who was reading a history of Italy in Italian—of course, he may have been an Italian but he spoke English without a trace of accent—we used to come out and have some cocktails and then have supper and stay till night—there was a great big full moon—we used to keep moving our blanket back as the water came further up till we were right up against the cliff and then the shale used to fall on us—This is the first time I've ever come to his place with an easy conscience—I've always been like the Ancient Mariner, don't you know? When he used to glance back for fear some terrible fiend was following him"—When we got dressed, our underclothes blew out with the tempered cold Pacific wind like sails about our bodies—the breakers so long and easy—the flapping white gulls close above us—"They make iodine out of the kelp." The shadow of Vera Cruz lay before us in the water.

The Drummonds of Boston. The father apparently a rounder—the mother imprisoned the children, refused to send them to school or college, made each learn a trade and compelled them periodically to wait upon the servants—one, according to Ted, was an archetypical old ape; another a great big masturbating moron who spread scandal about Dorothy Heydell; a third, who had studied to be an electrician, went to the war and never came back but got a job as an electrician after he was demobilized and the other children are forbidden to correspond with him; and a fourth, Ellen, is a strapping tomboy all Western but for a Boston pronunciation of *darn*—she gave him a kiss and said "Hello, Passion!" "Well, isn't it about time to coït?" Mrs. Drummond a woman with a red face and a red nose and a baleful eye. Mary Craig, Ted's cousin, used to remonstrate with him about Margaret Canby and tell him how terribly she (Mary) felt about her little child, etc., and on one occasion she enraged him by taking him to task for wasting his life in drunkenness, when he "had only been in swimming." She said, "Look at you now, your eyes are all bloodshot!" "I hadn't had a drink for a week." (Her mother was simple and nice and said things like "Oh, look at the mountainy—mountainy—mountains.") "Then she [Mary Craig] told me that I wouldn't listen to anybody's opinion on anything."

The spacious Pacific landscapes. The pink enormous mountains—the people grow to match the scenery—they expand out there more easily— they marry and divorce young—gigantic uncultivated beauties like the beauties of the prehistoric world—men playing and thriving in the raw magnificent landscapes of primordial processes and upheavals—the sun dropping into the Pacific and the red-gold holocaust of the sky.

Getting into New York by the Liberty Street ferry on a rainy day—a blotting of gray over everything, behind which the strong heavy colors of summer showed dark and dull—the green of trees in the Square, the red of the house fronts on the north side. Coming up, the ruddy roasted dark walls of factories overtowering and standing out among the lower build- ings—in a window of which one would see a livid but acrid and flint-like lime-green light. And the red and green lamps on the backs of taxis has a similar jewellike look.

Coming home down Broadway at night, as he passed under the windows of some nightclub, he was sprayed profusely with some cold evacuation of liquid from the second floor and thought at once of a nickel-silver cocktail shaker which it had been found advisable for some reason or other to empty. But, looking up, he beheld the drawn sallow face of a gentleman whose drinks had not agreed with him. With energy and virile disgust, he tried to wipe off his shoulder and his knee with his handkerchief.—Stripping off his contaminated clothes, he disclosed the white double box of his breast, which he admired in the glass. "Some *bastard vomited* on me!"—he stung her with the words like masculine stabs.

The fashion of large black hats that folded about the ears, like bonnets, and half concealed the face, with mysterious and provocative effect. The two girls at Thirty-fourth Street and Sixth Avenue, both in black, with white stockings and these black hats—the face of one was easy to be seen, Jewish and plain; that of the other hidden in her hat, as if from bashfulness—she was pretty, with a nose like Belle Gifford's and a deeper stronger voice than one expected—she was apparently governed by the other and always waited for her to make decisions on any proposition. At the same time, boyish bobs are fashionable, and you have a regular type of little girl who, with a bob, simply seems to tie her dress around the waist with a boyish leather belt. The little girl of this type at the Tango Gardens—the first night, I thought her slight, slender-legged, shrewd, gray-eyed and matter-of-fact. The next night, I found her amiable, honest and with a ready simple smile and I observed that her body was ample and thick—it was perhaps the bob, the dress and her black round-nosed slippers with a strap across the instep, of a model that looks old-fashioned but is now popular, which gave her the effect of being slight.—When she disappeared in the middle of the evening, at the instance, apparently, of the ticket taker, she came back with a different pair of shoes—light coffee brown.

Marie. I picked her up somewhere in the Forties or Fifties coming out of a hotel. We just looked at one another and began to talk. Looking out into the hot, the smothered summer night, the dark greenery of the park (Washington Square Park), its benches loaded with slowed and muted swarms of human beings, hundreds of them stupidly swarming in the night so close to my spacious empty room, my comparatively so much cooler apartment, just across the street, dirty, sweaty, giving out the sounds of life, but obscured by the darkness and restrained and keyed down by the heat.—When I first saw her on the street, I thought her whore-broken, hard-boiled—her dissatisfied, disagreeable look, as if she smelled a bad smell: but when I came to talk to her, I learned that her father was supposed to have come from Barcelona, and saw that her hands were strong, broad and thick, her fingers blunt and large. She had a simplicity and a feminine gentleness under her hard-boiled New York manner.— When she came to the apartment, I was amazed to see how much younger she looked and how much handsomer. She had the large soft tragic eyes (with the "nose all over my face" and the thick red sensual lips which she worked into vulgar grimaces as she talked) of the Italian whores and peasant women of whom the Renaissance painters made madonnas. She told me about her brother in jail in Brooklyn, falsely accused of rape—this kid who had him indicted hadn't yet appeared for a trial, the boy she had been going with and who had been jealous of Marie's brother who had made all the trouble—she had retained a lawyer who was supposed to be very good, having got somebody off in some well-known case (well-known in the tabloid dailes)—she had given him everything she had, $350 (her tactful way of asking for money).

A *gray day at the shore*—it was going to rain—sky and sea were both gray—a few gulls above the water—dry smell of salt dust in the nostrils above the breaking crests.—The next day, the girl on the sand whom I took at first for a boy—she had glossy black hair, boyish-bobbed, and wore a white shirt tucked inside a pair of black trunks like a boy—I first recognized her as a girl by the way she held her cigarette—her feminine gesture moving the upper half of her arm toward her body—later I saw the low roundness of her breasts.—A young boy and girl playing ball across one of the lifelines in the surf, she a blonde in a turquoise bathing suit and with her tanned summer skin not quite continuous with the edge of the slip at the shoulders and thighs.

QUESTIONS

1. In his journal entries, Edmund Wilson achieves great vividness. How does he create these pictures and experiences in words? What techniques does he use to bring his writing to life?

2. In "A Murder on Shipboard," Hawthorne gave a straightforward *account of an event.* In our selection from Merton's *Secular Journal,* we found opinions about the Second World War. How would you characterize the entries in Wilson's journal?

3. If you had been the author of Wilson's journal entries, what use might you have put them to? In what sense could one characterize these journal entries as "raw material"?

4. Which of these short entries was most difficult for you to read? Why was it difficult? Did you have trouble with the language? Did you need more "background" information about the situation?

5. Did you enjoy reading these selections? Explain why or why not.

HENRY DAVID THOREAU
From *Journals*

Thoreau's Walden *(1854) stands with such masterpieces as Mark Twain's*
Huckleberry Finn, *Nathaniel Hawthorne's* The Scarlet Letter, *and the poems of*
Emily Dickinson as one of the supremely important American books. Less well
known, but also important, is his record of A Week on the Concord and Merrimack
Rivers.

While attending Harvard, Thoreau discovered the writing of Ralph Waldo
Emerson, who later became his mentor and friend; Emerson's thought was a major
influence on the younger man. Thoreau and Emerson shared a transcendentalist
philosophy, viewing man and nature as divine.

The essay "Civil Disobedience" (1849), which served as a philosophical basis for
the Civil Rights Movement, resulted from Thoreau's being jailed for refusing to pay
a poll tax that supported the war with Mexico, which he believed was an attempt to
extend slavery.

Born in 1817, Thoreau lived in and around Concord, Massachusetts until his
death in 1862.

The selections that follow reflect Thoreau's keen interest in the natural world.
Like other writers whom we admire—Joan Didion, and Edmund Wilson, for
example—Thoreau paid attention to concrete details, and he brought his prose to life
with images.

June 4 . . . Today, June fourth, I have been tending a burning in
the woods. Ray was there. It is a pleasant fact that you will know no man
long, however low in the social scale, however poor, miserable, intemper-
ate, and worthless he may appear to be, a mere burden to society, but you
will find at last that there is something which he understands and can do
better than any other. I was pleased to hear that one man had sent Ray as
the one who had had the most experience in setting fires of any man in
Lincoln. He had experience and skill as a burner of brush.

You must burn against the wind always, and burn slowly. When the
fire breaks over the hoed line, a little system and perseverance will accomplish more toward quelling it than any man would believe. It fortunately
happens that the experience acquired is oftentimes worth more than the
wages. When a fire breaks out in the woods, and a man fights it too near
and on the side, in the heat of the moment, without the systematic
cooperation of others, he is disposed to think it a desperate case, and that
this relentless fiend will run through the forest till it is glutted with food;
but let the company rest from their labors a moment, and then proceed
more deliberately and systematically, giving the fire a wider berth, and the
company will be astonished to find how soon and easily they will subdue it.
The woods themselves furnish one of the best weapons with which to

contend with the fires that destroy them—a pitch pine bough. It is the best instrument to thrash it with. There are few men who do not love better to give advice than to give assistance.

However large the fire, let a few men go to work deliberately but perseveringly to rake away the leaves and hoe off the surface of the ground at a convenient distance from the fire, while others follow with pine boughs to thrash it with when it reaches the line, and they will finally get round it and subdue it, and will be astonished at their own success.

A man who is about to burn his field in the midst of woods should rake off the leaves and twigs for the breadth of a rod at least, making no large heaps near the outside, and then plow around it several furrows and break them up with hoes, and set his fire early in the morning, before the wind rises.

As I was fighting the fire today, in the midst of the roaring and crackling—for the fire seems to snort like a wild horse—I heard from time to time the dying strain, the last sigh, the fine, clear, shrill scream of agony, as it were, of the trees breathing their last, probably the heated air or the steam escaping from some chink. At first I thought it was some bird, or a dying squirrel's note of anguish, or steam escaping from the tree. You sometimes hear it on a small scale in the log on the hearth. When a field is burned over, the squirrels probably go into the ground. How foreign is the yellow pine to the green woods—and what business has it here?

The fire stopped within a few inches of a partridge's nest today, June fourth, whom we took off in our hands and found thirteen creamy-colored eggs. I started up a wood-cock when I went to a rill to drink, at the westernmost angle of R. W. E.'s[1] wood-lot.

June 5 . . . Tonight, June fifth, after a hot day, I hear the first peculiar summer breathing of the frogs.

When all is calm, a small whirlwind will suddenly lift up the blazing leaves and let them fall beyond the line, and set all the woods in a blaze in a moment. Or some slight almost invisible cinder, seed of fire, will be wafted from the burnt district on to the dry turf which covers the surface and fills the crevices of many rocks, and there it will catch as in tinder, and smoke and smoulder, perchance, for half an hour heating several square yards of ground where yet no fire is visible, until it spreads to the leaves and the wind fans it into a blaze.

Men go to a fire for entertainment. When I see how eagerly men will run to a fire, whether in warm or in cold weather, by day or by night, dragging an engine at their heels, I am astonished to perceive how good a purpose the love of excitement is made to serve. What other force, pray,

---

[1]R. W. E. is Ralph Waldo Emerson, Thoreau's friend and mentor. See pp. 282–98 of this book.

what offered pay, what disinterested neighborliness could ever effect so much? No, these are boys who are to be dealt with, and these are the motives that prevail. There is no old man or woman dropping into the grave but covets excitement.

Nov 8. The stillness of the woods and fields is remarkable at this season of the year. There is not even the creak of a cricket to be heard. Of myriads of dry shrub oak leaves, not one rustles. Your own breath can rustle them, yet the breath of heaven does not suffice to. The trees have the aspect of waiting for winter. The autumnal leaves have lost their color; they are now truly sere, dead, and the woods wear a sombre color. Summer and harvest are over. The hickories, birches, chestnuts, no less than the maples, have lost their leaves. The sprouts, which had shot up so vigorously to repair the damage which the choppers had done, have stopped short for the winter. Everything stands silent and expectant. If I listen, I hear only the note of a chickadee—our most common and I may say native bird, most identified with our forests—or perchance the scream of a jay, or perchance from the solemn depths of these woods I hear tolling far away the knell of one departed. Thought rushes in to fill the vacuum. As you walk, however, the partridge still bursts away. The silent, dry, almost leafless, certainly fruitless woods. You wonder what cheer that bird can find in them. The partridge bursts away from the foot of a shrub oak like its own dry fruit, immortal bird! This sound still startles us. Dry goldenrods, now turned gray and white, lint our clothes as we walk. And the drooping, downy seed-vessels of the epilobium remind us of the summer. Perchance you will meet with a few solitary asters in the dry fields, with a little color left. The sumach is stripped of everything but its cone of red berries.

Nov. 19. The first really cold day. I find, on breaking off a shrub oak leaf, a little life at the foot of the leaf-stalk, so that a part of the green comes off. It has not died quite down to the point of separation, as it will do, I suppose, before spring. Most of the oaks have lost their leaves except on the lower branches, as if they were less exposed and less mature there, and felt the changes of the seasons less. The leaves have either fallen or withered long since, yet I found this afternoon, cold as it is—and there has been snow in the neighborhood—some sprouts which had come up this year from the stump of a young black-looking oak, covered still with handsome fresh red and green leaves, very large and unwithered and unwilted. It was on the south side of Fair Haven in a warm angle, where the wood was cut last winter and the exposed edge of the still standing wood running north and south met the cliff at right angles and served for a fence to keep off the wind. There were one or two stumps here whose sprouts had fresh leaves which transported me back to October. Yet the surrounding shrub oak leaves were as dry and dead as usual. There were also some minute birches only a year old, their leaves still freshly yellow, and some young wild apple trees apparently still growing, their leaves as green and tender as in summer. The goldenrods, one or more species of the white and some yellow ones, were many of them still quite fresh, though elsewhere they are all whitish and dry. I saw one whose top rose above the edge of a rock, and so much of it was turned white and dry: but the lower part of its raceme was still yellow. Some of the white species seemed to have started again as if for another spring. They had sprung up freshly a foot or more, and were budded to blossom, fresh and green. And sometimes on the same stem were old and dry and white downy flowers, and fresh green blossom-buds not yet expanded. I saw there some *pale* blue asters still bright, and the mullein leaves still large and green, one green to its top. And I discovered that when I put my hand on the mullein leaves they felt decidedly warm, but the radical leaves of the goldenrods felt cold and clammy. There was also the columbine, its leaves still alive and green; and I was pleased to smell the pennyroyal which I had bruised, though this dried up long ago. Each season is thus drawn out and lingers in certain localities, as the birds and insects know very well. If you penetrate to some warm recess under a cliff in the woods, you will be astonished at the amount of summer life that still flourishes there. No doubt more of the summer's life than we are aware thus slips by and outmaneuvers the winter, gliding from fence to fence. I have no doubt that a diligent search in proper places would discover many more of our summer flowers thus lingering till the snow came, than we suspect. It is as if the plant made no preparation for winter.

Now that the grass is withered and the leaves are withered or fallen, it begins to appear what is evergreen: the partridge [-berry] and checkerberry, and wintergreen leaves even, are more conspicuous.

The old leaves have been off the pines now for a month.

I once found a kernel of corn in the middle of a deep wood by Walden, tucked in behind a lichen on a pine, about as high as my head, either by a crow or a squirrel. It was a mile at least from any corn field.

Several species plainly linger till the snow comes.

Nov. 20. It is a common saying among country people that if you eat much fried hasty pudding it will make your hair curl. My experience, which was considerable, did not confirm this assertion.

Nov. 24. Plucked a buttercup on Bear Hill today.

I have certain friends whom I visit occasionally, but I commonly part from them early with a certain bitter-sweet sentiment. That which we love is so mixed and entangled with that we hate in one another that we are more grieved and disappointed, aye, and estranged from one another, by meeting than by absence. Some men may be my acquaintances merely, but one whom I have been accustomed to regard, to idealize, to have dreams about as a friend, and mix up intimately with myself, can never degenerate into an acquaintance. I must know him on that higher ground or not know him at all. We do not confess and explain, because we would fain be so intimately related as to understand each other without speech. Our friend must be broad. His must be an atmosphere coextensive with the universe, in which we can expand and breathe. For the most part we are smothered and stifled by one another. I go and see my friend and try his atmosphere. If our atmospheres do not mingle, if we repel each other strongly, it is of no use to stay.

. . . It is remarkable, but nevertheless true, as far as my observation goes, that women, to whom we commonly concede a somewhat finer and more sibylline nature, yield a more implicit obedience even to their animal instincts than men. The nature in them is stronger, the reason weaker. There are, for instance, many young and middle-aged men among my acquaintance—shoemakers, carpenters, farmers, and others—who have scruples about using animal food, but comparatively few girls or women. The latter, even the most refined, are the most intolerant of such reforms. I think that the reformer of the severest, as well as finest, class will find more sympathy in the intellect and philosophy of man than in the refinement and delicacy of woman. It is, perchance, a part of woman's conformity and easy nature. Her savior must not be too strong, stern, and intellectual, but charitable above all things.

Dec. 1. It is quite mild and pleasant today. I saw a little green hemisphere of moss which looked as if it covered a stone, but, thrusting my cane into it, I found it was nothing but moss, about fifteen inches in diameter and eight or nine inches high. When I broke it up, it appeared as if the annual growth was marked by successive layers half an inch deep each. The lower ones were quite rotten, but the present year's quite green, the intermediate white. I counted fifteen or eighteen. It was quite solid, and I saw that it continued solid as it grew by branching occasionally, just enough to fill the newly gained space, and the tender extremities of each plant, crowded close together, made the firm and compact surface of the bed. There was a darker line separating the growths, where I thought the surface had been exposed to the winter. It was quite saturated with water, though firm and solid.

Dec. 2. The woodpeckers' holes in the apple trees are about a fifth of an inch deep or just through the bark and half an inch apart. They must be the decaying trees that are most frequented by them, and probably their work serves to relieve and ventilate the tree and, as well, to destroy its enemies.

The barberries are shrivelled and dried. I find yet cranberries hard and not touched by the frost.

QUESTIONS

1. If you could have joined Thoreau on one of the days he talks about, which one would you choose? Why?

2. Explain at least one principle of good writing that you learned from—or found in—Thoreau's journal.

3. In his journal, Thoreau gives instructions for putting out a forest fire. What does the author do to make these instructions exceptionally clear and easy to understand?

4. On the basis of clues that you find in his journal entries, characterize Thoreau. What sort of person do you think he was?

5. All of the entries from Thoreau's journal maintain a consistent attitude toward life and the world around the author. On the basis of what you find in the journal entries, how would you characterize Thoreau's "philosophy of life"? Refer to the text to support your ideas.

SUGGESTIONS FOR WRITING

1. All of us have had experiences of which, later, we wished we had kept a detailed account—a trip to an exotic place such as New York; a period in our lives when we met many interesting people; a moment of triumph, as when we finally mastered a skill such as fly casting or making the perfect quiche. Write a page or two about such a moment in your life, and write as if you were entering it into your journal shortly after it happened.

2. Write three brief "journal entries." In the first, try to write like Edmund Wilson. In the second, imitate Henry David Thoreau. And in the third, pretend that you are Joan Didion. To prepare for these writings, you will want to return to the originals and take a close look at the way Wilson, Thoreau, and Didion express themselves.

3. Choose a general word—such as "boredom," "freedom," "education," "honor"—and define it by relating a specific instance that illustrates the word. (For example, you might "define" boredom by telling in detail

about a boring episode in your life.) Don't forget physical details (sounds, smells, textures, colors) and the actions of the people involved.

4. One point that this book has made again and again so far is this: the uses of writing and the reasons for doing it are as various as the people who read and write. It would interest you to take a close look at the part writing plays in the life of your family. For one week, note in some detail each "writing event" that takes place in your family, and then classify these events and discuss them in a written report to the class.

Remember to note each event—from a business letter that your mother might write to a doodle that your brother makes as he talks on the telephone.

Most people who carry out this observation are amazed at how much writing goes on in the typical family and how important it is to daily life.

Autobiography

Autobiography, like biography, is life history, but in the case of autobiography the authors write about their own lives, not the lives of others. Journals are, of course, autobiographical, but they are not extended, carefully structured works, as are most autobiographies.

Public figures—presidents and generals—write *memoirs*, but these tend to focus on historical events and are not personal and introspective, as are autobiographies.

Examples of autobiographies in world literature are St Augustine's *Confessions*, Benvenuto Cellini's *Autobiography*, Benjamin Franklin's *Autobiography*, and *The Education of Henry Adams*.

Simulated autobiography is a common device in fiction. For instance, Daniel Defoe's *Moll Flanders* is presumably the title character's telling of her life story, but actually the book is a novel. On the other hand, many novels are autobiographical, closely paralleling the life stories of their authors. Examples are Thomas Wolfe's *Look Homeward Angel* and James Joyce's *Portrait of the Artist as a Young Man.*

MARGARET MEAD
On Being a Granddaughter

Coming of Age in Samoa (1928) and Growing Up in New Guinea (1930) were anthropological studies of "primitive" societies, but each gained tremendous popular success and established Margaret Mead as both a respected scholar and public figure. She followed these books with a steady series of others and during her lifetime became one of the leading American intellectuals, known by her colleagues in anthropology and by the general public.

Born in 1901, she completed her doctorate at Columbia in 1929. At Columbia she was a student of Ruth Benedict, whose Patterns of Culture *was a milestone in American anthropological studies.*

Since her death in 1978, Margaret Mead's works have become controversial, particularly her research methods, but her influence on our view of child rearing and development, which grew out of her studies in the south Pacific, will be lasting.

In her autobiography, Blackberry Winter, *she tells of her background and intellectual development. "On Being a Granddaughter" is an account of her grandmother, a lasting influence on her life.*

My paternal grandmother, who lived with us from the time my parents married until she died in 1927, while I was studying anthropological collections in German museums, was the most decisive influence in my life. She sat at the center of our household. Her room—and my mother always saw to it that she had the best room, spacious and sunny, with a fireplace if possible—was the place to which we immediately went when we came in from playing or home from school. There my father went when he arrived in the house. There we did our lessons on the cherry-wood table with which she had begun housekeeping and which, later, was my dining room table for twenty-five years. There, sitting by the fire, erect and intense, she listened to us and to all of Mother's friends and to our friends. In my early childhood she was also very active—cooking, preserving, growing flowers in the garden, and attentive to all the activities of the country and the farm, including the chickens that were always invading the lawn and that I was always being called from my book to shoo away.

My mother was trustworthy in all matters that concerned our care. Grandma was trustworthy in a quite different way. She meant exactly what she said, always. If you borrowed her scissors, you returned them. In like case, Mother would wail ineffectually, "Why does everyone borrow my scissors and never return them?" and Father would often utter idle threats. But Grandma never threatened. She never raised her voice. She simply commanded respect and obedience by her complete expectation that she would be obeyed. And she never gave silly orders. She became my model when, in later life, I tried to formulate a role for the modern parent who can no longer exact obedience merely by virtue of being a parent and yet must be able to get obedience when it is necessary. Grandma never said, "Do this because Grandma says so," or "because Grandma wants you to do it." She simply said, "Do it," and I knew from her tone of voice that it was necessary.

My grandmother grew up in the little town of Winchester, in Adams County, Ohio, which two of my great-great-grandfathers had founded. She was one of nine children who reached adulthood. Her father was a farmer, a small entrepreneur, a member of the state legislature, a justice of the peace, and the Methodist local preacher. His name was Richard Ramsay, and in our family there have been so many Richards that they have to be referred to as Uncle El's Richard, Grace Bradford's Richard, and so on.

My grandmother began school teaching quite young, at a time when it was still somewhat unusual for a girl to teach school. When my grandfather, who was also a teacher, came home from the Civil War, he married my grandmother and they went to college together. They also graduated together. She gave a graduation address in the morning and my grandfather, who gave one in the afternoon, was introduced as the husband of Mrs. Mead who spoke this morning.

My grandfather was a school superintendent who was such a vigorous innovator that exhausted school boards used to request him to leave after a one-year term—with the highest credentials—to undertake the reform of some other school. We have a few examples of my grandmother's letters to him while they were engaged, including admonitions not to go on picnics on the Sabbath. He died when my father was six. Two days later the principal took his place and my grandmother took the principal's place. From then on she taught, sometimes in high school, sometimes small children, until she came to live with us when my parents married. It was the small children in whom she was most interested, and I have the notes she took on the schools she observed during a visit to Philadelphia before my parents' marriage.

She understood many things that are barely recognized in the wider educational world even today. For example, she realized that arithmetic is injurious to young minds and so, after I had learned my tables, she taught me algebra. She also understood the advantages of learning both inductively and deductively. On some days she gave me a set of plants to analyze; on others, she gave me a description and sent me out to the woods and meadows to collect examples, say, of the "mint family." She thought that memorizing mere facts was not very important and that drill was stultifying. The result was that I was not well drilled in geography or spelling. But I learned to observe the world around me and to note what I saw—to observe flowers and children and baby chicks. She taught me to read for the sense of what I read and to enjoy learning.

With the exception of the two years I went to kindergarten, for Grandma believed in training the hands early, though not with too fine work, and the year I was eight, when I went to school for a half-day in the fourth grade in Swarthmore, she taught me until I went to high school and even then helped me with my lessons when my teachers were woefully inadequate, as they often were. I never expected any teacher to know as much as my parents or my grandmother did. Although my grandmother had no Greek, she had a good deal of Latin, and I remember that once, on the Fourth of July, she picked up one of my brother's Latin texts because she had never read Sallust.

She was conscious of the developmental differences between boys and girls and considered boys to be much more vulnerable and in need of patience from their teachers than were girls of the same age. This was part of the background of my learning the meaning of gender. And just as Grandma thought boys were more vulnerable, my father thought it was easier for girls to do well in school, and so he always required me to get two and a half points higher than my brother in order to win the same financial bonus.

Grandma had no sense at all of ever having been handicapped by being a woman. I think she played as strong a role among her brothers and sisters as her elder brother, who was a famous Methodist preacher. Between them they kept up an active relationship with their parents in Winchester and, returning often for visits, they supervised, stimulated, and advised the less adventurous members of the family. This has now become my role among some of the descendants of my grandmother's sisters, who still live in various small towns and large cities in Ohio.

QUESTIONS

1. Does Mead seem to have had more respect for her grandmother or her mother? Explain.

2. Mead assumes her readers know about her *before* they begin to read this selection. How does your knowledge about Margaret Mead (or your lack of such knowledge) affect your interest in and understanding of the narrative?

3. In your own words, outline the grandmother's educational theories.

4. Every serious author creates a unique style, as you can see if you glance back over the selections that have preceded this one. How would you characterize Mead's style? Think of adjectives such as clear, murky, plain, ornate, natural, and artificial. Explain the basis for your characterization by referring to word choice, sentence structure, and figures of speech.

5. Being as specific as possible, explain your own reactions to the piece.

FRANK CONROY

Savages

Stop-time, Frank Conroy's autobiography, was a great critical success when it was published in 1965. It was greeted as an honest evocation of youth that was written beautifully. In the selection that follows, a chapter from this autobiography, you will find that personal narrative can advance social criticism and opinions about human beings, developing these ideas as part of telling a life story. As you read, you should think about Conroy's attitudes toward certain kinds of education, toward the basic "savagery" of human beings, and toward families. As Conroy and other writers in this section demonstrate, autobiography is a way of presenting not only the "facts" about a life, but also beliefs, attitudes, and opinions.

My father stopped living with us when I was three or four. Most of his adult life was spent as a patient in various expensive rest homes for dipsomaniacs and victims of nervous collapse. He was neither, although he drank too much, but rather the kind of neurotic who finds it difficult to live for any length of time in the outside world. The brain tumor discovered and removed toward the end of his life could have caused the illness, but I suspect this easy out. To most people he seemed normal, especially when he was inside.

I try to think of him as sane, yet it must be admitted he did some odd things. Forced to attend a rest-home dance for its therapeutic value, he combed his hair with urine and otherwise played it out like the Southern gentleman he was. He had a tendency to take off his trousers and throw them out the window. (I harbor some secret admiration for this.) At a moment's notice he could blow a thousand dollars at Abercrombie and Fitch and disappear into the Northwest to become an outdoorsman. He spent an anxious few weeks convinced that I was fated to become a homosexual. I was six months old. And I remember visiting him at one of the rest homes when I was eight. We walked across a sloping lawn and he told me a story, which even then I recognized as a lie, about a man who sat down on the open blade of a penknife embedded in a park bench. (Why, for God's sake would he tell a story like that to his eight-year-old son?)

At one point in his life he was analyzed or took therapy with A. A. Brill, the famous disciple of Freud, whith no apparent effect. For ten or fifteen years he worked as a magazine editor, and built up a good business as a literary agent. He died of cancer in his forties.

I visited him near the end. Half his face was paralyzed from the brain-tumor operation and jaundice had stained him a deep yellow. We were alone, as usual, in the hospital room. The bed was high to my child's eye. With great effort he asked me if I believed in universal military training. Too young even to know what it was, I took a gamble and said yes. He seemed satisfied. (Even now I have no idea if that was the answer he wanted. I think of it as some kind of test. Did I pass?) He showed me some books he had gotten to teach himself to draw. A few weeks later he died. He was six feet tall and at the end he weighed eighty-five pounds.

Against the advice of his psychiatrists my mother divorced him, a long, tedious process culminating a year before his death. One can hardly blame her. At his worst he had taken her on a Caribbean cruise and amused himself by humiliating her at the captain's table. Danish, middle-class, and not nearly as bright, she was unable to defend herself. Late one night, on deck, his fun and games went too far. My mother thought he was trying to push her over the rail and screamed. (This might be the time to mention her trained mezzo-soprano voice and lifelong interest in opera.) My father was taken off the ship in a strait jacket, to yet another (Spanish-speaking) branch of the ubiquitous rest home he was never to escape.

I was twelve when my father died. From the ages of nine to eleven I was sent to an experimental boarding school in Pennsylvania called Freemont. I wasn't home more than a few days during these years. In the summer Freemont became a camp and I stayed through.

The headmaster was a big, florid man named Teddy who drank too much. It was no secret, and even the youngest of us were expected to sympathize with his illness and like him for it—an extension of the attitude that forbade the use of last names to make everyone more human. All of us knew, in the mysterious way children pick things up, that Teddy had almost no control over the institution he'd created, and that when decisions were unavoidable his wife took over. This weakness at the top might have been the key to the wildness of the place.

Life at Freemont was a perpetual semihysterical holiday. We knew there were almost no limits in any direction. A situation of endless, dreamlike fun, but one that imposed a certain strain on us all. Classes were a farce, you didn't have to go if you didn't want to, and there were no tests. Freedom was the key word. The atmosphere was heavy with the perfume of the nineteen-thirties—spurious agrarianism, group singing of proletarian chants from all countries, sexual freedom (I was necking at the age of nine), sentimentalism, naïveté. But above all, filtering down through the whole school, the excitement of the *new thing*, of the experiment—that peculiar floating sensation of not knowing what's going to happen next.

One warm spring night we staged a revolution. All the Junior boys, thirty or forty of us, spontaneously decided not to go to bed. We ran loose on the grounds most of the night, stalked by the entire faculty. Even old Ted was out, stumbling and crashing through the woods, warding off the nuts thrown from the trees. A few legitimate captures were made by the younger men on the staff, but there was no doubt most of us could have held out indefinitely. I, for one, was confident to the point of bravado, coming out in the open three or four times just for the fun of being chased. Can there be anything as sweet for a child as victory over authority? On that warm night I touched heights I will never reach again—baiting a thirty-year-old man, getting him to chase me over my own ground in the darkness, hearing his hard breath behind me (ah, the *wordlessness* of the chase, no words, just action), and finally leaping clean, leaping effortlessly over the brook at exactly the right place, knowing he was too heavy, too stupid as an animal, too old, and too tired to do what I had done. O God, my heart burst with joy when I heard him fall, flat out, in the water. Lights flashed in my brain. The chase was over and I had won. I was untouchable. I raced across the meadow, too happy to stop running.

Hours later, hidden in a bower, I heard the beginning of the end. A capture was made right below me. Every captured boy was to join forces with the staff and hunt the boys still out. My reaction was outrage. Dirty pool! But outrage dulled by recognition—"Of course. What else did you expect? They're clever and devious. Old people, with cold, ignorant hearts." The staff's technique didn't actually work as planned, but it spread confusion and broke the lovely symmetry of us against them. The revolution was no longer simple and ran out of gas. To this day I'm proud that I was the last boy in, hours after the others. (I paid a price though—some inexplicable loss to my soul as I crept around all that time in the dark, looking for another holdout.)

We went through a fire period for a couple of weeks one winter. At two or three in the morning we'd congregate in the huge windowless coat-room and set up hundreds of birthday candles on the floor. They gave a marvelous eerie light as we sat around telling horror stories. Fire-writing became the rage—paint your initials on the wall in airplane glue and touch a flame to it. At our most dramatic we staged elaborate take-offs on religious services, complete with capes and pseudo-Latin. We were eventually discovered by our bug-eyed counselor—a homosexual, I recognize in retrospect, who had enough problems caring for thirty-five boys at the brink of puberty. As far as I know he never touched anyone.

Teddy announced a punishment that made the hair rise on the backs of our necks. After pointing out the inadequacies of the fire-escape system he decreed that each of us would be forced to immerse his left hand in a pot of boiling water for ten seconds, the sentence to be carried out two days hence. Frightened, morbidly excited, we thought about nothing else, inevitably drawn to the image of the boiling water with unhealthy fascination. We discussed the announcement almost lovingly till all hours of the

night, recognizing a certain beauty in the phrasing, the formal specifica-
tion of the "left hand," the precision of "immersed for ten seconds"—it had
a medieval flavor that thrilled us.

But Teddy, or his wife (it was done in her kitchen), lost his nerve after
the screams and tears of the first few boys. The flame was turned off under
the pot and by the time my turn came it didn't hurt at all.

The only successful bit of discipline I remember was their system to
get us to stop smoking. We smoked corn silk as well as cigarettes. (The
preparation of corn silk was an important ritual. Hand-gathered in the field
from only the best ears, it was dried in the sun, rubbed, aged, and rolled
into pipe-sized pellets. We decimated Freemont's corn crop, ineptly
tended in the first place, by leaving ten stripped ears rotting on the ground
for every one eventually harvested. No one seemed to mind. Harvest day,
in which we all participated, was a fraudulent pastoral dance of symbolic
rather than economic significance.) With rare decisiveness Teddy got
organized about the smoking. The parents of the only non-scholarship
student in the school, a neat, well-to-do Chinese couple, removed him
without warning after a visit. The faculty believed it was the sight of
students lounging around the public rooms with cigarettes hanging expertly
from their rosy lips, while we maintained it was the toilet paper war. The
parents had walked through the front door when things were reaching a
crescendo—endless white rolls streaming down the immense curved stairway, cylindrical bombs hurtling down the stairwell from the third-floor
balcony to run out anticlimactically a few feet from the floor, dangling like
exhausted white tongues. The withdrawal of the only paying student was a
catastrophe, and the smoking would have to stop.

Like a witch doctor, some suburban equivalent of the rainmaker, Mr.
Kleinberg arrived in his mysterious black panel truck. Members of the staff
were Teddy, George, or Harry, but this outsider remained Mister Kleinberg, a form of respect to which it turned out he was entitled. We greeted
him with bland amusement, secure in the knowledge that no one could do
anything with us. A cheerful realist with a big smile and a pat on the
shoulder for every boy in reach, he was to surprise us all.

The procedure was simple. He packed us into a small, unventilated
garage, unloaded more cigarettes than the average man will see in a
lifetime, passed out boxes of kitchen matches, and announced that any of
us still smoking after ten packs and five cigars was excluded from the new,
heavily enforced ban on smoking. None of us could resist the challenge.

He sat behind his vast mound with a clipboard, checking off names as
we took our first, fresh packs. Adjusting his glasses eagerly and beaming with
friendliness, he distributed his fantastic treasure. The neat white cartons
were ripped open, every brand was ours for the asking—Old Gold, Pall
Mall (my brand), Chesterfields, Wings, Camels, Spud, Caporals, Lucky

Strike (Loose Sweaters Mean Floppy Tits),[1] Kools, Benson & Hedges. He urged us to try them all. "Feel free to experiment, boys, it may be your last chance," he said, exploding with benevolent laughter.

I remember sitting on the floor with my back against the wall. Bruce, my best friend, was next to me.

"We're supposed to get sick," he said.

"I know."

We lighted up a pair of fat cigars and surveyed the scene. Forty boys puffed away in every corner of the room, some of them lined up for supplies, keeping Mr. Kleinberg busy with his paperwork. The noise was deafening. Gales of nervous laughter as someone did an imitation of John Garfield, public speeches as so-and-so declared his intention to pass out rather than admit defeat, or his neighbor yelled that he'd finished his fourth pack and was still by God going strong. One had to scream through the smoke to be heard. It wasn't long before the first boys stumbled out, sick and shamefaced, to retch on the grass. There was no way to leave quietly. Every opening of the door sent great shafts of sunlight across the smoky room, the signal for a derisive roar—boos, hoots, whistles, razzberries—from those sticking it out. I felt satisfaction as an enemy of mine left early, when the crowd was at its ugliest.

The rest of us followed eventually, of course, some taking longer than others, but all poisoned. Mr. Kleinberg won and smoking ended at Freemont. With dazed admiration we watched him drive away the next day in his black truck, smiling and waving, a panetela clamped between his teeth.

A rainy day. All of us together in the big dorm except a fat boy named Ligget. I can't remember how it started, or if any one person started it. A lot of talk against Ligget, building quickly to the point where talk was not enough. When someone claimed to have heard him use the expression "nigger-lipping" (wetting the end of a cigarette), we decided to act. Ligget was intolerable. A boy was sent to find him.

I didn't know Ligget. He had no friends even though he'd been at school longer than the rest of us. There was some vagueness about his origins, probably his parents were dead and relatives cared for him. We knew he was in the habit of running away. I remember waking up one night to see three men, including a policeman, carrying him back to his bed. He fought with hysterical strength, although silently, as if he were afraid to wake the rest of us. All three had to hold him down for the hypodermic.

On this rainy day he didn't fight. He must have known what was up the moment he walked through the door, but he didn't try to run. The two

---

[1] LSMFT—"Lucky Strike means fine tobacco"—was an advertising slogan.

boys assigned to hold his arms were unnecessary. Throughout the entire trial he stood quite still, only his eyes, deep in the pudgy face, swiveling from side to side as he followed the speakers. He didn't say anything.

The prosecutor announced that first of all the trial must be fair. He asked for a volunteer to conduct Ligget's defense. When it became clear no one wanted the job a boy named Herbie was elected by acclamation. It seemed the perfect choice: Herbie was colorless and dim, steady if not inspired.

"I call Sammy as a witness," said the prosecutor. There was a murmur of approval. Sammy was something of a hero to us, as much for his experiences in reform school as for his fabulous condition. (An undescended testicle, which we knew nothing about. To us he had only one ball.) "The prisoner is charged with saying 'nigger-lip.' Did you hear him say it?"

"Yes. He said it a couple of days ago. We were standing over there in front of the window." Sammy pointed to the end of the room. "He said it about Mark Schofield." (Schofield was a popular athletic star, a Senior, and therefore not in the room.)

"You heard him?"

"Yes. I got mad and told him not to talk like that. I walked away. I didn't want to hear him."

"Okay. Now it's your turn, Herbie."

Herbie asked only one question. "Are you sure he said it? Maybe he said something else and you didn't hear him right."

"He said it, all right." Sammy looked over at Ligget. "He said it."

"Okay," said the prosecutor, "I call Earl." Our only Negro stepped forward, a slim, good-looking youth, already vain. (A sin so precocious we couldn't even recognize it.) He enjoyed the limelight, having grown used to it in the large, nervous, and visit-prone family that had spoiled him so terribly. He got a package every week, and owned a bicycle with gears, unheard of before his arrival.

"What do you know about this?" asked the prosecutor.

"What do you mean?"

"Did you ever hear him say what he said?"

"If he ever said that around me I'd kill him."

"Have you noticed anything else?"

"What?"

"I mean, well, does he avoid you or anything?"

Herbie suddenly yelled, "But he avoids everybody!" This was more than we had expected from old Herbie. He was shouted down immediately.

"I don't pay him no mind," said Earl, lapsing uncharacteristically into the idiom of his people.

The trial must have lasted two hours. Witness after witness came forward to take a stand against race prejudice. There was an interruption when one of the youngest boys, having watched silently, suddenly burst into tears.

"Look, Peabody's crying."

"What's wrong, Peabody?" someone asked gently.

Confused, overwhelmed by his emotions, Peabody could only stammer, "I'm sorry, I'm sorry, I don't know what's the matter. . . . It's so horrible, how could he . . ."

"What's horrible?"

"Him saying that. How could he say that? I don't understand," the boy said, tears falling from his eyes.

"It's all right, Peabody, don't worry."

"I'm sorry, I'm sorry."

Most of the testimony was on a high moral plane. Children are swept away by morality. Only rarely did it sink to the level of life. From the boy who slept next to Ligget: "He smells."

We didn't laugh. We weren't stupid boys, nor insensitive, and we recognized the seriousness of such a statement.

"His bed smells, and his clothes, and everything he has. He's a smelly, fat slob and I won't sleep next to him. I'm going to move my bed."

Sensing impatience in the room, the prosecutor called the prisoner himself. "Do you have anything to say?"

Ligget stood stock still, his hidden eyes gleaming. He was pale.

"This is your last chance, you better take it. We'll listen, we'll listen to your side of it." The crowd voiced its agreement, moved by an instant of homage to fair play, and false sympathy. "Okay then, don't say you didn't have a chance."

"Wait a second," said Herbie. "I want to ask him something. Did you say 'nigger-lip' to Sammy?"

It appeared for a moment that Ligget was about to speak, but he gave up the effort. Shaking his head slowly, he denied the charge.

The prosecutor stepped forward. "All those who find him guilty say aye." A roar from forty boys. "All those who find him innocent say nay." Silence. (In a certain sense the trial was a parody of Freemont's "town meetings" in which rather important questions of curriculum and school policy were debated before the students and put to a vote.)

The punishment seemed to suggest itself. We lined up for one punch apiece.

Although Ligget's beating is part of my life (past, present, and future coexist in the unconscious, says Freud), and although I've worried about it off and on for years, all I can say about it is that brutality happens easily. I learned almost nothing from beating up Ligget.

There was a tremendous, heart-swelling excitement as I waited. The line moved slowly, people were taking their time. You got only one punch and you didn't want to waste it. A ritual of getting set, measuring the distance, perhaps adjusting the angle of his jaw with an index finger—all this had to be done before you let go. A few boys had fluffed already, only grazing him. If you missed completely you got another chance.

It wasn't hurting Ligget that was important, but rather the unbelievable opportunity to throw a clean, powerful punch completely unhindered, and with none of the sloppiness of an actual fight. Ligget was simply a punching bag, albeit the best possible kind of punching bag, one in human form, with sensory equipment to measure the strength of your blows.

It was my turn. Ligget looked at me blankly. I picked a spot on his chin, drew back my arm, and threw as hard a punch as I could muster. Instant disappointment. I hadn't missed, there was a kind of snapping sound as my fist landed, and his head jerked back, but the whole complex of movements was too fast, somehow missing the exaggerated movie-punch finality I had anticipated. Ligget looked at the boy behind me and I stepped away. I think someone clapped me on the back.

"Good shot."

Little Peabody, tear-stained but sober, swung an awkward blow that almost missed, grazing Ligget's mouth and bringing a little blood. He moved away and the last few boys took their turns.

Ligget was still on his feet. His face was swollen and his small eyes were glazed, but he stood unaided. He had kept his hands deep in his pockets to prevent the reflex of defense. He drew them out and for a moment there was silence, as if everyone expected him to speak.

Perhaps it was because we felt cheated. Each boy's dreams-of-glory punch had been a shade off center, or not quite hard enough, or thrown at the wrong angle, missing perfection by a maddeningly narrow margin. The urge to try again was strong. Unconsciously we knew we'd never have another chance. This wild freedom was ours once only. And perhaps among the older boys there were some who harbored the dream of throwing one final, superman punch, the knock-out blow to end all knock-out blows. Spontaneously, the line formed again.

After three or four blows Ligget collapsed. He sank to the floor, his eyes open and a dark stain spreading in his crotch. Someone told him to get up but it became clear he couldn't understand. Eventually a boy was sent to get the nurse. He was taken to the hospital in an ambulance.

X rays revealed that Ligget's jaw was broken in four places. We learned this the day after the beating, all of us repentant, sincerely unable to understand how it had happened. When he was well enough we went to visit him in the hospital. He was friendly, and accepted our apologies. One could tell he was trying, but his voice was thin and stiff, without a person behind it, like a bad actor reading lines. He wouldn't see us alone, there had to be an adult sitting by him.

No disciplinary action was taken against us. There was talk for a while that Sammy was going to be expelled, but it came to nothing. Ligget never returned.

It is two o'clock in the morning. I lie in bed watching the back of my wife's neck. She sleeps, she is part of the night. The baby wakes at seven, her sleep is for both of them. Sleep is everywhere. I am like a bather at the edge of a pool.

My faith in the firmness of time slips away gradually. I begin to believe that chronological time is an illusion and that some other principle organizes existence. My memories flash like clips of film from unrelated movies. I wonder, suddenly, if I am alive. I know I'm not dead, but am I alive? I look into the memories for reassurance, searching for signs of life. I find someone moving. Is it me? My chest tightens.

I get so uncomfortable floating around like this that I almost gratefully accept the delusion that I've lived another life, remote from me now, and completely forgotten about it. Somewhere in the nooks and crannies of memory there are clues. As I chase them down a kind of understanding comes. I remember waking up in the infirmary at Freemont. I had been sick, unconscious for at least a day. Remembering it I rediscover the exact, spatial center of my life, the one still point. The incident stands like an open window looking out to another existence.

Waking in a white room filled with sunshine. The breeze pushes a curtain gently and I can hear the voices of children outside, far away. There's no one in the room. I don't know where I am or how long I've been there. It seems to be afternoon but it could be morning. I don't know who I am, but it doesn't bother me. The white walls, the sunlight, the voices all exist in absolute purity.

QUESTIONS

1. What was Conroy's attitude toward his father? How did the author convey this attitude in his autobiography? Refer to the text to support your answer.

2. What sort of school was Freemont? Did it have anything in common with schools you have attended? What school experiences can you relate that show how your school was like (or unlike) Freemont?

3. Conroy doesn't ever directly evaluate Freemont, but he conveys his opinion of it. How does he accomplish this?

4. The main part of this excerpt from Conroy's autobiography tells of the "Liggett" episode. What point is the author attempting to make? Can you state his "thesis" in a sentence or two?

5. Did you find this selection interesting or uninteresting? Explain your reaction.

ROGER WILKINS
Confessions of a Blue-Chip Black

Roger Wilkins, who was born in 1932, is now a journalist. After taking a law degree at the University of Michigan in 1956, he practiced law in New York City and held several government posts, including a period as assistant attorney general (1966–1969). He is the nephew of Roy Wilkins, who for many years was the executive director of the National Association for the Advancement of Colored People.

In this excerpt from his autobiographical essay, Wilkins relates the experience of growing up in a prosperous, educated black family. The next selection, from Manchild in the Promised Land, *by Claude Brown is an account of quite a different sort of childhood.*

Early in the spring of 1932—six months after Earl's brother, Roy, left Kansas City to go to New York to join the national staff of the National Association for the Advancement of Colored People, and eight months before Franklin Roosevelt was elected president for the first time—Earl and Helen Wilkins had the first and only child to be born of their union. I was born in a little segregated hospital in Kansas City called Phillis Wheatley. The first time my mother saw me, she cried. My head was too long and my color, she thought, was blue.

My parents never talked about slavery or my ancestors. Images of Africa were images of backwardness and savagery. Once, when I was a little boy, I said to my mother after a friend of my parents left the house: "Mr. Bledsoe is black, isn't he, mama."

"Oh," she exclaimed. "Never say anybody is black. That's a *terrible* thing to say."

Next time Mr. Bledsoe came to the house, I commented, "Mama, Mr. Bledsoe is navy blue."

When I was two years old and my father was in the tuberculosis sanitarium, he wrote me a letter, which I obviously couldn't read, but which tells a lot about how he planned to raise his Negro son.

Friday, March 22, 1934

Dear Roger—

Let me congratulate you upon having reached your second birthday. Your infancy is now past and it is now that you should begin to turn your thoughts upon those achievements which are expected of a brilliant young gentleman well on his way to manhood.

During the next year, you should learn the alphabet; you should learn certain French and English idioms which are a part of every cultivated person's vocabulary: you should gain complete control of those natural functions which, uncontrolled, are a source of worry and embarrassment to even the best of grandmothers: you should learn how to handle table silver so that you will be able to eat gracefully and conventionally: and you should learn the fundamental rules of social living—politeness, courtesy, consideration for others, and the rest.

This should not be difficult for you. You have the best and most patient of mothers in your sterling grandmother and your excellent mother. Great things are expected of you. Never, never forget that.

Love,

Your Father

We lived in a neat little stucco house on a hill in a small Negro section called Roundtop. I had no sense of being poor or of any anxiety about money. At our house, not only was there food and furniture and all the rest, there was even a baby grand piano that my mother would play sometimes. And there was a cleaning lady, Mrs. Turner, who came every week.

When it was time for me to go to school, the board of education provided us with a big yellow bus, which carried us past four or five perfectly fine schools down to the middle of the large Negro community, to a very old school called Crispus Attucks. I have no memories of those bus rides except for my resentment of the selfishness of the whites who wouldn't let us share those newer-looking schools near my home.

My father came home when I was four and died when I was almost nine. He exuded authority. He thought the women hadn't been sufficiently firm with me, so he instituted a spanking program with that same hard hairbrush that my grandmother had used so much to try to insure that I didn't have "nigger-looking" hair.

After my father's death, the family moved to New York. Our apartment was in that legendary uptown area called Sugar Hill, where blacks who had it made were said to live the sweet life. I lived with my mother, my grandmother, and my mother's youngest sister, Zelma. My Uncle Roy and his wife, Minnie, a New York social worker, lived on the same floor. My Aunt Marvel and her husband, Cecil, lived one floor down.

Sometime early in 1943 my mother's work with the YMCA took her to Grand Rapids, Michigan, where she made a speech and met a forty-four-year-old bachelor doctor who looked like a white man. He had light skin, green eyes, and "good hair"—that is, hair that was as straight and as flat as white people's hair. He looked so like a white person that he could have passed for white. There was much talk about people who had passed. They were generally deemed to be bad people, for they were not simply selfish, but also cruel to those whom they left behind. On the other hand, people who could pass, but did not, were respected.

My mother remarried in October 1943, and soon I was once more on a train with my grandmother, heading toward Grand Rapids and my new home. This train also took me, at the age of twelve, beyond the last point in my life when I would feel totally at peace with my blackness.

Creston High School, which served all the children from the north end of Grand Rapids, was all white and middle-class. Nobody talked to me that first day, but I was noticed. When I left school at the end of the day I found my bike leaning up against the fence where I had left it, with a huge glob of slimy spit on my shaggy saddle cover. People passed by on their way home and looked at me and the spit. I felt a hollowness behind my eyes, but I didn't cry. I just got on the bike, stood up on the pedals, and rode it home without sitting down. After the third day, I got rid of the saddle cover because the plain leather was a lot easier to clean.

But the glacier began to thaw. One day in class, the freckle-faced kid with the crewcut sitting next to me was asking everybody for a pencil. And then he looked at me and said, "Maybe you can lend me one." Those were the best words I had heard since I first met Jerry.[1] This kid had included me in the human race in front of everybody. His name was Jack Waltz.

And after a while when the spitters had subsided and I could ride home sitting down, I began to notice that little kids my size were playing pickup games in the end zones of the football field. It looked interesting, but I didn't know anybody and didn't know how they would respond to me. So I just rode on by for a couple of weeks, slowing down each day, trying to screw up my courage to go in.

But then one day, I saw Jack Waltz there. I stood around the edges of the group, watching. It seemed that they played forever without even noticing me, but finally somebody had to go home and the sides were unbalanced. Somebody said, "Let's ask him."

As we lined up for our first huddle, I heard somebody on the other side say, "I hope he doesn't have a knife." One of the guys on my side asked me, "Can you run the ball?" I said yes, so they gave me the ball and I ran three quarters of the length of the field for a touchdown. And I made other touchdowns and other long runs before the game was over. When I thought about it later that night, I became certain that part of my success was due to the imaginary knife that was running interference for me. But no matter. By the end of the game, I had a group of friends. Boys named Andy and Don and Bill and Gene and Rich. We left the field together and some of them waved and yelled, "See ya tomorra, Rog."

And Don De Young, a pleasant round-faced boy, even lived quite near me. So, after parting from everybody else, he and I went on together down

---

[1] Jerry was a white friend from an earlier period of Wilkins' life.

to the corner of Coit and Knapp. As we parted, he suggested that we meet to go to school together the next day. I had longed for that but I hadn't suggested it for fear of a rebuff for overstepping the limits of my race. I had already learned one of the great tenets of Negro survival in America: to live the reactive life. It was like the old Negro comedian who once said, "When the man asks how the weather is, I know nuff to look keerful at his face 'fore even I look out the window." So, I waited for him to suggest it, and my patience was rewarded. I was overjoyed and grateful.

I didn't spend all my time in the north end. Soon after I moved to Grand Rapids, Pop introduced me to some patients he had with a son my age. The boy's name was Lloyd Brown, and his father was a bellman downtown at the Pantlind Hotel. Lloyd and I often rode bikes and played basketball in his backyard. After a while, my mother asked me why I never had Lloyd come out to visit me. It was a question I had dreaded, but she pressed on. "After all," she said, "you've had a lot of meals at his house and it's rude not to invite him back." I knew she was right and I also hated the whole idea of it.

With my friends in the north, race was never mentioned. Ever. I carried my race around with me like an open basket of rotten eggs. I knew I could drop one at any moment and it would explode with a stench over everything. This was in the days when the movies either had no blacks at all or featured rank stereotypes like Stepin Fetchit, and the popular magazines like *Life, Look,* the *Saturday Evening Post,* and *Colliers* carried no stories about Negroes, had no ads depicting Negroes, and generally gave the impression that we did not exist in this society. I knew that my white friends, being well brought up, were just too polite to mention this disability that I had. And I was grateful to them, but terrified, just the same, that maybe someday one of them would have the bad taste to notice what I was.

It seemed to me that my tenuous purchase in this larger white world depended on the maintenance between me and my friends in the north end of our unspoken bargain to ignore my difference, my shame, and their embarrassment. If none of us had to deal with it, I thought, we could all handle it. My white friends behaved as if they perceived that bargain exactly as I did. It was a delicate equation, and I was terrified that Lloyd's presence in the North End would rip apart the balance.

I am so ashamed of that shame now that I cringe when I write it. But I understand that boy now as he could not understand himself then. I was an American boy, though I did not fully comprehend that either. I was fully shaped and formed by America, where white people had all the power in sight, and they owned everything in sight except our house. Their beauty was the real beauty; there wasn't any other beauty. A real human being had straight hair, a white face, and thin lips. Other people, who looked different, were lesser beings.

No wonder, then, that most black men desired the forbidden fruit of white loins. No wonder, too, that we thought that the most beautiful and worthy Negro people were those who looked most white. We blacks used to have a saying: "If you're white, you're all right. If you're brown, stick around. If you're black, stand back." I was brown.

It was not that we in my family were direct victims of racism. On the contrary, my stepfather clearly had a higher income than the parents of most students in my high school. Unlike those of most of my contemporaries, black and white, my parents had college degrees. Within Grand Rapids' tiny Negro community, they were among the elite. The others were the lawyer, the dentist, the undertaker, and the other doctor.

But that is what made race such exquisite agony. I did have a sense that it was unfair for poor Negroes to be relegated to bad jobs—if they had jobs at all—and to bad or miserable housing, but I didn't feel any great sense of identity with them. After all, the poor blacks in New York had also been the hard ones: the ones who tried to take my money, to beat me up, and to keep me perpetually intimidated. Besides, I had heard it intimated around my house that their behavior, sexual and otherwise, left a good deal to be desired.

So I thought that maybe they just weren't ready for this society, but that I was. And it was dreadfully unfair for white people to just look at my face and lips and hair and decide that I was inferior. By being a model student and leader, I thought I was demonstrating how well Negroes could perform if only the handicaps were removed and they were given a chance. But deep down I guess I was also trying to demonstrate that I was not like those other people; that I was different. My message was quite clear: I was not *nigger*. But the world didn't seem quite ready to make such fine distinctions, and it was precisely that fact—though at the time I could scarcely even have admitted it to myself—that was the nub of the race issue for me.

I would sometimes lie on my back and stare up at passing clouds and wonder why God had played a dirty trick by making me a Negro. It all seemed so random. So unfair to me. To *me*! But in school I was gaining more friends, and the teachers respected me. It got so that I could go for days not thinking very much about being Negro, until something made the problem unavoidable.

One day in history class, for instance, the teacher asked each of us to stand and tell in turn where our families had originated. Many of the kids in the class were Dutch with names like Vander Jagt, De Young, and Ripstra. My pal Andy was Scots-Irish. When it came my turn, I stood up and burned with shame and when I could speak, I lied. And then I was even more ashamed because I exposed a deeper shame. "Some of my family was English," I said—Wilkins is an English name—"and the rest of it came from . . . Egypt." Egypt!

QUESTIONS

1. According to the letter he wrote (pp. 103–04), what were Mr. Wilkins' expectations for his two-year-old son?

2. Characterize Roger Wilkins' attitude toward his experience of growing up in Grand Rapids. Compare his attitude with your attitude about where you grew up.

3. Characterize the family's attitude toward its own race. Cite specific evidence for your opinion.

4. In your own words, summarize the meaning of the incident with Jack Waltz.

5. According to Wilkins, what was "real beauty" for blacks ? Why would blacks hold this view?

6. A common theme of autobiography is often expressed as "You can't go home again." Can Roger Wilkins "go home" again? Can *you* go home again?

7. What similarities do you find between Wilkins' experiences and Eldridge Cleaver's (pp. 29–37)?

CLAUDE BROWN
From *Manchild in the Promised Land*

Claude Brown's autobiography was published in 1965, during the height of the Civil Rights Movement. It is the story of one person's struggle, against enormous odds, to become a part of the American Mainstream. After expending considerable effort, he succeeded. The irony is, of course, that after two decades, the Claude Browns are still exceptional, and many of the problems that he speaks of in his autobiography characterize the situation of minority Americans today in New York, Chicago, and Los Angeles; Keokuk, Salt Lake City, and Peoria.

Statistics are marvelously useful, but so are the personal accounts that we get through autobiography. Statistics are quantitative; autobiographies are qualitative. We need both kinds of knowledge to understand the human and the national situations.

"Run!"
Where?
Oh, hell! Let's get out of here!
"Turk! Turk! I'm shot!"
I could hear Turk's voice calling from a far distance, telling me not to go into the fish-and-chips joint. I heard, but I didn't understand. The only thing I knew was that I was going to die.

I ran. There was a bullet in me trying to take my life, all thirteen years of it.

I climbed up on the bar yelling, "Walsh, I'm shot. I'm shot." I could feel the blood running down my leg. Walsh, the fellow who operated the fish-and-chips joint, pushed me off the bar and onto the floor. I couldn't move now, but I was still completely conscious.

Walsh was saying, "Git outta here, kid. I ain't got no time to play."

A woman was screaming, mumbling something about the Lord, and saying, "Somebody done shot that poor child."

Mama ran in. She jumped up and down, screaming like a crazy woman. I began to think about dying. The worst part of dying was thinking about the things and the people that I'd never see again. As I lay there trying to imagine what being dead was like, the policeman who had been trying to control Mama gave up and bent over me. He asked who had shot me. Before I could answer, he was asking me if I could hear him. I told him that I didn't know who had shot me and would he please tell Mama to stop jumping up and down. Every time Mama came down on the shabby floor, the bullet lodged in my stomach felt like a hot poker.

Another policeman had come in and was struggling to keep the crowd outside. I could see Turk in the front of the crowd. Before the cops came, he asked me if I was going to tell them that he was with me. I never answered. I looked at him and wondered if he saw who shot me. Then his question began to ring in my head: "Sonny, you gonna tell'em I was with you?" I was bleeding on a dirty floor in a fish-and-chips joint, and Turk was standing there in the doorway hoping that I would die before I could tell the cops that he was with me. Not once did Turk ask me how I felt.

Hell, yeah, I thought, I'm gonna tell 'em.

It seemed like hours had passed before the ambulance finally arrived. Mama wanted to go to the hospital with me, but the ambulance attendant said she was too excited. On the way to Harlem Hospital, the cop who was riding with us asked Dad what he had to say. His answer was typical: "I told him about hanging out with those bad-ass boys." The cop was a little surprised. This must be a rookie, I thought.

The next day, Mama was at my bedside telling me that she had prayed and the Lord had told her that I was going to live. Mama said that many of my friends wanted to donate some blood for me, but the hospital would not accept it from narcotics users.

This was one of the worst situations I had ever been in. There was a tube in my nose that went all the way to the pit of my stomach. I was being fed intravenously, and there was a drain in my side. Everybody came to visit me, mainly out of curiosity. The girls were all anxious to know where I had gotten shot. They had heard all kinds of tales about where the bullet struck. The bolder ones wouldn't even bother to ask: they just snatched the cover off me and looked for themselves. In a few days, the word got around that I was in one piece.

On my fourth day in the hospital, I was awakened by a male nurse at about 3 A.M. When he said hello in a very ladyish voice, I thought that he had come to the wrong bed by mistake. After identifying himself, he told me that he had helped Dr. Freeman save my life. The next thing he said, which I didn't understand, had something to do with the hours he had put in working that day. He went on mumbling something about how tired he was and ended up asking me to rub his back. I had already told him that I was grateful to him for helping the doctor save my life. While I rubbed his back above the beltline, he kept pushing my hand down and saying, "Lower, like you are really grateful to me." I told him that I was sleepy from the needle a nurse had given me. He asked me to pat his behind. After I had done this, he left.

The next day when the fellows came to visit me, I told them about my early-morning visitor. Dunny said he would like to meet him. Tito joked about being able to get a dose of clap in the hospital. The guy with the tired back never showed up again, so the fellows never got a chance to meet him. Some of them were disappointed.

After I had been in the hospital for about a week, I was visited by another character. I had noticed a woman visiting one of the patients on the far side of the ward. She was around fifty-five years old, short and fat, and she was wearing old-lady shoes. While I wondered who this woman was, she started across the room in my direction. After she had introduced herself, she told me that she was visiting her son. Her son had been stabbed in the chest with an ice pick by his wife. She said that his left lung had been punctured, but he was doing fine now, and that Jesus was so-o-o good.

Her name was Mrs. Ganey, and she lived on 145th Street. She said my getting shot when I did "was the work of the Lord." My gang had been stealing sheets and bedspreads off clotheslines for months before I had gotten shot. I asked this godly woman why she thought it was the work of the Lord or Jesus or whoever. She began in a sermonlike tone, saying, "Son, people was gitting tired-a y'all stealing all dey sheets and spreads." She said that on the night that I had gotten shot, she baited her clothesline with two brand-new bedspreads, turned out all the lights in the apartment, and sat at the kitchen window waiting for us to show.

She waited with a double-barreled shotgun.

The godly woman said that most of our victims thought that we were winos or dope fiends and that most of them had vowed to kill us. At the end of the sermon, the godly woman said, "Thank the Lord I didn't shoot nobody's child." When the godly woman had finally departed, I thought, Thank the Lord for taking her away from my bed.

The next day, I asked the nurse why she hadn't changed my bed linen, and she said because they were evicting me. I had been in the hospital eleven days, but I wasn't ready to go home. I left the hospital on January 2 and went to a convalescent home in Valhalla, New York. After I had been there for three weeks, the activity director took me aside and told me that I was going to New York City to see a judge and that I might be coming back. The following morning, I left to see that judge, but I never got back to Valhalla.

I stood there before Judge Pankin looking solemn and lying like a professional. I thought that he looked too nice to be a judge. A half hour after I had walked into the courtroom, Judge Pankin was telling me that he was sending me to the New York State Training School for Boys. The judge said that he thought I was a chronic liar and that he hoped I would be a better boy when I came out. I asked him if he wanted me to thank him. Mama stopped crying just long enough to say, "Hush your mouth, boy."

Mama tried to change the judge's mind by telling him that I had already been to Wiltwyck School for Boys for two and a half years. And before that, I had been ordered out of the state for at least one year. She said that I had been away from my family too much; that was why I was always getting into trouble.

The judge told Mama that he knew what he was doing and that one day she would be grateful to him for doing it.

I had been sent away before, but this was the first time I was ever afraid to go. When Mama came up to the detention room in Children's Court,

I tried to act as though I wasn't afraid. After I told her that Warwick and where I was going were one and the same, Mama began to cry, and so did I.

Most of the guys I knew had been to Warwick and were too old to go back. I knew that there were many guys up there I had mistreated. The Stinky brothers were up there. They thought that I was one of the guys who had pulled a train on their sister in the park the summer before. Bumpy from 144th Street was up there. I had shot him in the leg with a zip gun in a rumble only a few months earlier. There were many guys up there I used to bully on the streets and at Wiltwyck, guys I had sold tea leaves to as pot. There were rival gang members up there who just hated my name. All of these guys were waiting for me to show. The word was out that I couldn't fight any more—that I had slowed down since I was shot and that a good punch in the stomach would put my name in the undertaker's book.

When I got to the Youth House, I tried to find out who was up at Warwick that I might know. Nobody knew any of the names I asked about. I knew that if I went up to Warwick in my condition, I'd never live to get out. I had a reputation for being a rugged little guy. This meant that I would have at least a half-dozen fights in the first week of my stay up there.

It seemed the best thing for me to do was to cop out on the nut. For the next two nights, I woke up screaming and banging on the walls. On the third day, I was sent to Bellevue for observation. This meant that I wouldn't be going to Warwick for at least twenty-eight days.

While I was in Bellevue, the fellows would come down and pass notes to me through the doors. Tito and Turk said they would get bagged and sent to Warwick by the time I got there. They were both bagged a week later for smoking pot in front of the police station. They were both sent to Bellevue. Two weeks after they showed, I went home. The judge still wanted to send me to Warwick, but Warwick had a full house, so he sent me home for two weeks.

The day before I went back to court, I ran into Turk, who had just gotten out of Bellevue. Tito had been sent to Warwick, but Turk had gotten a walk because his sheet wasn't too bad. I told him I would probably be sent to Warwick the next day. Turk said he had run into Bucky in Bellevue. He told me that he and Tito had voted Bucky out of the clique. I told him that I wasn't going for it because Bucky was my man from short-pants days. Turk said he liked him too, but what else could he do after Bucky had let a white boy beat him in the nutbox? When I heard this, there was nothing I could do but agree with Turk. Bucky had to go. That kind of news spread fast, and who wanted to be in a clique with a stud who let a paddy boy beat him?

The next day, I went to the Youth House to wait for Friday and the trip to Warwick. As I lay in bed that night trying to think of a way out, I began to feel sorry for myself. I began to blame Danny, Butch, and Kid for my present fate. I told myself that I wouldn't be going to Warwick if they hadn't taught me how to steal, play hookey, make homemades, and stuff like that. But then I thought, aw, hell, it wasn't their fault—as a matter of fact, it was a whole lotta fun.

I remembered sitting on the stoop with Danny, years before, when a girl came up and started yelling at him. She said that her mother didn't want her brother to hang out with Danny any more, because Danny had taught her brother how to play hookey. When the girl had gone down the street, I asked Danny what hookey was. He said it was a game he would teach me as soon as I started going to school.

Danny was a man of his word. He was my next-door neighbor, and he rang the doorbell about 7:30 A. M. on the second day of school. Mama thanked him for volunteering to take me to school. Danny said he would have taught me to play hookey the day before, but he knew that Mama would have to take me to school on the first day. As we headed toward the backyard to hide our books, Danny began to explain the great game of hookey. It sounded like lots of fun to me. Instead of going to school, we would go all over the city stealing, sneak into a movie, or go up on a roof and throw bottles down into the street. Danny suggested that we start the day off by waiting for Mr. Gordon to put out his vegetables; we could steal some sweet potatoes and cook them in the backyard. I was sorry I hadn't started school sooner, because hookey sure was a lot of fun.

Before I began going to school, I was always in the streets with Danny, Kid, and Butch. Sometimes, without saying a word, they would all start to run like hell, and a white man was always chasing them. One morning as I entered the backyard where all the hookey players went to draw up an activity schedule for the day, Butch told me that Danny and Kid had been caught by Mr. Sands the day before. He went on to warn me about Mr. Sands, saying Mr. Sands was that white man who was always chasing somebody and that I should try to remember what he looked like and always be on the lookout for him. He also warned me not to try to outrun Mr. Sands, "because that cat is fast." Butch said, "When you see him, head for a backyard or a roof. He won't follow you there."

During the next three months, I stayed out of school twenty-one days. Dad was beating the hell out of me for playing hookey, and it was no fun being in the street in the winter, so I started going to school regularly. But when spring rolled around, hookey became my favorite game again. Mr. Sands was known to many parents in the neighborhood as the truant officer. He never caught me in the street, but he came by my house many mornings to escort me to class. This was one way of getting me to school, but he never found a way to keep me there. The moment my teacher took her eyes off me, I was back on the street. Every time Dad got a card from Mr. Sands, I got bruises and welts from Dad. The beatings had only a temporary effect on me. Each time, the beatings got worse; and each time, I promised never to play hookey again. One time I kept that promise for three whole weeks.

The older guys had been doing something called "catting" for years. That catting was staying away from home all night was all I knew about the term. Every time I asked one of the fellows to teach me how to cat, I was told I wasn't old enough. As time went on, I learned that guys catted when they were afraid to go home and that they slept everywhere but in comfortable places. The usual places for catting were subway trains, cellars, unlocked cars, under a friends' bed, and in vacant newsstands.

One afternoon when I was eight years old, I came home after a busy day of running from the police, truant officer, and storekeepers. The first thing I did was to look in the mailbox. This had become a habit with me even though I couldn't read. I was looking for a card, a yellow card. That yellow card meant that I would walk into the house and Dad would be waiting for me with his razor strop. He would usually be eating and would pause just long enought to say to me, "Nigger, you got a ass whippin' comin'." My sisters, Carole and Margie, would cry almost as much as I would while Dad was beating me, but this never stopped him. After each beating I got, Carole, who was two years older than I, would beg me to stop playing hookey. There were a few times when I thought I would stop just to keep her and Margie, my younger sister, from crying so much. I decided to threaten Carole and Margie instead, but this didn't help. I continued to play hookey, and they continued to cry on the days that the yellow cards got home before I did.

Generally, I would break open the mailbox, take out the card, and throw it away. Whenever I did this, I'd have to break open two or three other mailboxes and throw away the contents, just to make it look good.

This particular afternoon, I saw a yellow card, but I couldn't find anything to break into the box with. Having some matches in my pockets, I decided to burn the card in the box and not bother to break the box open. After I had used all the matches, the card was not completely burned. I stood there getting more frightened by the moment. In a little while, Dad would be coming home; and when he looked in the mailbox, anywhere would be safer than home for me.

This was going to be my first try at catting out. I went looking for somebody to cat with me. My crime partner, Buddy, whom I had played hookey with that day, was busily engaged in a friendly rock fight when I found him in Colonial Park. When I suggested that we go up on the hill and steal some newspapers, Buddy lost interest in the rock fight.

We stole papers from newsstands and sold them on the subway trains until nearly 1 A. M. That was when the third cop woke us and put us off the train with the usual threat. They would always promise to beat us over the head with a billy and lock us up. Looking back, I think the cops took their own threats more seriously than we did. The third cop put us off the Independent Subway at Fifty-ninth Street and Columbus Circle. I wasn't afraid of the cops, but I didn't go back into the subway—the next cop might have taken me home.

In 1945, there was an Automat where we came out of the subway. About five slices of pie later, Buddy and I left the Automat in search of a place to stay the night. In the center of the Circle, there were some old lifeboats that the Navy had put on display.

Buddy and I slept in the boat for two nights. On the third day, Buddy was caught ringing a cash register in a five-and-dime store. He was sent to Children's Center, and I spent the third night in the boat alone. On the fourth night, I met a duty-conscious cop, who took me home. That ended my first catting adventure.

Dad beat me for three consecutive days for telling what he called "that dumb damn lie about sleeping in a boat on Fifty-ninth Street." On the fourth day, I think he went to check my story out for himself. Anyhow, the beating stopped for a while, and he never mentioned the boat again.

Before long, I was catting regularly, staying away from home for weeks at a time. Sometimes the cops would pick me up and take me to a Children's Center. The Centers were located all over the city. At some time in my childhood, I must have spent at least one night in all of them except the one on Staten Island.

The procedure was that a policeman would take me to the Center in the borough where he had picked me up. The Center would assign someone to see that I got a bath and was put to bed. The following day, my parents would be notified as to where I was and asked to come and claim me. Dad was always in favor of leaving me where I was and saying good riddance. But Mama always made the trip. Although Mama never failed to come for me, she seldom found me there when she arrived. I had no trouble getting out of Children's Centers, so I seldom stayed for more than a couple of days.

When I was finally brought home—sometimes after weeks of catting—Mama would hide my clothes or my shoes. This would mean that I couldn't get out of the house if I should take a notion to do so. Anyway, that's how Mama had it figured. The truth of the matter is that these measures only made getting out of the house more difficult for me. I would have to wait until one of the fellows came around to see me. After hearing my plight, he would go out and round up some of the gang, and they would steal some clothes and shoes for me. When they had the clothes and shoes, one of them would come to the house and let me know. About ten minutes later, I would put on my sister's dress, climb down the back fire escape, and meet the gang with the clothes.

If something was too small or too large, I would go and steal the right size. This could only be done if the item that didn't fit was not the shoes. If the shoes were too small or large, I would have trouble running in them and probably get caught. So I would wait around in the backyard while someone stole me a pair.

Mama soon realized that hiding my clothes would not keep me in the house. The next thing she tried was threatening to send me away until I was twenty-one. This was only frightening to me at the moment of hearing it. Ever so often, either Dad or Mama would sit down and have a heart-to-heart talk with me. These talks were very moving. I always promised to mend my bad ways. I was always sincere and usually kept the promise for about a week. During these weeks, I went to school every day and kept my stealing at a minimum. By the beginning of the second week, I had reverted back to my wicked ways, and Mama would have to start praying all over again.

The neighborhood prophets began making prophecies about my life-span. They all had me dead, buried, and forgotten before my twenty-first birthday. These predictions were based on false tales of policemen shooting at me, on truthful tales of my falling off a trolley car into the midst of oncoming automobile traffic while hitching a ride, and also on my uncontrollable urge to steal. There was much justification for these prophecies. By the time I was nine years old, I had been hit by a bus, thrown into the Harlem River (intentionally), hit by a car, severely beaten with a chain. And I had set the house afire.

While Dad was still trying to beat me into a permanent conversion, Mama was certain that somebody had worked roots on me. She was writing to all her relatives in the South for solutions, but they were only able to say, "that boy must have been born with the devil in him." Some of them advised Mama to send me down there, because New York was no place to raise a child. Dad thought this was a good idea, and he tried to sell it to Mama. But Mama wasn't about to split up her family. She said I would stay in New York, devil or no devil. So I stayed in New York, enjoying every crazy minute.

Mama's favorite question was, "Boy, why you so bad?" I tried many times to explain to Mama that I wasn't "so bad." I tried to make her understand that it was trying to be good that generally got me into trouble. I remember telling her that I played hookey to avoid getting into trouble in school. It seemed that whenever I went to school, I got into a fight with the teacher. The teacher would take me to the principal's office. After I had fought with the principal, I would be sent home and not allowed back in school without one of my parents. So to avoid all that trouble, I just didn't go to school. When I stole things, it was only to save the family money and avoid arguments or scolding whenever I asked for money.

Mama seemed silly to me. She was bothered because most of the parents in the neighborhood didn't allow their children to play with me.

What she didn't know was that I never wanted to play with them. My friends were all daring like me, tough like me, dirty like me, ragged like me, cursed like me, and had a great love for trouble like me. We took pride in being able to hitch rides on trolleys, buses, taxicabs and in knowing how to steal and fight. We knew that we were the only kids in the neighborhood who usually had more than ten dollars in their pockets. There were other people who knew this too, and that was often a problem for us. Somebody was always trying to shake us down or rob us. This was usually done by the older hustlers in the neighborhood or by storekeepers or cops. At other times, older fellows would shake us down, con us, or Murphy us out of our loot. We accepted this as the ways of life. Everybody was stealing from everybody else. And sometimes we would shake down newsboys and shoeshine boys. So we really had no complaints coming. Although none of my sidekicks was over twelve years of age, we didn't think of ourselves as kids. The other kids my age were thought of as kids by me. I felt that since I knew more about life than they did, I had the right to regard them as kids.

QUESTIONS

1. How did Claude Brown's experience of growing up differ from that of Roger Wilkins? What kinds of experiences did they have in common?

2. Roger Wilkins makes direct statements about the American dream and racism, but Claude Brown simply tells his story. What is Brown's attitude toward his own escapades, his parents' attitudes, the values of conventional society? How do you know?

3. Have you had experiences similar to Brown's? In what ways?

4. How did Brown's parents compare with Wilkins'?

5. In what ways is this selection a strong piece of writing? In what ways is it weak? State your opinions, and refer to the text for specific examples of strengths and weaknesses.

PETER DRUCKER

The Monster and the Lamb

Born in Vienna in 1909, Drucker came to the United States in 1937 to escape the Nazi regime, which had annexed Austria and would very soon plunge Europe into a brutal war. Before he fled Europe, Drucker had been a staff member of a daily newspaper in Frankfurt, Germany, through which connection he met the subjects of the following autobiographical narrative. Adventures of a Bystander *is a collection of Drucker's essays, showing both his great skill as a writer and his wide interests.*

The two people whom Drucker discusses become symbolic for him, one of the lust for power and the other of the sin of pride. Thus, the author uses his narrative like a fable or a parable, drawing a moral from the story.

In the days of Hitler Germany's collapse, a short item on an inside page of *The New York Times* caught my eye: It ran somewhat as follows:

> Reinhold Hensch, one of the most wanted Nazi war criminals, committed suicide when captured by American troops in the cellar of a bombed-out house in Frankfurt. Hensch, who was deputy head of the Nazi SS with the rank of Lieutenant General, commanded the infamous annihilation troops and was in charge of the extermination campaign against Jews and other "enemies of the Nazi state," of killing off the mentally and physically defective in Germany, and of stamping out resistance movements in occupied countries. He was so cruel, ferocious, and bloodthirsty that he was known as "The Monster" (*Das Ungeheuer*) even to his own men.

It was the first time since I had left Germany in the winter of 1933 that I had heard or seen Hensch's name. But I had thought of him often. For I had spent my last evening in Germany in the company of "The Monster."

A year earlier, in the spring of 1932, I had realized that I was not going to stay in Germany with the Nazis in power. An old friend had come to visit me in Frankfurt where I then lived. We spent the evening together talking out our fears for the future. Then suddenly I heard myself saying: "One thing I do know, Berthold. If the Nazis come to power, I shan't stay in Germany." I had not, I think, given conscious thought to the decision at all until then. But the moment I heard myself say this, I knew that I had made up my mind. And I also knew that I had become convinced in my heart—though not, perhaps, in my mind as yet—that the Nazis would get into power.

I had come to Germany in the fall of 1927 first as a trainee clerk in an export firm in Hamburg; then, fifteen months later, I moved to Frankfurt as a securities analyst in an old merchant bank that had become the European branch of a Wall Street brokerage firm. That job came to an end in the fall of 1929 with the New York Stock Exchange crash, and I was hired as a financial writer on Frankfurt's largest-circulation newspaper, the *Frankfurter General-Anzeiger*—an afternoon paper, somewhat similar to the Washington *Star* or the Detroit *Free Press* both in circulation and in editorial policy. . . . I had a full professional life outside the job too. . . . I was due, though still in my early twenties, to be appointed "Dozent"— Lecturer—at the University, the first and biggest step up the German academic ladder.

I had begun to write outside of my newspaper job. Two unbearably "learned" econometric papers, one on the commodity markets and one on the New York Stock Exchange, were written while I was still at the bank, in 1929. . . . The papers got published in a prestigious economics quarterly. My doctoral thesis came out as a book. And I wrote a fair number of magazine articles on economic and financial topics, none of which, fortunately, are still around.

When I realized that I would leave upon Hitler's coming to power— and also that I expected that to happen—I did not, of course, stop doing all these things: I did hope against hope. After all, it was not entirely wishful thinking in 1932 to believe that the Nazi wave was cresting; the Nazi vote actually did fall with every successive election. So I continued to work on the paper, teach international law and international affairs, and write for magazines. I even began to look around for another job; for I knew that I had outgrown the *Frankfurter General-Anzeiger*. I almost immediately got an offer from a prestigious German paper, the leading paper in Cologne, to take charge of everything foreign: politics, economics, literature, and culture. I was assured that with this appointment I could easily get a lecturership at Cologne University or at the neighboring university of Bonn.

But at the same time I began to prepare for leaving. I kept the offer from Cologne alive but did not act on it. I dragged my feet on the lecturership even though the international law professor urged it on me. I was officially a graduate assistant; as such I ran many of the meetings of the International Law Seminar and substituted for the professor in teaching his classes. But a "Dozent," while unpaid, had a university appointment and became automatically a German citizen, which I was not; and I had no intention of becoming Hitler's subject.

I also made up my mind to make sure that I could not waver and stay. The day after my evening with my friend Berthold, I began to write a book that would make it impossible for the Nazis to have anything to do with me, and equally impossible for me to have anything to do with them. It was a short book, hardly more than a pamphlet. Its subject was Germany's only Conservative political philosopher, Friedrich Julius Stahl—a prominent Prussian politician and conservative parliamentarian of the period before Bismark, the philosopher of freedom under the law, and the leader of the philosophical reaction against Hegel as well as Hegel's successor as professor of philosophy at Berlin. And Stahl had been a Jew! A monograph on Stahl, which in the name of conservatism and patriotism put him forth as the exemplar and preceptor for the turbulence of the 1930s, represented a frontal attack on Nazism. . . .

The book, I am happy to say, was understood by the Nazis exactly as I had intended; it was immediately banned and publicly burned. Of course it had no impact. I did not expect any. But it made it crystal-clear where I stood; and I knew I had to make sure for my own sake that I would be counted, even if no one else cared.

I was thus ready to leave when Hitler, already losing popular support precipitously, was put into power on January 31, 1933. . . . From the beginning I had few illusions as to what the Nazis were up to. I knew that my foreign passport would not protect me very long and that sooner or later I would be kicked out or jailed. I was determined to leave at my own discretion, not wait until I had to.

Yet I dawdled and hung on. One reason I gave to myself was that I had to check the page proofs of my book on Stahl, promised for just about that time. I feared—perhaps not entirely without cause—that my leaving the country might give the publisher the pretext for scuttling what had clearly become a risky project. But I also gave in to my bent for postponing the inevitable.

What then decided me to carry out my intention and to leave right away, several weeks after the Nazis had come to power, was the first Nazi-led faculty meeting at the University. Frankfurt was the first university the Nazis tackled, precisely because it was the most self-confidently liberal of major German universities, with a faculty that prided itself on its allegiance to scholarship, freedom of conscience, and democracy. The Nazis knew that control of Frankfurt University would mean control of German academia altogether. So did everyone at the University. Above all, Frankfurt had a science faculty distinguished both by its scholarship and by its liberal convictions; and outstanding among the Frankfurt scientists was a biochemist of Nobel Prize caliber and impeccable liberal credentials. When the appointment of a Nazi commissar for Frankfurt was announced—around February 25 of that year—and when not only every teacher but also every graduate assistant at the University was summoned to a faculty meeting to hear his new master, everybody knew that a trial of strength was at hand. I had never attended a faculty meeting but I did attend this one.

The new Nazi commissar wasted no time on the amenities. He immediately announced that Jews would be forbidden to enter university premises and would be dismissed without salary on March 15. This was something no one had thought possible despite the Nazis' loud anti-Semitism. Then he launched into a tirade of abuse, filth, and four-letter words such as had rarely been heard even in the barracks and never before in academia. It was nothing but "shit" and "fuck" and "screw yourself"—words the assembled scholars undoubtedly knew but had certainly never heard applied to themselves. Next the new boss pointed his finger at one department chairman after another and said: "You either do what I tell you or we'll put you into a concentration camp." There was dead silence when he finished; everybody waited for the distinguished biochemist. The great liberal got up, cleared his throat, and said: "Very interesting, Mr. Commissar, and in some respects very illuminating. But one point I didn't get too clearly. Will there be more money for research in physiology?"

The meeting broke up shortly thereafter with the commissar assuring the scholars that indeed there would be plenty of money for "racially pure science." A few of the professors had the courage to walk out with their Jewish colleagues; most kept a safe distance from these men who, only a few hours earlier, had been their close friends. I went out sick unto death—and I knew that I would leave Germany within forty-eight hours.

When I got home, there, thank God, were the page proofs of my Stahl book. I went to the office—I had taken special leave that morning to attend the faculty meeting—announced my resignation, and said goodbye to my colleagues. Then I went home and read the proofs. By that time it was about ten at night; I was drained. I decided to go to bed and start packing early in the morning to catch a train from Frankfurt to Vienna the next day. But just at that moment my doorbell rang. Outside stood somebody in the uniform of the Hitler storm troops. My heart missed a beat. Then I recognized my colleague Hensch, a fellow editor at the *Frankfurter General-Anzeiger* who had not been at the office when I was there earlier in the day. "I heard that you'd resigned," he said. "I happened to pass by and did want to take my leave. May I come in?"

Hensch was not a particular friend. Indeed he was somewhat of an outsider at the office. He covered local politics, City Hall; and while important, the assignment was not of interest to most of us who were not locals and who did not expect to spend the rest of our days in Frankfurt. He was not a particularly good journalist, and he was suspected of taking and giving political favors. Of middle height, with small close-set eyes and cropped hair that was already beginning to gray although he was not yet thirty, he came from local craftsman stock—his father was a stonemason, I believe. There were only two things noteworthy about him. First, he had a lovely girlfriend, Elise Goldstein, a commercial artist who did a lot of work for the paper—an outgoing, lively, effervescent young woman whom all of us thought most attractive. She and Hensch lived together and were going to be married; we had all attended their engagement party a year or so earlier. And second, Hensch, as everyone on the staff knew, held membership cards in both the Communist and the Nazi parties, both of course considered subversive and out of bounds for a reporter on a nonpartisan paper. When Hensch was challenged on this, he always said: "I have to get the news from them to know what goes on in City Hall—and they only talk to members of their own gang."

"I've spent most of the day," he now said, "at a meeting of the Nazi leadership in which I've been appointed adviser on the press to the new Nazi commissar for Frankfurt and the representative of the Party at the *General-Anzeiger*. Then I called a meeting of the editors to tell them that I'm in charge. That's how I learned that you had resigned earlier. I thought I'd come by to ask you to reconsider. I hope you do—we need you. Of course I have relieved the publisher. The biggest paper in Frankfurt can't have a Jewish publisher. I shan't keep the editor-in-chief very long. He's a leftist and married to a Jewish wife who is also the sister of a Socialist deputy. There would be a great opportunity for someone like you, for I won't be able to edit the paper myself; I'll be too busy supervising the press in the whole Frankfurt area." I replied that I was flattered but was sure it wouldn't work. "I thought you'd say that," he said. "But, Drucker, do sleep on it and let me know if you change your mind." He made as if to go, then sat down again and remained silent for five or ten minutes.

Then he began again. "If you go abroad, may I tell Elise where she can reach you? Of course, I had to break it off when Hitler came to power. I moved out of the apartment we had together, back to my parents, but I've paid the rent on the apartment until the end of March. I told Elise that she ought to get out of Germany as fast as possible. But she doesn't know anyone abroad. May I have your address so that she can get in touch with you when she leaves?" I agreed and he wrote down my parents' address in Vienna. Again he relapsed into silence after making as if to get up and leave.

Then he burst out: "My God, how I envy you! I only wish I could leave—but I can't. I get scared when I hear all that talk in the Nazi Party inner councils, and I do sit in now, you know. There are madmen there who talk about killing the Jews and going to war, and about jailing and killing anyone who holds a dissenting opinion and questions the Fuehrer's word.

"It's all insane. But it frightens me. I know you told me a year ago that the Nazis believed these things and that I ought to take them seriously. But I thought it was the usual campaign rhetoric and didn't mean a thing. And I still think so. Now that they're in power they'll have to learn that one can't do such things. After all, this is the twentieth century. My parents think so too; so does Elise. When I told her that she ought to get out of Germany she thought I was mad. And I probably am—they can't mean these things and get away with them. But I'm beginning to be scared. You can't imagine the things some of the higher-ups say to us when no one from the outside is listening."

I assured Hensch that I did not have to imagine these things; Hitler had written them out in great detail in his book *Mein Kampf* for anyone to read. Then I asked: "If you feel that way, why don't you leave? You aren't thirty yet and have no family that depends on you. You have a decent degree in economics and won't have any trouble finding work." "That's easy for you to say," he replied. "You know languages, you've been abroad. Do you realize I've never been away from Frankfurt, never even been to Berlin? And I have no connections—my father is a craftsman."

At that I got angry. "Look, Hensch, that's nonsense; who the hell cares who your father is? The father of the editor-in-chief was a prison guard someplace in East Prussia; Arne's father (Arne was the oldest senior editor) is a coal miner; Becker—the third senior editor—grew up as the child of an elementary schoolteacher; Bilz—the stock exchange editor—comes from a family of poor vintners with a small stony plot on the Rhine. All right, none of us would ever have been invited to a court ball by the Hohenzollerns or gotten a commission in one of their guards. But otherwise what difference can it possibly make?"

"You just don't understand, Drucker," he came back heatedly. "You never did. I'm not clever, I know that. I've been on the paper longer than you or Arne or Becker—you three are the senior editors and I still have the City Hall beat on which I started. I know I can't write. No one invites me to their homes. Even Elise's father—the dentist—thought his daughter too good for me. Don't you understand that I want power and money and to be somebody? That's why I joined the Nazis early on, four or five years ago when they first got rolling. And now I have a party membership card with a very low number and *I am going to be somebody!* The clever, well-born, well-connected people will be too fastidious, or not flexible enough, or not willing to do the dirty work. That's when I'll come into my own. Mark my word, you'll hear about me now." With that he stormed out of the room and started for the stairs. But before he slammed the door, he turned once more and shouted: "And don't forget, you promised to help Elise!"

I bolted the front door, something I had never done before in the three years I lived in the apartment. And suddenly I had a vision—a vision of things to come, of the horrible, bloody, and mean bestiality that was descending on the world. There and then I beheld as in a dream what was later to become my first major book, *The End of Economic Man*. I felt an almost irresistible urge to sit down and start typing. But I repressed it and started packing instead. I was on the train to Vienna by the following noon.

I never heard from Elise. And I did not hear from or about "The Monster" until twelve years later when I read of his end in the ruins of what had been his parents' house.

It was only a month later, in early April 1933, that I met "The Lamb." After a few weeks in Vienna I went to London where I knew nobody except for one German journalist, the London correspondent of the Ullstein publishing firm of Berlin, Count Albert Montgelas. Montgelas, scion of a Bavarian Whig family, had been in England for a good many years and was one of the most highly respected foreign correspondents there. I had been in contact with him for some time. On his last trip back to his head office in Berlin he had stopped over in Frankfurt for a few hours and we had found each other congenial despite the difference in ages, Montgelas being in his late thirties whereas I was only twenty-three. So I sent him a note from Vienna before leaving for London—and to my surprise got back a telegram saying: "Come as soon as you possibly can. I need you."

I found Montgelas packing. He too had resigned when the Nazis moved in, despite urgings by the new Nazi-appointed publisher to stay on. He was only waiting for his replacement. "I wired you to hurry up," he said, "because I'm expecting Paul Schaeffer within a day or two. He's due in from New York on the next fast boat. He's been offered the editorship of the *Berliner Tageblatt* and is inclined to accept it. But I made him stop over here and give it a final thought—it would be a tragedy if Paul took the offer. You've just come out of Germany. Maybe you can tell Paul what hell he's letting himself in for."

The *Berliner Tageblatt* had for almost half a century occupied a role in Germany and the German-speaking countries similar to that of *The New York Times* in America or The *Times* in England; not the biggest but the best and most visible daily paper. Founded in 1885, when Bismarck was still German Chancellor and the old Emperor William I was still on the throne, the paper had for all these years been run by its founder-editor, Theodore Wolff, a man renowned alike for his integrity and his independence. Wolff was getting old, of course, and so, beginning in the early 1920s, he had been grooming a successor—Paul Schaeffer, an extraordinarily incisive political writer and analyst. But before handing over to Schaeffer, Wolff sent him as correspondent of the *Berliner Tageblatt* to America in 1929 or 1930. . . .

Wolff had intended, as everyone in the small world of European journalism knew, to step down in 1935—the fiftieth year of his editorship and the eightieth year of his life. But Wolff was a Jew, so the Nazis threw him out two years ahead of schedule and asked Schaeffer to return to Berlin and take over the vacant position. Schaeffer stayed long enough in the United States to cover Roosevelt's inauguration. Then, in late March or early April, he sailed. But, upon Montgelas's urgings and still not totally decided, he was willing to stop over for a few days in London before making a final commitment.

Schaeffer, it turned out, did not need me to tell him what was going on in Germany. He knew, indeed much better than I did, and had no illusions. He had access, it seemed, both to the internal dispatches of *The New York Time*'s European correspondents and to the dispatches of the State Department in Washington. "It's precisely because this is such a horror," he said, "that I have to accept the job. I'm the only man who can prevent the worst. The Nazis will need me and the *Berliner Tageblatt*. They'll need loans from New York and London, trade with the West, understanding and a hearing. And then they'll need someone like me who knows the West, who knows whom to talk to and who's listened to. They'll need me because not one of them knows anything about the outside world. They are all know-nothing illiterates. They'll have to listen to me when I tell them that this or that of their barbarous policies will get them into trouble in the outside world and that they have to pay attention to public opinion in the Anglo-Saxon countries. They'll have to accept the restraints on their actions and their rhetoric that I know they need in order to enjoy a minimum of respect and acceptance. They know they depend on me and that the Americans will look to me. I had a long talk before I left with the Chicago historian whom President Roosevelt has just appointed as his ambassador in Berlin. He assured me he'd use me as his channel to the German Foreign Office and the Nazi hierarchy—and even the stupidest Nazi goon will have to respect and accept *that*."

"But, Paul," said Montgelas, "aren't you afraid the Nazis will just use you to give them a front of respectability and to bamboozle the outside world? They haven't shown much concern for world opinion so far." Schaeffer was indignant: "I wasn't exactly born yesterday. I'm a seasoned newspaperman. If they try to manipulate me, I'll up and leave; and that would hurt them and discredit them so completely that they couldn't take the risk. . . . I feel I have a duty. I owe it to Theodore Wolff to continue his life's work. The old man was like a father to me when he gave me my first job on my return from the trenches after the Great War. I owe it to the *Tageblatt* to make sure that it's not going to be prostituted and destroyed by savages. I owe it to the country to prevent these Nazi beasts from doing their worst. I don't look forward to Berlin under the Nazis, but I do know that no one else can have the influence for good I shall have, because no one else is quite as badly needed as I'll be when I take that job."

When Schaeffer arrived in Berlin a few days later he was received with great fanfare. Titles, money, and honors were heaped on him; and the Nazi press pointed to his appointment as editor-in-chief of the *Berlinger Tageblatt* as proof that all the stories about the Nazis and their treatment of the press that had appeared in foreign papers were just dirty Jewish lies. They immediately began to use him. He was granted interviews by Nazi bigwigs who solemnly assured him that, of course, they were not themselves anti-Semitic and had, indeed, good personal friends who were Jewish; and these interviews promptly appeared in the *Tageblatt* under Schaeffer's by-line. Whenever news of Nazi repression or Nazi atrocities filtered out, Schaeffer was dispatched to the foreign embassies in Berlin or to a meeting with foreign correspondents to assure them that these were "isolated excesses" that would not be allowed to recur. Whenever news of German rearmament appeared, it was again Schaeffer who wrote an article quoting "high-placed sources" for Hitler's intense desire for peace, and so on. For these services he was once in a while contemptuously thrown little goodies. He was allowed to keep two elderly Jewish editors on as rewrite men on the financial page, or as proofreaders—but only for two months. Or he was allowed to write a short editorial criticizing a proposed tax on oleomargarine, or on movie tickets. And when after two years the *Berliner Tageblatt* and Schaeffer had outlived their usefulness, both were liquidated and disappeared without a trace.

In her book on Eichmann, the Nazi mass murderer, the late German-American philosopher Hanna Arendt speaks of "the banality of evil." This is a most unfortunate phrase. Evil is never banal. . . . Evil works through the Hensches and the Schaeffers precisely because evil is monstrous and men are trivial. Popular usage is more nearly right than Miss Arendt was when it calls Satan *"Prince* of Darkness"; the Lord's Prayer knows how small man is and how weak, when it asks the Lord not to lead us into temptation but to deliver us from evil. And because evil is never banal and men so often are, men must not treat with evil on any terms—for the terms are always the terms of evil and never those of man. Man becomes the instrument of evil when, like the Hensches, he thinks to harness evil to his ambition; and he becomes the instrument of evil when, like the Schaeffers, he joins with evil to prevent worse.

I have often wondered which of these two did, in the end, more harm—the Monster or the Lamb; and which is worse, Hensch's sin of the lust for power or Schaeffer's hubris and sin of pride? But maybe the greatest sin is neither of these two ancient ones; the greatest sin may be the new twentieth-century sin of indifference, the sin of the distinguished biochemist who neither kills nor lies but refuses to bear witness when, in the words of the old gospel hymn, "They crucify my Lord."

QUESTIONS

1. In your own words, characterize Hensch.

2. In contrast with Hensch, what sort of person was Schaeffer?

3. What sort of person is Peter Drucker? On the basis of what you find in the selection, how would you characterize the author? (Refer to the text for support and examples.)

4. Drucker does not write a point-by-point comparison of the Monster and the Lamb. How would such a comparison have changed the essay and your response to it?

5. In your opinion, how would Drucker define "academic freedom"? In what way would his definition differ from one that might be offered by the distinguished biochemist, who at the faculty meeting described at the beginning of the essay asks the Nazi commissar only if there will be more money for research in his area?

6. How does the following quotation from *The Art of Readable Writing*, by Rudold Flesch, explain Drucker's technique in "The Monster and the Lamb"?

> Only stories are really readable. [A *Reader's Digest* editor said] "Whenever we want to draw attention to a problem, we wait until somebody does something about it. Then we print the story of how he did it."

7. In his conclusion, Drucker speculates about whether the Monster or the Lamb did more harm, but then he mentions that the greatest sin may be that of indifference. If Drucker had added another paragraph to continue his thoughts about indifference, what might he have written?

RICHARD RODRIGUEZ
From *Hunger of Memory*

Born to working-class Mexican immigrants in Sacramento, California, Richard Rodriguez spoke Spanish almost exclusively until he enrolled in school. He then came to think of Spanish as the language of his private life and English as the language of his public or school life. The book from which this excerpt is taken is an autobiographical account of the education of its author, who found himself a highly prized "minority student." When the book appeared, it created a furor because it seemed to speak against the minority targeting of education, and it challenged the popular view that minority students should be encouraged to use the language of their home even in school. For Rodriguez, alienation from his parents and his siblings was the result of his joining the mainstream.

I remember to start with that day in Sacramento—a California now nearly thirty years past—when I first entered a classroom, able to understand some fifty stray English words.

The third of four children, I had been preceded to a neighborhood Roman Catholic school by an older brother and sister. But neither of them had revealed very much about their classroom experiences. Each afternoon they returned, as they left in the morning, always together, speaking in Spanish as they climbed the five steps of the porch. And their mysterious books, wrapped in shopping-bag paper, remained on the table next to the door, closed firmly behind them.

An accident of geography sent me to a school where all my classmates were white, many the children of doctors and lawyers and business executives. All my classmates certainly must have been uneasy on that first day of school—as most children are uneasy—to find themselves apart from their families in the first institution of their lives. But I was astonished.

The nun said, in a friendly but oddly impersonal voice, 'Boys and girls, this is Richard Rodriguez.' (I heard her sound out: *Rich-heard Road-ree-guess.*) It was the first time I had heard anyone name me in English. 'Richard,' the nun repeated more slowly, writing my name down in her black leather book. Quickly I turned to see my mother's face dissolve in a watery blur behind the pebbled glass door.

Many years later there is something called bilingual education—a scheme proposed in the late 1960s by Hispanic-American social activists, later endorsed by a congressional vote. It is a program that seeks to permit non-English-speaking children, many from lower-class homes, to use their family language as the language of school. (Such is the goal its supporters announce.) I hear them and am forced to say no: It is not possible for a child—any child—ever to use his family's language in school. Not to understand this is to misunderstand the public uses of schooling and to trivialize the nature of intimate life—a family's 'language.'

Memory teaches me what I know of these matters; the boy reminds the adult. I was a bilingual child, a certain kind—socially disadvantaged—the son of working-class parents, both Mexican immigrants.

In the early years of my boyhood, my parents coped very well in America. My father had steady work. My mother managed at home. They were nobody's victims. Optimism and ambition led them to a house (our home) many blocks from the Mexican south side of town. We lived among *gringos* and only a block from the biggest, whitest houses. It never oc-curred to my parents that they couldn't live wherever they chose. Nor was the Sacramento of the fifties bent on teaching them a contrary lesson. My mother and father were more annoyed than intimidated by those two or three neighbors who tried initially to make us unwelcome. ('Keep your brats away from my sidewalk!') But despite all they achieved, perhaps because they had so much to achieve, any deep feeling of ease, the confidence of 'belonging' in public was withheld from them both. They regarded the people at work, the faces in crowds, as very distant from us. They were the others, *los gringos*. That term was interchangeable in their speech with another, even more telling, *los americanos*.

I grew up in a house where the only regular guests were my relations. For one day, enormous families of relatives would visit and there would be so many people that the noise and the bodies would spill out to the backyard and front porch. Then, for weeks, no one came by. (It was usually a salesman who rang the doorbell.) Our house stood apart. A gaudy yellow in a row of white bungalows. We were the people with the noisy dog. The people who raised pigeons and chickens. We were the foreigners on the block. A few neighbors smiled and waved. We waved back. But no one in the family knew the names of the old couple who lived next door; until I was seven years old, I did not know the names of the kids who lived across the street.

In public, my father and mother spoke a hesitant, accented, not always grammatical English. And they would have to strain—their bodies tense—to catch the sense of what was rapidly said by *los gringos*. At home they spoke Spanish. The language of their Mexican past sounded in counterpoint to the English of public society. The words would come quickly, with ease. Conveyed through those sounds was the pleasing, soothing, consoling reminder of being at home.

During those years when I was first conscious of hearing, my mother and father addressed me only in Spanish; in Spanish I learned to reply. By contrast, English (*inglés*), rarely heard in the house, was the language I came to associate with *gringos*. I learned my first words of English over-hearing my parents speak to strangers. At five years of age, I knew just enough English for my mother to trust me on errands to stores one block away. No more.

I was a listening child, careful to hear the very different sounds of Spanish and English. Wide-eyed with hearing, I'd listen to sounds more than words. First, there were English (*gringo*) sounds. So many words were still unknown that when the butcher or the lady at the drugstore said something to me, exotic polysyllabic sounds would bloom in the midst of their sentences. Often, the speech of people in public seemed to me very loud, booming with confidence. The man behind the counter would literally ask, "What can I do for you?' But by being so firm and so clear, the sound of his voice said that he was a *gringo*; he belonged in public society.

I would also hear then the high nasal notes of middle-class American speech. The air stirred with sound. Sometimes, even now, when I have been traveling abroad for several weeks, I will hear what I heard as a boy. In hotel lobbies or airports, in Turkey or Brazil, some Americans will pass, and suddenly I will hear it again—the high sound of American voices. For a few seconds I will hear it with pleasure, for it is now the sound of *my* society—a reminder of home. But inevitably—already on the flight headed for home—the sound fades with repetition. I will be unable to hear it anymore.

When I was a boy, things were different. The accent of *los gringos* was never pleasing nor was it hard to hear. Crowds at Safeway or at bus stops would be noisy with sound. And I would be forced to edge away from the chirping chatter above me.

I was unable to hear my own sounds, but I knew very well that I spoke English poorly. My words could not stretch far enough to form complete thoughts. And the words I did speak I didn't know well enough to make into distinct sounds. (Listeners would usually lower their heads, better to hear what I was trying to say.) But it was one thing for *me* to speak English with difficulty. It was more troubling for me to hear my parents speak in public: their high-whining vowels and guttural consonants; their sentences that got stuck with 'eh' and 'ah' sounds; the confused syntax; the hesitant rhythm of sounds so different from the way *gringos* spoke. I'd notice, moreover, that my parents' voices were softer than those of *gringos* we'd meet.

I am tempted now to say that none of this mattered. In adulthood I am embarrassed by childhood fears. And, in a way, it didn't matter very much that my parents could not speak English with ease. Their linguistic difficulties had no serious consequences. My mother and father made themselves understood at the county hospital clinic and at government offices. And yet, in another way, it mattered very much—it was unsettling to hear my parents struggle with English. Hearing them, I'd grow nervous, my clutching trust in their protection and power weakened.

There were many times like the night at a brightly lit gasoline station (a blaring white memory) when I stood uneasily, hearing my father. He was talking to a teenaged attendant. I do not recall what they were saying, but I cannot forget the sounds my father made as he spoke. At one point his words slid together to form one word—sounds as confused as the threads of blue and green oil in the puddle next to my shoes. His voice rushed through what he had left to say. And, toward the end, reached falsetto notes, appealing to his listener's understanding. I looked away to the lights of passing automobiles. I tried not to hear anymore. But I heard only too well the calm, easy tones in the attendant's reply. Shortly afterward, walking toward home with my father, I shivered when he put his hand on my shoulder. The very first chance that I got, I evaded his grasp and ran on ahead into the dark, skipping with feigned boyish exuberance.

But then there was Spanish. *Español*: my family's language. *Español*: the language that seemed to me a private language. I'd hear strangers on the radio and in the Mexican Catholic church across town speaking in Spanish, but I couldn't really believe that Spanish was a public language, like English. Spanish speakers, rather, seemed related to me, for I sensed that we shared—through our language—the experience of feeling apart from *los gringos*. It was thus a ghetto Spanish that I heard and I spoke. Like those whose lives are bound by a barrio, I was reminded by Spanish of my separateness from *los otros*, *los gringos* in power. But more intensely than for most barrio children—because I did not live in a barrio—Spanish seemed to me the language of home. (Most days it was only at home that I'd hear it.) It became the language of joyful return.

A family member would say something to me and I would feel myself specially recognized. My parents would say something to me and I would feel embraced by the sound of their words. Those sounds said: *I am speaking with ease in Spanish. I am addressing you in words I never use with* los gringos. *I recognize you as someone special, close, like no one outside. You belong with us.* In the family.

(*Ricardo.*)

At the age of five, six, well past the time when most other children no longer easily notice the difference between sounds uttered at home and words spoken in public, I had a different experience. I lived in a world magically compounded of sounds. I remained a child longer than most; I lingered too long, poised at the edge of language—often frightened by the sounds of *los gringos*, delighted by the sounds of Spanish at home. I shared with my family a language that was startlingly different from that used in the great city around us.

For me there were none of the gradations between public and private society so normal to a maturing child. Outside the house was public society; inside the house was private. Just opening or closing the screen door behind me was an important experience. I'd rarely leave home all alone or without reluctance. Walking down the sidewalk, under the canopy of tall trees, I'd warily notice the—suddenly—silent neighborhood kids who stood warily watching me. Nervously, I'd arrive at the grocery store to hear there the sounds of the *gringo*—foreign to me—reminding me that in this world so big, I was a foreigner. But then I'd return. Walking back toward our house, climbing the steps from the sidewalk, when the front door was open in summer, I'd hear voices beyond the screen door talking in Spanish. For a second or two, I'd stay, linger there, listening. Smiling, I'd hear my mother call out, saying in Spanish (words): 'Is that you, Richard?' All the while her sounds would assure me: *You are home now; come closer; inside. With us.*

'*Sí,*' I'd reply.

Once more inside the house I would resume (assume) my place in the family. The sounds would dim, grow harder to hear. Once more at home, I would grow less aware of that fact. It required, however, no more than the blurt of the doorbell to alert me to listen to sounds all over again. The house would turn instantly still while my mother went to the door. I'd hear her hard English sounds. I'd wait to hear her voice return to soft-sounding Spanish, which assured me, as surely as did the clicking tongue of the lock on the door, that the stranger was gone.

Plainly, it is not healthy to hear such sounds so often. It is not healthy to distinguish public words from private sounds so easily. I remained cloistered by sounds, timid and shy in public, too dependent on voices at home. And yet it needs to be emphasized: I was an extremely happy child at home. I remember many nights when my father would come back from work, and I'd hear him call out to my mother in Spanish, sounding relieved. In Spanish, he'd sound light and free notes he never could manage in English. Some nights I'd jump up just at hearing his voice. With *mis hermanos* I would come running into the room where he was with my mother. Our laughing (so deep was the pleasure!) became screaming. Like others who know the pain of public alienation, we transformed the knowledge of our public separateness and made it consoling—the reminder of intimacy. Excited, we joined our voices in a celebration of sounds. *We are speaking now the way we never speak out in public. We are alone—together,* voices sounded, surrounded to tell me. Some nights, no one seemed willing to loosen the hold sounds had on us. At dinner, we invented new words. (Ours sounded Spanish, but made sense only to us.) We pieced together new words by taking, say, an English verb and giving it Spanish endings. My mother's instructions at bedtime would be lacquered with mock-urgent tones. Or a word like *sí* would become, in several notes, able to convey added measures of feeling. Tongues explored the edges of words, especially the fat vowels. And we happily sounded that military drum roll, the twirling roar of the Spanish *r*. Family language: my family's sounds. The voices of my parents and sisters and brother. Their voices insisting: *You belong here. We are family members. Related. Special to one another. Listen!* Voices singing and sighing, rising, straining, then surging, teeming with pleasure that burst syllables into fragments of laughter. At times it seemed there was steady quiet only when, from another room, the rustling whispers of my parents faded and I moved closer to sleep.

QUESTIONS

1. Outline the author's argument in favor of his premise that "It is not possible for a child—any child—ever to use his family's language in school."
2. Discuss the similarities and differences in Roger Wilkins' and Richard Rodriguez' experiences.
3. Try to capture in literal language the meanings of the "color"metaphors in the paragraph beginning "There were many times like the night at a brightly lit gasoline station. . . ." What does the literal translation lose?
4. What did English and Spanish symbolize for the author?
5. What do you think Rodriguez means by "bilingual education"? Explain your own thoughts about this educational method.
6. By the conclusion of *Hunger of Memory*, Richard Rodriguez, in his own way, has, like Roger Wilkins, said, "You can't go home again":

   It is to those whom my mother refers to as the *gringos* that I write. The *gringos*. The expression reminds me that she and my father have not followed their children all the way down the path to full American-ization.

   Does integration always involve alienation? In becoming part of the mainstream, must blacks and Chicanos leave their native culture behind? Use evidence from the selections by Rodriguez, Wilkins, and Brown in answering this question.

MAXINE HONG KINGSTON
From *The Woman Warrior*

Maxine Hong Kingston was born in California in 1940 to a laundryman and a laundress-midwife, both of whom had held higher status in China. Kingston's childhood experiences are recounted in The Woman Warrior, *from which the following selection is taken. This book won widespread acclaim when it first appeared in 1976. Part of that approval derived from Kingston's vivid depiction of the mix of two cultures, as you will see in our selection. But also an important part of that approval was for her interesting use of stylistic devices for descriptive and narrative purposes in a work of nonfiction.*

Maybe because I was the one with the tongue cut loose, I had grown inside me a list of over two hundred things that I had to tell my mother so that she would know the true things about me and to stop the pain in my throat. When I first started counting, I had had only thirty-six items: how I had prayed for a white horse of my own—white, the bad, mournful color—and prayer bringing me to the attention of the god of the black-and-white nuns who gave us "holy cards" in the park. How I wanted the horse to start the movies in my mind coming true. How I had picked on a girl and made her cry. . . . How it was me who pulled up the onions in the garden out of anger. How I had jumped head-first off the dresser, not accidentally, but so I could fly. Then there were my fights at Chinese school. And the nuns who kept stopping us in the park, which was across the street from Chinese school, to tell us that if we didn't get baptized we'd go to a hell like one of the nine Taoist hells forever. . . . And the Mexican and Filipino girls at school who went to "confession," and how I envied them their white dresses and their chance each Saturday to tell even thoughts that were sinful. If only I could let my mother know the list, she—and the world—would become more like me, and I would never be alone again. I would pick a time of day when my mother was alone and tell her one item a day; I'd be finished in less than a year. If the telling got excruciating and her anger too bad, I'd tell five items once a week like the Catholic girls, and I'd still be through in a year, maybe ten months. My mother's most peaceful time was in the evenings when she starched the white shirts. The laundry would be clean, the gray wood floors sprinkled and swept with water and wet sawdust. She would be wringing shirts at the starch tub and not running about. My father and sisters and brothers could be at their own jobs mending, folding, packaging. Steam would be rising from the starch, the air cool at last. Yes, that would be the time and place for the telling. . . .

I hunkered down between the wall and the wicker basket of shirts. I had decided to start with the earliest item—when I had smashed a spider against the white side of the house: it was the first thing I killed. I said, clearly, "I killed a spider," and it was nothing; she did not hit me or throw hot starch at me. It sounded like nothing to me too. How strange when I had had such feelings of death shoot through my hand and into my body so that I would surely die. So I had to continue, of course, and let her know how important it had been. "I returned every day to look at its smear on the side of the house," I said. "It was our old house, the one we lived in until I was five. I went to the wall every day to look, I studied the stain." Relieved because she said nothing but only continued squeezing the starch, I went away feeling pretty good. Just two hundred and six more items to go. I moved carefully all the next day so as not to do anything or have anything happen to me that would make me go back to two hundred and seven again. I'd tell a couple of easy ones and work up to how I had pulled the quiet girl's hair and how I had enjoyed the year being sick. If it was going to be this easy, maybe I could blurt out several a day, maybe an easy one and a hard one. I could go chronologically, or I could work from easy to hard or hard to easy, depending on my mood. On the second night I talked about how I had hinted to a ghost[1] girl that I wished I had a doll of my own until she gave me a head and body to glue together—that she hadn't given it to me of her own generosity but because I had hinted. But on the fifth night (I skipped two to reward myself) I decided it was time to do a really hard one and tell her about the white horse. And suddenly the duck voice came out, which I did not use with the family. "What's it called, Mother"—the duck voice coming out talking to my own mother— "when a person whispers to the head of the sages—no, not the sages, more like the buddhas but not real people like the buddhas (they've always lived in the sky and never turned into people like the buddhas)—and you whisper to them, the boss of them; and ask for things? They're like magicians? What do you call it when you talk to the boss magician?"

"'Talking-to-the-top-magician,' I guess."

"I did that. Yes. That's it. That's what I did. I talked-to-the-top-magician and asked for a white horse." There. Said.

"Mm," she said, squeezing the starch out of the collar and cuffs. But I had talked, and she acted as if she hadn't heard.

Perhaps she hadn't understood. I had to be more explicit. I hated this. "I kneeled on the bed in there, in the laundry bedroom, and put my arms up like I was in a comic book"—one night I heard monsters coming through the kitchen, and I had promised the god in the movies, the one

---

[1] A Caucasian, especially a white Anglo-Saxon American.

the Mexicans and Filipinos have, as in "God Bless America," that I would not read comic books anymore if he would save me just once; I had broken that promise, and I needed to tell all this to my mother too—"and in that ludicrous position asked for a horse."

"Mm," she said, nodded, and kept dipping and squeezing.

On my two nights off, I had sat on the floor too but had not said a word.

"Mother," I whispered and quacked.

"I can't stand this whispering," she said looking right at me, stopping her squeezing. "Senseless gabbings every night. I wish you would stop. Go away and work. Whispering, whispering, making no sense. Madness. I don't feel like hearing your craziness."

So I had to stop, relieved in some ways. I shut my mouth, but I felt something alive tearing at my throat, bite by bite, from the inside. Soon there would be three hundred things, and too late to get them out before my mother grew old and died.

I had probably interrupted her in the middle of her own quiet time when the boiler and presses were off and the cool night flew against the windows in moths and crickets. Very few customers came in. Starching the shirts for the next day's pressing was probably my mother's time to ride off with the people in her own mind. That would explain why she was so far away and did not want to listen to me. "Leave me alone," she said.

The hulk, the hunching sitter, brought a third box now, to rest his feet on. He patted his boxes. He sat in wait, hunching on his pile of dirt. My throat hurt constantly, vocal cords taut to snapping. One night when the laundry was so busy that the whole family was eating dinner there, crowded around the little round table, my throat burst open. I stood up, talking and burbling. I looked directly at my mother and at my father and screamed, "I want you to tell that hulk, that gorilla-ape, to go away and never bother us again. I know what you're up to. You're thinking he's rich, and we're poor. You think we're odd and not pretty and we're not bright. You think you can give us away to freaks. You better not do that, Mother. I don't want to see him or his dirty boxes here tomorrow. If I see him here one more time, I'm going away. I'm going away anyway. I am. Do you hear me? I may be ugly and clumsy, but one thing I'm not, I'm not retarded. There's nothing wrong with my brain. Do you know what the Teacher Ghosts say about me? They tell me I'm smart, and I can win scholarships. I can get into colleges. I've already applied. I'm smart. I can do all kinds of things. I know how to get A's, and they say I could be a scientist or a mathematician if I want. I can make a living and take care of myself. So you don't have to find me a keeper who's too dumb to know a bad bargain. I'm so smart, if they say write ten pages, I can write fifteen. I can do ghost things even better than ghosts can. Not everybody thinks I'm nothing. I am not going to be a slave or a wife. Even if I am stupid and talk funny and get sick, I won't let you turn me into a slave or a wife. I'm getting out of here. I can't stand living here anymore. It's your fault I talk weird. The only reason I flunked kindergarten was because you couldn't teach me English, and you gave me a zero IQ. I've brought my IQ up, though. They say I'm smart now. Things follow in lines at school. They take stories and teach us to turn them into essays. I don't need anybody to pronounce English words for me. I can figure them out by myself. I'm going to get scholarships, and I'm going away. And at college I'll have the people I like for friends. I don't care if their great-great-grandfather died of TB. I don't care if they were our enemies in China four thousand years ago. So get that ape out of here. I'm going to college. And I'm not going to Chinese school anymore. I'm going to run for office at American school, and I'm going to join clubs. I'm going to get enough offices and clubs on my record to get into college. And I can't stand Chinese school anyway; the kids are rowdy and mean, fighting all night. And I don't want to listen to any more of your stories; they have no logic. They scramble me up. You lie with stories. You won't tell me a story and then say, 'This is a true story,' or, 'This is just a story.' I can't tell the difference. I don't even know what your real names are. I can't tell what's real and what you make up. Ha! You can't stop me from talking. You tried to cut off my tongue, but it didn't work." So I told the hardest ten or twelve things on my list all in one outburst.

My mother, who is champion talker, was, of course, shouting at the same time. "I cut it to make you talk more, not less, you dummy. You're still stupid. You can't listen right. I didn't say I was going to marry you off. Did I ever say that? Did I ever mention that? Those newspaper people were for your sister, not you. Who would want you? Who said we could sell you? We can't sell people. Can't you take a joke? You can't even tell a joke from real life. You're not so smart. Can't even tell real from false."

"I'm never getting married, never!"

"Who'd want to marry you anyway? Noisy. Talking like a duck. Disobedient. Messy. And I know about college. What makes you think you're the first one to think about college? I was a doctor. I went to medical school. I don't see why you have to be a mathematician. I don't see why you can't be a doctor like me."

"I can't stand fever and delirium or listening to people coming out of anesthesia. But I didn't say I wanted to be a mathematician either. That's what the ghosts say. I want to be a lumberjack and a newspaper reporter." Might as well tell her some of the other items on my list. "I'm going to chop down trees in the daytime and write about timber at night."

"I don't see why you need to go to college at all to become either one of those things. Everybody else is sending their girls to typing school. 'Learn to type if you want to be an American girl.' Why don't you go to typing school? The cousins and village girls are going to typing school."

"And you leave my sister alone. You try that with the advertising again, and I'll take her with me." My telling list was scrambled out of order. When I said them out loud I saw that some of the items were ten years old already, and I had outgrown them. But they kept pouring out anyway in the voice like Chinese opera. I could hear the drums and the cymbals and the gongs and brass horns.

"You're the one to leave your little sisters alone," my mother was saying. "You're always leading them off somewhere. I've had to call the police twice because of you." She herself was shouting out things I had meant to tell her—that I took my brothers and sisters to explore strange people's houses, ghost children's houses, and haunted houses blackened by fire. . . .

"You turned out so unusual. I fixed your tongue so that you could say charming things. You don't even say hello to the villagers."

"They don't say hello to me."

"They don't have to answer children. When you get old, people will say hello to you."

"When I get to college it won't matter if I'm not charming. And it doesn't matter if a person is ugly; she can still do schoolwork."

"I didn't say you were ugly."

"You say that all the time."

"That's what we're supposed to say. That's what Chinese say. We like to say the opposite."

It seemed to hurt her to tell me that—another guilt for my list to tell my mother, I thought. And suddenly I got very confused and lonely because I was at that moment telling her my list, and in the telling, it grew. No higher listener. No listener but myself.

QUESTIONS

1. In what ways does Kingston identify with her family? In what ways does she feel she is different from them?

2. How do Kingston's attitudes toward her family compare with Richard Rodriguez' attitudes toward his?

3. Why does Kingston give us so much detail about *setting*, the family's laundry? How does this scene affect our understanding of the narrative?

4. Explain why Kingston wanted to tell her list to her mother.

5. How does Kingston help readers share the experiences that she writes

about? What information does she include that she might not have put in if her work had been intended only for first-generation immigrants? Only for Orientals? Only for women?

6. In the first paragraph, Kingston uses some obvious stylistic devices. What are those devices, and what is their effect? (Think, for instance, about *repetition* of words and sentence structures.) Then look at the shouting match between mother and daughter that serves as the final scene of our excerpt. What are the stylistic devices that are used here? How do they affect your response to the narrative?

SUGGESTIONS FOR WRITING

1. Margaret Mead's autobiographical narrative presents a striking portrait of her grandmother. Write an account of one of your grandparents (or an uncle or aunt). What does your subject look like? sound like? wear? believe in? move like? What are some typical sayings or verbal tics?

2. The idea that children can be savages occurs again and again in literature, as it does in William Golding's *The Lord of the Flies* and Frank Conroy's autobiography. Write about a time when you, perhaps in conjunction with friends, were a savage.

3. One theme that Roger Wilkins, Claude Brown, Richard Rodriguez, and Maxine Hong Kingston have in common is this: Life as a cultural outsider is difficult. The authors bring that theme to life through their narratives. If you have ever been an "outsider" (and almost everyone has been at some time), tell of that experience. Focus on one or two significant events rather than trying to give a general outline of a long period in your life.

4. Tell about your relationship with either the most wicked or the most saintly person you have ever known. In your narrative, try to be judicious and not go overboard with either condemnation or praise. Before you write, think about the methods that Peter Drucker uses to portray the Monster and the Lamb.

5. Richard Rodriguez' autobiography is largely about language. Have you ever had language problems? Perhaps your native language is not Englsh, or maybe your home dialect is not one of those that carries prestige, as does "network standard" (spoken by newscasters on the national networks) or the upper class British dialect. In any case, write about a language problem that you (or a family member or close friend) have encountered.

6. Make a *setting* the main focus of an autobiographical narrative: your room, the kitchen at home, a place where you have worked. . . . You should pack your writing with concrete details so that the reader can visualize the place you are talking about and also understand why it is significant to you.

7. Recall a time when you discovered you were different from other people. Write about that time as a way of sharing with your readers part of a view of yourself.

CHAPTER THREE

Expository Writing

In personal writing (the kinds of selections included in Chapter Two), the focus is on the writer. The purpose of writers in the personal mode is to explain themselves—their attitudes, feelings, experiences, ideas—to readers. The selection by Frank Conroy in the "Autobiography" subsection of Chapter Two (pages 94–102) is a good example. Conroy is not telling of earth-shaking events, but of an intense and instructive episode in his own life. On the other hand, in "The Monster and the Lamb" Peter Drucker focuses not so much on himself as on two people he knew, each of whom became a symbol for him. In each case, however, we are keenly interested in what the writing tells us about the writer, for we take autobiography to be a *personal* statement.

By contrast, the focus in expository writing is on ideas, beliefs, concepts, processes, and things. Every explanation of an idea is expository; so too is every set of instructions (for assembling a barbecue or performing brain surgery) and every definition (either of the kind found in a dictionary or the sort that demands several pages). We could reasonably say, then, that the primary focus of the writer and reader of exposition is on the subject matter of the essay.

Because of its purpose—basically *to convey information* to a reader—expository writing generally follows certain principles, and these are well worth taking into account.

As regards the *writer*: obviously, highly personal elements in an essay will shift attention away from the information to be gained (for instance, how to do something or the facts concerning an event) and toward the personality of the writer. The more the writer calls attention to himself or herself, the more personal (and the less expository) the writing becomes. This is not to say that the best expository writing is cold and impersonal, machine-like.

The following diagram illustrates the place of the writer's personality in most exposition:

personal •••••••••••••••••••••••••••••• impersonal
:
:
:
exposition

In other words, most exposition falls at the midpoint between the most "bloodless" and the most intimate kinds of writing.

Since the goal of exposition is to explain, expository writers attempt to make their writings as easy to read as possible (which is not the same as being simpleminded). Effective expository writers produce clear, readable prose. They choose more familiar words rather than less familiar ones unless they have a good reason for using such words as "thaumaturgist" for "miracle worker," "ideation" for "thinking," and "piscivorous" for "fish-eating." They try to untangle "snarled" sentences (for example, "The child in the meantime pulled the picture that I had put up down" versus "In the meantime, the child pulled down the picture that I had put up"). And they help the reader by providing subheadings and other "guides" to reading when these are appropriate.

In expository writing, we usually apply certain criteria to the contents of a piece. As a rule, we expect all the information that we need to understand the subject and no more, and we also expect that this information will be true and accurate. Moreover, we want all of the contents to be relevant to the point that is being made.

There are, then, certain "rules of thumb"[1] that we can use to judge expository writing:

1. Has the writer made his or her prose as readable as possible?
2. Does the writer supply adequate examples, data, reasons, analysis? Or does he or she include too much, thus becoming redundant?
3. Is the content reliable? Up to date? Accurate? From trustworthy sources?

---

[1]See H. P. Grice, "Logic and Conversation," *Syntax and Semantics*, vol. 3; *Speech Acts*, ed. P. Cole and J. L. Morgan (New York: Seminar Press, 1975).

4. Does all of the content relate to the main point that the author is making?

These questions relate to the information that authors present and the methods they use to present it. Thus, if you keep the questions in the back of your mind as you read, you will have a guide for analysis and discussion and a set of criteria for evaluation.

Two "How-To" Essays

As we saw, exposition is prose that explains, and one of the most important kinds of explanations is instructions on *how to* do things. Instructions explain *how to* make fudge brownies and long distance calls, *how to* assemble barbecues and cyclotrons, *how to* get from Peoria to Pittsburgh and from earth to Saturn. (Many how-to writings include graphics: diagrams, equations, photographs, and so on.)

How-to writing is utilitarian. It systematically and clearly explains processes, often enumerating:

1. Insert the floppy disk in drive no. 1.
2. Turn the computer on by pushing the large red switch on the right-hand side upward.
3. When the "prompt" >A appears on your screen, type BASICA, then hit the "enter" key.

Not all how-to essays are as streamlined as this example, however; writers often give general information along with the instructions, thus informing readers about a subject as well as how to deal with it, and such is the case with the essays that follow.

EUELL GIBBONS

The Acorn: Ancient Food of Man

Born in the Red River Valley in Texas, Euell Gibbons has led an astoundingly varied life, having been, at one time or another, a cowboy, hobo, carpenter, surveyor, boat builder, beachcomber, newspaperman, schoolteacher, farmer, and staff member at a Quaker graduate school. It is not surprising that a man with such varied interests would write Stalking the Wild Asparagus, *a book about gathering food in forest and field.*

This essay not only gives background on the various kinds of acorns, but also explains several methods of preparing acorns for food. In its explanations, the essay is extremely clear, and can thus serve as an excellent introductory example of exposition.

Many of the sweet acorns borne by the White Oak group are not at all unpleasant eaten raw. Roasted acorns easily compete with roasted chestnuts in some parts of Spain, Portugal and North Africa. To primitive man in Europe, Asia and America, acorns were often the "staff of life." If we consider the whole sweep of his existence on earth, it seems likely that mankind has consumed many millions of tons more of acorns than he has of the cereal grains, which made their appearance only during the comparatively recent development of agriculture. It seems a pity that the food which nourished the childhood of our race is today nearly everywhere neglected and despised.

America is blessed with a great many species of oak, and many kinds of acorns were highly appreciated by our Indian predecessors. Our oaks can be very roughly divided into two kinds: (1) those with bristles at the tips and lobes of the leaves, taking two years to mature a crop of acorns, and (2) those without bristly terminal points on the leaves and maturing a crop of more or less edible acorns in a single year. Examples of the former class are the Red, Black and Willow oaks, and of the latter, White, Post and Chestnut oaks.

Primitive man everywhere preferred the sweet acorns when he could get them, but he never refused to gather and use even the bitterest kinds. The bitter and astringent qualities, when present, are due to tannin, which is a substance readily soluble in water, and therefore easily leached out by

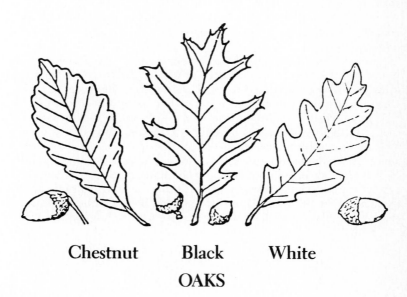

Chestnut   **Black**   **White**

OAKS

any one of several simple processes, leaving a sweet, nut-flavored product which can be prepared in a number of palatable ways.

I was a member of a party of six in the mountains of central Pennsylvania one autumn when the chestnut oaks, *Quercus Muhlenbergii*, had borne an extra heavy crop of acorns. We easily gathered a bushel in an hour. All of us tried them raw, and three members of the party liked them well enough to eat several. I thought them considerably improved when we roasted some in the oven of the wood stove that heated the cabin in which we were staying. This experience convinced me that even unleached acorns of some species are worth the attention of anyone who is really hungry.

We shelled out a number of the acorns and boiled the kernels whole for two hours, changing the water every time it became tea-colored. We kept a large kettle of fresh water boiling on the stove and used this for replacements, so the boiling was hardly interrupted by the water changes. The acorn meats turned a dark chocolate brown and were without a trace of their former bitterness and astringency. When they were roasted, or, more accurately, dried out, in a slow oven, they were enjoyed by every member of the group. I dipped some of the boiled and dried acorns in clarified sugar, in the same manner that the French prepare *marrons glacés*[1] from chestnuts, and after that the job of getting the party to eat acorns was replaced with the task of keeping enough candied acorns on hand. The extra sugar in the sirup was welcome, for much of the natural sugar in the acorn dissolves out during the leaching process.

I have since developed two standard materials from acorns to use in cooking., I call these Acorn Grits and Acorn Meal, and neither is very difficult to prepare.

Acorn Grits are made of shelled-out acorn kernels, boiled for two hours, with several changes of water, as described above, then thoroughly dried in a slow oven and ground rather coarsely. I often use Acorn Grits when a recipe calls for chopped nuts and find them very satisfactory.

Acorn Meal is made by grinding dry, raw acorn kernels, mixing the meal with boiling water and pressing out the liquid through a jelly bag. This process might have to be repeated several times with very bitter acorns. Then the meal is spread thinly in shallow pans and dried in the sun or in a very slow oven. It ordinarily becomes partly caked during this process so it must be reground, this time using the finest plate on your food chopper, or a hand gristmill, set very closely. Both the meal and the grits can be stored in sealed glass jars, where they seem to keep indefinitely.

Both Acorn Grits and Meal are very dark-colored with a sweet, nutlike

---

[1] *Marrons glacés* are glazed Spanish chestnuts.

flavor that nearly everyone enjoys. A lighter colored meal can be made with cold-water leaching. Use a tall can, such as those in which fruit juice is ordinarily sold, and punch the bottom full of holes with a nail. Fit a piece of filter paper or a pad of folded cheesecloth in the bottom and fill the can with coarsely ground meal made of well-dried, raw acorn meats. Fasten a wire bail to the top of the can and hang it over the sink faucet. Open the faucet just enough so the running water will stand above the meal and let the cold water filter through it all night. Dry and regrind as with the hot-water-leached Acorn Meal.

To make Acorn Glacé, put 2 cups of sugar, 1 cup of water, ⅛ teaspoon of cream of tartar and a pinch of salt in a small saucepan and boil until you see the very first hint of browning. Set the small saucepan in a kettle of boiling water to keep the contents liquid and dip in whole acorn kernels, which have been boiled and dried as described above, using a pair of tweezers; then place them on wax paper to harden. This improves the appearance as well as the taste of the acorns and they can be served either as a confection or with a meal, as a good hearty food.

For Acorn Bread sift together 1 cup of Acorn Meal, 1 cup of white flour, 3 teaspoons of baking powder, 1 teaspoon of salt and 3 tablespoons of sugar. Beat 1 egg, add 1 cup of milk and 3 tablespoons of salad oil. Add this to the dry ingredients and stir just enough to moisten everything. Pour into a greased pan, and bake in a 400° oven for 30 minutes. Or you can fill greased muffin tins two-thirds full of the same batter and bake only about 20 minutes for some excellent Acorn Muffins. These breads make a fine accompaniment to wild vegetables or wild fruit jams and marmalades, and taste as if they had already been buttered.

To make Acorn Griddle Cakes follow the recipe for Acorn Bread, but use instead 2 eggs and 1¼ cups of milk. Spoon the batter onto a hot griddle and spread thin. Brown both sides, turning only once. Serve with home-made maple sirup or wild fruit jellies.

For something special in acorn cookery, try Steamed Acorn Black Bread. Mix 1½ cups of Acorn Meal with ½ cup of Acorn Grits, 1 cup of white flour, ½ cup of sugar, 1 teaspoon of salt and 1 teaspoon of baking soda. When these ingredients are well mixed, add ½ cup of dark molasses, 1½ cups of sour milk and 2 tablespoons of salad oil. Wring out a pudding cloth in boiling water, spread it in a round-bottomed bowl and turn the batter into it. Tie up the corners and suspend the bag over boiling water in a closed kettle for 4 hours. This should be served hot from the bag, and a steaming slab of this rich, dark, moist bread is just right with a plate of baked beans.

Nowadays, when people are again coming to appreciate the dark, wholesome breads of our ancestors, maybe the acorn will come back into its own.

QUESTIONS

1. In his explanations of how to prepare acorns for eating, does Gibbons provide enough information? Are there irrelevancies?
2. What do you find in the essay that makes you think the information is reliable (or unreliable)? Why might you conclude that Gibbons knows (or doesn't know) what he's talking about?
3. What does Gibbons do to make his explanations clear?
4. What two forms of instruction does Gibbons use? (Compare the instructions beginning "We shelled out a number of acorns and boiled the kernels whole for two hours" with those beginning "For Acorn Bread sift together 1 cup of Acorn Meal."

T. J. RITTER M.D.
Sleeplessness

In the nineteenth century and the earlier part of the twentieth, the "doctor book"
was part of almost every home library and sometimes the only book in the house
besides the Bible. The following discussion of sleeplessness is from The People's
Home Medical Book, *by T. J. Ritter, M.D., which is one section of* The People's
Home Library, *containing, in addition to the "doctor book," a cookbook and a book*
on veterinary medicine. The publication date of this three-in-one volume is 1919.

Of course, you won't take the medical advice in "Sleeplessness" seriously; in
fact, the little essay is likely to make you grin, if not chuckle. However, the
explanations are clear and to the point. Enjoy "Sleeplessness" as a quaint part of
the American past.

Causes.—Often caused by nervousness and too much mental work,
especially at night.

TREATMENT:

"What to Do."—Get away from excitement. Go to the country and be
outdoors doing light work as much as possible. Tone up the system. Drink
hop tea or get a hop pillow to sleep on. Instead of hop tea you can take the
tincture of hops in 15-drop doses. Sleeping in the barn on the hay is often
conducive to sleep. Some people need big pillows and some need none.
Change of scene and work is generally beneficial. People who engage in
outdoor work, unless they work too hard, are generally good sleepers. Keep
the head cool and the feet warm.

"What Not to Do."—Do not take opiates. Do not eat much at night
and, on the other hand, do not go to bed with stomach entirely empty. Do
not do any mental work at night. Do not talk politics or religion and do not
get excited when you can avoid it. . . .

PEOPLE'S HOME REMEDIES:

1. *Onions*—Three or four small onions eaten just before going to bed
have a soothing narcotic effect and induce sleep.
2. *Cold Water Cloths*—Wet a towel in cold water and apply to the
back of the neck and lower part of the head and cover with a dry towel.
This is excellent where sleeplessness is the result of an overworked and
congested brain.
3. *Food and Mental Exercises*—Eat a few bites of light food. Recite
poetry or the multiplication table.
Physician's Remarks—The food draws the blood to the stomach and
thus relieves the congestion of the brain.

4. *Fresh Air and Sunshine*—Like all other afflictions the patient needs quiet, fresh air and clean, freshly aired bedding. Be out of doors in the sunshine as much as possible.

5. *Hot Water*—Drink hot water three times a day or at any time you are thirsty and bathe feet in hot water before going to bed.

Physician's Remarks—The hot water draws the blood to the stomach and the hot foot bath draws it to the feet, thus the blood is taken away from the brain and the congestion is relieved.

QUESTIONS

1. Suggest how the organization of the piece might be improved.

2. Did you find this selection amusing or humorous? Explain why.

3. The selection is very readable. Explain why it is so easy to read. (Think of such matters as vocabulary, sentence structure, and the layout and typography of the page.)

4. Speculate about why thousands of readers took *The People's Home Medical Book* very seriously, using it as a guide to health and even as a substitute for a family physician. You might want to know that the volume is bound in imitation leather and has handsome gold printing on the cover.

5. Are there modern equivalents of *The People's Home Medical Book?* What are they, and why are they successful?

A Change of Pace

From the gritty but useful world of how to, we turn briefly to some poems. In the first one, the English poet Henry Reed (1914–   ) gives an ironic account of rifle training in the army: as the world blossoms about him, he is learning the nomenclature of an instrument of death. In the second poem, the American poet John Ashbery (1927–   ) tells how he was distracted from the practical task of writing an instruction manual and let himself deviate into a rich fantasy.

These poems are intended to contrast with the prose selections in the how-to section, demonstrating that there are modes of perception other than "the facts and nothing but the facts."

As you will see, the devices that Reed and Ashbery use in their poems are very much like, and in some cases identical with, the methods that essayists employ to convey their points—metaphor and imagery, for example.

HENRY REED
Naming of Parts

Today we have naming of parts. Yesterday,
We had daily cleaning. And tomorrow morning,
We shall have what to do after firing. But today,
Today we have naming of parts. Japonica
Glistens like coral in all of the neighboring gardens,   5
    And today we have naming of parts.

This is the lower sling swivel. And this
Is the upper sling swivel, whose use you will see,
When you are given your slings. And this is the piling swivel,
Which in your case you have not got. The branches   10
Hold in the gardens in their silent, eloquent gestures,
    Which in our case we have not got.

This is the safety-catch, which is always released
With an easy flick of the thumb. And please do not let me

See anyone using his finger. You can do it quite easy   15
If you have any strength in your thumb. The blossoms
Are fragile and motionless, never letting anyone see
    Any of them using their finger.

And this you can see is the bolt. The purpose of this
Is to open the breech, as you see. We can slide it   20
Rapidly backwards and forwards: we call this
Easing the spring. And rapidly backwards and forwards
The early bees are assaulting and fumbling in the flowers:
    They call it easing the Spring.

They call it easing the Spring: it is perfectly easy   25
If you have any strength in your thumb: like the bolt,
And the breech, and the cocking-piece, and the point of balance,
Which in our case we have not got; and the almond-blossom
Silent in all of the gardens and the bees going backwards and forwards,
    For today we have naming of parts.   30

JOHN ASHBERY
The Instruction Manual

As I sit looking out of a window of the building
I wish I did not have to write the instruction manual on the uses of a new
    metal.
I look down into the street and see people, each walking with an inner
    peace,
And envy them—they are so far away from me!
Not one of them has to worry about getting out this manual on schedule.   5
And, as my way is, I begin to dream, resting my elbows on the desk and
    leaning out of the window a little,
Of dim Guadalajara! City of rose-colored flowers!
City I wanted most to see, and most did not see, in Mexico!
But I fancy I see, under the press of having to write the instruction manual,
Your public square, city, with its elaborate little bandstand!   10
The band is playing *Scheherazade* by Rimsky-Korsakov.
Around stand the flower girls, handing out rose-and lemon-colored
    flowers,
Each attractive in her rose-and-blue striped dress (Oh! such shades of rose
    and blue),
And nearby is the little white booth where women in green serve you green
    and yellow fruit.
The couples are parading; everyone is in a holiday mood.   15
First, leading the parade, is a dapper fellow
Clothed in deep blue. On his head sits a white hat
And he wears a mustache, which has been trimmed for the occasion.
His dear one, his wife, is young and pretty; her shawl is rose, pink, and
    white.
Her slippers are patent leather, in the American fashion,   20
And she caries a fan, for she is modest, and does not want the crowd to see
    her face too often.
But everybody is so busy with his wife or loved one
I doubt they would notice the mustachioed man's wife.
Here come the boys! They are skipping and throwing little things on the
    sidewalk
Which is made of gray tile. One of them, a little older, has a toothpick in
    his teeth.   25
He is silenter than the rest, and affects not to notice the pretty young girls
    in white.
But his friends notice them, and shout their jeers at the laughing girls.
Yet soon all this will cease, with the deepening of their years,

And love bring each to the parade grounds for another reason.
But I have lost sight of the young fellow with the toothpick.   30
Wait—there he is—on the other side of the bandstand,
Secluded from his friends, in earnest talk with a young girl
Of fourteen or fifteen. I try to hear what they are saying
But it seems they are just mumbling something—shy words of love,
    probably.
She is slightly taller than he, and looks quietly down into his sincere eyes.   35
She is wearing white. The breeze ruffles her long fine black hair against
    her olive cheek.
Obviously she is in love. The boy, the young boy with the toothpick, he is
    in love too;
His eyes show it. Turning from this couple,
I see there is an intermission in the concert.
The paraders are resting and sipping drinks through straws   40
(The drinks are dispensed from a large glass crock by a lady in dark blue),
And the musicians mingle among them, in their creamy white uniforms,
    and talk
About the weather, perhaps, or how their kids are doing at school.
Let us take this opportunity to tiptoe into one of the side streets.
Here you may see one of those white houses with green trim   45
That are so popular here. Look—I told you!
It is cool and dim inside, but the patio is sunny.
An old woman in gray sits there fanning herself with a palm leaf fan.
She welcomes us to her patio, and offers us a cooling drink.
"My son is in Mexico City," she says. "He would welcome you too   50
If he were here. But his job is with a bank there.
Look, here is a photograph of him."
And a dark-skinned lad with pearly teeth grins out at us from the worn
    leather frame.
We thank her for her hospitality, for it is getting late
And we must catch a view of the city, before we leave, from a good high
    place.   55
That church tower will do—the faded pink one, there against the fierce
    blue of the sky. Slowly we enter.
The caretaker, an old man dressed in brown and gray, asks us how long we
    have been in the city, and how we like it here.
His daughter is scrubbing the steps—she nods to us as we pass into the
    tower.
Soon we have reached the top, and the whole network of the city extends
    before us.
There is the rich quarter, with its houses of pink and white, and its
    crumbling, leafy terraces.   60

There is the poorer quarter, its homes a deep blue.
There is the market, where men are selling hats and swatting flies
And there is the public library, painted several shades of pale green and
     beige.
Look! There is the square we just came from, with the promenaders.
There are fewer of them, now that the heat of the day has increased,   65
But the young boy and girl still lurk in the shadows of the bandstand.
And there is the home of the little old lady—
She is still sitting in the patio, fanning herself.
How limited, but how complete withal, has been our experience of
     Guadalajara!
We have seen young love, married love, and the love of an aged mother for
     her son.   70
We have heard the music, tasted the drinks, and looked at colored houses.
What more is there to do, except stay? And that we cannot do.
And as a last breeze freshens the top of the weathered old tower, I turn
     my gaze
Back to the instruction manual which has made me dream of Guadalajara.

SUGGESTIONS FOR WRITING

1. As an in-class exercise, write a set of instructions for making a paper airplane. When you have finished, ask a fellow student to follow your instructions *exactly*, performing every operation that you specify and not performing any that you do not call for. (If your instructions result in a paper airplane that flies, you should treat yourself to a large ice cream sundae.)

   If your instructions are faulty—and an airworthy paper airplane is not the result—what was wrong with your instructions, and how could you fix them?

   Revise your how-to exercise, and ask someone else in the class to use your instructions as a guide to constructing a paper airplane.

2. In "The Acorn: Ancient Food of Man," Euell Gibbons explains how to prepare acorns for eating, but he also gives background information about acorns.

   Write an essay such as Gibbons'; explain how to do something and also include background information.

3. Does your family have any home remedies? If so, explain one or several of them.

4. Write "How to Survive the Freshman Year" for students who will be entering your college or university next year.

5. Much of what you do is so familiar that your methods have become automatic: driving a car, using a word processer, grooming, going from one familiar often-visited place to another. Now then, suppose an actor were going to portray you in a movie: he or she would want to capture the uniqueness of your activities, not their general nature—not the way most people drive an automobile, but the way you in particular do it; not a general scheme for going from one building on campus to another, but the way you navigate the course.

   Write a set of instructions for playing you as you do something. In order to succeed, you must defamiliarize the familiar; you must "stand back" and look at yourself as if the observed you were a stranger to you the observer.

6. You have decided to write a self-help piece for a Sunday newspaper magazine supplement. Your subject is "How to Relax." Write the article. (Or choose any other *how to* that you know about and that would interest readers of such publications as the Sunday magazine supplement.)

On Being Human

The following essays by Tom Wolfe and Mark Snyder are similar in one respect: they both focus on a human characteristic; Wolfe on what he calls "the right stuff" and Snyder on "self-fulfilling stereotypes." Each of the authors, however, uses a different perspective for understanding the human situation and for explaining it to readers.

In his essay, Wolfe is the creative artist, the humanist, attempting to create a rich, imaginative background for his ideas about the astronauts. Mark Snyder is writing as a social scientist, basing his conclusions and explanations on "laboratory" research.

The point is not, of course, that one method is better than the other. Each is appropriate for its given purpose and audience. Neither is more "true" than the other, but Snyder's rests more on "objective" evidence than does Wolfe's, which is an individual— and individualistic—view.

TOM WOLFE
The Right Stuff

Born in 1931, Tom Wolfe took his doctorate at Yale, but chose to pursue a career as a journalist and social critic rather than teach or do research. His intriguingly titled books are The Kandy-Kolored Tangerine Flake Streamline Baby *(1965),* The Pump House Gang *(1968),* The Electric Kool-Aid Acid Test *(1968),* Radical Chic & Mau-Mauing the Flak Catchers *(1970),* The Painted Word *(1975), and* Mauve Gloves & Madmen, Clutter & Vine *(1976).*

Wolfe is one of the leading writers in a group who interpret history from a personal viewpoint. Truman Capote was perhaps the first writer to give such a personal report of an event in history, and In Cold Blood *is a masterpiece of its kind. Norman Mailer also turned from "pure" fiction to history when he wrote* The Executioner's Song.

Wolfe completed The Right Stuff *before Sally Ride's historic mission, which proved that women as well as men have "the right stuff" to be astronauts.*

As you read this selection, notice how Wolfe uses concrete detail to define an abstract concept, "the right stuff."

What an extraordinary grim stretch that had been . . . and yet thereafter Pete and Jane would keep running into pilots from other Navy bases,
from the Air Force, from the Marines, who had been through their own
extraordinary grim stretches. There was an Air Force pilot named Mike
Collins, a nephew of former Army Chief of Staff J. Lawton Collins. Mike
Collins had undergone eleven weeks of combat training at Nellis Air Force
Base, near Las Vegas, and in that eleven weeks twenty-two of his fellow
trainees had died in accidents, which was an extraordinary rate of two per
week. Then there was a test pilot, Bill Bridgeman. In 1952, when Bridgeman was flying at Edwards Air Force Base, sixty-two Air Force pilots died
in the course of thirty-six weeks of training, an extraordinary rate of 1.7 per
week. Those figures were for fighter-pilot trainees only; they did not
include the test pilots, Bridgeman's own confreres, who were dying quite
regularly enough.

Extraordinary, to be sure; except that every veteran of flying small
high-performance jets seemed to have experienced these bad strings.

In time, the Navy would compile statistics showing that for a career
Navy pilot, i.e., one who intended to keep flying for twenty years as
Conrad did, there was a 23 percent probability that he would die in an
aircraft accident. This did not even include combat deaths, since the
military did not classify death in combat as accidental. Furthermore, there
was a better than even chance, a 56 percent probability, to be exact, that at
some point a career Navy pilot would have to eject from his aircraft and
attempt to come down by parachute. In the era of jet fighters, ejection
meant being exploded out of the cockpit by a nitroglycerine charge, like a
human cannonball. The ejection itself was so hazardous—men lost knees,
arms, and their lives on the rim of the cockpit or had the skin torn off their
faces when they hit the "wall" of air outside—that many pilots chose to
wrestle their aircraft to the ground rather than try it . . . and died that way
instead.

The statistics were not secret, but neither were they widely known,
having been eased into print rather obliquely in a medical journal. No
pilot, and certainly no pilot's wife, had any need of the statistics in order to
know the truth, however. The funerals took care of that in the most
dramatic way possible. Sometimes, when the young wife of a fighter pilot
would have a little reunion with the girls she went to school with, an odd
fact would dawn on her: *they* have not been going to funerals. And then
Jane Conrad would look at Pete . . . Princeton, Class of 1953 . . . Pete
had already worn his great dark sepulchral bridge coat more than most boys
of the Class of '53 had worn their tuxedos. How many of those happy
young men had buried more than a dozen friends, comrades, and co-
workers? (Lost through violent death in the execution of everyday duties.)
At the time, the 1950's, students from Princeton took great pride in going

into what they considered highly competitive, aggressive pursuits, jobs on Wall Street, on Madison Avenue, and at magazines such as *Time* and *Newsweek*. There was much fashionably brutish talk of what "dog-eat-dog" and "cutthroat" competition they found there; but in the rare instances when one of these young men died on the job, it was likely to be from choking on a chunk of Chateaubriand, while otherwise blissfully boiled, in an expense-account restaurant in Manhattan. How many would have gone to work, or stayed at work, on cutthroat Madison Avenue if there had been a 23 percent chance, nearly one chance in four, of dying from it? Gentlemen, we're having this little problem with chronic violent death. . . .

And yet was there any basic way in which Pete (or Wally Schirra or Jim Lovell or any of the rest of them) was different from other college boys his age? There didn't seem to be, other than his love of flying. Pete's father was a Philadelphia stockbroker who in Pete's earliest years had a house in the Main Line suburbs, a limousine, and a chauffeur. The Depression eliminated the terrific brokerage business, the house, the car, and the servants; and by and by his parents were divorced and his father moved to Florida. Perhaps because his father had been an observation balloonist in the First World War—an adventurous business, since the balloons were prized targets of enemy aircraft—Pete was fascinated by flying. He went to Princeton on the Holloway Plan, a scholarship program left over from the Second World War in which a student trained with midshipmen from the Naval Academy during the summers and graduated with a commission in the Regular Navy. So Pete graduated, received his commission, married Jane, and headed off to Pensacola, Florida for flight training.

Then came the difference, looking back on it.

A young man might go into military flight training believing that he was entering some sort of technical school in which he was simply going to acquire a certain set of skills. Instead, he found himself all at once enclosed in a fraternity. And in this fraternity, even though it was military, men were not rated by their outward rank as ensigns, lieutenants, commanders, or whatever. No, herein the world was divided into those who had it and those who did not. This quality, this *it*, was never named, however, nor was it talked about in any way.

As to just what this ineffable quality was . . . well, it obviously involved bravery. But it was not bravery in the simple sense of being willing to risk your life. The idea seemed to be that any fool could do that, if that was all that was required, just as any fool could throw away his life in the process. No, the idea here (in the all-enclosing fraternity) seemed to be that a man should have the ability to go up in a hurtling piece of machinery and put his hide on the line and then have the moxie, the reflexes, the experience, the coolness, to pull it back in the last yawning moment—and then to go up again *the next day*, and the next day, and every next day, even if the series should prove infinite—and, ultimately, in its best expression, do so in a cause that means something to thousands, to a people, a nation, to humanity, to God. Nor was there a *test* to show whether or not a pilot had this righteous quality. There was, instead, a seemingly infinite series of tests. A career in flying was like climbing one of those ancient Babylonian pyramids made up of a dizzy progression of steps and ledges, a ziggurat, a pyramid extraordinarily high and steep; and the idea was to prove at every foot of the way up that pyramid that you were one of the elected and annointed ones who had *the right stuff* and could move higher and higher and—ultimately, God willing, one day—that you might be able to join that special few at the very top, that elite who had the capacity to bring tears to men's eyes, the very Brotherhood of the Right Stuff itself.

None of this was to be mentioned, and yet it was acted out in a way that a young man could not fail to understand. When a new flight (i.e., a class) of trainees arrived at Pensacola, they were brought into an auditorium for a little lecture. An officer would tell them: "Take a look at the man on either side of you." Quite a few actually swiveled their heads this way and that, in the interest of appearing diligent. Then the officer would say: "One of the three of you is not going to make it!"—meaning, not get his wings. That was the opening theme, the *motif* of primary training. We already know that one-third of you do not have the right stuff—it only remains to find out who.

Furthermore, that was the way it turned out. At every level in one's progress up that staggeringly high pyramid, the world was once more divided into those men who had the right stuff to continue the climb and those who had to be *left behind* in the most obvious way. Some were eliminated in the course of the opening classroom work, as either not smart enough or not hardworking enough, and were left behind. Then came the basic flight instruction, in single-engine, propeller-driven trainers, and a few more—even though the military tried to make this stage easy—were washed out and left behind. Then came more demanding levels, one after the other, formation flying, instrument flying, jet training, all-weather flying, gunnery, and at each level more were washed out and left behind. By this point easily a third of the original candidates had been, indeed, eliminated . . . from the ranks of those who might prove to have the right stuff.

In the Navy, in addition to the stages that Air Force trainees went through, the neophyte always had waiting for him, out in the ocean, a certain grim gray slab; namely, the deck of an aircraft carrier; and with it perhaps the most difficult routine in military flying, carrier landings. He was shown films about it, he heard lectures about it, and he knew that carrier landings were hazardous. He first practiced touching down on the shape of a flight deck painted on an airfield. He was instructed to touch down and gun right off. This was safe enough—the shape didn't move, at least—but it could do terrible things to, let us say, the gyroscope of the soul. *That shape!—it's so damned small*! And more candidates were washed out and left behind. Then came the day, without warning, when those who remained were sent out over the ocean for the first of many days of reckoning with the slab. The first day was always a clear day with little wind and a calm sea. The carrier was so steady that it seemed, from up there in the air, to be resting on pilings, and the candidate usually made his first carrier landing successfully, with relief and even *élan*. Many young candidates looked like terrific aviators up to that very point—and it was not until they were actually standing on the carrier deck that they first began to wonder if they had the proper stuff, after all. In the training film the flight deck was a grand piece of gray geometry, perilous, to be sure, but an amazing abstract shape as one looks down upon it on the screen. And yet once the newcomer's two feet were on it . . . *Geometry*—my God, man, this is a . . . skillet! It *heaved*, it moved up and down underneath his feet, it pitched up, it pitched down, it rolled to port (this great beast *rolled*!) and it rolled to starboard, as the ship moved into the wind and, therefore, into the waves, and the wind kept sweeping across, sixty feet up in the air out in the open sea, and there were no railings whatsoever. This was a *skillet!*—a frying pan!—a short-order grill!—not gray but black, smeared with skid marks from one end to the other and glistening with pools of hydraulic fluid and the occasional jet-fuel slick, all of it still hot, sticky, greasy, runny, virulent from God knows what traumas—still ablaze!—consumed in detonations, explosions, flames, combustion, roars, shrieks, whines, blasts, horrible shudders, fracturing impacts, as little men in screaming red and yellow and purple and green shirts with black Mickey Mouse helmets over their ears skittered about on the surface as if for their very lives (you've said it now!), hooking fighter planes onto the catapult shuttles so that they can explode their afterburners and be slung off the deck in a red-mad fury with a *kaboom*! that pounds through the entire deck—a procedure that seems absolutely controlled, orderly, sublime, however, compared to what he is about to watch as aircraft return to the ship for what is known in the engineering stoicisms of the military as "recovery and arrest." To say that an F-4 was coming back onto this heaving barbecue from out of the sky at a speed of 135 knots . . . that might have been the truth in the training lecture, but it did not begin to get across the idea of what the newcomer saw from the deck itself, because it created the notion that perhaps the plane was gliding in. On the deck one knew differently! As the aircraft came closer and the carrier heaved on into the waves and the plane's speed did not diminish and the deck did not grew steady—indeed, it pitched up and down five or ten feet per greasy heave—one experienced a neural alarm that no lecture could have prepared him for: This is not an *airplane* coming toward me, it is a brick with some poor sonofabitch riding it (*someone much like myself!*), and it is not *gliding*, it is *falling*, a fifty-thousand-pound brick, headed not for a stripe on the deck but for *me*—and with a horrible *smash!* it hits the skillet, and with a blur of momentum as big as a freight train's it hurtles toward the far end of the deck—another blinding storm!—another roar as the pilot pushes the throttle up to full military power and another smear of rubber screams out over the skillet—and this is nominal!—quite okay!—for a wire stretched across the deck has grabbed the hook on the end of the plane as it hit the deck tail down, and the smash was the rest of the fifteen-ton brute slamming onto the deck, as it tripped up, so that it is now straining against the wire at full throttle, in case it hadn't held and the plane had "boltered" off the end of the deck and had to struggle up into the air again. And already the Mickey Mouse helmets are running toward the fiery monster. . . .

And the candidate, looking on, begins to *feel* that great heaving sun-blazing deathboard of a deck wallowing in his own vestibular system—and suddenly he finds himself backed up against his own limits. He ends up going to the flight surgeon with so-called conversion symptoms. Overnight he develops blurred vision or numbness in his hands and feet or sinusitis so severe that he cannot tolerate changes in altitude. On one level the symptom is real. He really cannot see too well or use his fingers or stand the pain. But somewhere in his subconscious he knows it is a plea and a beg-off; he shows not the slightest concern (the flight surgeon notes) that the condition might be permanent and affect him in whatever life awaits him outside the arena of the right stuff.

Those who remained, those who qualified for carrier duty—and even more so those who later on qualified for *night* carrier duty—began to feel a bit like Gideon's warriors. *So many have been left behind!* The young warriors were now treated to a deathly sweet and quite unmentionable sight. They could gaze at length upon the crushed and wilted pariahs who had washed out. They could inspect those who did not have that righteous stuff.

The military did not have very merciful instincts. Rather than packing up these poor souls and sending them home, the Navy, like the Air Force and the Marines, would try to make use of them in some other role, such as flight controller. So the washout has to keep taking classes with the rest of his group, even though he can no longer touch an airplane. He sits there in the classes staring at sheets of paper with cataracts of sheer human mortification over his eyes while the rest steal looks at him . . . this man reduced to an ant, this untouchable, this poor sonofabitch. And in what test had he been found wanting? Why, it seemed to be nothing less than *manhood* itself. Naturally, this was never mentioned, either. Yet there it was. *Manliness, manhood, manly courage* . . . there was something ancient, primordial, irresistible about the challenge of this stuff, no matter what a sophisticated and rational age one might think he lived in.

Perhaps because it could not be talked about, the subject began to take on superstitious and even mystical outlines. A man either had it or he didn't! There was no such thing as having *most* of it. Moreover, it could blow at any seam. One day a man would be ascending the pyramid at a terrific clip, and the next—bingo!—he would reach his own limits in the most unexpected way. Conrad and Schirra met an Air Force pilot who had had a great pal at Tyndall Air Force Base in Flordia. This man had been the budding ace of the training class; he had flown the hottest fighter-style trainer, the T-38, like a dream; and then he began the routine step of being checked out in the T-33. The T-33 was not nearly as hot an aircraft as the T-38; it was essentially the old P-80 jet fighter. It had an exceedingly small cockpit. The pilot could barely move his shoulders. It was the sort of airplane of which everybody said, "You don't get into it, you *wear* it." Once inside a T-33 cockpit this man, this budding ace, developed claustrophobia of the most paralyzing sort. He tried everything to overcome it. He even went to a psychiatrist, which was a serious mistake for a military officer if his superiors learned of it. But nothing worked. He was shifted over to flying jet transports, such as the C-135. Very demanding and necessary aircraft they were, too, and he was still spoken of as an excellent pilot. But as everyone knew—and, again, it was never explained in so many words—only those who were assigned to fighter squadrons, the "fighter jocks," as they called each other with a self-satisfied irony, remained in the true fraternity. Those assigned to transports were not humiliated like washouts—*somebody* had to fly those planes—nevertheless, they, too, had been *left behind* for lack of the right stuff.

Or a man could go for a routine physical one fine day, feeling like a million dollars, and be grounded for *fallen arches*. It happened!—just like that! (And try raising them.) Or for breaking his wrist and losing only *part* of its mobility. Or for a minor deterioration of eyesight, or for any of hundreds of reasons that would make no difference to a man in an ordinary occupation. As a result all fighter jocks began looking upon doctors as their natural enemies. Going to see a flight surgeon was a no-gain proposition; a pilot could only hold his own or lose in the doctor's office. To be grounded for a medical reason was no humiliation, looked at objectively. But it was a humiliation, nonetheless!—for it meant you no longer had that indefinable, unutterable, integral stuff. (It could blow at *any* seam.)

All the hot young fighter jocks began trying to test the limits themselves in a superstitious way. They were like believing Presbyterians of a century before who used to probe their own experience to see if they were truly among *the elect*. When a fighter pilot was in training, whether in the Navy or the Air Force, his superiors were continually spelling out strict rules for him, about the use of the aircraft and conduct in the sky. They repeatedly forbade so-called hotdog stunts, such as outside loops, buzzing, flat-hatting, hedgehopping and flying under bridges. But somehow one got the message that the man who truly *had* it could ignore those rules—not that he should make a point of it, but that he *could*—and that after all there was only one way to find out—and that in some strange unofficial way, peeking through his fingers, his instructor halfway expected him to challenge all the limits. They would give a lecture about how a pilot should never fly without a good solid breakfast—eggs, bacon, toast, and so forth—because if he tried to fly with his blood-sugar level too low, it could impair his alertness. Naturally, the next day every hot dog in the unit would get up and have a breakfast consisting of one cup of black coffee and take off and go up into a vertical climb until the weight of the ship exactly canceled out the upward pull of the engine and his air speed was zero, and he would hang there for one thick adrenal instant—and then fall like a rock, until one of three things happened: he keeled over nose first and regained his aerodynamics and all was well, he went into a spin and fought his way out of it, or he went into a spin and had to eject or crunch it, which was always supremely possible.

Likewise, "hassling"—mock dogfighting—was strictly forbidden, and so naturally young fighter jocks could hardly wait to go up in, say, a pair of F-100s and start the duel by making a pass at each other at 800 miles an hour, the winner being the pilot who could slip in behind the other one and get locked in on his tail ("wax his tail"), and it was not uncommon for some eager jock to try too tight an outside turn and have his engine flame out, whereupon, unable to restart it, he has to eject . . . and he shakes his fist at the victor as he floats down by parachute and his half-a-million dollar aircraft goes *kaboom!* on the palmetto grass or the desert floor, and he starts thinking about how he can get together with the other guy back at the base in time for the two of them to get their stories straight before the investigation: "I don't know what happened, sir. I was pulling up after a target run, and it just flamed out on me." Hassling was forbidden, and hassling that led to the destruction of an aircraft was a serious court-martial offense, and the man's superiors knew that the engine hadn't *just flamed out*, but every unofficial impulse on the base seemed to be saying: "Hell, we wouldn't give you a nickel for a pilot who hasn't done some crazy rat-racing like that. It's all part of the right stuff."

The other side of this impulse showed up in the reluctance of the young jocks to admit it when they had maneuvered themselves into a bad corner they couldn't get out of. There were two reasons why a fighter pilot hated to declare an emergency. First, it triggered a complex and very public chain of events at the field: all other incoming flights were held up, including many of one's comrades who were probably low on fuel; the fire trucks came trundling out to the runway like yellow toys (as seen from way up there), the better to illustrate one's hapless state; and the bureaucracy began to crank up the paper monster for the investigation that always followed. And second, to declare an emergency, one first had to reach that conclusion in his own mind, which to the young pilot was the same as saying: "A minute ago I still *had* it—now I need your help!" To have a bunch of young fighter pilots up in the air thinking this way used to drive flight controllers crazy. They would see a ship beginning to drift off the radar, and they couldn't rouse the pilot on the microphone for anything other than a few meaningless mumbles, and they would know he was probably out there with engine failure at a low altitude, trying to reignite by lowering his auxiliary generator rig, which had a little propeller that was supposed to spin in the slipstream like a child's pinwheel.

"Whiskey Kilo Two Eight, do you want to declare an emergency?"

This would rouse him!—to say: "Negative, negative, Whiskey Kilo Two Eight is not declaring an emergency."

Kaboom. Believers in the right stuff would rather crash and burn.

QUESTIONS

1. Give an extended definition of "the right stuff."

2. What methods does Wolfe use to demonstrate the perils of being a fighter pilot?

3. In the section that describes carrier landings (pp. 160–62), what techniques does Wolfe use to give readers a sense of what it must be like to bring an aircraft down on a carrier?

4. What devices of *style* in the essay most attract your attention? (Think of word-choice, sentence structure, and figurative language. For example, consider the ziggurat metaphor on page 160? Or take a look at the stylistic shift beginning on page 161 with, "*Geometry*—my God, man, this is a . . . skillet!") What are the effects of these devices?

5. How do the pilots avoid saying directly that they have "the right stuff"?

6. Which section of the essay was most interesting to you? Why?

7. The book from which this selection was taken is a nonfiction novel: an actual event that the writer presents *as if* it were fiction, using all of the novelist's devices of characterization, structure, and so on. Other books in this genre are *In Cold Blood*, by Truman Capote, and *The Executioner's Song*, by Norman Mailer. The interesting question is this: Where does history end and fiction begin? Discuss it.

MARK SNYDER

Self-Fulfilling Stereotypes

Mark Snyder, a professor of psychology at the University of Minnesota, originally published this article in Psychology Today. *In their guidelines for writers, the editors say that the "primary purpose is to provide the nonspecialist with accurate and readable information about society and behavior." This selection is a good example of how a specialist can write for nonspecialists, avoiding jargon and highly technical details.*

Whereas Tom Wolfe used the imaginative techniques of a novelist to explain "the right stuff," Mark Snyder is straightforward and businesslike.

Gordon Allport, the Harvard psychologist who wrote a classic work on the nature of prejudice, told a story about a child who had come to believe that people who lived in Minneapolis were called monopolists. From his father, moreover, he had learned that monopolists were evil folk. It wasn't until many years later, when he discovered his confusion, that his dislike of residents of Minneapolis vanished.

Allport knew, of course, that it was not so easy to wipe out prejudice and erroneous stereotypes. Real prejudice, psychologists like Allport argued, was buried deep in human character, and only a restructuring of education could begin to root it out. Yet many people whom I meet while lecturing seem to believe that stereotypes are simply beliefs or attitudes that change easily with experience. Why do some people express the view that Italians are passionate, blacks are lazy, Jews materialistic, or lesbians mannish in their demeanor? In the popular view, it is because they have not learned enough about the diversity among these groups and have not had enough contact with members of the groups for their stereotypes to be challenged by reality. With more experience, it is presumed, most people of good will are likely to revise their stereotypes.

My research over the past decade convinces me that there is little justification for such optimism—and not only for the reasons given by Allport. While it is true that deep prejudice is often based on the needs of pathological character structure, stereotypes are obviously quite common even among fairly normal individuals. When people first meet others, they cannot help noticing certain highly visible and distinctive characteristics: sex, race, physical appearance, and the like. Despite people's best intentions, their intitial impressions of others are shaped by their assumptions about such characteristics.

What is critical, however, is that these assumptions are not merely beliefs or attitudes that exist in a vacuum; they are reinforced by the behavior of both prejudiced people and the targets of their prejudice. In recent years, psychologists have collected considerable laboratory evidence about the processes that strengthen stereotypes and put them beyond the reach of reason and good will.

My own studies initially focused on first encounters between strangers. It did not take long to discover, for example, that people have very different ways of treating those whom they regard as physically attractive and those whom they consider physically unattractive, and that these differences tend to bring out precisely those kinds of behavior that fit with stereotypes about attractiveness.

In an experiment that I conducted with my colleagues Elizabeth Decker Tanke and Ellen Berscheid, pairs of college-age men and women met and became acquainted in telephone conversations. Before the conversations began, each man received a Polaroid snapshot, presumably taken just moments before, of the woman he would soon meet. The photograph, which had actually been prepared before the experiment began, showed either a physically attractive woman or a physically unattractive one. By randomly choosing which picture to use for each conversation, we insured that there was no consistent relationship between the attractiveness of the woman in the picture and the attractiveness of the woman in the conversation.

By questioning the men, we learned that even before the conversations began, stereotypes about physical attractiveness came into play. Men who looked forward to talking with physically attractive women said that they expected to meet decidedly sociable, poised, humorous, and socially adept people, while men who thought that they were about to get acquainted with unattractive women fashioned images of rather unsociable, awkward, serious, and socially inept creatures. Moreover, the men proved to have very different styles of getting acquainted with women whom they thought to be attractive and those whom they believed to be unattractive. Shown a photograph of an attractive woman, they behaved with warmth, friendliness, humor, and animation. However, when the woman in the picture was unattractive, the men were cold, uninteresting, and reserved.

These differences in the men's behavior elicited behavior in the women that was consistent with the men's stereotyped assumptions. Women who were believed (unbeknown to them) to be physically attractive behaved in a friendly, likeable, and sociable manner. In sharp contrast, women who were perceived as physically unattractive adopted a cool, aloof, and distant manner. So striking were the differences in the women's behavior that they could be discerned simply by listening to tape recordings of the women's side of the conversations. Clearly, by acting upon their stereotyped beliefs about the women whom they would be meeting, the men had initiated a chain of events that produced *behavioral confirmation* for their beliefs.

Similarly, Susan Andersen and Sandra Bem have shown in an experiment at Stanford University that when the tables are turned—when it is women who have pictures of men they are to meet on the telephone—many women treat the men according to their presumed physical attractiveness, and by so doing encourage the men to confirm their stereotypes. Little wonder, then, that so many people remain convinced that good looks and appealing personalities go hand in hand.

SEX AND RACE

It is experiments such as these that point to a frequently unnoticed power of stereotypes: the power to influence social relationships in ways that create the illusion of reality. In one study, Berna Skrypnek and I arranged for pairs of previously unacquainted students to interact in a situation that permited us to control the information that each one received about the apparent sex of the other. The two people were seated in separate rooms so that they could neither see nor hear each other. Using a system of signal lights that they operated with switches, they negotiated a division of labor, deciding which member of the pair would perform each of several tasks that differed in sex-role connotations. The tasks varied along the dimensions of masculinity and femininity: sharpen a hunting knife (masculine), polish a pair of shoes (neutral), iron a shirt (feminine).

One member of the team was led to believe that the other was, in one condition of the experiment, male; in the other, female. As we had predicted, the first member's belief about the sex of the partner influenced the outcome of the pair's negotiations. Women whose partners believed them to be men generally chose stereotypically masculine tasks; in contrast, women whose partners believed that they were women usually chose stereotypically feminine tasks. The experiment thus suggests that much sex-role behavior may be the product of other people's stereotyped and often erroneous beliefs.

In a related study at the University of Waterloo, Carl von Baeyer, Debbie Sherk, and Mark Zanna have shown how stereotypes about sex roles operate in job interviews. The researchers arranged to have men conduct simulated job interviews with women supposedly seeking positions as research assistants. The investigators informed half of the women that the men who would interview them held traditional views about the ideal woman, believing her to be very emotional, deferential to her husband, home-oriented, and passive. The rest of the women were told that their interviewer saw the ideal woman as independent, competitive, ambitious, and dominant. When the women arrived for their interviews, the researchers noticed that most of them had dressed to meet the stereotyped expectations of their prospective interviewers. Women who expected to see a traditional interviewer had chosen very feminine-looking makeup, clothes, and accessories. During the interviews (videotaped through a one-way mirror) these women behaved in traditionally feminine ways and gave traditionally feminine answers to questions such as "Do you have plans to include children and marriage with your career plans?"

Once more, then, we see the self-fulfilling nature of stereotypes. Many sex differences, it appears, may result from the images that people create in their attempts to act out accepted sex roles. The implication is that if stereotyped expectations about sex roles shift, behavior may change, too. In fact, statements by people who have undergone sex-change operations have highlighted the power of such expectations in easing adjustment to a new life. As the writer Jan Morris said in recounting the story of her transition from James to Jan: "The more I was treated as a woman, the more woman I became."

The power of stereotypes to cause people to confirm stereotyped expectations can also be seen in interracial relationships. In the first of two investigations done at Princeton University by Carl Word, Mark Zanna, and Joel Cooper, white undergraduates interviewed both white and black job applicants. The applicants were actually confederates of the experimenters, trained to behave consistently from interview to interview, no matter how the interviewers acted toward them.

To find out whether or not the white interviewers would behave differently toward white and black job applicants, the researchers secretly videotaped each interview and then studied the tapes. From these, it was apparent that there were substantial differences in the treatment accorded blacks and whites. For one thing, the interviewers' speech deteriorated when they talked to blacks, displaying more errors in grammar and pronunciation. For another, the interviewers spent less time with blacks than with whites and showed less "immediacy," as the researchers called it, in their manner. That is, they were less friendly, less outgoing, and more reserved with blacks.

In the second investigation, white confederates were trained to approximate either the immediate or the nonimmediate interview styles that had been observed in the first investigation as they interviewed white job applicants. A panel of judges who evaluated the tapes agreed that applicants subjected to the nonimmediate styles performed less adequately and were more nervous than job applicants treated in the immediate style. Apparently, then, the blacks in the first study did not have a chance to display their qualifications to the best advantage. Considered together, the two investigations suggest that in interracial encounters, racial stereotypes may constrain behavior in ways that cause both blacks and whites to behave in accordance with those stereotypes.

REWRITING BIOGRAPHY

Having adopted stereotyped ways of thinking about another person, people tend to notice and remember the ways in which that person seems to fit the stereotype, while resisting evidence that contradicts the stereotype. In one investigation that I conducted with Seymour Uranowitz, student subjects read a biography of a fictitious woman named Betty K. We constructed the story of her life so that it would fit the stereotyped images of both lesbians and heterosexuals. Betty, we wrote, never had a steady boyfriend in high school, but did go out on dates. And although we gave her a steady boyfriend in college, we specified that he was more of a close friend than anything else. A week after we had distributed this biography, we gave our subjects some new information about Betty. We told some students that she was now living with another woman in a lesbian relationship; we told others that she was living with her husband.

To see what impact stereotypes about sexuality would have on how people remembered the facts of Betty's life, we asked each student to answer a series of questions about her life history. When we examined their answers, we found that the students had reconstructed the events of Betty's past in ways that supported their own stereotyped beliefs about her sexual orientation. Those who believed that Betty was a lesbian remembered that Betty had never had a steady boyfriend in high school, but tended to neglect the fact that she had gone out on many dates in college. Those who believed that Betty was now a heterosexual tended to remember that she had formed a steady relationship with a man in college, but tended to ignore the fact that the relationship was more of a friendship than a romance.

The students showed not only selective memories but also a striking facility for interpreting what they remembered in ways that added fresh support for their stereotypes. One student who accurately remembered that a supposedly lesbian Betty never had a steady boyfriend in high school confidently pointed to that fact as an early sign of her lack of romance or sexual interest in men. A student who correctly remembered that a purportedly lesbian Betty often went out on dates in college was sure that these dates were signs of Betty's early attempts to mask her lesbian interests.

Clearly, the students had allowed their preconceptions about lesbians and heterosexuals to dictate the way in which they interpreted and reinterpreted the facts of Betty's life. As long as stereotypes make it easy to bring to mind evidence that undermines them, people will cling to erroneous beliefs.

STEREOTYPES IN THE
CLASSROOM AND WORK PLACE

The power of one person's beliefs to make other people conform to them has been well demonstrated in real life. Back in the 1960s, as most people well remember, Harvard psychologist Robert Rosenthal and his colleague Lenore Jacobson entered elementary-school classrooms and identified one out of every five pupils in each room as a child who could be expected to show dramatic improvement in intellectual achievement during the school year. What the teachers did not know was that the children had been chosen on a random basis. Nevertheless, something happened in the relationships between teachers and their supposedly gifted pupils that led the children to make clear gains in test performance.

It can also do so on the job. Albert King, now a professor of management at Northern Illinois University, told a welding instructor in a vocational training center that five men in his training program had unusually high aptitude. Although these five had been chosen at random and knew nothing of their designation as high-aptitude workers, they showed substantial changes in performance. They were absent less often than were other workers, learned the basics of the welder's trade in about half the usual time, and scored a full 10 points higher than other trainees on a welding test. Their gains were noticed not only by the researcher and by the welding instructor, but also by other trainees, who singled out the five as their preferred co-workers.

Might not other expectations influence the relationships between supervisors and workers? For example, supervisors who believe that men are better suited to some jobs and women to others may treat their workers (wittingly or unwittingly) in ways that encourage them to perform their jobs in accordance with stereotypes about differences between men and women. These same stereotypes may determine who gets which job in the first place. Perhaps some personnel managers allow stereotypes to influence, subtly or not so subtly, the way in which they interview job candidates, making it likely that candidates who fit the stereotypes show up better than job-seekers who do not fit them.

Unfortunately, problems of this kind are compounded by the fact that members of stigmatized groups often subscribe to stereotypes about themselves. That is what Amerigo Farina and his colleagues at the University of Connecticut found when they measured the impact upon mental patients of believing that others knew their psychiatric history. In Farina's study, each mental patient cooperated with another person in a game requiring teamwork. Half of the patients believed that their partners knew they were patients; the other half believed that their partners thought they were nonpatients. In reality, the nonpatients never knew a thing about anyone's psychiatric history. Nevertheless, simply believing that others were aware of their history led the patients to feel less appreciated, to find the task more difficult, and to perform poorly. In addition, objective observers saw them as more tense, more anxious, and more poorly adjusted than patients who believed that their status was not known. Seemingly, the belief that others perceived them as stigmatized caused them to play the role of stigmatized patients.

CONSEQUENCES FOR SOCIETY

Apparently, good will and education are not sufficient to subvert the power of stereotypes. If people treat others in such a way as to bring out behavior that supports stereotypes, they may never have an opportunity to discover which of their stereotypes are wrong.

I suspect that even if people were to develop doubts about the accuracy of their stereotypes, chances are they would proceed to test them by gathering precisely the evidence that would appear to confirm them.

The experiments I have described help to explain the persistence of stereotypes. But, as is so often the case, solving one puzzle only creates another. If by acting as if false stereotypes were true, people lead others, too, to act as if they were true, why do the stereotypes not come to *be* true? Why, for example, have researchers found so little evidence that attractive people are generally friendly, sociable, and outgoing and that the unattractive people are generally shy and aloof ?

I think that the explanation goes something like this: Very few among us have the kind of looks that virtually everyone considers either very attractive or very unattractive. Our looks make us rather attractive to some people but somewhat less attractive to other people. When we spend time with those who find us attractive, they will tend to bring out our more sociable sides, but when we are with those who find us less attractive, they will bring out our less sociable sides. Although our actual physical appearance does not change, we present ourselves quite differently to our admirers and to our detractors. For our admirers we become attractive people, and for our detractors we become unattractive. This mixed pattern of behavior will prevent the development of any consistent relationship between physical attractiveness and personality.

Now that I understand some of the powerful forces that work to perpetuate social stereotypes, I can see a new mission for my research. I hope, on the one hand, to find out how to help people see the flaws in their stereotypes. On the other hand, I would like to help the victims of false stereotypes find ways of liberating themselves from the constraints imposed on them by other members of society.

QUESTIONS

1. Briefly summarize Snyder's evidence for his thesis that stereotypes are self-fulfilling prophecies.

2. Explain how the following relates to Snyder's point:

> In highly stratified situations, where society is divided into two major groups, the values associated with the dominant group are assigned to the dominant language by all. Lambert and his colleagues at McGill University have shown how regular are such unconscious evaluations in the French-English situation of Quebec, in the Arabic-Hebrew confrontation in Israel, and in other areas as well. When English Canadians heard the same person speaking Canadian French, on the one hand, and English, on the other, they unhesitatingly judged him to be more intelligent, more dependable, kinder, more ambitious, better looking and taller—when he spoke English. Common sense would tell us that French-Canadians would react in the opposite manner, but in fact they do not. Their judgments reflect almost the same set of unconscious values as the English-Canadians show. This overwhelming negative evaluation of Canadian French is a property of the society as a whole. It is an omnipresent stigma which has a strong effect on what happens in school as well as in other social contexts.[1]

3. Are any of Snyder's terms unfamiliar to you? Why do you suppose Snyder or the editors of *Psychology Today* chose *not* to define these terms?

4. What purpose does the beginning of the essay—the story of a child's misunderstanding—serve? Propose some other ways in which Snyder could have begun his article and discuss the strengths and weaknesses of each.

5. Discuss a time when you tried to "keep an open mind" about some person or group. Were you successful, or did your stereotypes prove to be self-fulfilling? Alternatively, discuss a time when you felt unfairly treated as a result of someone's stereotype of you.

6. Explain how Snyder's subheadings help you read and understand the article.

7. Compare Snyder's style with Wolfe's. Think of word choice, sentence structure, and figurative language.

8. Does the personality of the author come through more strongly in *The Right Stuff* or in "Self-Fulfilling Stereotypes"? Explain.

---

[1]William Labov, *The Study of Nonstandard English* (Urbana: National Council of Teachers of English, 1970), p. 31.

A Change of Pace

The first poem in the following group laments the passing of youth into old age. The poet, Samuel Taylor Coleridge (1772–1834), one of the great nineteenth-century Romantics (the others being William Wordsworth, Percy Bysshe Shelley, George Gordon Lord Byron, and John Keats), is best known for *The Rime of the Ancient Mariner*.

"A Prayer for My Daughter" is by a poet generally regarded as one of the greats in our tradition, William Butler Yeats (1865–1939). The work is a verse essay, speaking of an ideal of human decency.

"Mr. Flood's Party" by Edwin Arlington Robinson (1869–1935) is a portrait of a lonely old man who copes.

Another way of looking at the poems: equate them with *The Right Stuff* and "Self-Fulfilling Stereotypes" as commentaries on what it means to be human. In other words, what *do* the five works have to say about the human situation?

SAMUEL TAYLOR COLERIDGE

Youth and Age

Verse, a breeze mid blossoms straying,
Where Hope clung feeding, like a bee—
Both were mine! Life went a-maying
      With Nature, Hope, and Poesy,
        When I was young!   5

When I was young?—Ah, woful When!
Ah! for the change 'twixt Now and Then!
This breathing house not built with hands,
This body that does me grievous wrong,
O'er aery cliffs and glittering sands,   10
How lightly then it flashed along:—
Like those trim skiffs,[1] unknown of yore,
On winding lakes and rivers wide,

---

[1] *those trim skiffs*: steamboats

That ask no aid of sail or oar,
That fear no spite of wind or tide!   15
Nought cared this body for wind or weather
When Youth and I lived in't together.

Flowers are lovely; Love is flower-like;
Friendship is a sheltering tree;
O! the joys, that came down shower-like,   20
Of Friendship, Love, and Liberty,
                                        Ere I was old!

Ere I was old? Ah woful Ere,
Which tells me, Youth's no longer here!
O Youth! for years so many and sweet,   25
'Tis known, that Thou and I were one,
I'll think it but a fond conceit—
It cannot be that Thou are gone!
Thy vesper-bell[2] hath not yet toll'd:—
And thou wert aye a masker[3] bold!   30
What strange disguise hast now put on,
To make believe, that thou are gone?
I see these locks in silvery slips,
This drooping gait, this altered size:
But Spring-tide blossoms on thy lips,   35
And tears take sunshine from thine eyes!
Life is but thought; so think I will
That Youth and I are house-mates still.

Dew-drops are the gems of morning,
But the tears of mournful eve!   40
Where no hope is, life's a warning
That only serves to make us grieve,
                                        When we are old:

That only serves to make us grieve
With oft and tedious taking-leave,   45
Like some poor nigh-related guest,
That may not rudely be dismist;
Yet hath outstay'd his welcome while,
And tells the jest without the smile.

---

[2] *vesper-bell*: the call to evening worship
[3] *masker*: participant in a masquerade or masked ball

W. B. YEATS
A Prayer for My Daughter

Once more the storm is howling, and half hid
Under this cradle-hood and coverlid
My child[1] sleeps on. There is no obstacle
But Gregory's wood[2] and one bare hill
Whereby the haystack- and roof-levelling wind,   5
Bred on the Atlantic, can be stayed;
And for an hour I have walked and prayed
Because of the great gloom that is in my mind.

I have walked and prayed for this young child an hour
And heard the sea-wind scream upon the tower,   10
And under the arches of the bridge, and scream
In the elms above the flooded stream;
Imagining in excited reverie
That the future years had come,
Dancing to a frenzied drum.   15
Out of the murderous innocence of the sea.

May she be granted beauty and yet not
Beauty to make a stranger's eye distraught,
Or hers before a looking-glass, for such,
Being made beautiful overmuch,   20
Consider beauty a sufficient end,
Lose natural kindness and maybe
The heart-revealing intimacy
That chooses right, and never find a friend.

Helen being chosen[3] found life flat and dull   25
And later had much trouble from a fool,[4]
While that great Queen,[5] that rose out of the spray,
Being fatherless could have her way

---

[1]Anne Butler Yeats, born on February 26, 1919.
[2]Yeats often visited the estate of Lady Augusta Gregory at Coole, which was not far from Thoor Ballylee,
the tower in which the poet lived when his daughter was born.
[3]*Helen being chosen*: having been chosen as a wife.
[4]The fool is Helen's husband, Menelaus, whom she deserted for Paris, an act that resulted in the Trojan
War.
[5]Venus, who rose from the sea.

Yet chose a bandy-leggèd smith for man.[6]
It's certain that fine women eat   30
A crazy salad with their meat
Whereby the Horn of Plenty is undone.

In courtesy I'd have her chiefly learned;
Hearts are not had as a gift but hearts are earned
By those that are not entirely beautiful;   35
Yet many, that have played the fool
For beauty's very self, has charm made wise,
And many a poor man that has roved,
Loved and thought himself beloved,
From a glad kindness cannot take his eyes.   40

May she become a flourshing hidden tree
That all her thoughts may like the linnet[7] be,
And have no business but dispensing round
Their magnanimities of sound,
Nor but in merriment begin a chase,   45
Nor but in merriment a quarrel.
O may she live like some green laurel[8]
Rooted in one dear perpetual place.

My mind, because the minds that I have loved,
The sort of beauty that I have approved,
Prosper but little, has dried up of late,   50
Yet knows that to be choked with hate
May well be of all evil chances chief.
If there's no hatred in a mind
Assault and battery of the wind
Can never tear the linnet from the leaf.   55

An intellectual hatred is the worst,
So let her think opinions are accursed.
Have I not seen the loveliest woman[9] born
Out of the mouth of Plenty's horn,

                                                                        60

---

[6]Vulcan was the blacksmith of the gods.
[7]A songbird
[8]The laurel is a tree, the leaves of which were used to make crowns of victory and honor. The leaves, called bay, are also used in cooking. Thus, the tree symbolizes both honor and domesticity.
[9]Maude Gonne, the great love of Yeats' life. Her increasing militancy in the cause of Irish independence alienated her from Yeats.

Because of her opinionated mind
Barter that horn and every good
By quiet natures understood
For an old bellows full of angry wind?

Considering that, all hatred driven hence,   65
The soul recovers radical innocence
And learns at last that it is self-delighting,
Self-appeasing, self-affrighting,
And that its own sweet will is Heaven's will;
She can, though every face should scowl   70
And every windy quarter howl
Or every bellows burst, be happy still.

And may her bridegroom bring her to a house
Where all's accustomed, ceremonious;
For arrogance and hatred are the wares   75
Peddled in the thoroughfares.
How but in custom and in ceremony
Are innocence and beauty born?
Ceremony's a name for the rich horn,   80
And custom for the spreading laurel tree.

EDWIN ARLINGTON ROBINSON
Mr. Flood's Party

Old Eben Flood, climbing alone one night
Over the hill between the town below
And the forsaken upland hermitage
That held as much as he should ever know
On earth again of home, paused warily.   5
The road was his with not a native near;
And Eben, having leisure, said aloud,
For no man else in Tilbury Town to hear:

"Well Mr. Flood, we have the harvest moon
Again, and we may not have many more;   10
The bird is on the wing, the poet says,
And you and I have said it here before.
Drink to the bird." He raised up to the light
The jug that he had gone so far to fill,
And answered huskily: "Well, Mr. Flood,   15
Since you propose it, I believe I will."

Alone, as if enduring to the end
A valiant armor of scarred hopes outworn,
He stood there in the middle of the road
Like Roland's ghost winding a silent horn.[1]   20
Below him, in the town among the trees,
Where friends of other days had honored him,
A phantom salutation of the dead
Rang thinly til old Eben's eyes were dim.

Then, as a mother lays her sleeping child   25
Down tenderly, fearing it may awake,
He set the jug down slowly at his feet
With trembling care, knowing that most things break;
And only when assured that on firm earth
It stood, as the uncertain lives of men   30
Assuredly did not, he paced away,
And with his hand extended paused again:

---

[1]In *Chanson de Roland* (*Song of Roland*), a medieval French poem, the hero, Roland, refused to blow his horn to call for aid from Charlemagne until the very moment of his death. As a result, Roland and his men were all slain.

"Well, Mr. Flood, we have not met like this
In a long time; and many a change has come
To both of us, I fear, since last it was   35
We had a drop together. Welcome home!"
Convivially returning with himself,
Again he raised the jug up to the light;
And with an acquiescent quaver said:
"Well, Mr. Flood, if you insist, I might.   40

"Only a very little, Mr. Flood—
For auld lang syne. No more, sir; that will do."
So, for the time, apparently it did,
And Eben evidently thought so too;
For soon amid the silver loneliness   45
Of night he lifted up his voice and sang,
Secure, with only two moons listening,
Until the whole harmonious landscape rang—

"For auld lang syne." The weary throat gave out,
The last word wavered, and the song was done.   50
He raised again the jug regretfully
And shook his head, and was again alone.
There was not much that was ahead of him,
And there was nothing in the town below—
Where strangers would have shut the many doors   55
That many friends had opened long ago.

SUGGESTIONS FOR WRITING

1. We can agree with Tom Wolfe that it takes "the right stuff" to succeed—not only as an astronaut, but as a student, a team member, a
   leader of an organization, a family member, an employee, and so forth.
   Keeping Tom Wolfe's techniques in mind, write about "the right stuff"
   in some endeavor with which you are familiar or in which you have
   succeeded.

2. You might turn the first assignment around and write about "the wrong
   stuff": how *not* to succeed without really trying. Possibly your essay will
   center on a "nerd" who, poor soul, seems to do everything wrong.
   (Perhaps that nerd will be you.)

3. In his essay Mark Snyder was an expert writing for nonexperts. You, of course, are an expert on many subjects: perhaps your hobby, the history of your home town, the schools that you attended, a sport, your genealogy, an organization to which you belong. In an essay, explain the subject about which you are expert to a specific audience of nonexperts (for example, high school students, university or college faculty members, a group of recent immigrants to the United States). On a cover sheet for your essay, explain what you did to make the subject understandable to your audience. (Did you avoid using technical vocabulary? Did you provide any definitions? How about explanations that would be unnecessary for an expert? Did you use examples to clarify your points? How did you go about getting the readers' interest? How did you make your subject meaningful for them?)

4. Write an essay in which you characterize the good life. In your discussion, be specific. Provide examples and explanations. For example, don't merely state that the good life includes serving others; give examples of such service by people whom you know and respect. If you think the good life involves gracious living, characterize that graciousness in detail. What kinds of activities and surroundings does it include?

5. Write a character sketch of one of your grandparents or of another older person whom you know. Be specific. Think about typical actions or movements, ways of talking, manner of dress, facial features, hair, posture, interests, opinions, and so on.

On Being a Member of Society

Three of the following essays are about places: two about the Pine Barrens of New Jersey and one about the small town of Milpitas in California. The fourth one, "Speedway," is about an American institution, the Indianapolis 500.

The four essays have a great deal in common. First, they are extremely informative, giving us information about specific places and about a major event. More than this, however, the authors— Elizabeth Kaye, John McPhee, Lewis Simons, and Paul Fussell— probe the significance of their subjects, asking always, "What is the wider meaning of this?" Thus these essays about specific places and events become explorations of what it means to live in America.

JOHN MCPHEE
From *The Pine Barrens*

A staff writer for the New Yorker *magazine, John McPhee was born in 1931 in New Jersey, the state where the Pine Barrens are located. As an author who writes about fairly unexpected subjects (one of his books provides a historical, geographical, botanical, and anecdotal study of oranges), McPhee has consistently been praised for his craftsmanship as a writer. (His writing process is discussed in this volume on pages 51–56.)*

The essay on the Pine Barrens is a good example of McPhee's technique: the patient amassing of detail after detail. Here, from The Pine Barrens, *is a typical McPhee scene:*

Fred Brown's house is on an unpaved road that curves along the edge of a wide cranberry bog. What attracted me to it was the pump that stands in his yard. It was something of a wonder that I noticed the pump, because there were, among other things, eight automobiles in the yard, two of them on their sides and one of them upside down, all ten years old or older. Around the cars were old refrigerators, vacuum cleaners, partly dismantled radios, cathode-ray tubes, a short wooden ski, a large wooden mallet, dozens of cranberry picker's boxes, many tires, an orange crate dated 1946, a cord or so of firewood, mandolins, engine heads, and maybe a thousand other things.

As you read, notice how McPhee uses detail to establish his points and to make his writing vivid.

The Pine Barrens are so close to New York that on a very clear night a bright light in the pines would be visible from the Empire State Building. A line ruled on a map from Boston to Richmond goes straight through the middle of the Pine Barrens. The halfway point between Boston and Richmond—the geographical epicenter of the developing megalopolis—is in the northern part of the woods, about twenty miles from Bear Swamp Hill.

Technically, the Pine Barrens are much larger than the thousand or so square miles of them that remain wild, and their original outline is formed by the boundaries of a thick layer of sand soils that covers much of central and southern New Jersey—down the coast from the outskirts of Asbury Park to the Cape May Peninsula, and inland more than halfway across the state. Settlers in the seventeenth and eighteenth centuries found these soils unpromising for farms, left the land uncleared, and began to refer to the region as the Pine Barrens. People in New Jersey still use the term, with variants such as "the pine belt," "the pinelands," and, most frequently, "the pines." Gradually, development of one kind or another has moved in over the edges of the forest, reducing the circumference of the wild land and creating a man-made boundary in place of the natural one. This transition line is often so abrupt that in many places on the periphery of the pines it is possible to be at one moment in farmland, or even in a residential development or an industrial zone, and in the next moment to be in the silence of a bewildering green country, where a journey of forty or fifty miles is necessary to get to the farms and factories on the other side. I don't know where the exact center of the pines may be, but in recent years I have spent considerable time there and have made outlines of the integral woodland on topographic maps and road maps, and from them I would judge that the heart of the pine country is in or near a place called Hog Wallow. There are twenty-five people in Hog Wallow. Some of them describe it, without any apparent intention to be clever, as a suburb of Jenkins, a town three miles away, which has forty-five people. . . .

In 1859, when the population of the central Pine Barrens was about as large as it has ever been, the area had nonetheless remained wild enough for the *Atlantic* to report, "It is a region aboriginal in savagery, grand in the aspects of untrammelled Nature; where forests extend in uninterrupted lines over scores of miles; where we may wander a good day's journey without meeting half-a-dozen human faces; where stately deer will bound across our path, and bears dispute our passage through the cedar-brakes; where, in a word, we may enjoy the undiluted essence, the perfect wildness, of woodland life." The magazine feared, however, that accelerated development would soon clear this wild country. "It is scarcely too much to anticipate that, within five years, thousands of acres, now dense with pines and cedars of a hundred rings, will be laid out in blooming market-gardens and in fields of generous corn," the article concluded. "Five years hence, bears and deer will be a tradition, panthers and raccoons a myth, partridges and quails a vain and melancholy recollection, in what shall then be known as what was once the pines." The trend the *Atlantic* anticipated was the reverse of the one that actually took place. As the last of the iron furnaces gradually blew out and the substitute industries failed, people either left the pines or began to lead self-sufficient backwoods lives, and while the rest of the State of New Jersey developed toward its twentieth-century aspect, the Pine Barrens all but returned to their pre-Colonial desolation, becoming, as they have remained, a distinct and separate world. The people of the pines came to be known as pineys—a term that is current today as it was at the turn of the century. After a generation or two had lived in isolation, the pineys began to fear people from the outside, and travellers often reported that when they approached a cabin in the pines the people scattered and hid behind trees. This was interpreted, by some, as a mark of lunacy. It was simply fear of the unknown.

The pineys had little fear of their surroundings, from which they drew an adequate living. A yearly cycle evolved that is still practiced, but by no means universally, as it once was. With the first warmth of spring, pineys took their drags—devices with tines, something like hand cultivators—and went into the lowland forests to gather sphagnum moss. This extraordinary material has such a capacity for absorbing water that one can squeeze it and twist it and wring it a dozen times and water will still come pouring out. Since the water is acidulous and somewhat antiseptic, sphagnum moss was used by soldiers during the Revolution when they lacked ordinary bandages. Florists provided a large part of the market for the pineys' moss. Boxes of cut flowers sent out by florists' shops all over the East used to contain—under and around the flowers—protective beds of sphagnum from the pines. Plastic moss has largely replaced sphagnum moss in the floral trade, but a market remains for it, and some people still gather it.

In June and July, when the wild blueberries of the Pine Barrens ripened on the bush, the pineys hung large homemade baskets around their necks, bent the blueberry bushes over the baskets, and beat the stems with short clubs. The berries, if just ripe enough, rained into the baskets. Fred Brown told me one day that he had knocked off his share of "huckleberries" in his time, and that many people still go out after them every summer. In the vernacular of the pines, huckleberries are blueberries, wild or cultivated. Huckleberries are also huckleberries, and this confuses outsiders but not pineys. Fred explained to me, when I pressed him, that "hog huckleberries" are huckleberries and "sugar huckleberries" are blueberries. He said, "Ain't nothing for a man to go out and knock off two hundred pounds in less than a day." In 1967, the average price for wild blueberries was fourteen cents a pound. People who gather wild blueberries now use No. 2 galvanized tubs instead of baskets. They beat the bushes with lengths of rubber hose. "Wild berries got a better taste than cultivated berries," Fred said. "Mrs. Wagner's Pies won't make pies with just cultivated berries." Millions of blueberry bushes grow wild in the pines, but when a forester who was doing field work for a doctoral thesis recently asked a piney assistant to cut one down, the piney refused.

Cranberries followed blueberries in the cycle of the pines. Cranberries grow wild along the streams and are white in the summer and red in the fall. In the eighteen-sixties and the eighteen-seventies, people began to transplant them to the cleared and excavated bogs where ore raisers had removed bog iron, and that was the beginning of commercial cranberry growing in the Pine Barrens, where about a third of the United States total is now grown. Cranberry bogs are shallow basins, dammed on all sides, so that streams can fill them in late autumn and keep cold winter winds from drying out the vines. The older bogs were turfed out by hand, and the dams were built from the turf. In the fall, the berries were harvested by hand, with many-tined wooden scoops that went through the vines like large claws. Cranberry scoops are so primitive in appearance that they are sold as antiques in shops on Third Avenue and in Bucks County. In a few bogs in the Pine Barrens, scoops are still used, and only five years ago all bogs used them.

In winter, the cycle moved on to cordwood and charcoal. Woodcutters, in the seventeenth century, were among the first people in the pines. They were needed in the iron era, they remained when it was over, and they are still there. They are getting a good price for their pulpwood—seven dollars a cord. With a chain saw, a man can cut a cord of pine in less than an hour. "Oak isn't worth nothing, but the pine is way up," Fred Brown said one day. Charcoal burning also continued beyond the iron era and was actually a major occupation in the Pine Barrens until the Second World War. In the eighteen-fifties, fifty schooners made regular runs with charcoal from the Pine Barrens to New York. Countless four-mule teams hauled charcoal over the sand roads to Philadelphia in covered wagons. Eight-mule teams hauled larger wagons, full of the best grade, to the Philadelphia mint. Almost any piney knew how to make charcoal, and the woods were full of little clearings, which is one reason that so many culs-de-sac branch from the sand roads. Full-time colliers specialized in charcoal to the exclusion of most of the other occupations in the yearly cycle. They frequently made their pits with someone else's wood. They moved around a lot, nomadically, living in shacks that had no floors, or in tepee-shaped structures made of cedar poles and turf. They stored their supplies—mainly salt pork and apple whiskey—in turf-covered dugouts, in which they hid and sometimes died when wildfires overcame the forest. Charcoal pits were actually above-ground. They had the shape of beehives and were twenty feet high. To make them, colliers stacked cordwood in vertical tiers and covered the wood with chunks of sandy turf, known as floats. The colliers dropped burning kindling into a hole in the top and then sealed it over. They poked holes in the sides with a stick called a fagan, and kept watch over the pit day and night. If blue smoke came out, too much oxygen was involved in the combustion, and the colliers plugged a few holes. If white steam came out, the wood inside was charring perfectly. This went on for about ten days. The late George Crummel, the Indian collier of Jenkins Neck, had a dog that could watch a pit and would awaken him if the ventilating holes needed attention. With Crummel gone, there are only two or three colliers left in the Pine Barrens. The last important market was for bagged charcoal for back-yard cooking, but the modern briquette has all but eliminated that. Most "charcoal" briquettes are made in gasoline refineries as a petroleum by-product. On this subject, Fred Brown said one day, "These here charcoal brick-a-bats, or whatever you call them, that they sell—look at them, all you have to do is *look* at them. You know they didn't come from no tree."

Venison, of course, was available the year round to pineys, who have always felt detached about game laws. The sphagnum-blueberry-cranberry-wood-and-charcoal cycle was supplemented in other ways as well—most notably in December, when shiploads of holly, laurel, mistletoe, ground pine, greenbriar, inkberry, plume grass, and boughs of pitch pine were sent to New York for sale as Christmas decorations. Small birch trees were cut in short lengths and turned into candle holders. People who specialized in pine cones became known as pineballers, and the term is still used. The Christmas business continues to be an important source of income in the pines. Modern pineballers pick about three thousand cones in a day. They like to get them from the dwarf forests—the Plains, as they are called—because the trees there are shorter than men, and can be picked clean. At the moment, pineballing is not as remunerative as huckleberrying. Pineballers are getting only three dollars and seventy-five cents per thousand cones, or about eleven dollars for a day's work. Pineys once sold rosin, turpentine, pitch tar, and shoemaker's wax. They cut laurel stems to sell to makers of pipes. They dug the roots of wild indigo for medicinal use (wild indigo is, among other things, a stimulant), and they cut the bark of wild cherry (a tonic) and collected pipsissewa leaves (an astringent). They sold laurel, ilex, and rhododendron to landscape gardeners. They sent wild flowers into the cities—trailing arbutus, swamp pinks, wild magnolias, lupine, azaleas, Pine Barrens gentians. They made birdhouses out of cedar slabs, and they still do. They sold box turtles by the gross to people in Philadelphia, who used the turtles to keep cellars free of snails—a market that has declined. . . .

In 1913, startling publicity was given to the most unfortunate stratum of the pine society, and the effects have not yet faded. In that year, Elizabeth Kite, a psychological researcher, published a report called "The Pineys," which had resulted from two years of visits to cabins in the pines. Miss Kite worked for the Vineland Training School, on the southern edge of the Pine Barrens, where important early work was being done with people of subnormal intelligence, and she was a fearless young woman who wore spotless white dresses as she rode in a horse-drawn wagon through the woods. Her concern for the people there became obvious to the people themselves, who grew fond of her, and even dependent upon her, and a colony for the care of the "feebleminded" was founded in the northern part of the Pine Barrens as a result of her work. Her report told of children who shared their bedrooms with pigs, of men who could not count beyond three, of a mother who walked nine miles with her children almost every day to get whiskey, of a couple who took a wheelbarrow with them when they went out drinking, so that one could wheel the other home. "In the heart of the region, scattered in widely separated huts over miles of territory, exists today a group of human beings as distinct in morals and manners as to excite curiosity and wonder in the mind of any outsider brought into contact with them," Miss Kite wrote. "They are recognized as a distinct people by the normal communities living on the borders of their forests." The report included some extremely gnarled family trees, such as one headed by Sam Bender, who conceived a child with his daughter, Mollie Bender Brooks, whose husband, Billie Brooks, sometimes said the child had been fathered by his wife's brother rather than her father, both possibilities being strong ones. When a district nurse was sent around to help clean up Mollie's house, chickens and a pig were found in the kitchen, and the first implement used in cleaning the house was a hoe. Mollie, according to Miss Kite, was "good-looking and sprightly, which fact, coupled with an utter lack of sense of decency, made her attractive even to men of otherwise normal intelligence." When Billie and all of their children were killed in a fire, Mollie said cheerfully, "Well, they was all insured. I'm still young and can easy start another family." Miss Kite reported some relationships that are almost impossible to follow. Of the occupants of another cabin, she wrote, "That May should call John 'Uncle' could be accounted for on the basis of a childish acceptance of 'no-matter-what' conditions, for the connection was that her mother was married to the brother of John's other woman's second man, and her mother's sister had had children by John. This bond of kinship did not, however, keep the families long together." Miss Kite also told of a woman who came to ask for food at a state almshouse on a bitter winter day. The people at the almshouse gave her a large burlap sack containing a basket of potatoes, a basket of turnips, three cabbages, four pounds of pork, five pounds of rye flour, two pounds of sugar, and some tea. The woman shouldered the sack and walked home cross-country through snow. Thirty minutes after she reached her home, she had a baby. No one helped her deliver it, nor had anyone helped her with the delivery of her nine other children.

Miss Kite's report was made public. Newspapers printed excerpts from it. All over the state, people became alarmed about conditions in the Pine Barrens—a region most of them had never heard of. James T. Fielder, the governor of New Jersey, travelled to the pines, returned to Trenton, and sought to increase his political momentum by recommending to the legislature that the Pine Barrens be somehow segregated from the rest of New Jersey in the interest of the health and safety of the people of the state at large. "I have been shocked at the conditions I have found," he said. "Evidently these people are a serious menace to the State of New Jersey because they produce so many persons that inevitably become public charges. They have inbred, and led lawless and scandalous lives, till they have become a race of imbeciles, criminals, and defectives." Meanwhile, H. H. Goddard, director of the research laboratory at the Vineland Training School and Miss Kite's immediate superior, had taken the genealogical charts that Miss Kite had painstakingly assembled, pondered them, extrapolated a bit, and published what became a celebrated treatise on a family called Kallikak—a name that Goddard said he had invented to avoid doing harm to real people. According to the theory set forth in the treatise, nearly all pineys were descended from one man. This man, Martin Kallikak, conceived an illegitimate son with an imbecile barmaid. Martin's bastard was said to be the forebear of generations of imbeciles, prostitutes, epileptics, and drunks. Martin himself, however, married a normal girl, and among their progeny were generations of normal and intelligent people, including doctors, lawyers, politicians, and a president of Princeton University. Goddard coined the name Kallikak from the Greek *kalós* and *kakós*—"good" and "bad." Goddard's work has been discredited, but its impact, like that of Governor Fielder's proposal to segregate the Pine Barrens, was powerful in its time. Even Miss Kite seemed to believe that there was some common flaw in the blood of all the people of the pines. Of one pinelands woman, Miss Kite wrote, "Strangely enough, this woman belonged originally to good stock. No piney blood flowed in her veins."

The result of all this was a stigma that has never worn off. A surprising number of people in New Jersey today seem to think that the Pine Barrens are dark backlands inhabited by hostile and semi-literate people who would as soon shoot an outsider as look at him. A policeman in Trenton who had never been to the pines—"only driven through on the way downa shore," as people usually say—once told me, in an anxious tone, that if I intended to spend a lot of time in the Pine Barrens I was asking for trouble. Some of the gentlest of people—botanists, canoemen, campers—spend a great deal of time in the pines, but their influence has not been sufficient to correct an impression, vivid in some parts of the state for fifty years, that the pineys are weird and sometimes dangerous barefoot people who live in caves, marry their sisters, and eat snakes. Pineys are, for the most part, mild and shy, but their resentment is deep, and they will readily and forcefully express it. The unfortunate people that Miss Kite described in her report were a minor fraction of the total population of the Pine Barrens, and the larger number suffered from it, and are still suffering from it. This appalled Elizabeth Kite, who said to an interviewer in 1940, some years before her death, "Nothing would give me greater pleasure than to correct the idea that has unfortunately been given by the newspapers regarding the pines. Anybody who lived in the pines was a piney. I think it a most terrible calamity that the newspapers publicly took the term and gave it the degenerate sting. Those families who were not potential state cases did not interest me as far as my study was concerned. I have no language in which I can express my admiration for the pines and the people who live there."

QUESTIONS

1. What use does McPhee make of statistics in this essay?
2. For what purpose does McPhee use comparison and contrast?
3. What was the nature of Elizabeth Kite's report? What was its effect?
4. Read the article on the Kallikaks in *The Encyclopedia Americana*. What does this episode in American scholarship tell you about evaluating sources of information?
5. How does Mark Snyder's concept of self-fulfilling stereotypes (pp. 166–73) apply to McPhee's essay?
6. Explain the concept "piney."
7. In a part of the essay not reprinted here, McPhee says, "The people of the Pine Barrens turn cold when they hear the word 'piney' spoken by anyone who is not a native." Why? Are there any other words like that in American society?
8. Characterize the values of the pineys. In what ways do those values fit in with or contradict typical American middle-class values?
9. On pages 51–56, William Howarth describes John McPhee's method of composing. How do the results that you find in "The Pine Barrens" compare to Howarth's explanations?

LEWIS SIMONS

New Jersey Shows a Different Face in This Bewitching Province of Pines

Lewis Simons, a newspaper reporter now stationed in Tokyo, writes about his reactions to the Pine Barrens.

This essay will give you an excellent chance to compare the techniques of two successful writers who have chosen the same subject. You will want to ask yourself in what ways the essays by McPhee and Simons are similar and in what ways different.

New Jersey, the most crowded state in the Union, has been the hapless butt of put-down jokes for years. (Question: What's worse than a weekend in Calcutta? Answer: A Saturday night in Secaucus.) My teen-age cousin, Craig, has spent his entire life in northern New Jersey and to him it is no laughing matter: row upon row of look-alike houses, congested highways lined with used-car lots and shopping centers, one dying city after another, and people, people, people. . . .

Given our decidedly urban impressions of New Jersey, the last thing Craig and I ever expected to find there was an authentic wilderness. But last summer, to our great surprise and everlasting delight, that is exactly what we did find—less than two hours away from downtown Manhattan. We drove for hours along sandy roads cutting through dense thickets and woods. We backpacked for miles on a winding path called the Batona Trail. We canoed down the enchanting Mullica River and seldom saw another soul. We knelt to drink cool water from fast-running streams— *New Jersey* streams, mind you!—as pure as any in the East.

The remarkable place where all of this happened is known as the Pine Barrens. . . .

Encompassing some 2,000 square miles in all, it is an intriguing patchwork of towns, farms, orchards, commercial cranberry bogs, forests and wetlands. For hikers, bird watchers and other nature lovers, its chief attraction is a 338,000-acre core of mostly undeveloped private and public land in and around the four state forests: Wharton, Bass River, Penn and Lebanon.

This territory, dotted with sparkling ponds and lakes, is considered the primeval heart and soul of the Pine Barrens. That name is a curious misnomer, because although the region is full of pitch pines, short-leaf pines and even pygmy pines, it is anything but barren. It sustains more than 80 bird species, dozens of reptiles and amphibians, including the endangered Pine Barrens tree frog, *Hyla andersoni*, and many deer, fox, raccoons and other creatures. The diverse vegetation includes, in addition to the ubiquitous pine trees, varieties of oak, cedar and magnolia, shoulder-high blueberry shrubs, myrtle, azaleas and a great many wild herbs.

The region's most abundant and, in some ways, most important natural resource is buried underground. The Pine Barrens' bristly surface stretches across beds of sand and gravel hundreds of feet deep. These contain about 17 trillion gallons of fresh water. The surface water is unappetizing in appearance because of its tea-brown color—the harmless result of dissolved organic materials—but it is drinkable in certain places. The Cohansey aquifer, as this huge subsurface reservoir is called, presently provides water for most of the area's 400,000 residents.

Another resource not to be overlooked in the Pine Barrens is the people who live there. Although much of the region is wild, it is not pristine and it hasn't been for a long time. The first settlers moved in more than two centuries ago. Since then, industries (iron for cannon balls was mined here during the Revolutionary War) and entire villages have come and gone, but some descendants of the earlier pioneers are still around. A number of them live at least partly off the land, farming, hunting, woodcutting and berry picking. They call themselves Pineys and in their woodsy lifestyle and characteristic speech patterns they are as culturally and sociologically distinct as the hill people of Appalachia and the briny island lobstermen of Maine. There is Piney music and even Piney cuisine, such as the thick, hearty snapping-turtle soup so highly esteemed by these locals.

The Pineys love their land in the same way that they love their families and, indeed, for most of them the two are almost inseparable. Some Pineys try to leave but, like Wilbur Higgenbothem, end up coming back. Wilbur played guitar and harmonica with a country band that traveled to Atlantic City and the Pennsylvania Dutch country. Then he started homesteading in Paisley, a handful of humble little homes in the woods. There, on nine acres which he says he bought in 1945 for less than $200, he built a house out of pine and cedar wood and raised seven children with his wife, Anna. He works part of the year in a nearby cranberry bog and raises strawberries, blueberries, raspberries and vegetables, some of which his family eats and some of which he sells. "It's hard to get by," Wilbur told Craig and me, "but out here at least you can always find something to eat. And you can always gather pine cones, moss and birch logs to sell. My brother-in-law does gathering full time."

Gathering! I thought it had gone out with the Indians of pre-Colonial America. Yet here were people who still earned a living gathering wild things in the forests. "We get $7 a thousand for pine cones," Anna told us. "Some people, if they're really fast, they gather 10,000 in a day. You can't afford to walk. You run from one tree to another, and you lose all the meat and skin off your shins, too." Once, Wilbur tied stovepipes around his shins to protect them. "But with them on," he said, "I couldn't run very much."

Wilbur paused for a moment. He had been weeding his strawberries and now he flicked a bead of sweat out of his eyebrow, slapped a mosquito and squinted into the sunset as he thoughtfully considered a broader issue. "One thing I can't understand is why anyone would ever want to develop this land," he said.

Some people see nothing wrong with development and quite a few are actively engaged in it. An hour's flight over the Pine Barrens in a light plane vividly reveals how successful they have been. Enormous retirement communities leap out of the deep green forests, their serried rows of little homes edged by red earth, gouged by bulldozers and backhoes. New housing developments, highways, powerlines and garbage dumps make their prominent marks on the fragile landscape, too. The sprawling glitter of Atlantic City lies only moments away from the peaceful center of an immense wetland. As the plane turns north we can see both the Garden State Parkway and the New Jersey Turnpike grasping the pinelands between them like a pair of giant calipers.

The trouble with all of this has mainly to do with its potentially devastating impact on the region's precious water supplies, and on the Pineys' bucolic way of life. To the extent that the Pineys depend on farming, berrying and gathering for their subsistence, any significant encroachment upon their lands casts a shadow over the future. As for the Pine Barrens' aquifer, it is, partly owing to it porous condition, particularly vulnerable to pollution and poisoning by septic-tank systems and garbage dumps. Another threat is posed by toxic dumps full of chemical wastes that have been delivered by trucks from industrial sites far beyond the Pine Barrens. Even now, experts say, this material is slowly but surely leaching into the water.

Development and land speculation have been going on in the area for decades, but it was not until the mid-1960s that conservationists began to fight for a more rational approach to growth. In 1978, largely as a result of their efforts, the Pine Barrens became one of the first "reserves" established under the National Parks and Recreation Act. A reserve differs from a park in that it may, like the Pine Barrens, consist of a smorgasbord of federal, state, local and private lands (about two-thirds of the Pine Barrens is privately owned). The point of creating this reserve is to reconcile preservation and development through enlightened land-use planning. . . . There is beauty in macrocosm, too, but some of those views struck me, at times, as a little forbidding. Some tracts of immature pygmy pines, for example, are about three feet tall, rough in texture and bizarre when you stand in their midst. Peering across their tops, I felt like Gulliver in Lilliput.

One night we bunked at an old Victorian house sandwiched between the pines and bogs. I was dead tired from all our wanderings and the mattress laid out on the floor felt positively luxurious. I was all but fast asleep when the sound began outside. Something like *quonk, quonk, quonk*. Deep. Big, in fact, though the creature that made it was not big at all. The noise came from the Pine Barrens tree frog, a finger-length creature, green in color with a distinctive lavender stripe running down each of its glistening sides. Its call was a lullaby I shall not soon forget.

One of the special things about the Pine Barrens wilderness is that it's so easy to get into. It is possible, for instance, to park your car next to the abandoned New Jersey Central Railroad bed just south of the hamlet of Atsion in Wharton State Forest and to strike off down the rusty tracks. Within minutes, you are in another world, a world of toads and turtles, buzzards and butterflies, skunks and snakes. Goldfinches are chipping and whistling in the pitch pines and redwinged blackbirds are *konk-la-reeing* in the bogs. Here and there, if you look carefully, you may even come upon the endangered Pine Barrens gentian.

At a junction of the tracks with a narrow dirt road, you may notice that the mud in a hollow looks like a page torn from a footprint field guide. Carelessly drawn just a few hours ago, these marks now appear almost fussy in their precision, and therefore they are unmistakable. That's the catlike imprint of a skunk and this is where a fox made its dainty way. The childlike business over there is a raccoon's fingery impression and, over there, next to the deer's cloven signature, this is a possum's tail dragging on the ground. It was, from the looks of it, a busy night for critters, but not for people; no sign of them here at all.

This is a good place for quiet encounters, if you are patient. Sit for a while on the bank of this soupy bog and the sunning turtles that slid off the log when you arrived a few minutes ago will return, hauling themselves back out one by one. You can hear their claws scratching on the wood. Get up now and watch them, startled, dump themselves in once again—all except that big one on the end. It looks, blinks, cranes its neck to make sure, seems almost to shrug, and reluctantly pivots on its belly, claws rasping. *Plop*.

A little farther down the tracks, with the sun warm on your back and the wind mussing up your hair, you find a couple of bleached fox scats lying between the ties and, digging with a stick, you separate the stiff outer hairs to reveal a core of olive-colored organic matter. It is powdery and flecked with fragments of bone. Nearby, at the base of a pine sapling, you find another scat—dried berries, mostly. Crushing several of them, you notice brown little buttonlike seeds, burnished as brightly as mother-of-pearl. These are the seeds of the greenbrier berry, a meager fruit raccoons and other animals usually don't bother with until winter, when there's little else to be had.

Still kneeling, you look up and see the deer. It is ambling across the tracks a couple of hundred feet upwind from you. It seems to be just moseying around, and when it heads down the embankment, you follow, walking softly, gaining on it. How close can you get? Suddenly a ruffed grouse explodes into flight ten feet away, scaring the daylights out of you and the deer. Flicking the white underside of its tail straight up, your quarry bolts for cover.

Walking back to the car, you notice that this part of the railroad bed is being absorbed by the wetlands on either side of it. It's sinking. The timbers are rotting. Grass is matting over the gravel; pine and oak saplings are taking firm root between the ties. Eventually, as the water continues to soften the embankment and the vegetation grows apace, even the rails will start to disappear and some day this conspicuous cut will be no more. It will be healed.

But although the healing process has indeed begun in certain parts of the Pine Barrens, some conservationists are concerned these days that unnecessary and perhaps even illegal damage is being inflicted elsewhere. In the past two years, they contend, there has been some serious slippage in the implementation of the master plan. Not surprisingly, some developers and municipal officials disagree.

"Conservation victories are never permanent," says Mary-Ann Thompson, the 34-year old daughter of a local cranberry grower and one of the area's leading activists. "I am worried because too many people are complacent."

Mary-Ann is another one of those who left the Pine Barrens only to return. She earned a law degree at Cornell and attended graduate school in London before working as a legal counsel for former New Jersey Governor Brendan Byrne and then as a Congressional aide in Washington. She's now practicing law in Vincentown and helping her father on the cranberry farm. The business employs 17 people at harvest time and helps support seven families, including that of Jimmy Bakely, age 38, who grew up in nearby Tabernacle and now lives on the premises.

What brought Mary-Ann back to her homeland in 1977 was the struggle to protect it. She is determined to see that the wilderness remains wild, that the water stays pure and that the area's 50 remaining cranberry growers (down from hundreds some 35 years ago) stay in business. That's just fine with Wilbur Higgenbothem, who works regularly for Mary-Ann's dad. "They've already taken away too many good farms," he grumbled when Craig and I stopped by. "People who don't even know how to grow a tomato."

With that, Wilbur reached out with a large, roughened hand and scooped up his young grandson, Nicky. Barefoot, white-blond and, like his granddad, red-faced, the little boy moved with the loose-limbed sure gait of the child at home in the woods. The grandfather hoisted him up, like a sack of pine cones, and bounced him on his knees. "This boy wouldn't know what to do without these pines," the grandfather said, and Nicky laughed and squealed.

QUESTIONS

1. Compare Simons' essay with McPhee's. What sort of "voice" or persona does each author project?
2. Do the two authors seem to have different purposes for their essays? Explain.
3. What do you learn from Simons that you don't from McPhee, and what do you learn from McPhee that you don't from Simons?
4. How do the styles of the two authors differ? (Think of sentence structure, word choice, and figures of speech.)
5. Which of the two essays did you like better? Why?

PAUL FUSSELL
Speedway

Paul Fussell (1924–   ) attended Harvard University and now teaches English at Rutgers. He has been active as a scholar and teacher, but at the same time has published widely for a broad nonspecialist audience. The Boy Scout Handbook and Other Observations *(a collection of his essays) was recently published,* Class: A Guide through the American Status System *appeared in the fall of 1983.*

John McPhee and Lewis Simons wrote about a region of America and the people in it, giving an account of the everyday life in the Pine Barrens. Paul Fussell observes that great American institution the Indianapolis 500, which he views almost as a national ritual. He gives a lively account of the people and events at the race, but he also comments on the meaning of this annual orgy of speed and power. As you read, you should ask yourself what the Indy 500 symbolizes for the author.

The violent death of driver Gordon Smiley at Indianapolis in May, only a week after the violent death of driver Gilles Villeneuve in Belgium, started a cascade of objections to motor racing, most of them based on the assumption that human beings are rational creatures, despite evidence to the contrary pouring in at the same time from the south Atlantic.[1] In *Time,* Tom Callahan deplored the whole Indy enterprise: "Some 450,000 people," he wrote, "will perch or picnic at the Speedway on Sunday. Nobody knows how many of them are ghouls spreading their blankets beside a bad intersection." This reprehension of ghoulishness was attended by four gruesome color photographs intended specifically to gratify the ghoul in all of us. At the same time, Frank Deford was setting off his anti-Indy blast in *Sports Illustrated,* finding the race not a sport but a mere hustling of automotive products ("The drivers at Indy look much less like athletes than like a lot of congested billboards"). He concluded that among the spectators lurk a significant number of "barbarians." George Vecsey, in the sports pages of *The New York Times,* suggested that the Indy race is becoming too dangerous to be regarded as a sport. "I can see accidents," he said, "on the Long Island Expressway."

Were these people right? Is the Indy 500 a sporting event, or is it something else? And if something else, is it evil or benign?

Although the automotive industry moved to Detroit early in this century, Indianapolis is still a motor city, swarming with car washes and auto-parts stores, and the sign on the road into town from the airport,

---

[1]During the spring and summer of 1982, Great Britain and Argentina went to war for control of the Falkland Islands, a British possession off the coast of Argentina.

WELCOME TO INDIANAPOLIS: CROSSROADS OF AMERICA, seems to imply that you're entering a place best reached by car. Here, nobody walks. One day I walked two and a half miles along Sixteenth Street to the Speedway, and in that one hour found myself literally the only person not in an automobile. Returning a few hours later, I was still the only walker, with the exception of a man who accosted me and tried to borrow sixty-two cents.

To a Northeasterner, Indianapolis seems at first to be a strangely retrograde repository of piety and patriotism. When I arrived, an editorial in the only paper in town was raising a populist voice in a call for school prayer, and a front-page box offered "Today's Prayer," just above "Today's Chuckle." After a short sojourn in Indianapolis one is no longer surprised at the imperious sign in the store window, GO TO CHURCH SUNDAY. Catholics wishing to arrive at the race very early Sunday morning, like everyone else, have their needs taken care of by the Archdiocese of Indianapolis, which has ruled that they may fulfill their holy Sunday obligation "by attending Mass the evening before." Indianapolis seemed to me the sort of place where President Reagan expects no one to guffaw when he asserts that someone or something is "in my prayers." In fact, the president would love the place. Driving to the Speedway, the motorist passes a billboard advertising (of course) cars, but shouting also GOD BLESS AMERICA. At the Speedway, even at qualifying trials weeks before the race, the national anthem is played at every opportunity, and the official program offers odd, vainglorious ads like one inserted by the International Association of Machinists and Aerospace Workers: "PRIDE—Pride helped build America into the greatest nation on earth."

"Naptown" is what many locals call Indianapolis, and it does seem a somnolent place. Although it's a city and not a town, it's hard not to think of the Hoosier Booth Tarkington[2] and those long, warm, sleepy afternoons when Penrod and Sam found nothing whatever to do. As I experienced the slowness of the Indianapolis pace—every transaction seems to drag on interminably, every delay welcomed with friendly patience—I began to wonder whether speed and danger were not celebrated there one day a year just for the sheer relief and the novelty of it, just because on all other days life was so safe and predictable and slow. But friendly as well, it must be said. An elderly man flushing the urinal next to mine at the Speedway Motel, astonished at the noisy vigor of the flush, turned to me and, although we'd not been introduced, kindly made me the audience for his observation, "Gawd, the *suction* on that son of a bitch! If you dropped it *in* there, you'd really lose it!" Ron Dorson, an authority on the anthropology of Indy, observes that although "in most public social settings . . . it is considered socially deviant for strangers to approach one another," at the

---

[2]Booth Tarkington was an early twentieth-century American writer of popular boys books that centered on the misadventures of two characters, Penrod and Sam.

Speedway things are different. There, "it becomes perfectly acceptable to engage total strangers in conversation about lap times, automotive technology, Speedway management, or race-driver intrigue." There's something of pioneer individualism lingering in this friendliness, and on race Sunday, when you see the infield crowded with campers, tents, trailers, and "recreational vehicles," their occupants cooking and drawing water and cosseting children and making love in the friendliest fashion, you realize what the Indy setting really is: it's an early-nineteenth-century American pioneer campsite surrounded, as if fortuitously, by an early-twentieth-century two-and-a-half-mile track. And you almost begin to wonder if it's not the camping out, that primeval American ceremony of innocence, rather than the race and its hazards, that has drawn these crowds here.

I'd say the people can be divided into three social classes: the middles, who on race day tend, in homage to the checkered flag, to dress all in black and white and who sit in reserved seats; the high proles, who watch standing or lolling in the infield, especially at the turns, "where the action is"; and the uglies, the overadvertised, black-leathered, beer-sodden, pot-headed occupiers of that muddy stretch of ground in the infield at the first turn, known as the Snake Pit. These are the ones who, when girls pass, spiritlessly hold up signs reading SHOW US YOUR TITS. The uglies are sometimes taken to be the essence of Indy, and they are the people who, I think, Frank Deford has in mind when he speaks of "barbarians." But they are not the significant Indy audience. The middle class is, all those people arriving at the Speedway in cars bearing Purdue and Indiana State stickers.

The middles are privileged to participate in an exclusive social event, the classy pit promenade. Beginning three hours before the start, anyone who can wangle a pit pass strolls slowly up and down in the space between the pits and the track proper, all dressed up and watched enviously, he imagines, by some tens of thousands of his social inferiors in the stands. On race morning in Indianapolis this is the stylish place to be, a place where one wouldn't dare show oneself unshaven or in dirty clothes. Many spandy-clean black-and-white getups are to be seen there, including trousers with two-inch black-and-white squares. Even though the social tone is compromised a bit by the presence of representatives of the press (that's how I got there), the thing struck me as comparable with some of the great snob social operations of the world, like appearing in or near the royal box at Ascot or nodding to well-dressed friends while strolling slowly down the Champs Elysées. But this promenade was for middle-class people. The upper-middle class is not to be found at Indy. If you're the sort of person drawn to Forest Hills, or the Test Matches at Lord's, or the Americas Cup Races in Newport, you're not likely to be seen at the Speedway.

From the outset, devotees of auto racing have felt anxieties about its place on the class-status ladder. Is motor racing on a par with cockfighting and mud wrestling, or up there with football and perhaps even badminton? The surprise registered by an Indianapolis paper after the 1912 race speaks volumes, socially: "There has been no better-mannered gathering in Indianapolis. . . . There was no pushing, no crowding, no profanity, no discourtesies." When the Chief Steward issues the portentous injunction, "Gentlemen, start your engines," we may feel that the first word insists a bit too much. Presumably, if women drivers were to become a regular feature in the Indy, the formula would have to include "Ladies and. . ." Janet Guthrie, who has been on the premises, and has so far been the only woman to participate (three times), says: "I think that racing's image needs all the help it can get. It has traditionally been a low brow image." Before being killed in the Austrian Grand Prix in 1975, Mark Donohue, who had graduated not just from college but from Brown, raced at Indy and sensed what an anomaly he was there. "I was considered different from the other drivers," he said. "I had gone to college, I was articulate, and I didn't swear a lot."

The sense that racing will naturally sink proleward unless rigorously disciplined is what one takes away from a reading of the rule book promulgated by the United States Auto Club, the official supervisor of Indy racing. Cars are not to bear "undignified names," "improper language or conduct" is forbidden, and everything must be neat and clean at all times, just the way a gentleman would want it: "*Appearance*: cars, crews, and all pit personnel whose appearance detracts from the character of the program may be excluded."

A similar aspiration to respectability seems to be partially responsible for euphemisms that abound at Indy. Just as the self-conscious middle class may remark that someone has "passed away" (sometimes "over"), the Indy public-address announcer will inform the spectators that "We have a fatality." Instead of saying there's been a terrible smash-up on the third turn, he'll say, "We have a yellow light." A car never hits the wall, it "gets into" it, or even "kisses" it, and speakers aspiring to even greater tastefulness might observe that the driver has "visited Cement City." Driver Danny Ongais, badly injured in a crash in 1981, spoke of it this year not as the crash or even the accident but as the "incident." Everywhere there is the gentleman's feeling that if you pretend something has not happened, it has not. Thus the rule prohibiting cars to add oil during a race. Adding oil would publicly acknowledge, as racing journalist Terry Reed points out, "that a car is blowing (or leaking) its original supply on the track, making the course even more hazardous." Almost immediately after Gordon Smiley's body nauseatingly stained the wall, it was repainted, white and pure. Now his tire marks on the third turn run oddly into a clean expanse of white.

As Danny Ongais's indirection suggests, there are psychological as well as social reasons for all this euphemism. Racing is deadly dangerous, especially now that speeds around 200 miles an hour are the rule, which makes more true than ever Jackie Stewart's point: "Motor racing will always be dangerous because you are always going too fast for things around you." Johnny Rutherford adds: "Very few drivers—maybe only a handful—are capable of running 200 miles an hour." An example of one guy who wasn't, some say in Indianapolis, was the late Gordon Smiley. At least that's the way they rationalize in order to admit no defect in the conditions, only in the weaker aspirants, thus making racing seem a wholesome and natural illustration of Darwinian selection. A pervasive atmosphere of risk enshrouds a top driver's professional life. Jackie Stewart had occasion to realize, in June 1970, that in the past months he'd "seen more of life and death than most people see in two lifetimes. Four weeks after Jimmy died, it was Mike Spence at Indianapolis; four weeks later, another friend, Ludovico Scarfiotti; four weeks more, to the day, it was Jo Schlesser in Rouen; and two weeks ago, Bruce McLaren at Goodwood. Now it's Piers. It just keeps on." The USAC rule book says explicitly that "Automobile racing is a hazardous undertaking," and it implies it all the way through, as when it notes that all drivers are required to remove dentures before starting or when it lays down precise specifications for easily detached steering wheels, "to aid in removing injured drivers from cars."

I have been genuinely scared quite a bit, most notably in the infantry during the Second World War, when shells whined inexorably closer and closer to my body and I waited for them finally to make contact and tear me to pieces. But a further moment of sheer terror occurred at eleven in the morning of May 22, 1982, the third day of qualifying at Indy, when I entered the Speedway through an underpass running beneath the track itself and for the first time heard those cars screaming by just overhead. They give off not just an almost unbearable sudden noise, but shocking heat and concussion as well. In their appalling whoosh is the quintessential menace of the Machine. Not even an observer feels entirely safe at the Speedway, and indeed the spectators are in literal danger all the time— from hurtling machines, tires, and fragments, and from the deadly methanol fuel, which burns with a scarcely visible flame, consuming ears and fingers before onlookers are even aware that the victim's on fire. No wonder "13" is, by USAC edict, never used in car numbering.

No wonder, either, that the rituals of the Indy world are strenuously male, macho as all get-out. Women, even wives and mistresses, weren't allowed in the pits until 1970. In 1976 Janet Guthrie was hoping to enter the race. She couldn't get her car to go fast enough to qualify, but on her way to her car to try, Dan Gerber, author of *Indy: The World's Fastest Carnival Ride*, remembers,

She is stopped by two slightly beer-crazed twenty-year-olds.

"Hey, Janet," one of them calls. "You gonna qualify?"

"I hope so," she replies, smiling, perhaps a little nervously.

"Well, we don't," the other boy calls back to her. "We hope you crash and burn where we can see you."

Actually, in order to understand precisely how male Indy is, you have only to scrutinize the famous Borg-Warner trophy, awarded annually to the winner. On top is a silver male figure ten inches tall, signaling the finish of a race by vigorously deploying a checkered flag, despite the curious fact that he's stark naked and exhibiting a complete set of realistic genital organs, instead of what we might expect, a *cache sexe* consisting maybe of a windblown bit of fabric. There he stands, quite undraped—unlike, say, the modest figure in front of Rockefeller Center—proclaiming for all to see the ideal maleness toward which Indy aspires.

The ideal whiteness, too. Indy, as Ron Dorson says, is "a show staged by white people for a white audience." Blacks are so rare among the spectators that you notice them specifically, and of course there are no black drivers, nor threat of any. (There was once a Jewish driver, Mauri Rose, but that's another story.) At a local cocktail party I broached the black topic as politely as I could and was told by one lady that blacks abjured the race because you had to sit for hours in the hot sun, and, as is well known, blacks can't bear to sit in the sun. Phoned for his views, the local NAACP spokesman fulminated, asserting that the situation is a scandal but that all black representations have been ineffective. Once Indy is over, and the Speedway emptied for another year, you see a lot of blacks there, working for a week to clear away the 6 million pounds of litter the crowd leaves (together with odd left-behinds like sets of teeth and, each time, two or three cars inexplicably abandoned forever in the infield).

The combined weight of the litter suggests the size of the crowd, estimated (since the Speedway does not issue a precise count) at around 400,000. And the size of the crowd suggests one other thing that's being celebrated. A name for it would be gigantism. It is the biggest of everything, "the largest single-day sporting event in the world," as local publicity says. And, as Roger Penske adds, for the drivers it's "the biggest race in the world to win"; both the purse and the publicity are the largest. There is more press coverage—over 4,000 media people are there—than of any similar event. So gigantic is the track that a spectator can see only a tiny segment of it. Thus the public-address announcer is indispensable, performing over (naturally) "the world's largest public-address system" to tell you what you're seeing. This means that every event is mediated through language: "We have a yellow light." The Indy public-address and radio announcers have always become public personages, even stars, and young

Paul Page, who succeeded Sid Collins as the radio "Voice of the Indianapolis Five Hundred," is as famous there as, say, George Steinbrenner in
New York.

It's not just the announcing that makes Indy so curiously a language
event. It's the advertising, the sight of grown men proud to be walking
around in caps that say VALVOLINE or GOODYEAR. The cars themselves,
plastered with decals (CHAMPION, DIEHARD, STP), have been called, by
somewhat heavy wits, "the world's fastest billboards." Officially, Indy is a
celebration of "progress" in the motor-car and rubber-tire industries, a
testing ground for improvements destined to make their way into your
passenger car. Unofficially, it's a celebration of the charm of brand names,
of their totemic power to confer distinction on those who wear, utter, or
display them. You achieve vicarious power by wearing the right T-shirt or
cap and thus allying yourself with successful enterprises like BUDWEISER or
GATORADE. By the use of "legible clothing," as Alison Lurie calls it, you
fuse your private identity with external commercial success, redeeming
your insignificance and becoming, for the moment, somebody. Even the
lucky wearers of the coveted pit passes are allowed to feel this sort of power,
for the badges, not content to be merely what they are, are also little ads for
CHEVROLET CAMARO. A person who couldn't read (a real "barbarian,"
maybe) would get very little out of Indy.

Obviously there's much more going on here than is commonly imagined by the "Eastern press," and there's certainly more going on than an
overpowering desire to see someone killed. There is a powerful and, in my
view, benign element of ritual purgation about Indy, and the things purged
are precisely such impurities as vulgarity, greed, snobbery, and sadism.

The events just preceding the race, presented always in the same order
and with the same deliberate, ample timing, are enough to hint at this
ritual element. It is a Sunday morning, a time once appropriated for rituals
of purgation. When I asked why the race was run on Sunday despite
protests from the local Baptists about profaning the Sabbath, and the
inconvenience of closed liquor stores, I was told that Monday, a holiday,
was always available as a rain date. But the race seems to gravitate to
Sunday for deeper reasons.

We've entered the Speedway very early, at 7:00 or 8:00 in the morning, although the crazies will have poured in, already blotto on beer and
clad in T-shirts proclaiming the wearer TOO DRUNK TO FUCK, when the
gates open at 5:00. We're all anticipating the hour of start, 11:00, the hour
when, formerly, church services began. By 9:30 virtually everyone involved in the unvarying prestart ceremonies is in place. At 9:45, as—I'm
quoting the official program—"the Purdue University Band plays 'On the
Banks of the Wabash,'" the cars, still inert, silent, dead things, a threat to
no one, are pushed by hand from the pits to their starting positions on the

too narrow track, where they are formed up in eleven rows of a viciously hazardous but thoroughly traditional three-abreast arrangement. At 10:34 the Chief Steward makes a stately circuit in the pace car, inspecting the track for impurities one last time. At 10:44, all rise: "The Star-Spangled Banner." At 10:47, heads bowed for the invocation, delivered by a local divine, who prays for a safe race and reminds us of the dead of all our wars—and of all past Indys. One minute later "Taps." It is Memorial Day, one suddenly remembers. Two minutes after "Taps," the band plays, quite slowly, "Back Home Again in Indiana." By this time I am crying, for me always an empirical indication, experienced at scores of weddings and commencements, that I am taking part in a ritual. By the time the booming voice issued its command to the gentlemen, I was ready to be borne out on a litter, and the race hadn't even started yet.

If, while witnessing these things, you come to understand that Indy has something more to do with Memorial Day than coincidence, you also realize that there's some evanescent ritual meaning in the event's occurring at the moment recognized as the division between spring and summer. For Dan Gerber, listening as a boy annually to the Voice of the Indianapolis Five Hundred meant—release. "It meant school was getting out and I could get sunburned and go fishing and spend three months on Lake Michigan." For me, likewise, as an adult, as far away I used to listen stretched out in the sun on that weekend, it meant school was out: university was over for that year, I'd finally turned the grades in, no more pressure, no more anxiety about treating someone unfairly until we resumed in the fall. Indy, says the man who for years has commanded the corps of 600 ushers, "is spring tonic to me." I know what he means.

As with a great many contemporary experiences, the meaning of Indy is elusive because it won't fit familiar schemes of classification. The rationalist, trying to make sense of its competitive elements, concludes that news about it belongs on the sports page. But then Warner Wolf, the TV sports commentator, appalled by the destruction of Villeneuve and Smiley, argues that racing's not a sport at all and indignantly defames it as merely a thing about machines. Although there probably is a legitimate sport called "motor sport," indulged in largely by amateurs, Wolf is right in perceiving that what takes place at Indy is not a sport. The true nature of Indy is in its resemblance to other rituals in which wild, menacing, nonhuman things are tamed.

I'm thinking of the rodeo and the bullfight. Subduing beasts that, unsubdued, would threaten man—that's the ritual of rodeo, and, with some additional deepening of the irrational element, of the bullfight as well. Just like at Indy, you can get hurt trying to subdue wild horses, killed trying to dominate bulls. Virility, *cojones* figure in each of these, as the little silver man indicates they do at Indy. Warner Wolf is also right when he notes that Indy is a thing about machines, but it's about machines only the way rodeos would be about broncos if no men were there to break them and bullfights about *toros* if no *toreros* were there to command them. Indy enacts the ritual taming and dominating of machines, emphasizing the crucial distinction between man and machine, the one soft and vulnerable but quick with courage and resource, the other hard and threatening but cold and stupid. The cars are at Indy so that men can be shown to be capable of dominating them, and the wonder and glory of the dominators is the point. Indy is thus a great Sunday-morning proclamation of the dignity of man, and no number of discarded chicken bones or trampled beer cans can change that. Like former Sunday-morning rituals, Indy insists that people are worth being saved.

Do some people, regardless, come to see drivers killed? Probably, but as irrelevant a tiny number of the sick as those who enjoy seeing a bullfight ruined by the bullfighter's being gored. If you see someone die at Indy, you are seeing that the machine has won, and that's opposed to everything the ritual is saying. A longtime student of the race, Sam Posey, seems to get the point when he addresses the pleasure spectators take in identifying themselves with the driver-tamer of the machine. When things go wrong and the crowd sees a driver killed, he says, "They are terribly shocked and extremely depressed. They wish they had not been there." What the spectator wants to see—needs to see?—is the machine crashing, disintegrating, wheels flying off, and in the end the man springing out and waving "I'm okay." "Because that's the moment of the greatest thrill," says Posey. "That's when man has conquered the machine. The machine has bitten back, but the man jumps out laughing and therefore the spectator's dream of immortality is confirmed." Immortality: hence, value, and value much longer lasting than the value conferred on congeries of steel, aluminum, and rubber by the mere age of the machine.

I was at Indy during a week when every day brought worse news of young people's limbs blown off in the south Atlantic, and perhaps the contrast between that spectacle and the Greatest Spectacle in Racing made Indy seem especially therapeutic. No one was hurt all the time I was there, the only injuries being sunburns and hangovers. I went there looking for something mean, but all I found was something innocent. The spectators were the innocents persuaded that the space shuttle promises great things, the same innocents who lost much of their money by putting it into United States Savings Bonds.

If Indy is in one sense about beer, in a deeper sense it's about milk. A full-page ad in the official program, inserted by "Your Local Indiana Dairy Farmer," announced that milk is "the Drink of Champions" and noted that "over the past six years milk has powered the 'Fastest Rookie.'" Indy, the program also said, is "An American Tradition." I'm glad it is.

QUESTIONS

1. In your own words, characterize the Indy as Fussell portrays it. For instance, according to the author, it's male and white. What else?

2. Fussell asks, "Is the Indy 500 a sporting event, or is it something else? And if something else, is it evil or benign?" Explain the conclusion that he comes to in answer to that question.

3. Fussell admits that the Indy 500 is not for everyone, yet he finishes the article by stating that the race is an "American tradition" and that he is glad it is. Does Fussell want to preserve the "ideal maleness" and "ideal whiteness" that seem central to the event? What evidence do you have for your answer?

4. In what ways are this essay and Wolfe's *The Right Stuff* similar in subject matter and attitude?

5. Explain why Fussell considers the Indy "a language event."

6. What point does Fussell establish with the following passage (p. 197)?

   When I arrived, an editorial in the only paper in town was raising a populist voice in a call for school prayer, and a front-page box offered "Today's Prayer," just above "Today's Chuckle."

7. What attitude does Fussell express in the following?

   Indianapolis seemed to me the sort of place where President Reagan expects no one to guffaw when he asserts that someone or something is "in my prayers." In fact, the president would love the place.

8. Why is camping out (p. 198) "that primeval American ceremony of innocence"?

9. According to Fussell, from which social classes do the Indy spectators come? How does he characterize these classes? In your opinion, is he fair in his judgments?

10. Explain the following (p. 202): "There is a powerful and, in my view, benign element of ritual purgation about Indy, and the things purged are precisely such impurities as vulgarity, greed, snobbery, and sadism."

11. What *analogies* does Fussell use to explain the Indy?

12. If you had the time and money, would you want to go to an Indy 500? Why or why not?

13. Do you agree or disagree with Fussell's values and judgments?

Elizabeth Kaye

Growing Up Stoned

Elizabeth Kaye published this article in California Magazine, *where an earlier article of hers on teenage alcoholics had appeared. Like* The Right Stuff, *by Tom Wolfe (pp. 157–63), Kaye's essay represents the "new journalism," which is very much like fiction in the richness of its interpretations, giving not just the "facts," but also the author's subjective viewpoint and the accoutrements of fiction such as scene and dialogue.*

If you want a sense of the new journalism, compare Kaye's essay with a newspaper report of a crime, and ask yourself how the two differ in technique and in what is included or excluded.

At the beginning of this selection, Kaye tells us that the events she relates assumed allegorical *significance. In allegory, events and characters symbolize general, abstract truths and values; we can read allegory both for the story itself and for its broader meaning. As you read this fascinating essay, keep in mind that the author views the events as allegorical.*

THE CIRCLE OF SILENCE

In the days that followed, the murder of Marcy Conrad assumed its allegorical significance and ultimately became that rare event of equal interest to newspaper reporters and to poets. It is at this stage in the narrative that the focus shifts and both the murderer and victim become oddly peripheral to its telling. Events center instead on nine young people, all of whom are self-described stoners.

In retrospect, it seemed inevitable that others be drawn into it. It was not all that likely that a sixteen year old could indefinitely keep to himself the amazing fact that he has just become a killer. So it was, on the day following the murder, that three teenage boys were told of it by Jacques Broussard himself. They did not believe him, so he took them up the hill and showed them what all the horror movies and all the televised violence they had ever seen could not have conceivably prepared them for, just as they had hardened them to it.

There was no requiem at the oak tree. There was only gazing. And there was this thought in the mind of one of the boys: "Jacques is in real trouble now."

The hours that followed were extraordinary only for their ordinariness, only for the way the three boys managed to proceed as if nothing had occurred that was in the least unusual. One fell asleep in his room listening to the radio and did not wake up for dinner. Another would later say he thought the body was a mannequin and didn't think anymore about it. The third was met at his door by his mother, who told him not to come in. She had discovered he had stolen her marijuana. This was something that had happened before; he had been warned that he would not be welcome in the house if it happened again.

The boy's name is John Hanson. He went out into the night and later met up with a friend named Robby Engle. He told Engle about the corpse, and when Engle wanted to see it, Hanson said he would show it to him the next day since it was now too dark to see anything. Instead they walked to Engle's house, went to his room to smoke some dope, and fell asleep. The night air was cool. In the hills where Marcy Conrad's body lay it was even cooler. Both boys slept dreamlessly.

All the next morning at Milpitas High, the huge bulk of Jacques Broussard traversed the grassy campus, telling students that he had killed Marcy and conveying that information with the reckless resolve of a man committing suicide because he is afraid of dying. Among the students, many of whom knew Marcy, though she had been enrolled at another school, the consensus was that Jacques couldn't have killed her, that he was simply "bragging" about it. Students at Milpitas High do not place too high a premium on the subtleties of words, which may be why the thought that bragging about a murder is kind of a contradiction in terms did not seem to occur to any of them.

Later in the day, Jacques, perhaps resenting that the most significant thing he had ever done had proven too significant to seem feasible, took a young girl and two boys up the hill so they might make witness to his claim, and having done so they, too, joined the circle of silence, increasing its number to six.

And now the passive silence was augmented by an action, when one of the boys aided Broussard in covering the corpse with a plastic bag and a scattering of leaves. Eventually he would be charged as an accessory after the fact, sentenced to three years at a county ranch for delinquent boys, and his existence would become a study in the curious way an entire life can be irrevocably altered in a single moment.

After lunch hour at the high school, John Hanson made a second sojourn to Old Marsh Road. He took Engle and two other friends, Mike Irvin and Dave Leffler, with him. Hanson was low on dope that day, so he bet Irvin a joint that the human form at the foot of the giant tree was an actual corpse. All right, he was told, but if it isn't, you give me your shoes and socks and walk home barefoot. It was on this note that they began to drive up the hill. They parked the car just as the oak tree became discernible. They scrambled down the incline. They stopped when they saw what they had come to see.

The four young men stared down at Marcy Conrad's earthly remains. Moments passed; nothing was said. The only sound was the insistent yammering of a few distant birds. Then Hanson wanted to collect on his bet. Leffler said, "This is no time to smoke," but they climbed up the incline and smoked anyway.

On the way down the hill Mike Irvin said he was going to the police. Hanson and Engle wanted to go back to class. "As far as we're concerned," Engle said, "the body doesn't exist." All Hanson could think of was that he had seen the corpse the day before and not reported it and that if he got involved at this point he might be arrested as an accessory. And he thought of how he had hated the time he once spent in juvenile hall after committing a burglary. And he thought of one of the terms of his parole, which was that he not associate with Mike Irvin, his alleged partner in that crime, the same young man who wanted to go to the police at this moment.

So Hanson and Engle went back to class, and Irvin and Leffler drove to the Milpitas police station. Leffler waited in the car. It was left to Irvin to walk alone up the sidewalk and to open the thick glass door and, once inside, tell of the incredible thing he had seen in the hills, so that 48 hours after the murder of Marcy Conrad, the silence of the young people who knew she had died would be forever broken.

While Mike Irvin was in the office of the Milpitas police, Sergeant Garry Meeker was driving on Interstate 680. Meeker is the homicide and assaults investigator for Santa Clara County, and at 42 has a slightly stocky frame and strong ruddy face that could get him a job in a beer commercial. He takes a cop's pride in being tough and when he is summoned to view a corpse tries to regard it not as a body but as a piece of evidence. He often apologizes for the coldness of that attitude but has never doubted that if he's going to do his job, that's the way to do it.

It was two-thirty in the afternoon when he got the radio dispatch about the body up on Old Marsh Road. Meeker knew the area well. For one thing, it was something of a dump ground for corpses. For another, it was a spot he drove to on occasion to watch hawks swoop and float above the expansive earth and sky. It was a good place to get away and think, even though you had to drive through Milpitas to get there. Milpitas is not exactly Meeker's favorite place, and he never drives through it without thinking of the song Pete Seeger sings about the little boxes on the hillside made of ticky-tacky.

When Meeker got to the oak tree, five of his colleagues were already there, men who were also paid to think of Marcy Conrad as a juvenile female, deceased. Before they left, two or three cars came up the hill and turned around when they drew near the police. Meeker did not give it much thought at the time; an hour or so would pass before he would learn of Broussard's boasts and the young people who had not reported the murder, and then he figured that the cars must have been those of young kids coming to see for themselves whether or not Broussard was lying.

The Milpitas police picked up Jacques Broussard later that evening. Shortly afterward Meeker questioned the young people who had gone up the hill to see Marcy's body. It had been an unsettling experience, though it was not the murder that was troubling. Meeker had seen a lot of murder victims, and murder itself was old as dirt. There was really nothing else you could say about it. But this case was different, and what made it so was the silence of the youngsters. "They were supposedly normal people," Meeker said. "But people who see dead bodies get shook. It bothers them. It still bothers me if you want to know the truth. But these kids . . . it didn't seem to bother them."

The silence of the children was the issue. The silence was the metaphor. And the only question of pertinence was, metaphor for what? "There's a moral breakdown somewhere," Meeker concluded. "That's what this thing represents. And it's not the kids' fault. The kids are a product of what we made them."

OUR TOWN

In the aftermath of these events I went to Milpitas, though not for the reason its citizens suspected, which was that my presence among them was indicative of a belief that Milpitas is an especially bad little town. That had certainly been the view of dozens of reporters from across the nation who trooped into the place, bringing with them notebooks, tape recorders, and a shared view that there was some special evil lurking in Milpitas, a belief that would inform stories about the murder and what followed it that found their way quite literally around the world, appearing in papers in Japan and on page one of the London *Times*. But these accounts missed the point, for they were mired in the assumption that Milpitas had contracted a disease the remainder of the nation was curiously immune to, when, quite to the contrary, what was of interest about the place was that there is nothing in the least atypical about Milpitas, not in a nation in which teenagers account for one-third of all the arrests made for violent crime.

It was precisely this resemblance to other places that made events there so awesome and so threatening. Now there was a possibility that the very name Milpitas, which had long stood as a pejorative meaning absolutely nowhere, would come to be a word that stood for Everyplace.

The buildings of the town are flat and mostly single level. Milpitas can be seen from a distance nonetheless because of three things that rise above it: two American flags that are never taken down, and a brick factory tower with the Ford emblem on it. It is located 9 miles north of San Jose and 36 miles south of Oakland.

The name Milpitas is an Indian word meaning "little cornfields," for originally this land was farmed and, in addition to plums, yielded corn and apricots. Early on it was inhabited by Castanoan Indians, who were routed out by Spanish settlers in the late 1820s. Following the gold rush, in the

1850s, American settlers moved in, presumably imbued with the pioneers' twin motivations of worldly greed and the spiritual longing to live in a place that could be likened to heaven on earth.

Milpitas was not incorporated until almost 100 years later, in 1954, when its population was 825 and the occasional building on Main Street included the Fat Boy restaurant and a pool hall that has since been torn down. The town's urban incarnation dates from 1956, when the Ford plant was opened, bringing enough people with it to establish Milpitas as one of those places chambers of commerce like to laud as "burgeoning." Its citizenry currently numbers 39,000, most of whom work in the nearby factories of Silicon Valley.

Of these citizens, 80 percent are white. The other 20 percent divides among blacks, Mexicans, Filipinos, and Vietnamese. But it was the psyche of the white community that was most relevant to the events that occurred in the wake of Marcy Conrad's murder, for those events involved white middle- and working-class youngsters whose behavior seemed the extreme manifestation of alienation and despair in the American white community. Ultimately I was to spend some time with one of the children directly involved in that incident, and with his mother, but in the beginning I wanted to understand its context.

The first place I went was the Reformation Lutheran Church, which is across the street from the K Mart and has a membership that is 96 percent white. Across from the church someone has written in chalk: STONERS DO IT BETTER AND LOOK BETTER DOING IT.

The Lutheran minister is a middle-aged man with a kindly face who is disturbed by a tendency he increasingly detects and describes as "an amorphous value system based primarily on 'if it feels good.'" One night a week, he teaches catechism class to seventh and eighth graders, and on this night four girls and three boys show up and are given a test. "This class is going to spend the year on the teaching of Jesus," he says, "so they realize they are part of the followers of the Way and that their lives are to be determined by the things He said."

The minister is sitting with his back to the class. I am facing him and watching the children take the test. They are cheating.

In the Serra Shopping Center, one of fourteen shopping centers in the town, are a weight control clinic, a rare coin store, an ice cream and sandwich parlor, and a gun shop. Here, too, is the only movie house in Milpitas, which contains two theaters. One of these theaters is showing *Halloween II* and *See No Evil*. As a rule, movies are changed every Friday, though horror movies are almost always held over for a second weekend. A sign on the cash register reads: CHILDREN UNDER FIVE NOT ADMITTED.

Inside the theater I sit between two ten-year-old girls. A man on the screen is saying, "Ladies are not very nice people. They're manipulative and deceitful." The woman he says this to is his wife. He then secures one end of a thick iron chain around her neck, the other end of which is attached to the bottom of an elevator. He pushes the button, and the elevator moves up and then down the elevator shaft while his wife dangles from it, hysterical and screaming. I ask one of the ten year olds what she thinks of all this. She says, "It's icky."

In the next movie a woman is killed by a man who sticks a knife in her back and then uses the knife as a lever to raise her off the floor. The fifteen-year-old boy behind me gives an appreciative grunt. "That dude is strong," he says.

One night I am sitting at the counter at Sambo's, across from the movie theater. Beside me a woman is talking with one of the waitresses. "How're things with Don?" the waitress asks her. "Not so hot," she says. "His wife just found out about us." At a nearby table, an eighteen-year-old girl and a boy the same age are eating pie a la mode and chocolate sodas.

Both May and Paul go to Milpitas High. Paul is white, May is Filipino, and, like Jacques Broussard, she is one of the few nonwhite stoners. She wears feather earrings and a marijuana leaf-shape necklace, presumably similar to the one Marcy Conrad used to wear. Her uncle gave it to her. Her aunt had one, and May admired it. May's aunt and uncle are 32 and 34.

May does not like school, does as little homework as possible, and has never read a book unless it was required for a class. "At least none that I can recall of," she says. "Oh, I know. A skin-care book. All about your skin."

May will go to junior college when she graduates from high school. In California such schools must accept anyone who applies to them. May thinks junior college will help her get a good job. "Like a cosmetologist or something."

Paul finishes his soda and orders another. He tells me that he and May "party" together frequently and that "party" means get high. "When I party," Paul says, "I like a lot of mirrors." "Inside joke," May says.

Paul does not like school any more than May does. "Kids aren't really good at school now," he says. "But they know more about the outside world. It's like, if you have a peer group that hangs out on street corners"— Paul pauses while he forms his thought—"well, then you learn a lot about hanging out on street corners."

The next night May is sitting in the same booth at Sambo's with another guy. He is wearing a Budweiser cap and wants to know what she'll do after high school. She says, "I think I'll probably be a singer."

There is one bookstore in Milpitas. Beneath certain books are cards that read: WE RECOMMEND. The bookstore recommends *No Love Lost* by

Helen Van Slyke. The card beneath *Scruples*, by Judith Krantz, reads: GREAT. The card beneath *The Other Side of Midnight* reads: ALL SIDNEY SHELDON'S BOOKS ARE TERRIFIC.

Debbi lives near the bookstore but is unaware of its existence. Debbi is in junior high school and is a B-plus student and an officer of her student body. She is a rocker but not a stoner, which means she likes rock music but doesn't smoke pot. She has blonde hair and a sweet smile. She is one of the young people who was cheating on the catechism test. Her favorite course is English because instead of having to read books the class reads plays written for television, which Debbi calls "teleplays."

The three-bedroom house where she, her older brother, and her parents live has a GOD BLESS OUR FAMILY plaque on the wall. On a recent afternoon her parents were having a cocktail party, and the kitchen table was covered with platters of sandwiches made of white and light wheat bread, filled with Underwood Deviled Ham and Cheez Whiz, and cut into quarters.

Debbi's father, a government worker, believes he and his wife have imparted good values to their children. "We teach them to be basically content and pleased with themselves," he says. "We haven't really emphasized material things and money. I think money will be a side issue for them."

"I want to be really rich," Debbi says. "My dad gave me a psychology test to see what career I'd be good in. It said maybe a talent scout or a judge. Someone who makes a lot of money. I would love to have a horse and take dancing lessons. I would love to have a big, big house and nice cars."

Aside from this list of potential acquisitions, the world at large is not of much interest to Debbi. Nor is it, she says, to her friends. Still, at school they are required to take current events classes. "We have movies about what's happening," Debbi says. "Like Leonid something, he wants to take over the United States or something like that. But I forget what happened in that last movie." Debbi gazes at one of the pink walls in her small room, which is decorated with pictures of John Travolta and many pictures of herself with her friends. "I guess the president's not doing such a good job," she says finally. "But I don't know. Like, I don't have any interest in what's going on with the president."

Debbi was interested, however, in the apparent lack of response on the part of those who saw Marcy Conrad's corpse. It had shocked her, and she was convinced that students at her junior high school would have responded differently. She went to all the classes at the school and asked, "Would you have been disturbed by seeing the corpse, or wouldn't you?" These were her findings: "50 percent would have been, 20 percent were half and half, and 30 percent could care less."

Mark is a stoner. He is small, thin, and sort of dirty looking, and wears a Van Halen cap and a Jack Daniel's T-shirt. "There's not much to being a stoner," he says. "All you gotta do is smoke pot." Mark is hanging out at Chuck E. Cheese Pizza, near the movie theater, about 100 yards from the site of the first Milpitas jail, where a Foster's Freeze now stands. A lot of kids hang out at Chuck E. Cheese because it has three rooms filled with computer games.

Mark is trying to score some pot. Despite this pressing concern he is willing to talk to me for a couple of minutes.

I ask Mark what he thinks of school. "I don't like nothin' about it."

I ask how he spends his time. "Doin' nothin'. Nothin' else to do." I ask if he is interested in anything. "Not too many things. Not too many."

I ask Mark how he spends his weekends. "Just go walkin' around. Visit friends."

"Do you ever feel the world may be more interesting than the way you see it?"

"Not really."

"Do you ever think there's anything wonderful in life?"

"Not really. Just bein' alive."

"But what's so great," I ask, "about being alive and doing nothing?"

"There's really not much great about it." Mark has dull, vacant eyes. There is no expression in his face. A long time seems to pass before he says, "It's better than being dead."

The other place in Milpitas that has a lot of computer games is Golfland, which achieved brief renown as the place where Jacques Broussard first announced that he had killed Marcy. Golfland is just a short way from Milpitas High, along a road littered with a collage of soggy trash: empty Granny Goose nacho bags, empty minidoughnut boxes, empty bottles of Magic Moments and Easy Night wines—the familiar debris of adolescent indulge.

There are 61 computer games and ten pinball machines at Golfland, and, naturally enough, the computer games all have space-age themes. The pinball machines, which once used to feature heroes of modern life such as Elton John and Hugh Hefner, have likewise joined the brave new world and are now based on *Star Trek*, Meteor, and Xenon, all appropriately reflective of the utter disinterest in the planet Earth on the part of most young people who play them.

The sounds in the arcade are as loud and discordant as they are endless, which seems only to add to the arcade's appeal, for, as anyone who watches teenagers play computer games must observe, they provide a whole new way for children to spend large portions of their time without burdening themselves by thinking about anything.

David Shawn is the father of two Milpitas teenagers. He is 37, a career navy man, and was stationed in I Corps in Viet Nam. He believed it was his duty to go there, though he has come to believe that the war was a tragic, misguided venture. Two years ago he and his wife divorced, after fourteen years of marriage, and now he visits his children on Sundays. Before returning to the navy base, he stops for a hamburger at the Milpitas Denny's, where pancakes are served with a parsley garnish.

"My daughter wears baggy pants and runs with the karate crowd," he says. "I keep telling myself she's going through a stage. My son recently told me he smokes dope and that he's sold it on occasion. I've talked to them. I've threatened them. I've tried to reward them. And after a few months of that the old man brought out the belt.

"My generation grew up in a rebellion of religion, ethics, morality. We just threw all that out the window, and now we're finding maybe we made a mistake. Everything is piling up on us. And it's horrifying. It's horrifying. And the thing is, there's no reversing it. We've got to live with what we produced."

I ask how he thinks his children will turn out. "It's scary as hell," he says, "but I can't predict that."

One day I go to Milpitas High, the school Broussard attended and that, after his arrest, had "been put on the map," a student told me. "The police map," another student said.

The place is a handsome arrangement of one-level buildings, each housing a different department, spread out around a large grassy campus. The one flaw in its structure is that there is no cafeteria, which leaves students free to wander off campus during lunch period. A lot of stoners go and get high in the park across the street. Other students spend lunchtime in the smoking area, as Broussard used to do, an outdoor place officially designated for smoking cigarettes, though from an occasional scent in the air it is obvious that students sometimes smoke other things.

I arrive at lunchtime, and some students in the smoking area are just hanging around. Some sit on the ground. Some sit on benches. Two boys and two girls sit side by side. Janet is fifteen, wears tight jeans, a T-shirt, and no makeup. Billy and Ralph are sixteen and wearing the outfit favored by Milpitas teenagers: jeans, a ski jacket, and tennis shoes. Sally is dressed like the boys and is very pretty, with long red nails and carefully applied mascara. She looks a lot older than she is.

"I told my Dad I smoke weed," Sally says. "He said he was glad I was being true with him but if he ever catches me he'll get me for it. But he can't control me. I mean, I'm fifteen."

"My mom knows I smoke," says Billy. "She smokes. So does my dad." I ask Billy if I could talk with his parents. "They don't like to talk about smoking much," he says, "when the subject goes around."

"My mom smokes," says Ralph. "My mom drinks," says Janet. All their parents are in their mid-thirties. "And she knows I smoke," Janet continues. "She says it's okay, just so I only do it in the house." I ask where they buy marijuana. "All kinds of places," says Janet. "Factories are real good places," says Billy. "That's where my dad gets it, and I get it from him."

At the end of the day I run into Sally and her friends at the bus stop. Like most students, they go right home after school. "You gotta go home. You gotta be real good all week. You change them Fs on your report card to Bs if you have to. Then on the weekend you can party." "School *is* partying," says another girl. "Yeah," says a sixteen-year-old boy, "it's partying and smoking and getting nookie." "Yeah," says another boy, "and without partying it'd be dead."

"See, that's why you act goody-goody at home," Sally explains, "so when you're out you can do what you want. Then you come home and act real goody-goody again. But sometimes you come home when you're high, and, oh, man, you gotta act as normal as you can. Just get upstairs! Like, 'Hi, Dad. Had a hard day! Gotta go to bed!'"

"Use that Visine," says Ralph.

"And you gotta munch first," says Janet.

"Hamburgers!" says Sally.

"Greasy french fries," says Janet.

"I love french fries," says Sally.

"With lots of catsup," says Ralph.

"And salt," says Sally.

They seem to have run out of things to say. I ask what they do after they eat. "Then you crash," says Sally.

Sally has lived with her father for two years. "My parents got divorced five years ago," she says. "Then I lived with my mother, but she couldn't handle it. So I moved in with my grandparents, but that didn't work, so I moved in with my dad. The divorce messed me up. Now I can handle it, but then I couldn't."

Joni, Anne, and Lynn have long hair and wear the standard uniform. All four girls work after school. This is not unusual in Milpitas, where the average working age last year was seventeen, in part because most adults work in other communities and also because many teenagers work to generate an income of their own. "Money's the only thing in our lives," says Lynn. "Money and guys," says Joni. "The only reason we come to school," says Anne, "is to get a good job when we get out of school. We all feel that way."

Teachers at Milpitas High are aware of this. "Kids today are point grubbers," says one of them. "They're interested in education only for what it will do for them in money-making terms." Another teacher says, "It's like that story about the professor who's talking about the glories of life, and a student puts up his hand and says, 'Excuse me, but is this going to be on the test?'"

A boy hovers at the edge of the smoking area. He is small, has a mustache and thick hair that looks like a wig. He wears a large silver cross on a chain around his neck. He has been watching me take notes, so even before I tell him, he has clearly figured out that I am a reporter. "I'm Robby Engle," he says.

Engle is the boy at whose house John Hanson spent the night after his mother kicked him out of his own home and who the following day went up the hill with Hanson, Irvin, and Leffler to view Marcy's corpse. "That's E-N-G-L-E," he says. A lot of reporters spelled his name wrong, as it happens.

"I found it," he says, "I found the body." He speaks in a soft, slightly oily, urgent voice, just a little louder than a whisper. "I heard about it. The guy told me."

I wonder what it was like to be told something like that. "No comment," says Robby Engle. "No personal opinions. I won't talk. My friend has a chance to make some money out of it. I'm getting a cut. I'd rather not say how much. And I ain't talkin'."

He talks anyway. "Mike Irvin. He's the one getting the money. Fifty thousand dollars. From *60 Minutes*." I say that sounds a little unlikely. "It's pretty true," says Robby Engle. "It's been in the *L.A. Times* and everything. Plus, they called Mike's brother, and he goes, 'How do I know this isn't a hoax?' and they go 'It isn't.'"

While I was in Milpitas the *World Almanac* released a study of 2,000 eighth graders who had named the 30 people they most admire. Their list was absolutely devoid of people in any field of human endeavor other than show business and athletics. The man most admired by these young people is Burt Reynolds, who is closely followed by Richard Pryor, Erik Estrada, Robin Williams, Kenny Rogers, Magic Johnson, Lou Ferrigno [sic], Steve Martin, George Burns, and Brooke Shields, a list that seems a little thin on compelling role models.

One day I ask literally dozens of Milpitas students if there is anyone they look up to. "You mean who smokes weed?" someone says. Another girl says, "I look up to myself, I guess." Two Filipino girls say they look up to their fathers. One girl says she looks up to Auntie Kathy. A lot of kids like Auntie Kathy because she lets them come over to her house and smoke weed and drink. Another says, "I look up to Matt Dillon. He's a teenager." A tall attractive girl named Peggy giggles. Peggy is a fine student and was recently part of the nine-person Milpitas High Academic Decathlon Team. "Ronald Reagan is my *idol*," she says, and everyone laughs.

The other students say they look up to nobody.

On Park Victoria Drive there is a 7-Eleven. A lot of kids hang out there and shoulder-tap beer. "Shoulder tapping's simple," I am told. "You just go up to someone, tap on their shoulder and say, "'Scuse me, mister, will you buy me some beer?' and give them the money." The boy telling me this is fourteen.

Down the street from the 7-Eleven, in the window of a T-shirt store called New York Fashions, a T-shirt bears the familiar legend DRUGS, SEX, AND ROCK AND ROLL. Up the street from the 7-Eleven, across Calaveras Boulevard, a shopping center houses Rainbow Records, where Louise works several days a week.

Louise is wearing a miniskirt and high boots and has lively blue eyes and brilliant red hair. She and her friends write songs that sound a little like the Go-Go's. One is called, "California's Just One Long Stretch of Beach."

Louise is one of the best students at Milpitas High and may go to Stanford when she graduates. She is mercurial, laughing one moment, serious a moment later. "I'm very upset about our current society," she says. "It's just awful. I'm so afraid Reagan is going to get us into a nuclear war." This apprehension is one I hear voiced by every single teenager I meet in Milpitas, regardless of how otherwise uninvolved they may be in the outside world. "We're not going to last much longer." She bursts into tears. "I'm sorry, but I get so upset. I think of all the things I'll miss. But I suppose it wouldn't really matter if I died tomorrow. I've had a nice life, I guess."

Jack Weinstein is one of the most popular teachers at Milpitas High. "We have 1,650 students here, and I teach 125 of them," he says. "A lot of my students are smart and caring—kids who could quote Joyce to you. So I'm optimistic. In the past I've been called a Pollyanna, but I choose optimism because it's the posture that allows me the most flexibility.

"I was in college from 1971 to 1974. There was a lot of cynicism then, and I found that I could not function with it. So I repudiate the cynicism I could feel if I allowed myself to now. A lot of my students are solid kids."

I say I believe him but that I also believe that maybe 50 percent of the students at Milpitas High are not solid at all. He says, "You're probably right." And when I say it seems to me that he forces himself to be more optimistic than is realistic, he says, "You're probably right."

One afternoon Weinstein assembles a group of his most intelligent and articulate students. The distinct difference between them and most of the others I have met is that they are capable of conceptual thought and are able to express ideas other students frequently cannot articulate but nonetheless have. "I mean," a girl says at one point, "we would rather watch TV or see a movie than read a book." Later, I ask how they view their lives. The girl who answers is seventeen. She says, "You're raised to work and raise a family and make money and then die. That's the American dream."

On Saturday night there is a party at Kenny's. He lives with his father, who is going out that night. I ask what Kenny's father does for a living. "Spot welder," says Kenny, "whatever the hell that is."

The house is small, with not much furniture in it, aside from two couches in the living room, both covered in plaid material. There is also a green shag rug and, beside the fireplace, a large plant that has five leaves on it. On the mantelpiece there are six trophies that Kenny's father won playing softball. One was awarded to the United Auto Workers team, another to the team from Tony's Pool Hall. Above the mantelpiece is a sign for Olympia beer, the kind often seen in bars, which lights up from the inside.

About 30 kids come to the party. One is Jerry Epperson, who saw Marcy Conrad's corpse, did not report it, and maintained he thought the body was a mannequin. He and his girlfriend are necking on the couch. They both wear tight jeans and have combs protruding from their back pockets. He is leaning over her so the most visible parts of him are his long blonde hair and the back of his T-shirt, which reads: IF YOU THINK SEX IS A PAIN IN THE ASS THEN YOU'RE DOING IT WRONG.

In the living room practically everyone sits on the floor, drinking beer and getting high and listening repeatedly to their favorite song, which is "Centerfold" by the J. Geils Band. Others stand in the kitchen, where there is a cheesecloth-covered table and, in the sink, leftover sweet and sour pork from a Chinese takeout place.

Jill shows up at the party. She is pretty and popular with a lot of kids, although some think she's really dumb because she likes soul music better than rock. Jill immediately starts eyeing Fred, who at 22 is the oldest person Kenny has invited. Fred works for the government. I ask in what capacity. "Right now I'm in maintenance," he says.

Craig walks around the room with his shirt off. He is a well-built sixteen year old with a slight facial resemblance to Mick Jagger. "Don't you think Craig's fine?" Jill's friend Tracy says to her.

"F——, yeah," says Jill. "Oh baby!" Fred walks by Jill and rubs her hair. "He's petting me like a little doggy," says Jill. "Arf, arf!" she says to Fred, then whispers to Tracy, "I'm gonna go for it." "It" is Fred.

"Listen," Tracy asks Jill, "you think I should go for that?" "That" is Craig.

"Hell, yeah," Jill says, eyeing Craig's naked chest.

"He's so fine, ain't he?" says Tracy. "Oh my God."

On the couch, three couples are locked in embrace, kissing with the peculiarly teenage intensity that resembles passion less than it does a kissing contest. One of the girls extracts herself from her boyfriend's grip and gets up to get them both a drink. She asks if anyone has a cigarette. I give her one. "My mother smokes that brand," she says, "because Barbara Mandrell does."

The kissing goes on awhile. Then one by one the couples separate like amoebas slowly splitting. The music is loud. No one says anything. They just sit there.

"Everybody's getting all bummed out," says Jill.

"No, they're just getting mellow," says Jack.

"Why?" says Tracy. "I want to get radical."

"Ken's dad doesn't want us to," says Jack. "That's why this is a two kegger and not a four kegger. It's better like this. You don't get cops. I don't want no cops now that I'm eighteen and you go to jail, not juvy."

"I'm so high I can't maintain," Jill announces from her perch on Fred's lap. She calls to Tracy, "Trace, I'm freaking out. How 'bout you?"

"Me too," says Tracy.

"I see two heads. I swear to God."

"Hey, Jill," says Tracy. "Don't go home. You guys stay at my house. We'll get drunk again." Tracy's mother does not mind when her daughter and her friends drink.

"F———, yeah," says Jill. "Scotch. That's what I want. I haven't had enough to drink yet."

Tracy stares drunkenly at Craig, who stands by the kitchen table talking to Steve, who is 20. Steve is wearing overalls and prides himself on hating communists. "I got the solution to the Russian problem," he is saying. "I know how to get everyone to fight them. When their tanks come over the hills, you set up a loudspeaker and say, 'Attention all stoners! They're coming to take your weed!'"

Later in the evening everyone is drunk and stoned. Jill can't maintain anymore. She thinks she is going to throw up, so she goes into the bathroom and locks the door. After she throws up she thinks she's going to pass out, so she goes into the bedroom and lies down. She does not know the boy who follows her there. They are kissing a moment later. Fred goes looking for Jill. When he sees her kissing another guy he gets upset, walks back into the living room, rolls himself a joint, and drinks a beer. Everyone is just kind of staring into space. The motion Fred makes while smoking the joint is the only movement in the room. It's just about midnight now.

"You probably think we're gangsters," Fred says to me. "Miniature gangsters or something like that. But we're just victims of society." Fred rolls another joint. He makes a gesture that includes all the stoned youngsters in the room. He says, "Everything is so hard-core these days, you just can't compare it to anything."

The United Pentecostal Church of California counts 4,000 to 5,000 young people among its members. Its congregation in San Jose has close to

100 young people, many of them from nearby Milpitas. "A lot of kids have turned to Christian," a sixteen-year-old boy says. "They used to fight each other and smoke weed. Now they sit up here and read the Bible to each other."

"In the Bible," says another boy, "Peter said, 'Repent and be baptized, all of you, in Jesus' name, and ye shall receive the gift of the Holy Ghost.'"

"That's Acts, chapter 2, verse 38," says a fifteen-year-old girl. "'For the promises unto you and your children to all those who are far off God shall call.'"

"All of us were far off," the first boy says. "Smoking dope. I worked in a liquor store and stole liquor and did everything a normal delinquent would do. I got the Holy Ghost in March and everything is different."

The service begins. "Oh, Lord," the minister intones, "there are hearts that are hard and cold and don't care anything about your church. How many people," he shouts to the congregation, "does it take to carry a coffin?" "Six," they shout back. "So it takes six live men," shouts the minister, "to carry a dead one. And you're dead if you haven't prayed. That's a good place to say amen!"

The sermon continues along these lines. The congregation's love of the Lord seems equaled only by their contempt for those who do not believe as they do. Later I mention that the United States was founded on the precept of freedom of worship. "Which would you rather believe," a boy asks, "your country or your God?"

"The Bible says the way of a trangressor is harsh," says a sixteen-year-old girl. "Like my mother was raised in the Pentecostal Church, but she turned her back on God and went in the way of the world. That's a sin. She'll get eternal damnation if she doesn't repent and change her wicked ways." To buttress this assertation, they continue to invoke the Scriptures. "It's not our idea," they keep saying. "It's in the Bible."

And that is the point: they have no ideas. They simply have committed the Scriptures to memory, and they continue to quote them with the fervor reserved for those who have received deliverance by accepting a belief system unquestionably and wholeheartedly as a substitute for their own.

Anyone who wonders what may ultimately befall a nation whose children are lost in trouble should remember that there comes a time when the living must find a way to live, and when that time comes they will seek their solution where it is available. That is the lesson of history, which also teaches that a society's problems are sometimes less lethal than its answers.

"Kids are in trouble today because they generally know less substantive information than any generation up to now," says Dr. Paul Wrubel, assistant principal in charge of educational services at Milpitas High.

"Things like knowing who the sixteenth president was, or what the Bill of Rights really says, or what was John Locke's influence on the Declaration of Independence. I'm talking about knowing some reason why you have the kind of values you have, I'm talking about some beliefs, about a foundation for one's set of values. And kids have a lack of direction because they don't *know* anything. They don't know *anything*. This lack of substantive underpinnings to their thinking means most kids are going through life in a closet.

"And they're dumb because of *us*, and us collectively, the collective human community. We're talking about a totally irresponsible public media, we're talking about teachers, we're talking about parents.

"How can you realistically expect adolescents to act like adults when so many adults act like adolescents? So many people sit back in righteous indignation over what happened here, but to me it's such hypocrisy on the part of the adult community. We're somehow outraged that kids could cover up a murder. Well, correct me if I'm wrong, but we had a president a few years ago who spent a hell of a lot of taxpayers' money covering up. So, yes, what they did was monstrous. But it can't come as a surprise. My God.

"And you and I can go quietly home and hold Milpitas as an example of the callousness of man and feel self-satisfied in our own communities where it didn't happen. By sheer luck, I might add."

From the time I arrived in Milpitas I was obsessed with the thought that if I could be magically dropped into the eighties from the early sixties, like some updated female version of Rip Van Winkle, I would be horrified by things I have come to accept in a relatively acquiescent manner. I thought this the morning I arrived, when the cab driver who took me from the airport apologized for being "all smoked out" for the day and having no dope to offer me. I thought it at the horror movie, and the party, and the church, and each time I talked to young people in Milpitas, whether they spoke of drugs, or sex, or doing nothing, or the state of the nation, or any of the other topics that ultimately express their own prevailing feeling that everything is futile.

Of course, I did not discuss this with them. Nor did I mention its corollaries: the feeling that we somehow did not become what we set out to be, and the sorrow that stems from realizing that it is possible to slowly acclimate oneself to situations and ideas that are fundamentally unacceptable, to gradually accustom oneself to that which one would have absolutely rebuffed at the outset.

But there was someone I discussed this with, and that was Dr. Wrubel, to whom I told this fable: it is said that if you take a frog and place it in boiling water, the frog will jump out and save its life. But if you take the same frog and place it in water that is heated degree by degree the frog will adapt to the ever rising temperature until it boils to death. However mechanistic this process may be, it applies equally to nations and to people. "And what you may be seeing here," Dr. Wrubel replied, "is the water slowly being heated."

QUESTIONS

1. In the first sentence of this selection, Elizabeth Kaye says, "In the days that followed, the murder of Marcy Conrad assumed its allegorical significance and ultimately became that rare event of equal interest to newspaper reporters and to poets." In what sense were the murder and its aftermath allegorical? Why would both reporters and poets be interested in the crime?

2. In her essay, to what extent is Elizabeth Kaye a reporter, and to what extent a novelist?

3. Explain "The silence of the children was the issue. The silence was the metaphor. And the only question of pertinence was, metaphor for what?"

4. Explain what Milpitas symbolizes.

5. The "Our Town" section is a series of largely self-contained vignettes. What does the author accomplish with this technique?

6. In your own words—referring to the essay for evidence—explain Kaye's characterization of American teenagers.

7. In what ways is Milpitas like some community with which you are familiar, perhaps your home town? In what ways different?

8. By adapting her word choice to her subject, Kaye gives a sense of authenticity to her writing; by demonstrating that she knows how her subjects talk, she shows her understanding of them. For instance, in writing about Mark, she says that he is a "stoner" and that he "is trying to score some pot." Find other examples of Kaye's using special vocabulary to achieve authenticity.

A Change of Pace

The great satirist Jonathan Swift (1667–1745), whose best known work is "A Modest Proposal," wrote a short impression of the morning in the 1700's. Clearly, his view of society, even in the morning, was not very hopeful.

You might want to imitate Swift, using his verse form and some of his ideas to write a poem about a typical morning that you experience. Notice that Swift writes in iambic pentameter rhyming couplets. That is to say, the lines consist of five iambs, and an iamb is an unstressed syllable followed by one that is stressed.

The WATCHful BAILiffs TAKE their SILent *STANDS*,
And SCHOOL-Boys LAG with SATCHels IN their *HANDS*.

In "Dover Beach," Matthew Arnold (1822–1888) expressed enormous pessimism about the prospects for society, concluding with the thought that only in human relations—in love—could there be hope for the individual.

Finally, in "Brass Spittoons" Langston Hughes (1902–1967) expresses the situation that many blacks have faced in our society.

You might like to "imitate" Hughes by choosing an object—a shovel, for instance—and writing a poem about what it stands for, using "Brass Spittoons" as a rough model.

JONATHAN SWIFT

A Description
Of The Morning

Now hardly here and there an Hackney-Coach[1]
Appearing, show'd the Ruddy Morns Approach.
Now *Betty* from her Masters Bed had flown,
And softly stole to discompose her own.
The Slipshod Prentice[2] from his Masters Door,   5
Had par'd the Dirt, and Sprinkled round the Floor.

---

[1] *hackney-coach*: a coach kept for hire, usually a four-wheeled vehicle drawn by two horses.
[2] *prentice*: apprentice; one legally bound to a master while learning a trade such as carpentry.

Now *Moll* had whirl'd her Mop with dext'rous Airs,
Prepar'd to Scrub the Entry and the Stairs.
The Youth with Broomy Stumps began to trace
The Kennel-Edge,[3] where Wheels had worn the Place.   10
The Smallcoal-Man[4] was heard with Cadence deep,
'Till drown'd in Shriller Notes of Chimney-Sweep,
Duns[5] at his Lordships Gate began to meet,
And Brickdust *Moll*[6] had Scream'd through half the Street.
The Turnkey[7] now his Flock returning sees,   15
Duly let out a Nights to Steal for Fees.[8]
The watchful Bailiffs take their silent Stands,
And School-Boys lag with Satchels in their Hands.

---

[3] *kennel*: gutter
[4] *small-coal man*: one who sells small pieces of coal
[5] *duns*: bill collectors
[6] *Brickdust Moll*: a seller of powdered brick dust, used for sharpening knives.
[7] *turnkey*: jail keeper
[8] In return for special privileges, such as extra food and drink, jailers regularly accepted bribes ("fees") from prisoners.

MATTHEW ARNOLD
Dover Beach

The sea is calm tonight,
The tide is full, the moon lies fair.
Upon the straits;—on the French coast the light
Gleams and is gone; the cliffs of England stand,
Glimmering and vast out in the tranquil bay.   5
Come to the window, sweet is the night-air!

Only, from the long line of spray
Where the sea meets the moon-blanched land,
Listen! you hear the grating roar
Of pebbles which the waves draw back, and fling,   10
At their return, up the high strand,
Begin, and cease, and then again begin,
With tremulous cadence slow, and bring
The eternal note of sadness in.

Sophocles[1] long ago   15
Heard it on the Aegean,[2] and it brought
Into his mind the turbid ebb and flow
Of human misery; we
Find also in the sound a thought,
Hearing it by this distant northern sea.   20

The Sea of Faith
Was once, too, at the full, and round earth's shore
Lay like the folds of a bright girdle furled.
But now I only hear
Its melancholy, long, withdrawing roar,   25
Retreating, to the breath
Of the night-wind, down the vast edges drear
And naked shingles of the world.

Ah, love, let us be true
To one another! for the world, which seems   30
To lie before us like a land of dreams,
So various, so beautiful, so new,

---

[1] *Sophocles*: fifth century B. C. Greek tragic dramatist whose best know work is *Oedipus Rex*.
[2] *Aegean*: the arm of the Mediterranean Sea that separates Asia Minor and Greece.

Hath really neither joy, nor love, nor light,
Nor certitude, nor peace, nor help for pain;
And we are here as on a darkling plain   35
Swept with confused alarms of struggle and flight,
Where ignorant armies clash by night.

Langston Hughes
Brass Spittoons

Clean the spittoons, boy.
    Detroit,
    Chicago,
    Atlantic City,
    Palm Beach.   5
Clean the spittoons.
The steam in hotel kitchens,
And the smoke in hotel lobbies,
And the slime in hotel spittoons:
Part of my life.   10
    Hey, boy!
    A nickel,
    A dime,
    A dollar,
Two dollars a day.   15
    Hey, boy!
    A nickel,
    A dime,
    A dollar,
    Two dollars   20
Buy shoes for the baby.
House rent to pay.
Gin on Saturday,
Church on Sunday.
    My God!   25
Babies and gin and church
And women and Sunday
All mixed with dimes and
Dollars and clean spittoons
And house rent to pay.   30
    Hey, boy!
A bright bowl of brass is beautiful to the Lord.
Bright polished brass like the cymbals
Of King David's dancers,
Like the wine cups of Solomon.   35
    Hey, boy!
A clean spittoon on the altar of the Lord.
A clean bright spittoon all newly-polished—
At least I can offer that.
    Com'mere, boy!   40

SUGGESTIONS FOR WRITING

1. Rules (laws) regarding the operation of a car govern how we drive: how fast we may go, when we must stop, the lanes that we can drive in, and so on. The rules of a game are different, for they not only regulate the game; they constitute it. Chess is the set of rules that both defines and is the game, as with bridge, football, or lacrosse. Driving a car in the wilds of Baja California where there are no traffic laws is nonetheless driving; moving chess pieces randomly around the board is *not* playing chess.

   Many of our daily activities are constituted by rules—of which we, paradoxically, may not be aware. For example, a conversation is defined by "rules" of taking turns at speaking and listening, so that the person who does not observe these rules is carrying on a monologue, not a conversation. There are many social rules we abide by. For example, if I request a meeting with a colleague, we must negotiate the meeting place, his office or mine; but if I request a meeting with the dean, the rule is that I must go to his office.

   Analyze and explain a set of rules that governs your behavior in some situation—as a member of a family or organization, as a student, as a "lover," as a guest of some sort, as a doctor's patient, as an employee or employer, and so forth. Be specific and concrete, giving examples wherever possible.

2. Explain why a group to which you currently belong is important to you. What is the exact nature of the group? Why does the group appeal to you? How does it fit your needs and personality?

3. Many of you have been thinking about a major in college and a career after graduation. In an essay, explain why you have chosen your career goal and why you expect to enjoy a lifetime in that career. You might want to interview successful practitioners of the career that you have chosen. In all likelihood you can find articles about your field in the library.

4. The needs of certain groups of people come to our attention daily: the homeless displaced by urban renewal, children starving to death in Africa, victims of mistreatment and abuse at the hands of others. You undoubtedly have strong feelings concerning such a group and might even know of an organization that has been effective in dealing with their plight. Write a paper in which you explain the problems of the group that concerns you.

5. Using John McPhee's essay on the Pine Barrens of New Jersey as a model, characterize some place or area with which you are familiar. Your subject might be your own backyard or neighborhood, or it could be a wider geographical location, such as a county or district. What

values are associated with the place you choose to discuss? How is it representative of our society as a whole?

6. Using Paul Fussell's essay as a model, characterize some American "institution," for example, a rodeo or circus, a concert of pop music, an amusement park.

On Language

Language is so much a part of us that stepping back to examine it objectively is difficult. (In fact, some peoples that have not yet become literate do not even have a word for "word," let alone "sentence." The idea that language is an object to be analyzed and discussed is completely foreign to them.) We know that language has changed over time and that it continues to change; every day we learn the lesson that the way people talk marks them socially and, to a certain extent, determines their economic futures; common sense tells us that certain strings of words are English and that others aren't ("Mary had a little lamb" versus "little a had Mary lamb"). However, many of the principles of language are not so obvious.

One of these is that language is in many respects a game like chess or baseball. The rules of these games not only regulate what can be done, but also make up the game. That is, chess *is* the rules by which it is played. Language results from the *rules* by which the game can be played.

The "markers" or "pieces" within the network of rules that make up a language are words, which enter the language from a variety of sources, some of them going back to the first written records of the languages that developed into modern English (modern English "house" from Old English *hus*), some having been borrowed from other languages ("kimono" from Japanese, "ranch" from Spanish *rancho*), some having been invented (Kodak, Lewis Carroll's "chortle").

In "The Play and the Players," Peter Farb presents a complex linguistic theory in a way that is both understandable and socially meaningful, while Michael Olmert makes the great *Oxford English Dictionary* appealing as a repository of hidden facts about English words and their histories.

These two essays are excellent examples of how specialized subjects can be presented in ways that interest general audiences.

PETER FARB

The Play and the Players

Peter Farb (1929–1980) studied comparative Mediterranean languages as an undergraduate at Vanderbilt University, collected folk ballads and speech styles in the South, and as a graduate student at Columbia University studied anthropological linguistics. He served as consultant to the Smithsonian Institution and as curator of American Indian Cultures at the Riverside Museum in New York City.

In this essay, Peter Farb alerts us to the rules of the game that we all must play: using language. He does so in a way that a person with no linguistic background can understand, but he manages not to "talk down" to his readers. The essay is a superb example of how an expert in a subject can explain complex ideas to intelligent nonexperts. You should note that one of Farb's techniques is explaining through concrete examples.

Immediately after the scene in which Hamlet hires players to act out his theory about the murder of his father, Guildenstern attempts to manipulate Hamlet with words. But Hamlet rebukes him:

> Why, look you now, how unworthy a thing you make of me! You would play upon me; you would seem to know my stops; you would pluck out the heart of my mystery; you would sound me from my lowest note to the top of my compass . . . 'Sblood, do you think I am easier to be played on than a pipe? Call me what instrument you will, though you can fret me, you cannot play upon me.

Hamlet fires off a barrage of puns and employs other forms of word play to make it perfectly clear that he has seen through Guildenstern's attempt to play upon him with words. In this passage, and throughout his works, Shakespeare demonstrates that he understood how people play a game with language to achieve certain ends: to cajole or convince, to display their own wisdom to an audience, to win honor or esteem. He often states his thoughts about language with poetic intensity and apt detail—yet they are nonscientific, merely common-sense observations, no matter how artfully they are expressed.

Beginning about 1960, and at an accelerating pace since then, a scientific approach has replaced common sense in interpreting the way human beings use their various tongues. Some linguists, intrigued by the social and psychological environments in which people manipulate language, have begun to look upon speech behavior as an interaction, a game in which both speakers and listeners unconsciously know the rules of their speech communities and the strategies they may employ. In the same way that every speaker has an intuitive grasp of the grammar of his native language, the speaker also intuitively understands the correct way to use his language in various situations. This approach—which has engaged a number of recently established fields of interest known by such names as sociolinguistics, psycholinguistics, the ethnography of speaking, the sociology of language, and so on—provides a new way to view language, one so new in fact that almost none of the material in this book has previously been available to the reader untutored in linguistics. Recent as this perspective is, it has already gone far toward revealing the remarkable ability of human beings to play upon one another with their speech. It is what this book is about.

The scene is a southern city in the United States; the speakers are a police officer and Dr. Alvin Poussaint, a black psychiatrist from Harvard. Exactly fifteen words are spoken in an interaction that has long been typical of black-white relations in the South:

> "What's your name, boy?" the policeman asked.
> "Doctor Poussaint. I'm a physician."
> "What's your first name, boy?"
> . . . As my heart palpitated, I muttered in profound humiliation: "Alvin."

To most readers, this exchange is simply an obvious insult offered by a policeman to a black person—but they might find it difficult to describe exactly the mechanism of the insult offered and the subtleties involved.

The explanation resides in the fact that the American speech community, like speech communities in every part of the world, employs a particular set of rules when one person addresses another, especially when that person is a stranger. The speaker may base his form of address on age (such as saying *mister* to an adult, *sonny* or *boy* to a child), on rank (*sir* to someone of equal or higher status, *buddy* or *Jack* to someone of lower status), or professional identity (*doctor* or *father* if it is apparent that the person being addressed is a physician or a priest). The American speech community considers certain other forms of address to be insulting—such as addressing someone on the basis of a visible physical deformity (*gimpy*), race (*nigger*), or national origin (*wop*)—although some speech communities in various parts of the world do not find these forms insulting at all. As a speaker who belongs to the American community, the policeman was expected to use one of the three acceptable selectors: age, rank, or professional identity. Instead he selected race by addressing Doctor Poussaint as *boy*—which, of course, is a southern white man's common form of address to blacks.

Doctor Poussaint replied by reminding the policeman that the formula for professional identity in address in the American speech community is *Doctor* + Last Name. But the policeman treated *Doctor* + Last Name as a failure to reply, as a nonmove in the game of interaction between them. He made no concession at all to the rule, and he failed even to compromise by addressing Doctor Poussaint as *Doc*. Instead he indicated a second time that he intended to play by different rules. He repeated his question, specified that he wanted the first name only, and also repeated the race-selected form of address, *boy*. Only because both the policeman and Doctor Poussaint shared a knowledge of the rules could the policeman's insult and condescension be clear. And Doctor Poussaint felt humiliated because he acquiesced in the policeman's game by agreeing to supply his first name. He collaborated in negating the American rules of address, one of the social cements that is supposed to hold our society together.

Even such a brief interaction illustrates how speakers play with the rules of their speech community. The word "play," however, should not be misinterpreted. Playing with words does not refer solely to entertainments like anagrams or crossword puzzles. Nor is "word play"–which usually refers to riddles, puns, jokes, wise sayings, verbal dueling, and so forth—a trivial pastime. In fact, "play" and "games" are two of life's very serious and complex activities, despite the apparent frivolousness of card games, board games like chess and checkers, sports like baseball. People are in the habit of saying *I'm in the advertising game* or *My game is life insurance*, but such statements do not mean that they look upon their livelihoods as "fun." Rather, the word *game* in these contexts—as well as in others, such as strategic *game plans* or fierce *war games*—refers to an interaction according to well-defined rules, in which something is at stake that both sides are attempting to win.

The language game shares certain characteristics with all other true games. First of all, it has a minimum of two players (the private, incomprehensible speech of a schizophrenic is no more a true game than is solitaire). Second, a person within speaking distance of any stranger can be forced by social pressure to commit himself to play, in the same way that a bystander in the vicinity of any other kind of game may be asked to play or to look on. Third, something must be at stake and both players must strive to win it—whether the reward be a tangible gain like convincing an employer of the need for a raise or an intangible one like the satisfaction of beating someone in an argument. Fourth, a player of any game has a particular style that distinguishes him as well as the ability to shift styles depending upon where the game is played and who the other players are. In the case of the language game, the style might be a preference for certain expressions or a folksy way of speaking, and the style shift might be the bringing into play of different verbal strategies when speaking in the home, at the office, on the street, or in a place of worship.

Variables such as these make the language game unpredictable. Just as a five of hearts may be used in a poker game to make a pair, a straight, a flush, or a full house, so the same word may turn up in many different contexts or environments. The speech situation gives the word meaning, just as the five of hearts has no meaning in itself until it is placed in the environment of other cards in the game. English offers the speaker *automobile, auto, car, buggy, jalopy, wheels,* and so forth as alternative ways to say virtually the same thing. The speaker's choice of one word in place of all other possibilities is often determined by an array of subtle social and psychological factors. He may, for example, say *buggy* if he wishes to deprecate his new Mercedes or *wheels* if he wants to show that he is with it in rapping with the younger generation.

Finally, the language game is similar to other games in that it is structured by rules, which speakers unconsciously learn simply by belonging to a particular speech community. Although players of the language game command a vast repertory of moves—that, is, a virtually infinite number of things that they could possibly say in many grammatical combinations—nevertheless the number of possibilities is severely limited by the situation in which the speaker finds himself. A speaker may no more switch to gibberish in mid-sentence than a poker player may apply the rules of chess in mid-game. The rules exist for the speaker and he must play by them—or else use the strategy of consciously breaking them.

The previous sentence illustrates one of these rules which make many utterances in English appear to result from male chauvinism. Note that I first said "for the speaker" and then "*he* must play." I expressed myself that way because the rules of English dictate that *he* (and not *she* or *it*) must be used to refer back to a sexually ambiguous antecedent. I might have rephrased the sentence to employ *one,* but that is awkward—or even referred to some hypothetical person, but that still would not have solved the problem because an English speaker also uses *he* as the pronoun to signify a hypothetical person. From a strictly linguistic point of view, of course, it would not matter if I used *it,* or *he* or *she,* or even some new word like *shis;* but centuries of social convention have made *he* the acceptable word here. Similarly, throughout this book English has forced me to use other apparently sexist words—*man, mankind,* and *human* (derived ultimately from the Latin *homo,* "man")—when I refer to both sexes of our species, words that appear to ignore the female sex.

An important thing about rules is that they do more than merely police behavior. The rules of chess do, of course, define who is playing fair—but they also actually create the game. This is borne out by the obvious fact that a chimpanzee might be taught to move chess pieces correctly, but the animal would not really be playing chess any more than a parrot faultlessly repeating an English sentence is really speaking English. The parrot, like the player of chess, must understand the interaction and the options available to express things in alternative ways. And a player, whether of the language game or of chess, must also be committed to the rule of winning—a commitment utterly lacking in the chimpanzee who moves pieces around a board. We show that we unconsciously sense this commitment by our similar disapproval of the player who throws a game and of the player who cheats. These players have broken quite different rules, but we condemn them equally because each has broken, in his own way, the rules of winning. Similarly, we close our ears to the speaker who utters a nonsensical statement as well as to the speaker who calculatingly lies—because both have violated their commitment to use language properly in the speech community.

When I talk about knowing the rules of a language, I do not mean that a speaker is able to state clearly the rules that govern his speech at any particular moment. In fact, unless he is a specialist in the subject of language, he most likely is unaware that he is following various complicated sets of rules which he has unconsciously acquired and internalized. Yet it is clear that he had incorporated such rules, for he recognizes speech that is "wrong"—that is, speech that departs from rules—even though he does not consciously know the rules themselves. Furthermore, when confronted with a need to say something he has never heard before, he unconsciously applies to the new case the same rules that he unconsciously applied to similar previous cases.

For an obvious example of the way speakers unconsciously internalize rules, take the way *linger* and *singer, anger* and *hanger,* and similar pairs of words are pronounced in many dialects of English. Careful listening reveals that speakers often pronounce the words in each pair in quite different ways. Both *linger* and *anger* are pronounced as if they were spelled with an additional hard *g* after the *ng* sound, somewhat like *ling-ger* and *ang-ger.* This additional *g* sound, though, is missing from both *singer* and *hanger.* If we examine many such pairs of words, a rule finally emerges: When a word is formed by the addition of *-er* to a verb, the *g* sound is not present; when the word is not derived from a verb, an additional *g* is pronounced. Probably no native speaker of a dialect of English that recognizes this rule consciously knows it unless he is a linguist or a teacher of speech. Yet, when the native speaker sees the word *bringer,* he automatically pronounces it without the additional *g* because it is derived from the verb *bring.* And when he sees the word *longer,* not derived from a verb, he introduces the hard *g* sound.

. . . .

Language is both a system of grammar and a human behavior which can be analyzed according to theories of interaction, play, and games. It also can be viewed as a shared system of rules and conventions mutually intelligible to all members of a particular community, yet a system which nevertheless offers freedom and creativity in its use. Further, only human beings—no matter the language they speak or the simplicity of their culture—have the capacity to play the language game because all human beings are born to speak.

QUESTIONS

1. According to Farb, "the language game shares certain characteristics with all other true games." What are those characteristics, according to Farb?

2. The term "game" implies competition and winners and losers, yet Farb does not discuss this aspect of the language game. In what respect is the game competitive? Who are the losers in the language game, and why do they lose? Who are the winners, and why do they win?

3. Explain why Farb characterizes language as "a game in which both speakers and listeners unconsciously know the rules of their speech communities and the strategies they may employ."

4. Explain the concept of "rules" in the language game. Are these more like the rules for chess or like those that govern drivers? Explain.

5. How much knowledge of language does Farb assume his readers already have? How do you know?

6. Farb is an expert writing for laypersons. What are some of the ways in which he makes his subject understandable to readers who have little background in the field of linguistics?

7. What analogies does Farb use to help explain his subject?

MICHAEL OLMERT
[*The Oxford English Dictionary*]

The Oxford English Dictionary is one of the great works of scholarship in language. Its main editor and compiler, James A. H. Murray, devoted 38 years to his task, from 1879 until his death in 1915.

Though one might not believe that so "dry" a subject as a dictionary would be good material for an article to be published in a general circulation magazine like the Smithsonian, *Olmert's assemblage of interesting facts and offbeat stories demonstrates that a person who has lively curiosity and writing ability can make unlikely subjects appealing for his readers.*

The strength of the essay is in its details, but it also gives a respectable introduction to the nature of the OED.

On January 18, 1884, at the Clarendon Press, Oxford, appeared the first volume of a work that has become the indispensable tool of writers and wordsmiths, scholars, critics and the congenitally curious for nearly a century. The work's title page proclaimed it as A *New English Dictionary on a Historical Basis,* of which this was to be the first part, covering "A" through "Ant-." Truly, this was a modest start for a project that appeared at the same time as *Huckleberry Finn,* Brahm's Symphony No. 3 and Rodin's *The Burghers of Calais.*

The "Historical Basis" noted in the title is what aroused so much interest in the work and what keeps it alive today. That means each word is not only described in all of its meanings, but is also presented in its original context, with a line or two for poetry, a phrase or sentence for prose. Further, the listing for each sense is continued, through time, from the first appearance of the word in the English language to the close of the 19th century.

For example, the dictionary begins with the first English use of the word "A," in its meaning as a letter of the alphabet. It appeared around the year 1340, in a poem called "The Pricke of Conscience" by the English mystical writer Richard Rolle of Hampole. The text presents the belief that you can determine a newborn's sex by the sound of its first cry:

> If it be man it says a!a!,
> That the first letter is of the name
> of our forme-fader Adam.
> And if the child a woman be,
> When it is born it says e!e!
> E. is the first letter and the head
> Of the name of Eve. . . .

Here is no bland start for the dictionary but a riveting one, reflecting an ancient custom obviously promulgated by nervous fathers outside the birthing chambers. The entry continues with other significant uses for the letter "A"—Chaucer in 1386, Samuel Butler in 1678, Tennyson in 1842.

Each such entry in the dictionary—known today as the *Oxford English Dictionary*, or more simply the *OED*—gives, in addition to the year and author, the quoted work's title and a line or page reference, so the interested reader can fill out the complete context of the passage (although it takes a rather full library).

Actually the need for such a dictionary had been seriously discussed since 1857, when the work was first sponsored by Britain's fledgling Philological Society and its early director, F. J. Furnival. Right off, Furnival recognized the importance of having reliable texts for the dictionary's quotations and so founded the Early English Text Society in 1864 (which is still publishing more than a century later) and the Chaucer Society in 1868 (now moved to America and the University of Oklahoma in Norman).

But a projected work of this scale needed a full-time editor and, by degrees, the job was turned over to a 42-year-old schoolmaster, James A. H. Murray, in 1879. Murray directed the project until his death in 1915. Still, the *OED* was not complete until April 1928, when the last section, "Wise" through "Wyzen," was printed (an easier task, "XYZ," had been completed in October 1921). A catchall supplementary volume for words missed the first time round appeared in 1933.

The continuity alone is impressive—54 years of production and 44 years of continuous publication. It is rumored that one of the Oxford University Press compositors set nothing else in type for the whole of his working life. Murray himself gave 38 years of labor to the dictionary and was knighted for his trouble—and achievement—in 1908.

One reason the *OED* is so valuable to us today is that so much unalloyed hard work went into its production. Under the direction of the indefatigable Murray and his editorial staff at Oxford, a corps of readers from around the globe undertook to read the entire body of English literature, as well as legal and historical documents, private papers, tracts and other ephemera. Five million such excerpts were collected on thin slips of paper that constantly engulfed the staff; about 1.8 million of those quotations appear in print. The result is a 12-volume work of 15,487 oversize pages, nearly half of them written by Murray.

And, oh, what you can do with those pages, where the outcome is so much more than just looking up words! Take as a test case my favorite passage in the films of W. C. Fields. There is a point in *The Bank Dick* where Fields' patience wears thin and he is forced to scowl at his great lummox of a prospective son-in-law (played to insouciant perfection by

Grady Sutton): "Don't be a mooncalf. Don't be a jobbernowl. You're not one of those, are you?" Mooncalf. Jobbernowl. We can hear in Fields' intonation that those are terms of derision, but what is their linguistic heritage? Who first capitalized on their load of derisive meaning?

Jobbernowl, the *OED* advises us, signifies "a blockish or stupid head; a ludicrous term for the head, usually connoting stupidity." Its first use was in 1599, when John Marston used it in his collection of verse satires called *The Scourge of Villanie*. There, he characterized the very type of a phony poet, the simpleton ballad maker whose "guts are in his brains, huge Jobbernoul,/Right gurnet's-head; the rest without all soul." Gurnet's-head, we learn elsewhere in the *OED*, is a term of contempt, used with reference to the disproportionate head of a certain fish, the gurnard (of the genus *Trigala*, typically with a large spiny head and armored cheeks).

And mooncalf? Shakespeare used it in Act II of *The Tempest* (1611) to mean a misshapen child, a monstrosity, as was his character Caliban: "How now, mooncalf!" Shakespeare's contemporary Ben Jonson used it in a play of 1620 to signify a born fool: "Moone Calves! what Monster is that . . .?/Monster? none at all; a very familiar thing, like our foole here on earth." The extension of the word's meaning to suggest one who gazes at the moon, a "mooning," absentminded person, was made by Thomas Middleton in his 1613 play, *No Wit like Woman's*: "One Weatherwise . . . Observes the full and change [of the moon], an arrant moon-calf."

The great advantage of the *OED*, of course, is that is shows, dramatically, how some words have been transformed from their former meanings. Pedagogue, for example, originally meant a type of Roman slave who accompanied patrician youths on their walks to school each day. The *OED* derives the word from Greek roots meaning "child-leader." Yet the original pedagogues were in no sense leaders or tutors, but merely escorts who drilled the children as they walked and who often sat in on the day's classes in a vain attempt to improve themselves. Such men became boring, moralistic, platitudinous dolts. In the *OED* entries, one can watch the early use of the English word connoting contempt and hostility (1735: "Cow'd by the ruling Rod, and haughty Frowns of Pedagogues severe"), watered down to the point in comparatively recent times when some educators would actually seek to have the practice of education called "pedagogy."

Conversely, the *OED* can make us feel good about the way we use our language. It is comforting to see that the word "decimate," a derivation from the Roman custom of executing every tenth man in a mutinous legion (and a current bête noire of popular commentators on "the decline of the English language," who claim we use the word too loosely) has in fact been very loosely applied since the beginning. In the 17th century,

Oliver Cromwell "decimated" the Royalist Cavaliers, the losers in the Great Civil War, merely by forcing them to give up a tenth of their estates to the victorious government. Decimate seems only to have been used "properly" when it was cited by historians referring to the original Roman custom. Only a "scowling pedagogue" would insist that it be strictly reserved for that historical purpose.

A particularly attractive word category is represented by the so-called onomatopoetic words, those that imitate actual sounds in nature. Such words had early appearances: mum (1377), buzz (1530), ding-dong (about 1560), to name a few. But my particular favorite is bow-wow, which was not used to stand for the dog itself—only its bark—until around 1800 in a poem by William Cowper, the rural poet. Cowper had earlier written a slight bit of verse that he entitled "On a Spaniel, Called Beau, Killing a Young Bird." He then responded with "Beau's Reply," which coined the new usage and still give us a smile in the bargain:

> Sir, when I flew to seize the bird
>> In spite of your command,
> A louder voice than yours I heard,
>> And harder to withstand . . .
>
> Well knowing him a sacred thing,
>> Not destined to my tooth,
> I only kiss'd his ruffled wing
>> And lick'd the feathers smooth.
>
> Let my obedience then excuse
>> My disobedience now,
> Nor some reproof yourself refuse
>> From your aggrieved bow-wow. . . .

In the face of this wealth of detail, the *OED*'s editors were constantly aware that their work would be closely followed by future dictionaries. And it has been. But to put off the truly sedulous apes, the editors, it is rumored, concocted a single spurious word, complete with false etymology and meanings. It may even lie somewhere in those 15,487 pages to this day, a lexicographic time bomb waiting to catch a slavish imitator (as indeed it may already have done). A scholar could spend a lifetime hunting down that word, with no more chance of success than a Boy Scout on a "snipe hunt."

QUESTIONS

1. Producing the 15,487 pages of the *OED* was a titanic labor. Why is the *OED* considered so important?

2. How does Olmert go about convincing his readers that the *OED* is valuable in part because it is enjoyable to use?

3. From Olmert's description, how does the *OED* differ from your present desk dictionary? How does your use of your dictionary differ from the way Olmert suggests the *OED* can be used?

4. Olmert says, "The great advantage of the *OED*, of course, is that it shows, dramatically, how some words have been transformed from their former meanings." Explain why this would be a great advantage. To what use might such knowledge be put?

5. What techniques does Olmert use to make his essay interesting to readers who normally would have no concern with lexicography (dictionary making)?

A Change of Pace

In "Creation Myth," the great American thinker Kenneth Burke (born 1897) boils his language theory down to its essence: "no" implies "yes" and vice versa. Once there is "no," "Thou shalt not" is inevitable: hence guilt. And "Finally, History fell a-dreaming and dreamed about Language—" for history *is* language.

And, in fact, Wallace Stevens (1879–1955) says much the same thing in "The Idea of Order at Key West." Language makes the world or at least our perception of it.

When Howard Neverov (born 1920) says that style is the "fire that eats what it illuminates," he is suggesting an important principle of language: the more you pay attention to style (for example, meter, rhyme, sentence structure), the harder it is to get the meaning—which is not to say that all writing should be completely transparent, for, after all, one of the great joys of poetry is the *way* in which poets convey their messages.

These poems are really philosophical statements about language, posing basic questions.

KENNETH BURKE
Creation Myth

In the beginning, there was universal Nothing.
Then Nothing said No to itself and thereby begat
        Something,
Which called itself Yes.

Then No and Yes, cohabitating, begat Maybe.
Next all three, in a ménage à trois, begat Guilt.   5

And Guilt was of many names:
Mine, Thine, Yours, Ours, His, Hers, Its, Theirs—
        and Order.

In time things so came to pass
That two of its names, Guilt and Order,
Honoring their great progenitors, Yes, No, and Maybe,   10
Begat History.

Finally, History fell a-dreaming
And dreamed about Language—

(And that brings us to critics-who-write-critiques-of-
        critical-criticism.)

WALLACE STEVENS
The Idea of Order at Key West

She sang beyond the genius of the sea.
The water never formed to mind or voice,
Like a body wholly body, fluttering
Its empty sleeves; and yet its mimic motion
Made constant cry, caused constantly a cry,   5
That was not ours although we understood,
Inhuman, of the veritable ocean.

The sea was not a mask. No more was she.
The song and water were not medleyed sound
Even if what she sang was what she heard,   10
Since what she sang was uttered word by word.
It may be that in all her phrases stirred
The grinding water and the gasping wind;
But it was she and not the sea we heard.

For she was the maker of the song she sang.   15
The ever-hooded, tragic-gestured sea
Was merely a place by which she walked to sing.
Whose spirit is this? we said, because we knew
It was the spirit that we sought and knew
That we should ask this often as she sang.   20

If it was only the dark voice of the sea
That rose, or even colored by many waves;
If it was only the outer voice of sky
And cloud, of the sunken coral water-walled,
However clear, it would have been deep air,   25
The heaving speech of air, a summer sound
Repeated in a summer without end
And sound alone. But it was more than that,
More even than her voice, and ours, among
The meaningless plungings of water and the wind,   30
Theatrical distances, bronze shadows heaped
On high horizons, mountainous atmospheres
Of sky and sea.
                    It was her voice that made
The sky acutest at its vanishing.
She measured to the hour its solitude.   35

She was the single artificer of the world
In which she sang. And when she sang, the sea,
Whatever self it had, became the self
That was her song, for she was the maker. Then we,
As we beheld her striding there alone,   40
Knew that there never was a world for her
Except the one she sang and, singing, made.

Ramon Fernandez,[1] tell me, if you know,
Why, when the singing ended and we turned
Toward the town, tell why the glassy lights,   45
The lights in the fishing boats at anchor there,
As the night descended, tilting in the air,
Mastered the night and portioned out the sea,
Fixing emblazoned zones and fiery poles,
Arranging, deepening, enchanting night.   50

Oh! Blessed rage for order, pale Ramon,
The maker's rage to order words of the sea,
Words of the fragrant portals, dimly-starred,
And of ourselves and of our origins,
In ghostlier demarcations, keener sounds.   55

---

[1]Stevens tells us that "Ramon Fernandez was not intended to be anyone at all." The poet simply combined
two popular Spanish names to create a fictitious character.

HOWARD NEMEROV
Style

Flaubert[1] wanted to write a novel
About nothing. It was to have no subject
And be sustained upon style alone,
Like the Holy Ghost cruising above
The abyss, or like the little animals   5
In Disney cartoons who stand upon a branch
That breaks, but do not fall
Till they look down. He never wrote that novel,
And neither did he write another one
That would have been called *La Spirale*,   10
Wherein the hero's fortunes were to rise
In dreams, while his waking life disintegrated.

Even so, for these two books
We thank the master. They can be read,
With difficulty, in the spirit alone,   15
Are not so wholly lost as certain works

Burned at Alexandria, flooded at Florence,[2]
And are never taught at universities.
Moreover, they are not deformed by style,
That fire that eats what it illuminates.   20

SUGGESTIONS FOR WRITING

1. Do a study of the language of menus. What kind of language do various restaurants employ on their menus? What sort of appeal do you think this language is attempting to make? Write a report of your findings.

   If you gather enough data, this writing assignment will be relatively easy, for you can set up categories: fast-food restaurants, "family" restaurants, "sophisticated" restaurants, and so on. Your essay will, to a certain extent, be based on comparison and contrast.

---

[1] Gustave Flaubert (1821–1880), French novelist, author of *Madame Bovary*.
[2] The library at Alexandria, Egypt, which contained more than 400,000 volumes, was burned in 651 A.D. The Laurentian library in Florence has several times been flooded by the river Arnó.

2. For several days, observe the language used by a preschool child. Make extensive notes, or tape-record the child's language use. Do you find any distinctive features in this language? What about vocabulary? Does the child use strange "grammar"—for instance, adding -ed to form the past of *all* verbs, not only walk*ed* and talk*ed*, but also runn*ed*, fli*ed*, and sitt*ed*? Write a short essay describing your observations.

3. Write a report on current teenage or college slang. What are the fashionable terms, and what do they mean? When are they used? Classify your terms according to meaningful categories: for example, terms having to do with food, school, home, and so forth. On the other hand, you could organize your material on the basis of the terms themselves, rather than according to their reference—for example, terms that contain rhymes, terms based on animals, and so on.

4. Write a report on the technical jargon of some field. For example, the field of computers is full of specialized terms that "outsiders" don't know: RAM, ROM, bus, boot, byte, bit, microprocessor, and so on. Organize your discussion according to some logical system.

5. In some source (perhaps a newspaper or magazine), find an example of what you consider to be the unfair use of language, and do an analysis of that piece of writing. What is the nature of the unfairness? Why is the language used unfair? What sorts of substitutions would you recommend in order to do away with the unfairness?

On Mind

In a book called *Philosophical Explanations*, Robert Nozick poses this question: How can you prove that what you think is you is *not* merely a brain floating in nourishing broth and controlled by someone else, who sends the necessary impulses to make you believe that you have a body and that it does certain things in given places? This is simply a modern way of asking a very old question: Is there any way of proving that we are anything but mind?

Regardless of how that basic question is answered, another one puzzles both scientists and philosophers: can one define the mind as the electrochemical reactions in the brain, or is it something beyond mere biology?

The two selections that follow discuss the nature of the mind. In the first one, Isaac Asimov explores reasoning and concludes that the ability to reason does not adequately explain the difference between human and animal behavior. In the second essay, D. N. Perkins discusses creativity.

ISAAC ASIMOV

Our Mind

Isaac Asimov (1920–   ) was born in the USSR but was brought to the United States in 1923. He has published many scientific works, particularly in the field of chemistry, but he is also a prolific writer of science fiction and essays and books on science for lay readers. (Among his works are The Chemicals of Life, The Living River, The Wellsprings of Life, Life and Energy, The Human Body: Its Structure and Operation.) *Some of Asimov's fans suspect that he knows everything, and certainly he has written on a great many subjects, including Shakespeare and the Bible.*

In his essay, Asimov reasons about reasoning. Step by step he builds toward his conclusion—that "Reason alone does not explain the gulf that lies between man and other animals." This selection is a superb example of logical organization and clear prose.

LEARNING

Men have in the past sometimes tended to set up a firm and impassable wall separating the behavior of man from that of all creatures other than man and to label the wall "reason." Creatures other than man we might suppose to be governed by instincts or by an inborn nature that dictates their actions at every step; actions which it is beyond their power to modify. In a sense, from such a viewpoint animals are looked upon as machines: very complicated machines, to be sure, but machines nevertheless.

Man, on the other hand, according to this view, has certain attributes that no animal has. He has the capacity to remember the past in great detail, to foresee possible futures in almost equal detail, to imagine alternatives, to weigh and judge in the light of past experience, to deduce consequences from premises—and to base his behavior upon all of this by an act of "free will." In short, he has the power of reason; he has a "rational mind," something, it is often felt, not possessed by any other creature.

That man also has instincts, blind drives, and, at least in part, an "animal nature" is not to be denied; but the rational mind is supposed to be capable of rising above this. It can even rise superior to the reflex. If prepared, and if there is a purpose to be served, a man can grasp a hot object and maintain the grasp although his skin is destroyed. He can steel himself not to blink if a blow is aimed at his eyes. He can even defy the "first law of nature," that of self-preservation, and by a rational act of free will give his life for a friend, for a loved one, or even for an abstract principle.

Yet this division between "rational man" and "irrational brute" cannot really be maintained. It is true that as one progresses along the scale of living species in the direction of simpler and less intricately organized nervous systems innate behavior plays a more and more important role, and the ability to modify behavior in the light of experience (to "learn," that is) becomes less important. The difference in this respect between man and other animals is not that between "yes" and "no" but, rather, that between "more" and "less."

Even some of the more complicated protozoa—one-celled animals—do not invariably make the same response to the same stimulus as would be expected of them if they were literally machines. If presented with an irritant in the water, such a creature might respond in a succession of different ways, 1, 2, 3, 4, each representing a more strenuous counter. If the irritant is repeated at short intervals, the creature may eventually counter with response 3 at once, without bothering to try 1 or 2. It is as though it has given up on halfway measures and, in a sense, has learned something.

And, of course, more complex animals are easily conditioned in such a fashion as to modify their behavior, sometimes in quite complex manner. Nor must we think of conditioning only as something imposed by a human experimenter; natural circumstances will do as well or better. The common rat was alive and flourishing long before man was civilized. It lived then without reference to man and his habitations. It has learned, however, to live in man's cities and is now as much a city creature as we are; better in some ways. It has changed its "nature" and learned as we have; and not with our help, either, but in the face of our most determined opposition.

To be sure, a lion cannot be conditioned, either by man or by circumstance, to eat grass, since it lacks the teeth required to chew grass properly or the digestive system to handle it even if it could be chewed and swallowed. It is, one could say, the lion's inborn nature to eat zebras and not grass, and this cannot be changed. This sort of physical limitation enslaves man too. A man cannot "by taking thought" add one cubit unto his stature, as is stated in the Sermon on the Mount. Nor can he by mere thought decide to become transparent or to flap his arms and fly. For all his rational mind, man is as much bound by his physical limitations as the amoeba is.

If we confine ourselves to behavior within physical limitations, does the fact that behavior can be modified even in simple animals wipe out the distinction between man and other creatures? Of course it doesn't. That the gap (only man can compose a symphony or deduce a mathematical theorem) exists is obvious and incontrovertible. The only question is whether the gap exists by virtue of man's exclusive possession of reason. What, after all, is reason?

In the case of simple organisms, it seems quite clear that learning, in the sense of the development of behavior not innate, takes place through conditioning, and we are not trapped into believing that anything resembling human reason is involved. A bee has no innate tendency to go to blue paper rather than gray paper, but it can be "taught" to do so by conditioning it to associate blue paper, but not gray paper, with food. The new behavior is as mechanical as the old. The machine is modified by a machinelike method and remains a machine.

In mammals, with more complicated nervous systems than are possessed by any creatures outside the class and with, therefore, the possibility of more complex behavior patterns, matters are less clear-cut. We begin to recognize in mammalian behavior a similarity to our own and consequently may begin to be tempted to explain their activity by using the word "reason." A cat trapped in an enclosure from which an exit is possible if a lever is pushed or a latch is pulled will behave in a manner so like our own under similar circumstances as to convince us that it is disturbed at being enclosed and anxious to be free. And when it finds the exit we may say to ourselves, "Ah, she's figured it out."

But has she? Or is this an overestimate of the cat's mental powers? Apparently the latter. A trapped cat makes random moves, pushing, jumping, squeezing, climbing, pacing restlessly. Eventually, it will make some move that will by accident offer a way out. The next time it is enclosed, it will go through the same random movements until it once again pushes the lever or raises the latch; the second time, after a shorter interval of trial and error, the cat will do the same. After enough trials, it will push the lever and escape at once. The simplest explanation is that it has conditioned itself to push the lever by associating this, finally, with escape. However, there would seem to be also a matter of memory involved; a dim process that makes the cat discover the exit more quickly (usually) the second time than the first.

Animal memory has been tested by experiment. Suppose a raccoon is conditioned to enter a lighted door as opposed to an unlighted one. (It will get food in the first and an electric shock in the second.) Suppose it is barred from entering either door while the light is on and is allowed to make its choice only after the light has gone out. It will nevertheless go to the door which *had been* lit, clearly remembering. If the interval between the light's going out and the liberation of the raccoon is too great, the raccoon sometimes does not go to the correct door. It has forgotten. A raccoon can be relied on to remember for up to half a minute; this interval increases as animals with a more complex nervous system are chosen. A monkey may sometimes remember for a full day.

The English biologist Lloyd Morgan took the attitidue that in interpreting animal behavior as little "humanity" as possible should be read into the observations. In the case of the cat in the enclosure, it is possible to avoid humanity just about altogether. A combination of trial-and-error with dim memory and conditioning is quite sufficient to explain the cat's behavior. The question is: How far up the scale of developing nervous system can we safely exclude humanity altogether? Memory improves steadily and surely that has an effect. We might conclude that it does not have too great an effect, since even in man, who certainly has the best memory in the realm of life, trial-and-error behavior is common. The average man, having dropped a dime in the bedroom, is very likey to look for it randomly, now here now there. If he then finds it, that is no tribute to his reasoning powers. Nevertheless, let us not downgrade memory. After all, a man does not have to indulge in trial-and-error only, even in searching for a dropped dime. He may look only in the direction in which he heard the dime strike. He may look in his trousers-cuff because he knows that in many cases a falling dime may end up there and defy all attempts to locate it on the floor. Similarly, if he were in a closed place, he might try to excape by beating and kicking on the walls randomly; but he would also know what a door would look like and would concentrate his efforts on that.

A man can, in short, simplify the problem somewhat by a process of reasoning based on memory. In doing so, however (to jump back to the other side of the fence again), it is possible that the trial-and-error method does not truly disappear but is etherealized—is transformed from action to thought. A man doesn't actually look everywhere for a lost dime. He visualizes the position and looks everywhere mentally, eliminating what his experience tells him are unlikely places (the ceiling, a distant room) and shortening the actual search by that much.

In moving up the scale of animal behavior we find that modification of behavior goes through the stages of (1) conditioning by circumstance, (2) conditioning after trial-and-error, and (3) conditioning after an etherealized trial-and-error. If it seems fair to call this third and most elaborate form of modification "reason" it next remains to decide whether only human beings make use of it.

Monkeys and apes remember accurately enough and long enough to make it seem unlikely that they can be thoroughly bereft of such etherealization, and indeed they are not. A German psychologist, Wolfgang Köhler, trapped in German southwestern Africa during World War I, spent his time working with chimpanzees and showed that they could solve problems by flashes of intuition, so to speak. Faced with a banana suspended in air and two sticks, each of which was too short to reach the banana and knock it down, a chimpanzee, after a period of trial-and-error that established the shortness of the sticks, would do nothing for a while, then would hook the sticks together to form a combined tool that would reach the banana. Chimpanzees will pile boxes or use a short stick to get a large stick, and do so in such a fashion as to make it impossible to deny that reason is at work.

At what point in the animal kingdom, trial-and-error is etherealized to a sufficient degree to warrant the accolade of "reason" is uncertain. Not enough animals have been tested thoroughly. If the chimpanzee can reason, what about the other apes? What about the elephant or the dolphin?

One thing is sure. Reason alone does not explain the gulf that lies between man and other animals.

QUESTIONS

1. According to Asimov, is the division between "rational man" and "irrational brute" a yes-no situation? Explain.
2. Explain why Asimov concludes that cats do not reason.
3. Explain "etherealized trial-and-error."
4. If you do not know what the term "behaviorism" means, look it up in an encyclopedia. How does Asimov's view of learning and reasoning differ from that of the behaviorists?

5. In the book from which this selection was taken, Asimov goes on to argue that speech (language) "fixes the gulf between man and non-man." But can animals "talk"? In the last two decades or so, experimenters have taught chimpanzees and apes various kinds of signing systems—for instance, the sort of sign language used by the deaf. You might be interested in reading some of the many articles on these "talking" apes. (You'll find the listings, of course, in *The Reader's Guide to Periodical Literature*.) Once you have read the articles, give a full explanation of your opinion about the question "Can animals talk?"

6. In your opinion, what are the most important techniques that Asimov uses to make his essay convincing?

D. N. PERKINS
The Shape of Making

In The Mind's Best Work, *of which "The Shape of Making" is a chapter, D. N. Perkins argues that creativity arises from making the best use of mental abilities that everyone possesses, not from some kind of special endowment that only a few have inherited.*

Perkins' essay is about the nature of creative work in general, but it can be applied directly to writing. For example, the creative person plans ahead, gets new ideas from the details of the work as it progresses, revises frequently, and is interested in the work itself, not just in the final product.

The author is a member of Project Zero, a group at Harvard who are studying creativity. He is a senior research associate and lecturer in the Graduate School of Education at Harvard.

How can we understand the creative process? Not just by understanding creativity, because creativity and creating are different matters. Whereas creativity involves traits that make a person creative, creating calls upon many resources not intrinsically creative. The ordinary acts of recognition that warn us away from open manholes can, in the right situation, warn us away from pitfalls in problem solving. Acts of recollection that tell us where we last used the pen with the blue cap can, in different circumstances, give us a word of poetry. Such resources are not what makes people creative, but they are what does much of the work of creating. And some of the factors that do make people creative do not do the work. Understanding that creative ideas are there to be found sets the stage for the inquirer to seek them but does nothing to find them.

To understand creating is to understand how the originality and other qualities get into the product. . . .

So now let us look at the shape of making, the logic behind the complexity of our mental resources and their best work. Viewed in the right way, the logic turns out to be simple, the shape an elegant one. For a preview, creating can be seen as a process of gradually selecting from an infinity of possibilities an actual product. The properties the maker selects for include originality and other kinds of quality. The process of selecting is roundabout, because of limits on human mental resources and the human will to push those resources to their limits. Creating goes beyond what a person can simply, straightforwardly and effortlessly do because of four fundamental moves.

Planning: instead of producing the work directly, the maker produces a plan for it, or for part of it. Abstracting: instead of always working from general intent to particulars, the maker abstracts new ideas from the particulars of the work in progress or other sources. Undoing: instead of getting everything right the first time, the maker undoes and redoes parts of the work. Making means into ends: instead of always being preoccupied with the final product, the maker often addresses a means as an end in itself.

The guiding force that puts these moves together and gets something worthwhile out of them is purpose—the purpose to create or to resolve problems that require invention. This is the teleological view of creating I've emphasized before. Such a view does not mean that the maker knows at some level just what the product will be before making it. On the contrary, products are vaguely and tentatively conceived, groped for, caught at, discovered in process. However, all this is part of the teleology, part of the purposeful striving toward something that will become increasingly specified and realized. Now for the details.

CREATING AS SELECTING

Imagine a monkey sitting at a typewriter and poking randomly at the keys. Eventually, just by chance, this monkey will type *Hamlet*. The only further requirement for a literature factory is a sharp critic, someone to select *Hamlet* or something just as good when it comes along. The catch, of course, lies in how long the critic would have to wait and the monkey would have to type. In fact, if the monkey had been typing since the beginning of the universe, at, say, one character per second, the chances of his having hammered out a single line anywhere in *Hamlet* are essentially zero. This simply reflects the vast number of typographical sequences the keys can make and the very small number of those, comparatively speaking, that are even meaningful, much less a part of Shakespeare's play.

The trouble with the monkey, of course, is that he doesn't have enough teleology. Beyond operating at the typewriter, his actions are not channeled by conditions that favor a literary product. The literary critic who does the selecting does most of the work of creating, while the monkey merely supplies very raw material. This artificial division of labor demonstrates how a creative product can be thought of as a very special selection out of a chaos of possibilities. A mathematical proof, like *Hamlet*, is a selection from the possible sequences of typographical characters. A painting is a selection from the possible distributions of pigment on a surface. A physical invention, the pilot model of a new engine, say, is one choice from among the infinity of ways that matter could be arranged into an object.

Admittedly, this is an odd way of describing what a creator does. After all, neither poet nor mathematician would be likely to think about that infinity of character sequences they could be said to select from. Even if we took a narrower field of possibilities, ones the mathematician might come close to considering, the mathematician certainly would not arrive at a proof by lining up candidate proofs and choosing. Likewise, Shakespeare did not choose *Hamlet* from a large set of alternative dramas, like pulling out the best chocolate from an assortment. Makers build up their products rather than pick them out.

One could say, of course, that makers select *by* building up. This is what I will say. But why should the notion of selecting be stretched so far? The answer is that, pursued persistently and artfully enough, the notion begins to pay off in an integrated picture of the way creating works.

One immediate gain is a sense of perspective on how special something like a good play or a good proof is. By seeing a play or proof as a choice from a chaos of possibilities, we remind ourselves how remote these products of human genius are from the mere anarchy of particles and radiation in a vacuum, where it all began. We remind ourselves that behind the building up the mathematician and poet do on a particular occasion lies a whole saga of preselection—years of training and striving for the individual maker, centuries of history in the discipline, millennia of general cultural evolution, billions of years of biological evolution, and, behind all that, the physical evolution of the universe. Taking this long perspective, we discover that the maker's work on the occasion is the least part of the work. The language, the symbols, the concepts, the cultural and personal style, even the particular task, already have been chosen. The maker of the moment merely puts the last block on the top of a pyramid of selection, a tower of ever higher and narrower ranges of possibility which finally finds its summit in a particular creative product.

There's a seeming pardox here. Is it right that so much credit go to preselecting, that is, to the selection already implicit or explicit when the maker begins? After all, we are talking about creating, where the maker ought not be hampered by conditions that limit the work of hacks. Challenging the preselection ought to be business as usual for the genuinely creative person.

That is true, but not entirely true. Yes, along the way to proving one theorem, a mathematician may depart from his or her preselection by discovering another theorem more worthy of attention, or perhaps some insight will lead the mathematician to challenging the axioms that so far have guided the work. However, the fact remains that no one can depart from much of the preselection at once and expect to make progress. The mathematician cannot discard the familiar axioms *and* conventional notation *and* traditions about which sorts of questions are worthwhile *and* the usual format for proofs. People in such a position would find themselves trapped by the self-made vacuum around them as much as if they had been frozen in blocks of ice. Such radical assaults on preselection simply don't occur. What we perceive as revolutionary innovation in a field always challenges only a little of the preselection. Only because we focus on the contrast rather than the continuity does innovation seem so much of a departure.

THE NECESSITY OF COMPLEXITY

Imagine that a time machine takes us to the far future, where we could walk among our descendants, evolved a million years beyond us. We are glad to find that this difficult business of creating is easier for them. They talk in perfect poetry, or with the rigor of mathematical proofs, quite as easily as you or I remember our phone numbers. Whatever strains our brains they carry off handily. Too bad things aren't that easy for us. But why aren't they? Some tasks, like holding an informal conversation, we accomplish readily. Why does creating get so complicated? The simple answer is that we do what we have to.

Planning is one of those necessities. When we cannot simply write out our poems or proofs—as we usually can't—we rely on an inbetween step, a plan. Then we try to go the rest of the way. Here I want to use the word plan very broadly. Included are painstakingly developed overt plans like outlines or blueprints. But also included is the sudden conjecture that points toward the complex experiment, the fleeting intention that guides a poet to the next word, the spontaneous idea for an image almost as quickly added to the painting in progress.

All these plans share an interesting feature: they all amount to selection. None selects its outcome yet—the article, the building, the experiment, the word, the image. Even less does any select the completed work—the article as finally revised, the building with paint job, the experiment plus results, the finished poem or painting. But each one delimits the range of the final result, narrowing down its possibilities. In short, a plan is a kind of divide-and-conquer strategy applied to the work of selection. Part of the selecting is done by making the plan, and then we try to continue with the guidance of the plan. Probably we need another plan, a little more specific than the first, that divides up the work of selection even more finely. So we proceed, from the first initial idea vaguely grasped to the final product, narrowing down and narrowing down through a chain of plans for the whole work and its parts.

Abstracting is another necessity. It would be most convenient if we could just narrow down until the work of selection were done. But expecting matters to be so neat ignores the way that selections already made can have unanticipated impact. One equation requires another, one part of a mechanical invention demands that another keep out of its way, one stroke of pigment calls for a neighbor with contrasting color. Besides requirements, opportunities appear. Such requirements and opportunities are plans we didn't think of, until the work in progress or some other situation suggested them. So plans arise not only by narrowing down more general plans, but by abstracting from particulars. In fact, often whole works grow from the first particulars, the plans arising mostly by abstraction. The initial words or brushstrokes suggest a plan for the next, and so on. Part way through, the maker abstracts a unifying conception, a plan which guides the completion of the work. This may happen quite spontaneously. Again, as with plans, I'm using "abstract" in a very broad sense to include simple and complex, spontaneous and deliberate, low-level and high-level abstractions.

Thus we narrow down toward the final work, translating plans into more particular plans or parts of the work and getting more plans by abstracting from the work of prior plans. Eventually we get there—but only if we're lucky. Allowance has to be made for mistakes, and that introduces the third necessity—undoing. We have to be able to undo parts of the work and redo them, as well as undo plans that don't turn out well in favor of new plans. Such acts are the opposite of selection. They open up possibilities again, after we thought things were suitably narrowed down. At first thought, this seems only a regrettable consequence of human error, but not so. Often there simply is no reasonable way to detect difficulties other than by working through a situation until they appear. For instance, a mathematician may set out to prove a theorem that in fact is false. Only by attempting to prove it, failing, and searching long and hard for a counterexample can the mathematician finally discover that the mission is futile. Trial and error permeates human thought not just because people are less alert than they might be but because a trial selection often is the only way to give an error a chance to show itself.

Planning, abstracting, and undoing might seem to provide enough flexibility to get anything done. But there is one more complication. In narrowing down, the maker often encounters problems that really don't concern the final product. Rather, a means is needed to overcome an obstacle along the way. So the maker addresses the means as an end. For instance, a writer may have to check the meaning of a word in a dictionary, a physicist may seek the exact formula in a book, a painter may mix pigments to get the right hue. Such minor detours get more interesting as they snowball. A writer may decide a dictionary has to be written, a physicist try to derive a formula that would illuminate many problems besides the one at hand, a painter invent the pigment that will have the flexibility and durability desired. Sometimes means may become entirely detached from their ends. Sculpture has its origins in religion and ritual, but has become a worthwhile pursuit in its own right. Mechanics began with the practical tools of moving things about—the wheel, the lever, the ramp—but has become a sophisticated theoretical discipline concerned with the motions of planets and atoms.

Planning, abstracting, undoing, and making means into ends are the basic organizing tactics of selection. They are what we compose our actions out of when we cannot narrow down to the result we want in a single fluent motion of mind and hand. In a superficial sense, the four all are symptoms of the limited maker, roundabout ways of doing what the maker would rather accomplish directly. But this disgruntled view is also misguided. It makes more sense to see the roundabout tactics as symptoms of a refusal to settle for what can be done directly. If creating were limited by the convenience of the process, convenience and not excellence would shape its nature. But the teleological view implies that the excellence of the results dominates. Inevitably and appropriately, behavior is pushed toward its complicated limits to achieve such results.

Remember our descendants a million years hence rattling off poems and proofs? Serious creating for these far evolved beings would not be those easy poems or proofs. It would be something grander and more subtle, something we could not even imagine, something that makes them plan, abstract, undo, and convert means into ends—something that keeps them as roundabout as we are.

SELECTING FOR WHAT?

With all this talk of teleology, I've said little about what makes a course of selection creative. The question is crucial, since the general description of creating as selecting could apply just as well to uncreative activities, such as building an ordinary bird feeder or a picket fence. For example, room appears for undoing as a measurement taken earlier turns out to be wrong or a nail bends over in the driving.

What, then, makes creating special among other courses of selection? Simply, what is selected *for*. The maker selects for creative products, meaning original high-quality products. Sometimes originality gets into the creative product by being selected for directly. Over the last decades visual artists have doggedly sought innovative modes of expression. On the other hand, sometimes originality is not selected for—it's a spinoff from other characteristics closer to the maker's intent. As I said several chapters ago, originality often results when people put "unreasonable" demands on themselves and their products, demands that have to be met with originality if at all.

However, let's not overestimate the significance of originality. Although necessary by definition for a creative product, originality is one of the most dispensable ingredients for a simply worthwhile product. Cleverly building a bird feeder out of a tin can or a milk carton may be original, but hardly very worthwhile if the tin can sizzles the birds under the summer sun or the milk carton turns soggy with the first rain. The mundane bird feeder that works outdoes the original one that doesn't. The same can be said for paintings, poems, mathematical proofs, and theories in physics. In essence, originality only counts for much when the product achieves quality in other respects.

Furthermore, although any field will have its individual standards, those "other respects" include some general ones for substantial creative achievement. Products judged highly creative by the society will have such features as scope and significance. Qualities of these sorts, in addition to originality, imbue creative products with value. Anything but easy to achieve, such qualities impose demands that push the person seeking them toward originality even if the person does not strive for originality as such.

THE IMPORTANCE OF ACCIDENT

James Austin's encounters with chance remind us that accident has much to do with invention. There is no guaranteed pattern to the problems or the opportunities noticed in a developing work. Where the maker's eye falls, at what particular time, with what particular mind set, may send the maker in a wholly unforeseen direction. At first thought, this much room for accident seems at odds with the teleological view of creating. But not so. First of all, accident realizes purpose. The plans that constrain the work to come don't usually determine it. Rarely is a range of alternatives well enough defined or small enough for the maker to survey them all and somehow choose the best. Satisficing[1] rather than maximizing is the mainstay of creating. This means that most narrowings down are acts of commitment rather than wholly calculation. They are taken not because the conditions allow only that selection, but because the only effective way to proceed is to settle for something. Such chance selections are a way of fulfilling the plan and carrying forward the teleological process.

Also, accident arises out of purpose or, as Pasteur said, chance favors the prepared mind. The accidents that carry the work along because the maker encounters an opportunity in the work so far, or in another experience altogether, are not mere accidents. The opportunity would never have been recognized had the maker not been saturated in the subject. So accidents are reflections of the teleology of the maker and the making.

Finally, accident is assimilated to purpose. A naive view would have accidents directing the maker down utterly new paths to utterly unexpected consequences. This can happen, of course. However, much more often accident deflects, enlarges, sharpens, simplifies, rather than radically altering. This is not because accidents always fit the context, but because the maker makes them fit.

---

[1]*Satisfice* "means that people strive until they achieve so much and then stop. They work to satisfy standards of adequacy," not to achieve absolute perfection.

HOW SELECTION HAPPENS

Chapter after chapter, we've looked at psychological processes that do the work of creating. We pondered everything from a poet capturing the essence of her poem in a few seconds of insight to Darwin remaking his problem over many months. Doing the work of creating means doing the work of selection that leads toward a creative result. In fact, most of the processes relate to the basic selective moves I've outlined—planning, abstracting, undoing, and making means into ends. To understand how this is so is to understand how the splendidly varied resources of the human creature fit together, a mosaic of potentials out of which creative products appear. A few cases in point:

Noticing opportunities. Noticing meant detecting relevant features spontaneously, without having to seek them out. Noticing an opportunity is a kind of abstracting, which adds to the plan another direction to be pursued.

Noticing flaws. This too is abstracting, but the result also is an undoing. The flaw must be removed and something better put in its place.

Directed remembering. This named the everyday ability to retrieve information from memory satisfying several constraints at once. Directed remembering often realizes plans, providing the poet with the word to match the need, for instance.

Reasons in judgment. Critical reactions to a work underway typically come with reasons. The reasons amount to plans for what to undo, better plans than if the maker experienced a vague pro or con reaction without reasons.

Looking harder. This meant evaluating a work with certain features or categories in mind. The maker has taken the trouble to think out what to look for, and so that "what" is an example of a means that temporarily was made into an end. The usual result of looking harder is new plans abstracted from the work.

Setting a work aside. This does no selecting by itself, of course. However, it contributes to later selecting because the flaws and opportunities of the work may prove more obvious when the maker returns to it.

Long searches. These reflected the maker's high standards, not chronic fluency. In its simplest form, a long search amounts to a chain of selections and undoings, as the maker generates and rejects option after option until one proves sound.

Hill climbing. The entire process of selecting can be seen as hill climbing. A narrowing down is a step up the hill, an undoing a step backwards in hopes of finding a way up an even higher hill nearby.

Schemata. The schemata that stand behind a creative effort are part of the maker's preselection. Some schemata appear in a final product with little variation, as with a word in a writer's vocabulary, a standard scientific formula, or a stock image a painter uses again and again. These provide a repertoire of specific selections; the maker need only plug them in. Many schemata have a much more open structure, one filled out in context-dependent ways. The schemata of English syntax are an example. These schemata provide a repertoire of plans that, often quite quickly and unconsciously, guide the making of more specific selections. Schemata do the work of selecting by having it already done. Schemata substitute preselected units and structures for selecting the maker otherwise would have to do at the time.

Problem finding. This is an example of a means temporarily becoming an end. What problem to address is itself taken as the problem.

THE SUM OF IT ALL

Let me attempt a terse summary of the points in this chapter and the general view of creating they offer. Those who like to think from generalizations to particulars might well have started here and read the book backwards. Here is what creating seems to be all about.

- Creating is the process by which a maker achieves a creative product.
- The process is a teleological one, governed by plans restricting the final product that exist at the outset and plans that arise during the course of creating. The plans lead to the marshalling of the maker's resources to realize them. Accident occurs abundantly, but realizes, arises out of, or is assimilated to purpose.
- Understanding how creating occurs requires understanding how originality and other qualities that make a product creative get put into the developing product.
- To explain this, it is useful to view creating as a process of selecting from among the many possible outcomes—arrays of words, formulas, pigments on a surface, and so on.
- The preselections of the makers's personal history and the histories of the culture, the species, and the physical world channel what the maker will attempt and equip the maker with skills and schemata to attempt it.
- Although the simplest sort of making would involve a direct jump from preselection to a final selection, makers, by adopting roundabout tactics of selection, can drastically increase the reach of their efforts. The basic roundabout tactics are planning, abstracting, undoing, and making means into ends.

- The resources of mind discussed throughout the book—noticing, realizing, directed remembering, problem finding, schemata, hill climbing, critical reasons, and many more—each contribute to creating by helping to accomplish selection.

- These same resources of selection explain masterly and more ordinary creating. The master will notice more, remember more, exercise better critical judgment, and so on, but the processes involved are the same in kind.

- The creative quality gets put into a work primarily through skillful selecting for it or selecting for features that favor it. The selective processes involved need not be intrinsically creative, but simply responsive to what is being selected for.

- Originality may occur through direct selecting for it or as a spinoff, a side effect of selecting for other qualities.

- In any case, selecting for originality cannot dominate the selective process, because originality adds little worth to the product unless the product achieves competence in other respects.

- Creativity involves a style, values, beliefs, and tactics that specifically favor selecting for a creative product.

- Creating at an extraordinary level depends on superior learned and inborn abilities to do the relevant work of selection. However, for the most part, these abilities shouldn't be considered a part of the maker's creativity, since other persons equally able may function quite uncreatively. Creativity concerns what we do with our abilities. Any normal person can be creative in terms of whatever abilities he or she has or can acquire.

- To understand creating as a process of selection, to understand how various psychological phenomena contribute to the work of selection, and to understand that products become creative because that is what is selected for, to understand all this is to grasp, in one way at least, the nature of creating.

AN IMAGE OF WIDE SCOPE

Of course, a neat description is not everything. It may not provide something the mind can grasp as a whole and entertain as essence. In fact, we know a way to do that job better—Howard Gruber's notion of images of wide scope. Such images, remember, included Darwin's tree of nature which guided him to his theory of natural selection, and, I suggested, the glow of radium with its puzzle of energy resident in matter. Then why not an image of wide scope for creating?

The image comes with a story. A couple of years ago, my oldest son accosted me with news from kindergarten as I came home from the office. He had learned something about apples and wanted to demonstrate. Out of the drawer came a knife, one of those he was not supposed to handle, and out of the refrigerator a McIntosh. "Dad," he said, "Let me show you what's inside an apple."

"I know what's inside an apple," I said, riding for a fall.

"C'mon, just let me show you."

"Listen, I've cut open lots of apples. Why ruin an apple just to show me something I already know?"

"Just take a look."

Ungracefully, I gave in. He cut the apple in half, the wrong way. We all know the right way to cut apples. One starts at the stem and slices through to the dimple on the bottom. However, he turned the apple on its side, sliced the apple in half perpendicular to the stem, and displayed the result. "See Dad. There's a star inside."

Sure enough, there was. In cross-section, the core of the apple made a distinct five-pointed star. How many apples I had eaten in my life, cutting them in half the right way and never suspecting the hidden pattern waiting for me until one day my child brought news of it home, out to convert the infidel—and he did.

I have not tried to find out, but I'm sure this star-shaped structure is common knowledge in botany, where no doubt there are students of apples who do dissections of McIntosh and Golden Delicious, nibbling the scraps as they go. Whoever first sliced an apple the wrong way may well have had a good reason to do so, curiosity being one good reason. Or it might have been one of those fruitful—I choose the word carefully—mistakes all of us make sometimes. Whatever the case, no matter. The occasion and process of discovery are not my concerns at this moment. What struck me then and still impresses me now is that this hidden pattern fascinated enough to make its way around. The knowledge of it traveled from unknown origins to my son's kindergarten class and so to me and you. Its very survival and vigor as something to know about vouches for the engagement we find in discovery.

So, if you want to know what creating is for, in part it's for an apple—sliced the wrong way.

QUESTIONS

1. Explain what Perkins means by "Planning, abstracting, undoing, and making means into ends are the basic organizing tactics of selection."

2. In your own words, answer this question: "What, then, makes creating special among other courses of selection?"

3. Explain Perkins' conclusion: "So, if you want to know what creating is for, in part it's for an apple—sliced the wrong way."

4. How much of Perkins' discussion can you turn into advice about writing? For example, you might say: "Writers should learn to 'satisfice' because if they look always for absolute perfection, they will never complete any task."

5. Was Asimov's or Perkins' essay easier for you to understand? Explain why. (What about subject matter? Which of the two developed his points more fully and explicitly? Which used examples more effectively?)

6. Explain how the following definitions either support or contradict Perkins' concept of creativity.
   a. ". . . creativity is the ability to see (or to be aware) and to respond." —Erich Fromm
   b. ". . . the emergence in action of a novel relational product, growing out of the uniqueness of the individual on the one hand, and the materials, events, people, or circumstances of his life on the other." —Carl R. Rogers
   c. ". . . the occurrence of a composition which is both new and valuable." —Henry A. Murray
   d. "An act that produces *effective surprise*—this I shall take as the hallmark of a creative enterprise." —Jerome Bruner
   e. ". . . the ability to abstract without giving up concreteness and the ability to be concrete without giving up abstractness." —Abraham Maslow

A Change of Pace

Issac Asimov and D. N. Perkins wrote objectively, scientifically, about mind. In the following poems, Louis Untermeyer (1885–1977), Emily Dickinson (1830–1886), Ted Hughes (1930–   ), and Andrew Marvell (1621–1678) give their metaphorical visions of mind as a dark chamber, a machine running within a groove, a universe in itself, a fox, and an endless ocean.

An interesting topic for discussion—or writing—is the views of mind presented by the two essayists and four poets in this section. Just what are those views? In what ways are they similar? In what ways different?

LOUIS UNTERMEYER

The Dark Chamber

The brain forgets, but the blood will remember.
    There, when the play of sense is over,
The last, low spark in the darkest chamber
    Will hold all there is of love and lover.

The war of words, the life-long quarrel   5
    Of self against self will resolve into nothing;
Less than the chain of berry-red coral
    Crying against the dead black of her clothing.

What has the brain that it hopes to last longer?
    The blood will take from forgotten violence,   10
The groping, the break of her voice in anger.
    There will be left only color and silence.

These will remain, these will go searching
    Your veins for life when the flame of life smolders:
The night that you two saw the mountains marching   15
    Up against dawn with the stars on their shoulders—

The jetting poplars' arrested fountains
    As you drew her under them, easing her pain—
The notes, not the words, of a half-finished sentence—
    The music, the silence. . . . These will remain.   20

EMILY DICKINSON
The Brain, Within Its Groove

The Brain, within its Groove
Runs evenly—and true—
But let a Splinter swerve—
'Twere easier for You—

To put a Current back—   5
When Floods have slit the Hills—
And scooped a Turnpike for Themselves—
And trodden out the Mills—

TED HUGHES

The Thought-Fox

I imagine this midnight moment's forest:
Something else is alive
Beside the clock's loneliness
And this blank page where my fingers move.

Through the window I see no star: 5
Something more near
Though deeper within darkness
Is entering the loneliness:

Cold, delicately as the dark snow,
A fox's nose touches twig, leaf: 10
Two eyes serve a movement, that now
And again now, and now, and now

Sets neat prints into the snow
Between trees, and warily a lame
Shadow lags by stump and in hollow   15
Of a body that is bold to come

Across clearings, an eye,
A widening deepening greenness,
Brilliantly, concentratedly,
Coming about its own business   20

Till, with a sudden sharp hot stink of fox
It enters the dark hole of the head.
The window is starless still; the clock ticks,
The page is printed.

ANDREW MARVELL
The Garden

How vainly men themselves amaze
To win the palm, the oak, or bays;
And their uncessant labors see
Crowned from some single herb or tree,
Whose short and narrow verged shade
Does prudently their toils upbraid;
While all flow'rs and all trees do close
To weave the garlands of repose.

Fair Quiet, have I found thee here,
And Innocence, thy sister dear?
Mistaken long, I sought you then
In busy companies of men.
Your sacred plants, if here below,
Only among the plants will grow.
Society is all but rude
To this delicious solitude.

No white nor red was ever seen
So am'rous as this lovely green.
Fond lovers, cruel as their flame,
Cut in these trees their mistress' name.   20
Little, alas, they know, or heed,
How far these beauties hers exceed!
Fair trees! where s'eer[1] your barks I wound,
No name shall but your own be found.

When we have run our passions' heat,
Love hither makes his best retreat.
The gods, that mortal beauty chase,
Still in a tree did end their race.
Apollo hunted Daphne so,
Only that she might laurel grow.   30
And Pan did after Syrinx speed
Not as a nymph, but for a reed.[2]

---

[1] *where s'eer*: where soever (wherever)
[2] Daphne, a river god's daughter, was pursued by Apollo and changed into a laurel tree to escape him. To escape from Pan, Syrinx turned into a reed, from which Pan made his pipes.

What wond'rous life in this I lead!
Ripe apples drop about my head;
The luscious clusters of the vine
Upon my mouth do crush their wine;
The nectarine, and curious³ peach
Into my hands themselves do reach;
Stumbling on melons, as I pass,
Ensnared with flow'rs, I fall on grass.   40

Meanwhile the mind from pleasure less
Withdraws into its happiness:
The mind, that Ocean where each kind
Does straight its own resemblance find;
Yet it creates, transcending these,
Far other worlds, and other seas;
Annihilating all that's made
To a green thought in a green shade.

Here at the fountain's sliding foot,
Or at some fruit-tree's mossy root,   50
Casting the body's vest aside,
My soul into the boughs does glide;
There, like a bird, it sits and sings,
Then whets,⁴ and combs its silver wings,
And, till prepared for longer flight,
Waves in its plumes the various light.

Such was that happy Garden-state
While man there walked without a mate;
After a place so pure, and sweet,
What other help could yet be meet!
But 'twas beyond a mortal's share
To wander solitary there:
Two Paradises 'twere in one
To live in Paradise alone.

How well the skilful Gard'ner drew
Of flow'rs and herbs this dial new;⁵
Where, from above, the milder sun
Does from a fragrant Zodiac run;

³*curious*: exquisite
⁴*whets*: preens
⁵Gardeners designed clocks, with flowers that opened at different times.

And, as it works, th' industrious bee
Computes its time as well as we.
How could such sweet and wholesome hours
Be reckoned, but with herbs and flow'rs!

SUGGESTIONS FOR WRITING

1. Recently you have learned something complex and important: a skill (such as driving a golf ball), a concept (such as the nature of Platonism), a body of information (for example, the history of the United Nations). In an essay, explain in as much detail as possible how you went about the learning, your reason for wanting to learn, and the difficulties that you had in the process.

   Before you begin to write, do some thinking and question-asking. For example, did time and place have any influence on the learning process or the reasons for learning? Did anyone assist you? How? Did you need any special "equipment," such as books, tools, a computer? Did the learning process have stages or parts? What were they? What was your purpose? Did you have several purposes? Were any of them hidden agendas?

2. Think of an argument you've had recently. If you and the person you argued with reached an agreement, what happened that made one or the other of you change your mind? If you did not reach agreement, what thoughts, feelings, or attitudes kept the two of you from agreeing? Drawing on this experience, explain what happened to make you or your opponent adopt a new opinion, or if you did not agree, explain what prevented the change of opinion.

3. Medical and religious ethicists often discuss "quality of life" issues as they bear on decisions to continue life by extraordinary measures. The term "brain dead" often comes up in such discussions. If a friend or relative of yours were seriously brain damaged, would you argue for or against the continuance of life support systems? Present your argument in an essay.

Two Exploratory Essays

Tradition says that essays should end with a bang, a clincher that ties up all the loose ends and leaves no questions unanswered, yet we know that life is full of uncertainties and unresolved problems. The two essays that follow reflect this frustrating, fascinating human situation: that sometimes no final answers are available.

An important use of writing is to explore problems, to find out where we stand, without reaching premature conclusions. The essays that follow illustrate such writing-as-thinking.

A Simplified Income Tax

The essay on the following page appeared as a United Technologies advertisement in the Atlantic.

In one sense this essay is an argument—in favor of a flat-rate income tax. However, the piece explores problems and alternatives and concludes not with a bang, but with the quiet recommendation that the idea of a flat-rate tax "merits full scrutiny and debate."

As you read, you might keep this question in the back of your mind: why did United Technologies, a major corporation, run the ad in the first place? When you have finished reading the proposal, consider the questions below.

QUESTIONS

1. What issues concerning a simplified income tax are raised in this essay?

2. Both "advocates" and "proponents" are used in this essay, yet "opponents" is not used. In what ways does the article treat the views of opponents to the proposal?

3. The article mentions that several options are being discussed, yet explores only one option even briefly. Why?

4. The article ends "It's an idea that merits full scrutiny and debate." Explain why you think that the writers of the article do or do not intend to encourage "full scrutiny and debate"?

5. Defend one of the following evaluations of "A Simplified Income Tax":

   Pro: The essay, though short, is exceptionally clear, and it contains enough data and other backing to develop its point convincingly.
   Con: The essay is too short to deal adequately with its subject, and in places is confusing.

A Simplified Income Tax

Imagine an income tax so simple and straightforward that all you do is add up your income for the year and send a modest percentage of it to Uncle Sam. No deductions. No shelters. No loopholes. The same rate would apply to all, across the board.

The idea of a flat-rate tax has been around for years. Today it's bubbling up afresh in the mounting frustration over budget deficits and the nation's economic troubles, along with public disaffection with the existing tax system.

The flat tax has supporters in both parties and across the political spectrum. Several bills on it have been introduced in Congress. The tax rates being discussed generally range below 25%. The top rate is now 50%.

Advocates see the flat tax as a way to stimulate productive enterprise and steer the economy back on a growth path. The idea is that people would be encouraged to work harder, take greater risks, and invest and save more because they'd be able to keep more of what they earned. No longer would they be taxed at ever-higher rates as their income rose.

In addition, proponents say, there would be more equity in the tax system. All would pay their fair share. Shelters and loopholes would be done away with. Cheating through fraudulent deductions would be eliminated.

In pure form, a flat tax would have no exemptions or deductions. But purity would have to give way to practicality. There should be an element of progressiveness: higher rates for higher income earners.

Most current discussion centers on providing for a base of exempt income. The exemption, for example, could be the first $10,000 of income. With a flat rate of 10%, someone with an income of $20,000 would pay a tax of $1,000. The effective rate would be 5%. A person with $100,000 in income would pay a tax of $9,000, or an effective rate of 9%.

Greater progressivity could be achieved through a tax of two or three tiers. One proposal calls for no tax on income below $17,500, a rate of 18% on incomes from $17,500 to $50,000, and 25% above $50,000.

Numerous options are being discussed. One is to have no income exempted from taxation. Instead, each person would get a $250 tax credit. For a family of four, total credit of $1,000 would be equivalent to an exemption of $10,000, given a 10% rate.

Arriving at a simple flat tax would be anything but simple. State and local governments depend on their ability to issue tax-free bonds. Institutions, organizations, and causes of all sorts need contributions that are now tax-deductible. Homeowners cherish the deductibility of their mortgage interest. All these things would have to be worked out carefully.

A streamlined tax has considerable appeal in its potential for simplicity, fairness, and revenue-raising effectiveness. It's an idea that merits full scrutiny and debate.

JOHN P. WILEY, JR.
[A Daydream]

In the following essay, Mr. Wiley is saying, "What if? . . ." His daydream is an attempt to assess the severity of the ecological crisis and the possibility of avoiding disaster. Wiley's method of exploring a problem is vivid and engaging, reminding one of the current "futurist" movies, in which the earth is portrayed as it might be a hundred or a thousand years hence.

The author writes "Phenomena, comment and notes," a monthly column in the Smithsonian.

A dark forest used to stand silent just inside the National Museum of Natural History, a growth of hemlocks four to five feet in diameter. Through the trees you could see a river, a wooded island on the right, and acres of wild rice to the left. No bridges crossed the river. It was the spot where Rock Creek empties into the Potomac River in Washington, and you were seeing it as the Indians saw it before Europeans arrived. Malls and memorials stand now where once the wild rice grew; a seawall keeps the river in its place.

When I walk the seawall, I try to see the river as it was. I do the same on Chesapeake Bay or along the Hudson River, remembering accounts of the extraordinarily abundant fish and wildlife found by the early explorers. And I wonder how well they might recover if we went away for a few centuries. Would hemlocks grow again in what is now a boathouse parking lot at Rock Creek?

My only empirical data comes from a 5-by-20-foot bank alongside my driveway. A rock garden planted with lilies and irises when I moved in six years ago, I abandoned it in the press of other business. Today, thanks to the wind and the birds, it is crowded with oaks, maples, dogwoods and a yellow poplar already 15 feet high. A living wall. All I had to do was stand back out of the way.

To find out what would happen on a larger scale, one could consult the literature on plant succession, study abandoned highways, visit ruins in Mexico, travel to lost cities in Asia. Or one could make evacuating the entire Earth the premise for a science-fiction story, and let the special-effects people fill in the details when the story is snapped up for a major motion picture. New York City 10,000 years after the last human left would be a new challenge for the model makers.

The scenario goes something like this: the time comes when, despite our best efforts, the only way left to save Earth is to leave it. Everybody. For a long time. So many species have been lost, so many ecosystems impoverished, that the whole biological life-support system is close to collapse. The natural waste-removal systems, the recyclers, the air filters and water holders are being overwhelmed.

In this fantasy future, field biologists are the new elite. They are paid more than Congressmen, although less than basketball players. Biologists have been multiplying as fast as species have been disappearing. In 1980 one expert had told Congress that there were only 1,500 people in the world competent to identify tropical organisms; when brown leafhoppers destroyed several billion dollars worth of rice in Southeast Asia in the late 1970s, only a dozen people in the world could distinguish with certainty the 20,000 species that make up that insect group.

Now, some decades later, armies of biologists carry on with a wartime intensity, desperate to learn more about how the natural systems work before they disappear. They need to know not only what should be saved first on Earth, but what should be added to the recycling systems on the space colonies and asteroid mines overhead which, like some of the most carefully assembled home aquariums, do not quite work. By now humans live as far away as the moons of Jupiter, but all the secrets of life remain on Earth.

At some point it becomes clear that the race is being lost. True, human numbers are dropping. Heavy industry has moved into space. But so much tropical forest has already been cut, so many watersheds destroyed, so much topsoil washed away that the biological decline has unstoppable momentum. it is too late for management, no matter how wise.

Thus a decision once made by bands and tribes, to pack up and move, is now made by the population of a planet. The actual mechanics are a little fuzzy in my fantasy, except that more and more people would move into space to build more and more colonies for more and more people to move into space.

With a little suspension of disbelief one can see the story unfold. Grass appears in the boathouse parking lot. A small section of the seawall collapses and, with no one around to fix it, the river moves in like a silent bulldozer. The noblest experiment of all as begun.

Now the story moves in fast-forward, time-lapse photography; we watch nature reclaim itself through the eyes of appropriate creatures. Early on we see city streets through the eyes of a rat; we follow the feral dogs and cats that roam the suburbs along with the raccoons and skunks. A century later a coyote hunts in the streets of Manhattan; five centuries after that a panther uses the pinnacle of a rubble pile to search for prey. A pigeon's eye view of a city changes to a falcon's.

Humans will not be able to leave the planet completely alone, of course, any more than an editor can pass on a manuscript without making a mark. The luckiest biologists of their generations will be landed at monitoring stations. Remote sensors will be maintained, camera lenses cleaned. A little crisis intervention might be allowed at first: aerial tankers putting out a fire about to destroy the last known stand of some special plant. But as far as humanly possible, the biologists would keep their hands off, acting only as passive receptors. Nature would be the protagonist and the star. A living Earth regenerating from the ruins. The miracle that struggles to happen in every vacant lot happening everywhere. All with appropriate inspirational music, of course.

Conflict for a story line should be easy. At the start the conflict would be over whether to leave; I could stoop to a line something like: "Gazing out into the dark—30 stories above the East River—after a day of hearing out the biologists' deputations, the Secretary-General became biologically literate." Later the conflict over whether it was time to return would grow stronger: The latter argument would not sound entirely unfamiliar to anyone who follows today's debates over multiple use versus preserving wilderness areas unsullied. A writer might suffer the temptation to inject ideological harangues into the dialogue.

In the meantime, the miracle would be fact. The biological crisis would be past. Nothing would have returned from extinction, but the several million species left would be plenty to keep the bio in biosphere. An optimist would end the movie with humans returning to live in gentle coexistence. A pessimist might have us come back to ravish the Earth all over again. Something in between seems more reasonable.

I'm completely over my head in every part of this fantasy, of course. If we flew 100,000 people off this Earth every day, it would take 125 years to move the current population. I certainly don't know if hemlocks could or would ever grow again in that boathouse parking lot.

But I like the uniting of what are now inimical factions: the high technologists who believe the future of our species lies in space, and the environmentalists who fear we would foul the rest of the solar system just as we have fouled the planet. Environmentalists might be a little humbler if the spacers save the world. I also like the idea of a species, grown out of its infancy, given a second chance at husbanding a remarkable place to live. Possibly even the only place to live.

But the strongest appeal is really the vision I started with—fish leaping in clear water, forests growing to the water's edge, swamps and marshes pulsating with life. The way things were here just five or six lifetimes ago.

To some people today, an environmentalist is a monomaniac. Worse, still, is a preservationist: an elitist unconcerned with people. Perhaps I am most unspeakable of all: a preservationist who not only wants to keep what we still have but would like to bring back what we once had. I don't feel antipeople at all. We people need the life support of the biosphere. The whole system is slowly failing, but still has the power to regenerate without any help from us. All we have to do is stand back. Now, if only that were somehow possible.

QUESTIONS

1. Wiley's style is highly metaphorical. For example, he sees "A living Earth regenerating from the ruins. The miracle that struggles to happen in every vacant lot happening everywhere" (p. 277). Point out and explain the meaning of other metaphors in the essay.

2. Some authors in this section have attempted to be completely objective and have not expressed their own personalities in their writing (e.g., Mark Snyder). Others have written in a style that makes us feel they are expressing their own personalities (e.g., John P. Wiley, Jr. and Tom Wolfe). Compare the writing of Snyder, Wolfe, and Wiley. What makes for a personal as compared with an objective style? How do authors express their personalities in their writings?

3. When might an objective style such as Snyder's be preferable to the personal style of Wiley and Wolfe?

4. The body of the essay is controlled by the motion picture scenario metaphor. What are the advantages of this metaphor in conveying Wiley's "message" to his readers?

5. Explain the implications of this passage: "An optimist would end the movie with humans returning to live in gentle coexistence. A pessimist might have us come back to ravish the Earth all over again. Something in between seems more reasonable."

SUGGESTIONS FOR WRITING

1. Choose a controversial topic about which you are undecided—for example, capital punishment, abortion, decriminalization of drug addiction, school prayer—and explore your attitudes and beliefs in an essay. You needn't reach a decision.

2. Recently you noticed someone you did not know, walking past in a store or sitting at a bus stop. Perhaps you wondered briefly what that person did for a living or how he or she relaxed. Using the details that you so briefly took in, write two or three scenarios about what the person's life may be like.

From the Tradition

In the words of George L. Dillon,

The expository essay . . . has a rhetorical purpose beyond "conveying information": it attempts to convince the reader that its model of experience or the world is valid. It does not seek to engage the reader in a course of action, however, but rather in a process of reflection, and its means of convincing are accordingly limited to the use of evidence and logical proof and the posture of openmindedness.[1]

The purpose of the expository essay, then, is very much like the purpose of a liberal education: to view human concerns rationally and to bring about understanding.

The four selections that follow in this section illustrate the traditional concerns of the expository essay and give some idea of the development of this genre, from Francis Bacon in the seventeenth century to George Orwell and E. B. White three hundred years later.

The essays by Bacon and Emerson are formal, the authors developing their points logically, without interjecting narratives of personal experience. The essays by Orwell and White are based on such narratives and are, in fact, "personal" essays. You cannot fail to notice the differences between the two types.

FRANCIS BACON
Of Studies

Francis Bacon (1561–1626), the first essayist in English, takes a lofty view of human concerns, writing magesterially about truth, marriage and single life, fame, and, in the essay that follows, the uses of learning. His star rose steadily during the reigns of Elizabeth and James I, but in 1621 he fell with a crash, having been accused of taking bribes. He spent the last five years of his life in retirement.

Bacon had projected a huge philosophical work, but completed only two parts of it, The Advancement of Learning *(1605) and the* Novum Organum. *Bacon's great contribution to philosophy was applying the inductive methods of science to*

---

[1]George L. Dillon, *Constructing Texts* (Bloomington: Indiana University Press, 1981), p.23.

questions that prior to his time had been answered on the basis of the authority of the "ancients," the Greek and Roman philosophers. Bacon argued that all questions should be carefully investigated and that thinkers should avoid conclusions based on insufficient evidence. In many ways, his works mark the beginning of modern thinking.

"Of Studies" is typically Baconian: pithy, to the point, as if he had extracted the essence of his thought and had thrown away the pulp. No writer in English is more economical than Bacon.

Studies serve for delight, for ornament, and for ability. Their chief use for delight is in privateness and retiring; for ornament, is in discourse; and for ability, is in the judgment and disposition of business. For expert men can execute, and perhaps judge of particulars, one by one; but the general counsels, and the plots and marshaling of affairs, come best from those that are learned. To spend too much time in studies is sloth; to use them too much for ornament is affectation; to make judgment wholly by their rules is the humor of a scholar. They perfect nature, and are perfected by experience; for natural abilities are like natural plants, that need pruning by study; and studies themselves do give forth directions too much at large, except they be bounded in by experience. Crafty men contemn studies, simple men admire them, and wise men use them, for they teach not their own use; but that is a wisdom without them, and above them, won by observation. Read not to contradict and confute, nor to believe and take for granted, nor to find talk and discourse, but to weigh and consider. Some books are to be tasted, others to be swallowed, and some few to be chewed and digested; that is, some books are to be read only in parts; others to be read, but not curiously;[1] and some few to be read wholly, and with diligence and attention. Some books also may be read by deputy and extracts made of them by others, but that would be only in the less important arguments and the meaner sort of books; else distilled books are like common distilled waters, flashy things. Reading maketh a full man, conference a ready man, and writing an exact man. And therefore, if a man write little, he had need have a great memory; if he confer little, he had need have a present wit; and if he read little, he had need have more cunning, to seem to know that he doth not. Histories make men wise; poets, witty; the mathematics, subtle; natural philosophy, deep; moral, grave; logic and rhetoric, able to contend. *Abeunt studia in mores.*[2] Nay, there is no stond[3] or impediment in the wit but may be wrought out by fit studies, like as diseases of the body may have appropriate exercises. Bowl-

---

[1] *curiously:* in detail.
[2] *Abeunt Studia in mores:* Studies change into habits.
[3] *stond:* stand, i.e., impediment

ing is good for the stone and reins, shooting for the lungs and breast, gentle walking for the stomach, riding for the head, and the like. So if a man's wit be wandering, let him study the mathematics; for in demonstrations, if his wit be called away never so little, he must begin again. If his wit be not apt to distinguish or find differences, let him study the schoolmen, for they are *Cymini sectores*. If he be not apt to beat over matters and to call up one thing to prove and illustrate another, let him study the lawyer's cases. So every defect of the mind may have a special receipt.

QUESTIONS

1. Explain the three uses of studies. Give one or two examples of how you have studies for delight, ornament, or ability.
2. In what way is Bacon's handling of his subject different from the ways in which modern essayists handle theirs? For instance, how important are specific examples to modern essayists? To Bacon?
3. What are the dangers of studies, according to Bacon? Have you encountered any of these dangers?
4. According to Bacon, how should one read books? Give examples from your own, contemporary experience of the kinds of books that Bacon is talking about.
5. Explain your opinion about Bacon's purpose in writing "Of Studies."

RALPH WALDO EMERSON

The American Scholar

Ralph Waldo Emerson (1803–1882) was, with Henry David Thoreau, a leading American transcendentalist, believing that God is everywhere in nature and that one's own intuition is the highest source of knowledge. During his career, Emerson was pastor of the Old North Church in Boston, until, in a conflict with his congregation, he was forced to resign. After his resignation, he traveled in Europe, meeting the essayist Thomas Carlyle and the poets William Wordsworth and Samuel Taylor Coleridge, all of whom were an influence on his transcendentalism.

Emerson considered himself a poet, but is best remembered for his essays, the most famous of which, aside from "The American Scholar," are "The Over-Soul," "Compensation," and "Self-Reliance."

This essay, which in its own time was a declaration of independence proclaiming the American scholar's freedom from European norms, is as timely now as when it was written; it raises the important issues about the nature and the uses of scholarship. It is also a memorable piece of writing, as when Emerson says, "The first in time and the first in importance of the influences upon the mind is that of nature. Every day, the sun; and, after sunset, Night and her stars. Ever the wind blows; ever the grass grows. Every day, men and women, conversing—beholding and beholden."

AN ORATION DELIVERED BEFORE THE PHI BETA KAPPA SOCIETY,
AT CAMBRIDGE AUGUST 31, 1837

Mr. President and Gentlemen:

I greet you on the recommencement of our literary year. Our anniversary is one of hope, and, perhaps, not enough of labor. We do not meet for games of strength or skill, for the recitation of histories, tragedies, and odes, like the ancient Greeks; for parliaments of love and poesy, like the Troubadours; nor for the advancement of science, like our contemporaries in the British and European capitals. Thus far, our holiday has been simply a friendly sign of the survival of the love of letters amongst a people too busy to give to letters any more. As such it is precious as the sign of an indestructible instinct. Perhaps the time is already come when it ought to be, and will be, something else; when the sluggard intellect of this continent will look from under its iron lids and fill the postponed expectation of the world with something better than the exertions of mechanical skill. Our day of dependence, our long apprenticeship to the learning of other lands, draws to a close. The millions that around us are rushing into life, cannot always be fed on the sere remains of foreign harvests. Events, actions arise, that must be sung, that will sing themselves. Who can doubt that poetry will revive and lead in a new age, as the star in the constellation

Harp, which now flames in our zenith, astronomers announce, shall one day be the pole-star for a thousand years?

In this hope I accept the topic which not only usage but the nature of our association seem to prescribe to this day,—the AMERICAN SCHOLAR. Year by year we come up hither to read one more chapter of his biography. Let us inquire what light new days and events have thrown on his character and his hopes.

It is one of those fables which out of an unknown antiquity convey an unlooked-for wisdom, that the gods, in the beginning, divided Man into men, that he might be more helpful to himself; just as the hand was divided into fingers, the better to answer its end.

The old fable covers a doctrine ever new and sublime; that there is One Man,—present to all particular men only partially, or through one faculty; and that you must take the whole society to find the whole man. Man is not a farmer, or a professor, or an engineer, but he is all. Man is priest, and scholar, and statesman, and producer, and soldier. In the *divided* or social state these functions are parcelled out to individuals, each of whom aims to do his stint of the joint work, whilst each other performs his. The fable implies that the individual, to possess himself, must sometimes return from his own labor to embrace all the other laborers. But, unfortunately, this original unit, this fountain of power, has been so distributed to multitudes, has been so minutely subdivided and peddled out, that it is spilled into drops, and cannot be gathered. The state of society is one in which the members have suffered amputation from the trunk, and strut about so many walking monsters,—a good finger, a neck, a stomach, an elbow, but never a man.

Man is thus metamorphosed into a thing, into many things. The planter, who is Man sent out into the field to gather food, is seldom cheered by any idea of the true dignity of his ministry. He sees his bushel and his cart, and nothing beyond, and sinks into the farmer, instead of Man on the farm. The tradesman scarcely ever gives an ideal worth to his work, but is ridden by the routine of his craft, and the soul is subject to dollars. The priest becomes a form; the attorney a statute-book; the mechanic a machine; the sailor a rope of the ship.

In this distribution of functions the scholar is the delegated intellect. In the right state he is *Man Thinking*. In the degenerate state, when the victim of society, he tends to become a mere thinker, or still worse, the parrot of other men's thinking.

In this view of him, as Man Thinking, the theory of his office is contained. Him Nature solicits with all her placid, all her monitory[1] pictures; him the past instructs; him the future invites. Is not indeed every

---

[1] *monitory*: warning

man a student, and do not all things exist for the student's behoof? And, finally, is not the true scholar the only true master? But the old oracle said, "All things have two handles: beware of the wrong one." In life, too often, the scholar errs with mankind and forfeits his privilege. Let us see him in his school, and consider him in reference to the main influences he receives.

I. The first in time and the first in importance of the influences upon the mind is that of nature. Every day, the sun; and, after sunset, Night and her stars. Ever the winds blow; ever the grass grows. Every day, men and women, conversing—beholding and beholden. The scholar is he of all men whom this spectacle most engages. He must settle its value in his mind. What is nature to him? There is never a beginning, there is never an end, to the inexplicable continuity of this web of God, but always circular power returning into itself. Therein it resembles his own spirit, whose beginning, whose ending, he never can find,—so entire, so boundless. Far too as her splendors shine, system on system shooting like rays, upward, downward, without centre, without circumference,—in the mass and in the particle, Nature hastens to render account of herself to the mind. Classification begins. To the young mind every thing is individual, stands by itself. By and by, it finds how to join two things and see in them one nature; then three, then three thousand; and so, tyrannized over by its own unifying instinct, it goes on tying things together, diminishing anomalies, discovering roots running under ground whereby contrary and remote things cohere and flower out from one stem. It presently learns that since the dawn of history there has been a constant accumulation and classifying of facts. But what is classification but the perceiving that these objects are not chaotic, and are not foreign, but have a law which is also a law of the human mind? The astronomer discovers that geometry, a pure abstraction of the human mind, is the measure of planetary motion. The chemist finds proportions and intelligible method throughout matter; and science is nothing but the finding of analogy, identity, in the most remote parts. The ambitious soul sits down before each refractory fact; one after another reduces all strange constitutions, all new powers, to their class and their law, and goes on forever to animate the last fibre of organization, the outskirts of nature, by insight.

Thus to him, to this schoolboy under the bending dome of day, is suggested that he and it proceed from one root; one is leaf and one is flower; relation, sympathy, stirring in every vein. And what is that root? Is not that the soul of his soul? A thought too bold; a dream too wild. Yet when this spiritual light shall have revealed the law of more earthly natures,—when he has learned to worship the soul, and to see that the natural philosophy that now is, is only the first gropings of its gigantic hand, he shall look forward to an ever expanding knowledge as to a becoming creator. He shall see that nature is the opposite of the soul, answering to it part for part. One is seal and one is print. Its beauty is the beauty of his own mind. Its laws are the laws of his own mind. Nature then becomes to him the measure of his attainments. So much of nature as he is ignorant of, so much of his own mind does he not yet possess. And, in fine, the ancient precept, "Know thyself," and the modern precept, "Study nature," become at last one maxim.

II. The next great influence into the spirit of the scholar is the mind of the Past,—in whatever form, whether of literature, of art, of institutions, that mind is inscribed. Books are the best type of the influence of the past, and perhaps we shall get at the truth,—learn the amount of this influence more conveniently,—by considering their value alone.

The theory of books is noble. The scholar of the first age received into him the world around; brooded thereon; gave it the new arrangement of his own mind, and uttered it again. It came into him life; it went out from him truth. It came to him short-lived actions; it went out from him immortal thoughts. It came to him business; it went from him poetry. It was dead fact; now, it is quick thought. It can stand, and it can go. It now endures, it now flies, it now inspires. Precisely in proportion to the depth of mind from which it issued, so high does it soar, so long does it sing.

Or, I might say, it depends on how far the process had gone, of transmuting life into truth. In proportion to the completeness of the distillation, so will the purity and imperishableness of the product be. But none is quite perfect. As no air-pump can by any means make a perfect vacuum, so neither can any artist entirely exclude the conventional, the local, the perishable from his book, or write a book of pure thought, that shall be as efficient, in all respects, to a remote posterity, as to contemporaries, or rather to the second age. Each age, it is found, must write its own books; or rather, each generation for the next succeeding. The books of an older period will not fit this.

Yet hence arises a grave mischief. The sacredness which attaches to the act of creation, the act of thought, is transferred to the record. The poet chanting was felt to be a divine man: henceforth the chant is divine also. The writer was a just and wise spirit; henceforward it is settled the book is perfect; as love of the hero corrupts into worship of his statue. Instantly the book becomes noxious: the guide is a tyrant. The sluggish and perverted mind of the multitude, slow to open to the incursions of Reason, having once so opened, having once received this book, stands upon it, and makes an outcry if it is disparaged. Colleges are built on it. Books are written on it by thinkers, not by Man Thinking; by men of talent, that is, who start wrong, who set out from accepted dogmas, not from their own sight of principles. Meek young men grow up in libraries, believing it their duty to accept the views which Cicero, which Locke,[2] which Bacon, have given; forgetful that Cicero, Locke, and Bacon were only young men in libraries when they wrote these books.

Hence, instead of Man Thinking, we have the bookworm. Hence the book-learned class, who value books, as such; not as related to nature and the human constitution, but as making a sort of Third Estate with the world and the soul. Hence the restorers of readings, the emendators, the bibliomaniacs of all degrees.

Books are the best of things, well used; abused, among the worst. What is the right use? What is the one end which all means go to effect? They are for nothing but to inspire. I had better never see a book than to be warped by its attraction clean out of my own orbit, and made a satellite instead of a system. The one thing in the world, of value, is the active soul. This every man is entitled to; this every man contains within him, although in almost all men obstructed and as yet unborn. The soul active sees absolute truth and utters truth, or creates. In this action it is genius; not the privilege of here and there a favorite, but the sound estate of every man. In its essence it is progressive. The book, the college, the school of art, the institution of any kind, stop with some past utterance of genius. This is good, say they,—let us hold by this. They pin me down. They look backward and not forward. But genius looks forward: the eyes of man are set in his forehead, not in his hind-head: man hopes: genius creates. Whatever talents may be, if the man create not, the pure efflux of the Deity is not his;—cinders and smoke there may be, but not yet flame. There are creative manners, there are creative actions, and creative words; manners, actions, words, that is, indicative of no custom or authority, but springing spontaneous from the mind's own sense of good and fair.

On the other part, instead of being its own seer, let it receive from another mind its truth, though it were in torrents of light, without periods of solitude, inquest, and self-recovery, and a fatal disservice is done. Genius is always sufficiently the enemy of genius by over-influence. The literature of every nation bears me witness. The English dramatic poets have Shakspearized now for two hundred years.

Undoubtedly there is a right way of reading, so it be sternly subordinated. Man Thinking must not be subdued by his instruments. Books are for the scholar's idle times. When he can read God directly, the hour is too precious to be wasted in other men's transcripts of their readings. But when the intervals of darkness come, as come they must,—when the sun is hid and the stars withdraw their shining,—we repair to the lamps which were kindled by their ray, to guide our steps to the East again, where the dawn is.

---

[2]Marcus Tullius Cicero (106–43 B. C.), Roman orator, rhetorical theorist, and statesman. John Locke (1632–1704), English philosopher.

We hear, that we may speak. The Arabian proverb says, "A fig tree, looking on a fig tree, becometh fruitful."

It is remarkable, the character of the pleasure we derive from the best books. They impress us with the conviction that one nature wrote and the same reads. We read the verses of one of the great English poets, of Chaucer, of Marvell, of Dryden,[3] with the most modern joy,—with a pleasure, I mean, which is in great part caused by the abstraction of all *time* from their verses. There is some awe mixed with the joy of our surprise, when this poet, who lived in some past world, two or three hundred years ago, says that which lies close to my own soul, that which I also had wellnigh thought and said. But for the evidence thence afforded to the philosophical doctrine of the identity of all minds, we should suppose some preëstablished harmony, some foresight of souls that were to be, and some preparation of stores for their future wants, like the fact observed in insects, who lay up food before death for the young grub they shall never see.

I would not be hurried by any love of system, by any exaggeration of instincts, to underrate the Book. We all know, that as the human body can be nourished on any food, though it were boiled grass and the broth of shoes, so the human mind can be fed by any knowledge. And great and heroic men have existed who had almost no other information than by the printed page. I only would say that it needs a strong head to bear that diet. One must be an inventor to read well. As the proverb says, "He that would bring home the wealth of the Indies, must carry out the wealth of the Indies." There is then creative reading as well as creative writing. When the mind is braced by labor and invention, the page of whatever book we read become luminous with manifold allusion. Every sentence is doubly significant, and the sense of our author is as broad as the world. We then see, what is always true, that as the seer's hour of vision is short and rare among heavy days and months, so is its record, perchance, the least part of his volume. The discerning will read, in his Plato or Shakspeare, only that least part,—only the authentic utterances of the oracle;—all the rest he rejects, were it never so many times Plato's and Shakspeare's.

Of course there is a portion of reading quite indispensable to a wise man. History and exact science he must learn by laborious reading. Colleges, in like manner, have their indispensable office,—to teach elements. But they can only highly serve us when they aim not to drill, but to create; when they gather from far every ray of various genius to their hospitable halls, and by the concentrated fires, set the hearts of their youth on flame. Thought and knowledge are natures in which apparatus and pretension avail nothing. Gowns and pecuniary foundations, though of

---

[3]Geoffrey Chaucer (1340?–1400), English poet, author of *The Canterbury Tales*. John Dryden (1631–1700), English poet and dramatist.

towns of gold, can never countervail the least sentence or syllable of wit. Forget this, and our American colleges will recede in their public importance, whilst they grow richer every year.

III. There goes in the world a notion that the scholar should be a recluse, a valetudinarian,—as unfit for any handiwork or public labor as a penknife for an axe. The so-called "practical men" sneer at speculative men, as if, because they speculate or *see*, they could do nothing. I have heard it said that the clergy,—who are always, more universally than any other class, the scholars of their day,—are addressed as women; that the rough, spontaneous conversation of men they do not hear, but only a mincing and diluted speech. They are often virtually disfranchised; and indeed there are advocates for their celibacy. As far as this is true of the studious classes, it is not just and wise. Action is with the scholar subordinate, but it is essential. Without it he is not yet man. Without it thought can never ripen into truth. Whilst the world hangs before the eye as a cloud of beauty, we cannot even see its beauty. Inaction is cowardice, but there can be no scholar without the heroic mind. The preamble of thought, the transition through which it passes from the unconscious to the conscious, is action. Only so much do I know, as I have lived. Instantly we know whose words are loaded with life, and whose not.

The world,—this shadow of the soul, or *other me*,—lies wide around. Its attractions are the keys which unlock my thoughts and make me acquainted with myself. I run eagerly into this resounding tumult. I grasp the hands of those next me, and take my place in the ring to suffer and to work, taught by an instinct that so shall the dumb abyss be vocal with speech. I pierce its order; I dissipate its fear; I dispose of it within the circuit of my expanding life. So much only of life as I know by experience, so much of the wilderness have I vanquished and planted, or so far have I extended my being, my dominion. I do not see how any man can afford, for the sake of his nerves and his nap, to spare any action in which he can partake. It is pearls and rubies to his discourse. Drudgery, calamity, exasperation, want, are instructors in eloquence and wisdom. The true scholar grudges every opportunity of action past by, as a loss of power. It is the raw material out of which the intellect moulds her splendid products. A strange process too, this by which experience is converted into thought, as a mulberry leaf is converted into satin. The manufacture goes forward at all hours.

The actions and events of our childhood and youth are now matters of calmest observation. They lie like fair pictures in the air. Not so with our recent actions,—with the business which we now have in hand. On this we are quite unable to speculate. Our affections as yet circulate through it. We no more feel or know it than we feel the feet, or the hand, or the brain of our body. The new deed is yet a part of life,—remains for a time immersed in our unconscious life. In some contemplative hour it detaches itself from the life like a ripe fruit, to become a thought of the mind. Instantly it is raised, transfigured; the corruptible has put on incorruption. Henceforth it is an object of beauty, however base its origin and neighborhood. Observe too the impossibility of antedating this act. In its grub state, it cannot fly, it cannot shine, it is a dull grub. But suddenly, without observation, the selfsame thing unfurls beautiful wings, and is an angel of wisdom. So is there no fact, no event, in our private history, which shall not, sooner or later, lose its adhesive, inert form, and astonish us by soaring from our body into the empyrean. Cradle and infancy, school and playground, the fear of boys, and dogs, and ferules, the love of little maids and berries, and many another fact that once filled the whole sky, are gone already; friend and relative, profession and party, town and country, nation and world, must also soar and sing.

Of course, he who has put forth his total strength in fit actions has the richest return of wisdom. I will not shut myself out of this globe of action, and transplant an oak into a flowerpot, there to hunger and pine; nor trust the revenue of some single faculty, and exhaust one vein of thought, much like those Savoyards,[4] who, getting their livelihood by carving shepherds, shepherdesses, and smoking Dutchmen, for all Europe, went out one day to the mountain to find stock, and discovered that they had whittled up the last of their pine trees. Authors we have, in numbers, who have written out their vein, and who, moved by a commendable prudence, sail for Greece or Palestine, follow the trapper into the prairie, or ramble round Algiers, to replenish their merchantable stock.

If it were only for a vocabulary, the scholar would be covetous of action. Life is our dictionary. Years are well spent in country labors; in town; in the insight into trades and manufactures; in frank intercourse with many men and women; in science; in art; to the one end of mastering in all their facts a language by which to illustrate and embody our perceptions. I learn immediately from any speaker how much he has already lived, through the poverty or the splendor of his speech. Life lies behind us as the quarry from whence we get tiles and copestones for the masonry of to-day. This is the way to learn grammar. Colleges and books only copy the language which the field and the work-yard made.

But the final value of action, like that of books, and better than books, is that it is a resource. That great principle of Undulation in nature, that shows itself in the inspiring and expiring of the breath; in desire and satiety; in the ebb and flow of the sea; in day and night; in heat and cold; and, as yet more deeply ingrained in every atom and every fluid, is known to us

---

[4]*Savoyards*: residents of Savoy, an alpine region of Eastern France.

under the name of Polarity,—these "fits of easy transmission and reflection," as Newton called them, are the law of nature because they are the law of spirit.

The mind now thinks, now acts, and each fit reproduces the other. When the artist has exhausted his materials, when the fancy no longer paints, when thoughts are no longer apprehended and books are a weariness,—he has always the resource *to live*. Character is higher than intellect. Thinking is the function. Living is the functionary. The stream retreats to its source. A great soul will be strong to live, as well as strong to think. Does he lack organ or medium to impart his truths? He can still fall back on this elemental force of living them. This is a total act. Thinking is a partial act. Let the grandeur of justice shine in his affairs. Let the beauty of affection cheer his lowly roof. Those "far from fame," who dwell and act with him, will feel the force of his constitution in the doings and passages of the day better than it can be measured by any public and designed display. Time shall teach him that the scholar loses no hour which the man lives. Herein he unfolds the sacred germ of his instinct, screened from influence. What is lost in seemliness is gained in strength. Not out of those on whom systems of education have exhausted their culture, comes the helpful giant to destroy the old or to build the new, but out of unhandselled savage nature; out of terrible Druids and Berserkers[5] come at last Alfred[6] and Shakspeare.

I hear therefore with joy whatever is beginning to be said of the dignity and necessity of labor to every citizen. There is virtue yet in the hoe and the spade, for learned as well as for unlearned hands. And labor is everywhere welcome; always we are invited to work; only be this limitation observed, that a man shall not for the sake of wider activity sacrifice any opinion to the popular judgments and modes of action.

I have now spoken of the education of the scholar by nature, by books, and by action. It remains to say somewhat of his duties.

They are such as become Man Thinking. They may all be comprised in self-trust. The office of the scholar is to cheer, to raise, and to guide men by showing them facts amidst appearances. He plies the slow, unhonored, and unpaid task of observation. Flamsteed and Herschel,[7] in their glazed observatories, may catalogue the stars with the praise of all men, and the results being splendid and useful, honor is sure. But he, in his private observatory, cataloguing obscure and nebulous stars of the human mind,

---

[5]*Druids*: pre-Christian priests who appear in Welsh and Irish sagas. *Berserkers*: ancient Scandinavian warriors who became frantic in battle and were thought to be invincible.
[6]Alfred: King of the West Saxons (849–899)
[7]John Flamsteed (1646–1719), English astronomer, appointed by King Charles II as royal astronomer. Sir William Herschel (1738–1822), the German-born British astronomer who discovered the planet Uranus.

which as yet no man has thought of as such,—watching days and months sometimes for a few facts; correcting still his old records;—must relinquish display and immediate fame. In the long period of his preparation he must betray often an ignorance and shiftlessness in popular arts, incurring the disdain of the able who shoulder him aside. Long he must stammer in his speech; often forego the living for the dead. Worse yet, he must accept— how often!—poverty and solitude. For the ease and pleasure of treading the old road, accepting the fashions, the education, the religion of society, he takes the cross of making his own, and, of course, the self-accusation, the faint heart, the frequent uncertainty and loss of time, which are the nettles and tangling vines in the way of the self-relying and self-directed; and the state of virtual hostility in which he seems to stand to society, and especially to educated society. For all this loss and scorn, what offset? He is to find consolation in exercising the highest functions of human nature. He is one who raises himself from private considerations and breathes and lives on public and illustrious thoughts. He is the world's eye. He is the world's heart. He is to resist the vulgar prosperity that retrogrades ever to barbarism, by preserving and communicating heroic sentiments, noble biographies, melodious verse, and the conclusions of history. Whatsoever oracles the human heart, in all emergencies, in all solemn hours, has uttered as its commentary on the world of actions,—these he shall receive and impart. And whatsoever new verdict Reason from her inviolable seat pronounces on the passing men and events of to-day,—this he shall hear and promulgate.

These being his functions, it becomes him to feel all confidence in himself, and to defer never to the popular cry. He and he only knows the world. The world of any moment is the merest appearance. Some great decorum, some fetish of a government, some ephemeral trade, or war, or man, is cried up by half mankind and cried down by the other half, as if all depended on this particular up or down. The odds are that the whole question is not worth the poorest thought which the scholar has lost in listening to the controversy. Let him not quit his belief that a popgun is a popgun, though the ancient and honorable of the earth affirm it to be the crack of doom. In silence, in steadiness, in severe abstraction, let him hold by himself; add observation to observation, patient of neglect, patient of reproach, and bide his own time,—happy enough if he can satisfy himself alone that this day he has seen something truly. Success treads on every right step. For the instinct is sure, that prompts him to tell his brother what he thinks. He then learns that in going down into the secrets of his own mind he has descended into the secrets of all minds. He learns that he who has mastered any law in his private thoughts, is master to that extent of all men whose language he speaks, and of all into whose language his own can be translated. The poet, in utter solitude remembering his spontaneous thoughts and recording them, is found to have recorded that which men in crowded cities find true for them also. The orator distrusts at first the fitness of his frank confessions, his want of knowledge of the persons he addresses, until he finds that he is the complement of his hearers;—that they drink his words because he fulfils for them their own nature; the deeper he dives into his privatest, secretest presentiment, to his wonder he finds this is the most acceptable, most public, and universally true. The people delight in it; the better part of every man feels, This is my music; this is myself.

In self-trust all the virtues are comprehended. Free should the scholar be,—free and brave. Free even to the definition of freedom, "without any hindrance that does not arise out of his own constitution." Brave; for fear is a thing which a scholar by his very function puts behind him. Fear always springs from ignorance. It is a shame to him if his tranquility, amid dangerous times, arise from the presumption that like children and women his is a protected class; or if he seek a temporary peace by the diversion of his thoughts from politics or vexed questions, hiding his head like an ostrich in the flowering bushes, peeping into microscopes, and turning rhymes, as a boy whistles to keep his courage up. So is the danger a danger still; so is the fear worse. Manlike let him turn and face it. Let him look into its eye and search its nature, inspect its origin,—see the whelping of this lion,—which lies no great way back; he will then find in himself a perfect comprehension of its nature and extent; he will have made his hands meet on the other side, and can henceforth defy it and pass on superior. The world is his who can see through its pretension. What deafness, what stone-blind custom, what overgrown error you behold is there only by sufferance,—by your sufferance. See it to be a lie, and you have already dealt it its mortal blow.

Yes, we are the cowed,—we the trustless. It is a mischievous notion that we are come late into nature; that the world was finished a long time ago. As the world was plastic and fluid in the hands of God, so it is ever to so much of his attributes as we bring to it. To ignorance and sin, it is flint. They adapt themselves to it as they may; but in proportion as a man has any thing in him divine, the firmament flows before him and takes his signet and form. Not he is great who can alter matter, but he who can alter my state of mind. They are the kings of the world who give the color of their present thought to all nature and all art, and persuade men by the cheerful serenity of their carrying the matter, that this thing which they do is the apple which the ages have desired to pluck, now at last ripe, and inviting nations to the harvest. The great man makes the great thing. Wherever Macdonald sits, there is the head of the table. Linnæus[8] makes botany the most alluring of studies, and wins it from the farmer and the

---

[8]Carolus Linnæus, (1707–1778), Swedish botanist.

herb-woman; Davy,[9] chemistry; and Cuvier,[10] fossils. The day is always his who works in it with serenity and great aims. The unstable estimates of men crowd to him whose mind is filled with a truth, as the heaped waves of the Atlantic follow the moon.

For this self-trust, the reason is deeper than can be fathomed,—darker than can be enlightened. I might not carry with me the feeling of my audience in stating my own belief. But I have already shown the ground of my hope, in adverting to the doctrine that man is one. I believe man has been wronged; he has wronged himself. He has almost lost the light that can lead him back to his prerogatives. Men are become of no account. Men in history, men in the world of to-day, are bugs, are spawn, and are called "the mass" and "the herd." In a century, in a millennium, one or two men; that is to say, one or two approximations to the right state of every man. All the rest behold in the hero or the poet their own green and crude being,—ripened; yes, and are content to be less, so *that* may attain to its full stature. What a testimony, full of grandeur, full of pity, is borne to the demands of his own nature, by the poor clansman, the poor partisan, who rejoices in the glory of his chief. The poor and the low find some amends to their immense moral capacity, for their acquiescence in a political and social inferiority. They are content to be brushed like flies from the path of a great person, so that justice shall be done by him to that common nature which it is the dearest desire of all to see enlarged and glorified. They sun themselves in the great man's light, and feel it to be their own element. They cast the dignity of man from their downtrod selves upon the shoulders of a hero, and will perish to add one drop of blood to make that great heart beat, those giant sinews combat and conquer. He lives for us, and we live in him.

Men, such as they are, very naturally seek money or power; and power because it is as good as money,—the "spoils," so called, "of office." And why not? for they aspire to the highest, and this, in their sleep-walking, they dream is highest. Wake them and they shall quit the false good and leap to the true, and leave governments to clerks and desks. This revolution is to be wrought by the gradual domestication of the idea of Culture. The main enterprise of the world for splendor, for extent, is the upbuilding of a man. Here are the materials strewn along the ground. The private life of one man shall be a more illustrious monarchy, more formidable to its enemy, more sweet and serene in its influence to its friend, than any kingdom in history. For a man, rightly viewed, comprehendeth the particular natures of all men. Each philosopher, each bard, each actor has

---

[9]Sir Humphry Davy (1778–1829), English chemist.
[10]Baron Georges Léopold Chrétien Frédéric Dogobert Cuvier (1967–1832), French naturalist.

only done for me, as by a delegate, what one day I can do for myself. The books which once we valued more than the apple of the eye, we have quite exhausted. What is that but saying that we have come up with the point of view which the universal mind took through the eyes of one scribe; we have been that man, and have passed on. First, one, then another, we drain all cisterns, and waxing greater by all these supplies, we crave a better and more abundant food. The man has never lived that can feed us ever. The human mind cannot be enshrined in a person who shall set a barrier on any one side to this unbounded, unboundable empire. It is one central fire, which, flaming now out of the lips of Etna, lightens the capes of Sicily, and now out of the throat of Vesuvius, illuminates the towers and vineyards of Naples. It is one light which beams out of a thousand stars. It is one soul which animates all men.

But I have dwelt perhaps tediously upon this abstraction of the Scholar. I ought not to delay longer to add what I have to say of nearer reference to the time and to this country.

Historically, there is thought to be a difference in the ideas which predominate over successive epochs, and there are data for marking the genius of the Classic, of the Romantic, and now of the Reflective or Philosophical age. With the views I have intimated of the oneness or the identity of the mind through all individuals, I do not much dwell on these differences. In fact, I believe each individual passes through all three. The boy is a Greek; the youth, romantic; the adult, reflective. I deny not, however, that a revolution in the leading idea may be distinctly enough traced.

Our age is bewailed as the age of Introversion. Must that needs be evil? We, it seems, are critical; we are embarrassed with second thoughts; we cannot enjoy any thing for hankering to know whereof the pleasures consists; we are lined with eyes; we see with our feet; the time is infected with Hamlet's unhappiness,—

"Sicklied o'er with the pale cast of thought."

It is so bad then? Sight is the last thing to be pitied. Would we be blind? Do we fear lest we should outsee nature and God, and drink truth dry? I look upon the discontent of the literary class as a mere announcement of the fact that they find themselves not in the state of mind of their fathers, and regret the coming state as untried; as a boy dreads the water before he had learned that he can swim. If there is any period one would desire to be born in, is it not the age of Revolution; when the old and the new stand side by side and admit of being compared; when the energies of all men are searched by fear and by hope; when the historic glories of the old can be compensated by the rich possibilities of the new era? This time, like all times, is a very good one, if we but know what to do with it.

I read with some joy of the auspicious signs of the coming days, as they glimmer already through poetry and art, through philosophy and science, through church and state.

One of these signs is the fact that the same movement which effected the elevation of what was called the lowest class in the state, assumed in literature a very marked and as benign an aspect. Instead of the sublime and beautiful, the near, the low, the common, was explored and poetized. That which had been negligently trodden under foot by those who were harnessing and provisioning themselves for long journeys into far countries, is suddenly found to be richer than all foreign parts. The literature of the poor, the feelings of the child, the philosophy of the street, the meaning of the household life, are the topics of the time. It is a great stride. It is a sign—is it not?—of new vigor when the extremities are made active, when currents of warm life run into the hands and the feet. I ask not for the great, the remote, the romantic; what is doing in Italy or Arabia; what is Greek art, or Provençal minstrelsy,[11] I embrace the common, I explore and sit at the feet of the familiar, the low. Give me insight into to-day, and you may have the antique and future worlds. What would we really know the meaning of? The meal in the firkin; the milk in the pan; the ballad in the street; the news of the boat; the glance of the eye; the form and the gait of the body;—show me the ultimate reason of these matters; show me the sublime presence of the highest spiritual cause lurking, as always it does lurk, in these suburbs and extremities of nature; let me see every trifle bristling with the polarity that ranges it instantly on an eternal law; and the shop, the plough, and the ledger referred to the like cause by which light undulates and poets sing;—and the world lies no longer a dull miscellany and lumber-room, but has form and order; there is no trifle, there is no puzzle, but one design unites and animates the farthest pinnacle and the lowest trench.

This idea has inspired the genius of Goldsmith, Burns, Cowper,[12] and, in a newer time, of Goethe, Wordsworth, and Carlyle.[13] This idea they have differently followed and with various success. In contrast with their

---

[11]Provençal was a language spoken in the south of France during medieval times. Minstrels sang verses to the accompaniment of a harp. Provençal minstrelsy flourished during the 11th and 12th centuries.

[12]Oliver Goldsmith (1728–1774), Robert Burns (1759–1796), and William Cowper (1731–1800), British writers. Goldsmith is best known for his novel *The Vicar of Wakefield*. Burns, a Scots, wrote some of the most popular poetry in the English language, including "Flow gently sweet Afton." William Cowper is less well known; his major work is *The Task*, a long poem.

[13]Johann Wolfgang von Goethe (1749–1832), German writer and intellectual whose most widely read work is *Faust*. William Wordsworth (1770–1850), British Romantic poet and poet laureate from 1843 until his death. Thomas Carlyle (1795–1881), Scotch essayist and historian who became a close friend of Emerson and influenced his thinking.

writing, the style of Pope, of Johnson, of Gibbon,[14] looks cold and pedantic. This writing is blood-warm. Man is surprised to find that things near are not less beautiful and wondrous than things remote. The near explains the far. The drop is a small ocean. A man is related to all nature. This perception of the worth of the vulgar is fruitful in discoveries. Goethe, in this very thing the most modern of the moderns, has shown us, as none ever did, the genius of the ancients.

There is one man of genius who has done much for this philosophy of life, whose literary value has never yet been rightly estimated;—I mean Emanuel Swedenborg.[15] The most imaginative of men, yet writing with the precision of a mathematician, he endeavored to engraft a purely philosophical Ethics on the popular Christianity of his time. Such an attempt of course must have difficulty which no genius could surmount. But he saw and showed the connection between nature and the affections of the soul. He pierced the emblematic or spiritual character of the visible, audible, tangible world. Especially did his shade-loving muse hover over and interpret the lower parts of nature; he showed the mysterious bond that allies moral evil to the foul material forms, and has given in epical parables a theory of insanity, of beasts, of unclean and fearful things.

Another sign of our times, also marked by an analogous political movement, is the new importance given to the single person. Every thing that tends to insulate the individual,—to surround him with barriers of natural respect, so that each man shall feel the world is his, and man shall treat with man as a sovereign state with a sovereign state,—tends to true union as well as greatness. "I learned," said the melancholy Pestalozzi,[16] "that no man in God's wide earth is either willing or able to help any other man." Help must come from the bosom alone. The scholar is that man who must take up into himself all the ability of the time, all the contributions of the past, all the hopes of the future. He must be an university of knowledges. If there be one lesson more than another which should pierce his ear, it is, The world is nothing, the man is all; in yourself is the law of all nature, and you know not yet how a globule of sap ascends; in yourself slumbers the whole of Reason; it is for you to know all; it is for you to dare all. Mr. President and Gentlemen, this confidence in the unsearched might of man belongs, by all motives, by all prophecy, by all preparation, to the American Scholar. We have listened too long to the courtly muses of

---

[14]Alexander Pope (1688–1744), British poet, author of "Essay on Man." Samuel Johnson (1709–1784), British author and intellectual, compiler of the first comprehensive dictionary in English. Edward Gibbon (1737–1794), English historian, author of *The History of the Decline and Fall of the Roman Empire.*

[15]Emanuel Swedenborg (1688–1772), Swedish scientist, religious teacher, and mystic whose thought influenced Emerson.

[16]Johann Heinrich Pestalozzi (1746–1827), Swiss educator.

Europe. The spirit of the American freeman is already suspected to be timid, imitative, tame. Public and private avarice make the air we breathe thick and fat. The scholar is decent, indolent, complaisant. See already the tragic consequence. The mind of this country, taught to aim at low objects, eats upon itself. There is no work for any but the decorous and the complaisant. Young men of the fairest promise, who begin life upon our shores, inflated by mountain winds, shined upon by all the stars of God, find the earth below not in unison with these, but are hindered from action by the disgust which the principles on which business is managed inspire, and turn drudges, or die of disgust, some of them suicides. What is the remedy? They did not yet see, and thousands of young men as hopeful now crowding to the barriers for the career do not yet see, that if the single man plant himself indomitably on his instincts, and there abide, the huge world will come round to him. Patience,—patience; with the shades of all the good and great for company; and for solace the perspective of your own infinite life; and for work the study and the communication of principles, the making those instincts prevalent, the conversion of the world. Is it not the chief disgrace in the world, not to be an unit;—not to be reckoned one character;—not to yield that peculiar fruit which each man was created to bear, but to be reckoned in the gross, in the hundred, or the thousand, of the party, the section, to which we belong; and our opinion predicted geographically, as the north, or the south? Not so, brothers and friends— please God, ours shall not be so. We will walk on our own feet; we will work with our own hands; we will speak our own minds. The study of letters shall be no longer a name for pity, for doubt, and for sensual indulgence. The dread of man and the love of man shall be a wall of defence and a wreath of joy around all. A nation of men will for the first time exist, because each believes himself inspired by the Divine Soul which also inspires all men.

QUESTIONS

1. What is Emerson's opinion of specialization? Explain why you agree or disagree with that opinion.

2. What are the main concerns of the scholar? What is the value of these concerns?

3. What sort of person should the scholar be? What sort of life should he or she lead?

4. What are the duties of the scholar?

5. In what ways is "The American Scholar" like "Of Studies" in method and tone? In what ways radically different?

6. Emerson frequently uses striking metaphors to make his points—for instance, this one: "The state of society is one in which the members have suffered amputation from the trunk, and strut about to many walking monsters,—a good finger, a neck, a stomach, an elbow, but never a man." Point out other metaphors in the essay, and explain what Emerson means by them.

7. What striking features of style do you find in the following paragraph? What are the effects of these stylistic devices?

> The theory of books is noble. The scholar of the first age received into him the world around; brooded thereon; gave it the new arrangement of his own mind, and uttered it again. It came into him life; it went out from him truth. It came to him short-lived actions; it went out from him immortal thoughts. It came to him business; it went from him poetry. It was dead fact; now, it is quick thought. It can stand, and it can go. It now endures, it now flies, it now inspires. Precisely in proportion to the depth of mind from which it issued, so high does it soar, so long does it sing.

8. *Personification* gives human attributes to animals, inanimate objects, or concepts. Thus, "My dog is a perfect gentleman," "The old automobile pants and sweats up the hill," and "Love speaks with a thousand tongues" are personifications. Point out instances of personification in "The American Scholar." Do you find this device effective or not? Explain.

GEORGE ORWELL
Shooting an Elephant

George Orwell (1903–1950), the pseudonym of Eric Arthur Blair, is best known for his two novels, Animal Farm *and* 1984. *After service in the British Imperial Police in Burma from 1922 to 1927, Orwell lived from hand to mouth in Paris and London. Fighting on the side of the Republicans in the Spanish Civil War, he was seriously wounded. All of Orwell's writings show his political and social concerns. (See also "Why I Write" on pp. 15–21 of this volume.)*

"Shooting an Elephant" is, first of all, a gripping and unforgettable narrative. No image could be more vivid than that of the elephant crumpling as the bullets hit home. However, the narrative is the basis that Orwell uses to convey his attitudes about colonialism and social class; he tells his story not just for the sake of the tale itself, but to establish a point about his feelings and beliefs.

In Moulmein, in Lower Burma, I was hated by large numbers of people— the only time in my life that I have been important enough for this to happen to me. I was sub-divisional police officer of the town, and in an aimless, petty kind of way anti-European feeling was very bitter. No one had the guts to raise a riot, but if a European woman went through the bazaars alone somebody would probably spit betel juice over her dress. As a police officer I was an obvious target and was baited whenever it seemed safe to do so. When a nimble Burman tripped me up on the football field and the referee (another Burman) looked the other way, the crowd yelled with hideous laughter. This happened more than once. In the end the sneering yellow faces of young men met me everywhere, the insults hooted after me when I was at a safe distance, got badly on my nerves. The young Buddhist priests were the worst of all. There were several thousands of them in the town and none of them seemed to have anything to do except stand on street corners and jeer at Europeans.

All this was perplexing and upsetting. For at that time I had already made up my mind that imperialism was an evil thing and the sooner I chucked up my job and got out of it the better. Theoretically—and secretly, of course—I was all for the Burmese and all against their oppress- ors, the British. As for the job I was doing, I hated it more bitterly than I can perhaps make clear. In a job like that you see the dirty work of Empire at close quarters. The wretched prisoners huddling in the stinking cages of the lock-ups, the grey, cowed faces of the long-term convicts, the scarred buttocks of the men who had been flogged with bamboos—all these oppressed me with an intolerable sense of guilt. But I could get nothing into perspective. I was young and ill-educated and I had had to think out my problems in the utter silence that is imposed on every Englishman in the East. I did not even know that the British Empire is dying, still less did I know that it is a great deal better than the younger empires that are going to supplant it. All I knew was that I was stuck between my hatred of the empire I served and my rage against the evil-spirited little beasts who tried to make my job impossible. With one part of my mind I thought of the British Raj as an unbreakable tyranny, as something clamped down, *in saecula saeculorum*,[1] upon the will of prostrate peoples; with another part I thought that the greatest joy in the world would be to drive a bayonet into a Buddhist priest's guts. Feelings like these are the normal by-products of imperialism; ask any Anglo-Indian official, if you can catch him off duty.

One day something happened which in a roundabout way was enlightening. It was a tiny incident in itself, but it gave me a better glimpse than I had had before of the real nature of imperialism—the real motives for which despotic governments act. Early one morning the sub-inspector at a police station the other end of the town rang me up on the phone and said that an elephant was ravaging the bazaar. Would I please come and do something about it? I did not know what I could do, but I wanted to see what was happening and I got on to a pony and started out. I took my rifle, an old .44 Winchester and much too small to kill an elephant, but I thought the noise might be useful *in terrorem*.[2] Various Burmans stopped me on the way and told me about the elephant's doings. It was not, of course, a wild elephant, but a tame one which had gone "must." It had been chained up as tame elephants always are when their attack of "must" is due, but on the previous night it had broken its chain and escaped. Its mahout,[3] the only person who could manage it when it was in that state, had set out in pursuit, but he had taken the wrong direction and was now twelve hours' journey away, and in the morning the elephant had suddenly reappeared in the town. The Burmese population had no weapons and were quite helpless against it. It had already destroyed somebody's bamboo hut, killed a cow and raided some fruit-stalls and devoured the stock; also it had met the municipal rubbish van, and, when the driver jumped out and took to his heels, had turned the van over and inflicted violence upon it.

The Burmese sub-inspector and some Indian constables were waiting for me in the quarter where the elephant had been seen. It was a very poor quarter, a labyrinth of squalid bamboo huts, thatched with palm-leaf, winding all over a steep hillside. I remember that it was a cloudy stuffy morning at the beginning of the rains. We began questioning the people as to where the elephant had gone, and, as usual, failed to get any definite information. That is invariably the case in the East; a story always sounds clear enough at a distance, but the nearer you get to the scene of events the

---

[1] *in saecula saeculorum*: for all eternity, literally "into ages of ages."
[2] *in terrorem*: as a means of frightening.
[3] *mahout*: elephant handler.

vaguer it becomes. Some of the people said that the elephant had gone in one direction, some said that he had gone in another, some professed not even to have heard of any elephant. I had almost made up my mind that the whole story was a pack of lies, when we heard yells a little distance away. There was a loud, scandalised cry of "Go away, child! Go away this instant!" and an old woman with a switch in her hand came round the corner of a hut violently shooing away a crowd of naked children. Some more women followed, clicking their tongues and exclaiming; evidently there was something there that the children ought not to have seen. I rounded the hut and saw a man's dead body sprawling in the mud. He was an Indian, a black Dravidian[4] coolie, almost naked, and he could not have been dead many minutes. The people said that the elephant had come suddenly upon him round the corner of the hut, caught him with its trunk, put its foot on his back and ground him into the earth. This was the rainy season and the ground was soft, and his face had scored a trench a foot deep and a couple of yards long. He was lying on his belly with arms crucified and head sharply twisted to one side. His face was coated with mud, the eyes wide open, the teeth bared and grinning with an expression of unendurable agony. (Never tell me, by the way, that the dead look peaceful. Most of the corpses I have seen looked devilish.) The friction of the great beast's foot had stripped the skin from his back as neatly as one skins a rabbit. As soon as I saw the dead man I sent an orderly to a friend's house nearby to borrow an elephant rifle. I had already sent back the pony, not wanting it to go mad with fright and throw me if it smelled the elephant.

The orderly came back in a few minutes with a rifle and five cartridges, and meanwhile some Burmans had arrived and told us that the elephant was in the paddy fields below, only a few hundred yards away. As I started forward practically the whole population of the quarter flocked out of their houses and followed me. They had seen the rifle and were all shouting excitedly that I was going to shoot the elephant. They had not shown much interest in the elephant when he was merely ravaging their homes, but it was different now that he was going to be shot. It was a bit of fun to them, as it would be to an English crowd; besides, they wanted the meat. It made me vaguely uneasy. I had no intention of shooting the elephant—I had merely sent for the rifle to defend myself if necessary—and it is always unnerving to have a crowd following you. I marched down the hill, looking and feeling a fool, with the rifle over my shoulder and an evergrowing army of people jostling at my heels. At the bottom, when you got away from the huts, there was a metalled road and beyond that a miry waste of paddy fields a thousand yards across, not yet ploughed but soggy

---

[4]*Dravidian*: member of an Australoid race in southern India.

from the first rains and dotted with coarse grass. The elephant was standing eighty yards from the road, his left side towards us. He took not the slightest notice of the crowd's approach. He was tearing up bunches of grass, beating them against his knees to clean them and stuffing them into his mouth.

I had halted on the road. As soon as I saw the elephant I knew with perfect certainty that I ought not to shoot him. It is a serious matter to shoot a working elephant—it is comparable to destroying a huge and costly piece of machinery—and obviously one ought not to do it if it can possibly be avoided. And at that distance, peacefully eating, the elephant looked no more dangerous than a cow. I thought then and I think now that his attack of "must" was already passing off; in which case he would merely wander harmlessly about until the mahout came back and caught him. Moreover, I did not in the least want to shoot him. I decided that I would watch him for a little while to make sure that he did not turn savage again, and then go home.

But at that moment I glanced round at the crowd that had followed me. It was an immense crowd, two thousand at the least and growing every minute. It blocked the road for a long distance on either side. I looked at the sea of yellow faces above the garish clothes—faces all happy and excited over this bit of fun, all certain that the elephant was going to be shot. They were watching me as they would watch a conjuror about to perform a trick. They did not like me, but with the magical rifle in my hands I was momentarily worth watching. And suddenly I realised that I should have to shoot the elephant after all. The people expected it of me and I had got to do it; I could feel their two thousand wills pressing me forward, irresistibly. And it was at this moment, as I stood there with the rifle in my hands, that I first grasped the hollowness, the futility of the white man's dominion in the East. Here was I, the white man with his gun, standing in front of the unarmed native crowd—seemingly the leading actor of the piece; but in reality I was only an absurd puppet pushed to and fro by the will of those yellow faces behind. I perceived in this moment that when the white man turns tyrant it is his own freedom that he destroys. He becomes a sort of hollow, posing dummy, the conventional-ised figure of a sahib.[5] For it is the condition of his rule that he shall spend his life in trying to impress the "natives" and so in every crisis he has got to do what the "natives" expect of him. He wears a mask, and his face grows to fit it. I had got to shoot the elephant. I had committed myself to doing it when I sent for the rifle. A sahib has got to act like a sahib; he has got to appear resolute, to know his own mind and do definite things. To come all that way, rifle in hand, with two thousand people marching at my heels,

---

[5]*sahib*: "master," formerly used by the people of India in referring to British colonials.

and then to trail feebly away, having done nothing—no, that was impossible. The crowd would laugh at me. And my whole life, every white man's life in the East, was one long struggle not to be laughed at.

But I did not want to shoot the elephant. I watched him beating his bunch of grass against his knees, with that preoccupied grandmotherly air that elephants have. It seemed to me that it would be murder to shoot him. At that age I was not squeamish about killing animals, but I had never shot an elephant and never wanted to. (Somehow it always seems worse to kill a *large* animal.) Besides, there was the beast's owner to be considered. Alive, the elephant was worth at least a hundred pounds; dead, he would only be worth the value of his tusks—five pounds, possibly. But I had got to act quickly. I turned to some experienced-looking Burmans who had been there when we arrived, and asked them how the elephant had been behaving. They all said the same thing: he took no notice of you if you left him alone, but he might charge if you went too close to him.

It was perfectly clear to me to what I ought to do. I ought to walk up to within, say, twenty-five yards of the elephant and test his behavior. If he charged I could shoot, if he took no notice of me it would be safe to leave him until the mahout came back. But also I knew that I was going to do no such thing. I was a poor shot with a rifle and the ground was soft mud into which one would sink at every step. If the elephant charged and I missed him, I should have about as much chance as a toad under a steam-roller. But even then I was not thinking particularly of my own skin, only the watchful yellow faces behind. For at that moment, with the crowd watching me, I was not afraid in the ordinary sense, as I would have been if I had been alone. A white man mustn't be frightened in front of "natives"; and so, in general, he isn't frightened. The sole thought in my mind was that if anything went wrong those two thousand Burmans would see me pursued, caught, trampled on and reduced to a grinning corpse like that Indian up the hill. And if that happened it was quite probable that some of them would laugh. That would never do. There was only one alternative. I shoved the cartridges into the magazine and lay down on the road to get a better aim.

The crowd grew very still, and a deep, low, happy sigh, as of people who see the theatre curtain go up at last, breathed from innumerable throats. They were going to have their bit of fun after all. The rifle was a beautiful German thing with cross-hair sights. I did not then know that in shooting an elephant one should shoot to cut an imaginary bar running from ear-hole to ear-hole. I ought therefore, as the elephant was sideways on, to have aimed straight at his ear-hole; actually I aimed several inches in front of this, thinking the brain would be further forward.

When I pulled the trigger I did not hear the bang or feel the kick—one never does when a shot goes home—but I heard the devilish roar of glee that went up from the crowd. In that instant, in too short a time, one would have thought, even for the bullet to get there, a mysterious, terrible change had come over the elephant. He neither stirred nor fell, but every line of his body had altered. He looked suddenly stricken, shrunken, immensely old, as though the frightful impact of the bullet had paralysed him without knocking him down. At last, after what seemed a long time—it might have been five seconds, I dare say—he sagged flabbily to his knees. His mouth slobbered. An enormous senility seemed to have settled upon him. One could have imagined him thousands of years old. I fired again into the same spot. At the second shot he did not collapse but climbed with desperate slowness to his feet and stood weakly upright, with legs sagging and head drooping. I fired a third time. That was the shot that did for him. You could see the agony of it jolt his whole body and knock the last remnant of strength from his legs. But in falling he seemed for a moment to rise, for as his hind legs collapsed beneath him he seemed to tower upwards like a huge rock toppling, his trunk reaching skyward like a tree. He trumpeted, for the first and only time. And then down he came, his belly towards me, with a crash that seemed to shake the ground even where I lay.

I got up. The Burmans were already racing past me across the mud. It was obvious that the elephant would never rise again, but he was not dead. He was breathing very rhythmically with long rattling gasps, his great mound of a side painfully rising and falling. His mouth was wide open—I could see far down into caverns of pale pink throat. I waited a long time for him to die, but his breathing did not weaken. Finally I fired my two remaining shots into the spot where I thought his heart must be. The thick blood welled out of him like red velvet, but still he did not die. His body did not even jerk when the shots hit him, the tortured breathing continued without a pause. He was dying, very slowly and in great agony, but in some world remote from me where not even a bullet could damage him further. I felt that I had got to put an end to that dreadful noise. It seemed dreadful to see the great beast lying there, powerless to move and yet powerless to die, and not even to be able to finish him. I sent back for my small rifle and poured shot after shot into his heart and down his throat. They seemed to make no impression. The tortured gasps continued as steadily as the ticking of a clock.

In the end I could not stand it any longer and went away. I heard later that it took him half an hour to die. Burmans were arriving with dahs and baskets even before I left, and I was told they had stripped his body almost to the bones by the afternoon.

Afterwards, of course, there were endless discussions about the shooting of the elephant. The owner was furious, but he was only an Indian and could do nothing. Besides, legally I had done the right thing, for a mad elephant has to be killed, like a mad dog, if its owner fails to control it. Among the Europeans opinion was divided. The older men said I was right, the younger men said it was a damn shame to shoot an elephant for killing a coolie, because an elephant was worth more than any damn Coringhee coolie. And afterwards I was very glad that the coolie had been killed; it put me legally in the right and it gave me a sufficient pretext for shooting the elephant. I often wondered whether any of the others grasped that I had done it solely to avoid looking a fool.

QUESTIONS

1. Explain Orwell's feelings about empire and its subjects.

2. On the surface, this essay appears merely to be a narrative, Orwell's autobiographical account of an event from his past. How does "Shooting an Elephant" fit George Dillon's characterization of the expository essay? (See p. 279.)

3. Orwell's essay is quite different from those by Bacon and Emerson. Discuss the differences. What are the effects of the different methods of development? Which sort of essay do you find most interesting, the "classical" sort written by Bacon and Emerson or the "modern" kind represented by Orwell?

4. Note the variety of kinds of sentences in the paragraph beginning "When I pulled the trigger I did not hear the bang. . . ." For example,

   I fired a third time.
   That was the shot that did for him.
   You could see the agony of it jolt his whole body and knock the last remnant of strength from his legs.
   But in falling he seemed for a moment to rise, for as his hind legs collapsed beneath him he seemed to tower upward like a huge rock toppling, his trunk reaching skywards like a tree.

5. If Orwell had stated his thesis or main point directly, what might it have been? Is there any advantage in not stating one's thesis? Explain.

E. B. WHITE
Once More to the Lake

A graduate of Cornell University, White (1899–   ) became a staff member on the
New Yorker and, during his career, established himself as one of America's foremost
essayists. He is also the author of the children's classic Charlotte's Web.

One of the most frequently reprinted of all modern essays, "Once More to the
Lake" is in the tradition of the "familiar essay," a kind of writing that deals,
sometimes humorously, with personal opinion, experiences, and prejudices. The
familiar essay often gives a new slant to everyday occurrences, as does White in
"Once More to the Lake." Among other writers in the familiar essay tradition were
Oliver Goldsmith (1728–1774), Charles Lamb (1775–1834), and Robert Louis
Stevenson (1850–1894).

One summer, along about 1904, my father rented a camp on a lake in
Maine and took us all there for the month of August. We all got ringworm
from some kittens and had to rub Pond's Extract on our arms and legs night
and morning, and my father rolled over in a canoe with all his clothes on;
but outside of that the vacation was a success and from then on none of us
ever thought there was any place in the world like that lake in Maine. We
returned summer after summer—always on August 1 for one month. I
have since become a salt-water man, but sometimes in summer there are
days when the restlessness of the tides and the fearful cold of the sea water
and the incessant wind that blows across the afternoon and into the
evening make me wish for the placidity of a lake in the woods. A few weeks
ago this feeling got so strong I bought myself a couple of bass hooks and a
spinner and returned to the lake where we used to go, for a week's fishing
and to revisit old haunts.

I took along my son, who had never had any fresh water up his nose
and who had seen lily pads only from train windows. On the journey over
to the lake I began to wonder what it would be like. I wondered how time
would have marred this unique, this holy spot—the coves and streams, the
hills that the sun set behind, the camps and the paths behind the camps. I
was sure that the tarred road would have found it out, and I wondered in
what other ways it would be desolated. It is strange how much you can
remember about places like that once you allow your mind to return into
the grooves that lead back. You remember one thing, and that suddenly
reminds you of another thing. I guess I remembered clearest of all the early
mornings, when the lake was cool and motionless, remembered how the
bedroom smelled of the lumber it was made of and of the wet woods whose
scent entered through the screen. The partitions in the camp were thin and

did not extend clear to the top of the rooms, and as I was always the first up I would dress softly so as not to wake the others, and sneak out into the sweet outdoors and start out in the canoe, keeping close along the shore in the long shadows of the pines. I remembered being very careful never to rub my paddle against the gunwale for fear of disturbing the stillness of the cathedral.

The lake had never been what you would call a wild lake. There were cottages sprinkled around the shores, and it was in farming country although the shores of the lake were quite heavily wooded. Some of the cottages were owned by nearby farmers, and you would live at the shore and eat your meals at the farmhouse. That's what our family did. But although it wasn't wild, it was a fairly large and undisturbed lake and there were places in it that, to a child at least, seemed infinitely remote and primeval.

I was right about the tar: it led to within half a mile of the shore. But when I got back there, with my boy, and we settled into a camp near a farmhouse and into the kind of summertime I had known, I could tell that it was going to be pretty much the same as it had been before—I knew it, lying in bed the first morning, smelling the bedroom and hearing the boy sneak quietly out and go off along the shore in a boat. I began to sustain the illusion that he was I, and therefore, by simple transposition, that I was my father. This sensation persisted, kept cropping up all the time we were there. It was not an entirely new feeling, but in this setting it grew much stronger. I seemed to be living a dual existence. I would be in the middle of some simple act, I would be picking up a bait box or laying down a table fork, or I would be saying something, and suddenly it would be not I but my father who was saying the words or making the gesture. It gave me a creepy sensation.

We went fishing the first morning. I felt the same damp moss covering the worms in the bait can, and saw the dragonfly alight on the tip of my rod as it hovered a few inches from the surface of the water. It was the arrival of this fly that convinced me beyond any doubt that everything was as it always had been, that the years were a mirage and that there had been no years. The small waves were the same, chucking the rowboat under the chin as we fished at anchor, and the boat was the same boat, the same color green and the ribs broken in the same places, and under the floorboards the same fresh-water leavings and débris—the dead helgramite, the wisps of moss, the rusty discarded fishhook, the dried blood from yesterday's catch. We stared silently at the tips of our rods, at the dragonflies that came and went. I lowered the tip of mine into the water, tentatively, pensively dislodging the fly, which darted two feet away, poised, darted two feet back, and came to rest again a little farther up the rod. There had been no years between the ducking of this dragonfly and the other one—the one that was part of memory. I looked at the boy, who was silently watching his fly, and it was my hands that held his rod, my eyes watching. I felt dizzy and didn't know which rod I was at the end of.

We caught two bass, hauling them in briskly as though they were mackerel, pulling them over the side of the boat in a businesslike manner without any landing net, and stunning them with a blow on the back of the head. When we got back for a swim before lunch, the lake was exactly where we had left it, the same number of inches from the dock, and there was only the merest suggestion of a breeze. This seemed an utterly enchanted sea, this lake you could leave to its own devices for a few hours and come back to, and find that it had not stirred, this constant and trustworthy body of water. In the shallows, the dark, water-soaked sticks and twigs, smooth and old, were undulating in clusters on the bottom against the clean ribbed sand, and the track of the mussel was plain. A school of minnows swam by, each minnow with its small individual shadow, doubling the attendance, so clear and sharp in the sunlight. Some of the other campers were in swimming, along the shore, one of them with a cake of soap, and the water felt thin and clear and unsubstantial. Over the years there had been this person with the cake of soap, this cultist, and here he was. There had been no years.

Up to the farmhouse to dinner through the teeming, dusty field, the road under our sneakers was only a two-track road. The middle track was missing, the one with the marks of the hooves and the splotches of dried, flaky manure. There had always been three tracks to choose from in choosing which track to walk in; now the choice was narrowed down to two. For a moment I missed terribly the middle alternative. But the way led past the tennis court, and something about the way it lay there in the sun reassured me; the tape had loosened along the backline, the alleys were green with plantains and other weeds, and the net (installed in June and removed in September) sagged in the dry noon, and the whole place steamed with midday heat and hunger and emptiness. There was a choice of pie for dessert, and one was blueberry and one was apple, and the waitresses were the same country girls, there having been no passage of time, only the illusion of it as in a dropped curtain—the waitresses were still fifteen; their hair had been washed, that was the only difference—they had been to the movies and seen the pretty girls with the clean hair.

Summertime, oh, summertime, pattern of life indelible, the fade-proof lake, the woods unshatterable, the pasture with the sweetfern and the juniper forever and ever, summer without end; this was the background, and the life along the shore was the design, the cottagers with their innocent and tranquil design, their tiny docks with the flagpole and the American flag floating against the white clouds in the blue sky, the little paths over the roots of the trees leading from camp to camp and the paths leading back to the outhouses and the can of lime for sprinkling, and at the souvenir counters at the store the miniature birch-bark canoes and the postcards that showed things looking a little better than they looked. This was the American family at play, escaping the city heat, wondering whether the newcomers in the camp at the head of the cove were "common" or "nice," wondering whether it was true that the people who drove up for Sunday dinner at the farmhouse were turned away because there wasn't enough chicken.

It seemed to me, as I kept remembering all this, that those times and those summers had been infinitely precious and worth saving. There had been jollity and peace and goodness. The arriving (at the beginning of August) had been so big a business in itself, at the railway station the farm wagon drawn up, the first smell of the pine-laden air, the first glimpse of the smiling farmer, and the great importance of the trunks and your father's enormous authority in such matters, and the feel of the wagon under you for the long ten-mile haul, and at the top of the last long hill catching the first view of the lake after eleven months of not seeing this cherished body of water. The shouts and cries of the other campers when they saw you, and the trunks to be unpacked, to give up their rich burden. (Arriving was less exciting nowadays, when you sneaked up in your car and parked it under a tree near the camp and took out the bags and in five minutes it was all over, no fuss, no loud wonderful fuss about trunks.)

Peace and goodness and jollity. The only thing that was wrong now, really, was the sound of the place, an unfamiliar nervous sound of the outboard motors. This was the note that jarred, the one thing that would sometimes break the illusion and set the years moving. In those other summertimes all motors were inboard; and when they were at a little distance, the noise they made was a sedative, an ingredient of summer sleep. They were one-cylinder and two-cylinder engines, and some were make-and-break and some were jump-spark, but they all made a sleepy sound across the lake. The one-lungers throbbed and fluttered, and the twin-cylinder ones purred and purred, and that was a quiet sound, too. But now the campers all had outboards. In the daytime, in the hot mornings, these motors made a petulant, irritable sound; at night, in the still evening when the afterglow lit the water, they whined about one's ears like mosquitoes. My boy loved our rented outboard, and his great desire was to achieve single-handed mastery over it, and authority, and he soon learned the trick of choking it a little (but not too much), and the adjustment of the needle valve. Watching him I would remember the things you could do with the old one-cylinder engine with the heavy flywheel, how you could have it eating out of your hand if you got really close to it spiritually. Motorboats in those days didn't have clutches, and you would make a landing by shutting off the motor at the proper time and coasting in with a dead rudder. But there was a way of reversing them, if you learned the trick, by cutting the switch and putting it on again exactly on the final dying revolution of the flywheel, so that it would kick back against compression and begin reversing. Approaching a dock in a strong following breeze, it was difficult to slow up sufficiently by the ordinary coasting method, and if a boy felt he had complete mastery over his motor, he was tempted to keep it running beyond its time and then reverse it a few feet from the dock. It took a cool nerve, because if you threw the switch a twentieth of a second too soon you would catch the flywheel when it still had speed enough to go up past center, and the boat would leap ahead, charging bull-fashion at the dock.

We had a good week at the camp. The bass were biting well and the sun shone endlessly, day after day. We would be tired at night and lie down in the accumulated heat of the little bedrooms after the long hot day and the breeze would stir almost imperceptibly outside and the smell of the swamp drift in through the rusty screens. Sleep would come easily and in the morning the red squirrel would be on the roof, tapping out his gay routine. I kept remembering everything, lying in bed in the mornings— the small steamboat that had a long rounded stern like the lip of a Ubangi, and how quietly she ran on the moonlight sails, when the older boys played their mandolins and the girls sang and we ate doughnuts dipped in sugar, and how sweet the music was on the water in the shining night, and what it had felt like to think about girls then. After breakfast we would go up to the store and the things were in the same place—the minnows in a bottle, the plugs and spinners disarranged and pawed over by the youngsters from the boys' camp, the Fig Newtons and the Beeman's gum. Outside, the road was tarred and cars stood in front of the store. Inside, all was just as it had always been, except there was more Coca-Cola and not so much Moxie and root beer and birch beer and sarsaparilla. We would walk out with the bottle of pop apiece and sometimes the pop would backfire up our noses and hurt. We explored the streams, quietly, where the turtles slid off the sunny logs and dug their way into the soft bottom; and we lay on the town wharf and fed worms to the tame bass. Everywhere we went I had trouble making out which was I, the one walking at my side, the one walking in my pants.

One afternoon while we were there at that lake a thunderstorm came up. It was like the revival of an old melodrama that I had seen long ago with childish awe. The second-act climax of the drama of the electrical disturbance over a lake in America had not changed in any important respect. This was the big scene, still the big scene. The whole thing was so familiar, the first feeling of oppression and heat and a general air around camp of not wanting to go very far away. In midafternoon (it was all the same) a curious darkening of the sky, and a lull in everything that had made life tick; and then the way the boats suddenly swung the other way at their moorings with the coming of a breeze out of the new quarter, and the premonitory rumble. Then the kettle drum, then the snare, then the bass drum and cymbals, then cracking light against the dark, and the gods grinning and licking their chops in the hills. Afterward the calm, the rain steadily rustling in the calm lake, the return of light and hope and spirits, and the campers running out in joy and relief to go swimming in the rain, their bright cries perpetuating the deathless joke about how they were getting simply drenched, and the children screaming with delight at the new sensation of bathing in the rain, and the joke about getting drenched linking the generations in a strong indestructible chain. And the comedian who waded in carrying an umbrella.

When the others went swimming, my son said he was going in, too. He pulled his dripping trunks from the line where they had hung all through the shower and wrung them out. Languidly, and with no thought of going in, I watched him, his hard little body, skinny and bare, saw him wince slightly as he pulled up around his vitals the small, soggy, icy garment. As he buckled the swollen belt, suddenly my groin felt the chill of death.

QUESTIONS

1. What is White's main point or thesis? How do you know?
2. In your own words, explain, "As he buckled the swollen belt, suddenly my groin felt the chill of death."
3. How would you characterize White's style? Is it plain? Ornate? Straightforward? Poetic? Think of word choice, sentence structure, and figurative language.
4. What is unique about the style in the paragraph beginning "One afternoon while we were there at the lake a thunderstorm came up"?
5. In what sense is White's essay a *parable*? What does he gain by presenting his "thesis" in this way rather than directly?
6. What do the essays by Orwell and White have in common?

SUGGESTIONS FOR WRITING

1. Use a narrative to convey your attitudes toward and opinions regarding some situation. "Shooting an Elephant" should be your inspiration if not your guide. Through providing a detailed account of some event in which you have been involved, you can express attitudes and opinions in regard to local, national, or international issues. For example, by telling about an incident that happened in church, you can make your points about religion; by narrating an event from your college or university, you can criticize either higher education in general or the way your institution dispenses education.

2. Give new meaning to an everyday event, as does E. B. White in "Once More to the Lake." Choose something that happened to you or that you participated in—at home, among friends, or on campus. By providing ample detail, as does E. B. White, you can make the familiar seem new and revealing.

3. Using the ideas that Bacon expresses in "Of Studies," write your own version of the essay—but flesh your discussion out with example and analyses.

CHAPTER FOUR

Argument and Persuasion

$\mathbf{T}$he differences among expository, argumentative, and persuasive writing are those of degree, not of absolutes. The primary goal of exposition is *to explain*. The primary goal of argument is *to convince*. The primary goal of persuasion is *to move readers to action*.

For example, if I impartially explain the position of two candidates for the United States Senate, I am writing exposition. If I present reasons for judging one candidate's platform better than that of the other, I am writing argumentation. If I urge you to vote for one of the candidates, I am writing persuasion.

A syllogism is the best example of a pure argument. If the syllogism is valid, you must accept its conclusion even if you do not agree with its premises.

Major Premise:	Everyone residing in the United States should attend church each Sunday.
Minor Premise:	You reside in the United States.
Conclusion:	You should attend church each Sunday.

Even though the argument itself is valid, it is not persuasive.

Both argument and persuasion depend on adequate evidence and valid logic, but persuasion goes beyond argument in appealing directly to readers. An ideal argument, one might say, is addressed to "all intelligent people"; persuasion is addressed to someone specifically or to a particular group of readers who may or may not know one another personally but who share goals, values, or concerns. Persuasion must therefore begin on a point of agreement between the writer and the readers. To persuade you to vote against a candidate who advocates gun control, a writer might begin thus: "Americans have traditionally agreed that citizens are entitled to bear arms; in fact, the Second Amendment to the Constitution grants that right. However, the absolute right to bear arms must be considered in the context of the wording of the Second Amendment and of the current storm of violence that is sweeping this country." With this beginning, the person who believes in gun control has become identified with the persuader and is ready to read on.

Most advertisements are directly persuasive, aimed at bringing about definite actions on the part of those who read them. Propaganda is a special sort of persuasion, using biased viewpoints, symbols such as flags and banners, and slogans to influence opinion. It is obviously not argument, for its "logic" and "data" do not stand analysis; it is a direct appeal to emotion, attempting by-pass the audience's critical ability.

The examples that follow have been classed as either argumentation or persuasion, but remember that clearcut distinctions are hard to draw and usually break down if pressed too far.

MARTIN E. MARTY
The Problem of Taste in TV Christianity

The author argues that religion has been relegated to a ghetto on television: public broadcasting and the networks largely avoid religious programming, with the result that the whole subject is left to shoddy sensationalists whose theology is shallow and whose taste is bad.

Martin E. Marty is a professor of the history of modern Christianity at the University of Chicago and the associate editor of The Christian Century *magazine. This article originally appeared in* Dial, *a magazine for viewers of public broadcasting television stations.*

America has a Theologian of the Year. Tammy Faye Bakker won the title for her expertise on the currently fashionable topic of death. In a recent book that echoes the style of Mrs. Bakker's television discourses, the theologian mused about her naughty little Chi Chi, a dog who died after overeating lima beans.

"I thought my world had come to an end because that was the first time death had ever entered into me." Bakker begged her husband: "Please don't let them bury him right away because I know God can raise things from the dead. . . . I prayed . . . 'Oh, Jesus, please raise Chi Chi from the dead.'" Chi Chi did not budge. The Theologian of the Year bade him good-bye and remembered that he often "wet on our drapes. . . . But you see, God knew . . . that if He took him then that would be the end of the wetting all over the room."

The Theologian of the Year received her title from some puckish Protestant evangelicals who publish *The Wittenburg Door,* a rather irreverent journal whose readership is predominantly young ministers who are born-again Christians. Some TV viewers may know her better as the wife of Jim Bakker, host of the world-famous PTL Club. ("PTL" is the acronym for the Pentecostal slogan "Praise the Lord.") The pair presides over a talk show that, along with its competitors and a number of shows featuring celebrity evangelists, is part of what almost everyone today calls the electronic church.

The spectrum of tastes represented by the electronic church, a Christian ministry, moves beyond Mrs. Bakker to self-parodies such as the unctuous television faith healer Ernest Angley on one end and to respectable figures such as Los Angeles pastor Robert Schuller on the other. The critical evangelicals at *The Wittenburg Door* do not admire Schuller's taste, which they feel is a waste of money that could otherwise be spent feeding the hungry and healing the sick, as well as being too ostentatious to match the simplicity of the Christian gospel. Yet the public knows that he engaged noted architect Philip Johnson to build his Crystal Cathedral and persuaded organist Virgil Fox and opera singer Beverly Sills to help dedicate it.

TV preachers defend their goals, if not their taste. Perhaps their aim is too low, so runs the argument. Nevertheless, they have discovered an audience for bad taste in millions of new followers. Aim too high, and you miss the public. With a full generation of television opportunities, main line Catholics, Protestants, and Jews settled for low-budget public service time during Sunday-morning "graveyard hours." Give those staid, drab, churchy culture snobs a camera, and they tend to focus on a panel discussion over the "thees" and "thous" of the Episcopal Book of Common Prayer or on a debate about whether to change the title of Jesus from Son of God to Child of God in order to please feminists. Is it any wonder, then, that main line religion on TV is as lifeless as poor Chi Chi?

It is a sobering thought that the aesthetic dimension of religion is so large a determinant of faith. The great art of the ages from the Alhambra through Michelangelo and Bach was a response to the tremendous mysteries of the sacred. Now we find the columnists and the journals from Art Buchwald through Nicholas von Hoffman to *Playboy* able to make sport of a television gospel for the pink-flamingo set at spiritual Tupperware parties.

Most nonreligious Americans ignore, or feel they can ignore, this battle over taste. Some of them may worry about the new political power of television evangelists, but that subject seems unconnected to aesthetics. Typical viewers of public or commercial television may be aware that on UHF channels or cable TV there exists the netherworld of the electronic church. They spin their dials past such broadcasting on their way to *Masterpiece Theatre* or *Dallas*, where other battles over taste can rage.

For a time, only practitioners of main line religions served as critics of the electronic church's taste. Recognizing losses in their followings, main liners were demoralized through the early 1970s. According to Arbitron ratings, the electronic-church clientele grew from 9,803,000 to 20,806,000 at mid-decade until it crested, in 1978, at 22,538,000. By 1980, however, there was a change in direction as the response group dropped to 20,538,000. One well-informed observer, Rice University sociologist William Martin, wrote in *The Atlantic* in June 1981 that only about ten million make up the hard-core audience. The main line is not being chipped away to any great extent by the religious broadcasters to the right.

Taste is especially important in churchly worlds. For decades, many have worked to restore the creative interplay between art and religion. The American Guild of Organists, the Interfaith Forum on Religion, Art and

Architecture, the periodic encouragement of talented artists and architects and playwrights, were designed to pay off in aesthetic improvements in the churches. Now the whole effort seems jeopardized by the electronic church, with its screenful of pastel polyester tuxedoes and bouffant hairdos, phallic candles and burbling fountains.

TV belongs to the "play" part of life. (Despite the impression evangelizers give, according to studies published by Fuller Theological Seminary, in Pasadena, California, television is a statistically proved poor instrument for conversion.) Television amuses. It builds loyalties. It makes the already converted happy to be represented on a medium that—let us emphatically grant their point—at worst abused them and at best neglected them. A "play" medium can have serious intentions, of course. But while TV does have instrumentalities to help us confront the serious and grave issues of life, those aspects of television that are most lulling and soporific appeal to the standards of taste the audience has previously picked up from Lawrence Welk and soap opera. Now we can see that electronic-church styles of apparel, music, celebrity, and entertainment are affecting evangelical churches and conventional churches as well.

Theology, of course, has a cognitive dimension. One believes "in," and one believes "that." Theology connects with the meaning of the universe. This is naturally tied up with taste, which is the experience of the universe. Taste is part of the experience of God, so that the two, taste and religion, are inextricably wed. The electronic church must create an impression of instantaneous conversion, must offer healing and parade success stories, or viewers' offerings will not come in, and the cameras will be shuttered. The critics, including other evangelicals, ask what room there is in TV entertainment's often giddy, always summery and sunny world for what Karl Rahner, a preeminent Roman Catholic theologian, points to as an equally biblical, "wintry sort of spirituality." Catering to pop-culture tastes, they argue, *does* reduce the Christian faith. Not all aspects of the church translate easily to electronic media. To take only main line-Catholic examples from our decades: Thomas Merton at quiet prayer, Dorothy Day with the poor, Dom Helder Pessoa Câmara (the justice-minded archbishop) at the side of the Brazilian outcasts, Mother Teresa among the dying in Calcutta, Pope John Paul II in the crowds— these are marvelous TV communicators before cameras that eavesdrop on them as they make the rounds. But you cannot convert these events into regularly scheduled nightly- or weekly-entertainment draws.

Evangelical and main line critics alike must take care lest their criticisms of taste smack of an un-Christian snobbery. The electronic-church clientele have genuine needs that merit ministering to. If they are organized in politics today as resentful and revengeful forces, until recently they were culturally marginal and overlooked. This may be their turn.

What the war over taste, at least in evangelicalism, is calling for now is a turning away from plastic culture but not from culturally plain people. The new challenge, the conservative church critics say, is to upgrade the electronic church, to raise standards and detrivialize it without losing its clientele.

One question remains: Why should anyone in the larger, semisecular culture that public television represents care about the issue of taste in religion? If I had a housetop, I would holler: "Because religion is important to humans"—and how people experience it, which is a matter of taste, determines much of the rest of their way of life. Religion is part of the wars and the tensions in Lebanon, Israel, Iran, Italy, India, Africa, Ireland, in American politics, and on and on. There are good reasons to believe that religious loyalty will organize much of the world and more of America in the future, and woe to those who fail to read the signs of those times. Human rites of passage escort the world's billions through puberty and mating to death, under sacred banners. Far from disappearing, religion is a growing force.

Public television until now has hardly touched religion, not even in its relatively safe historical or cultural dimensions. Network television is wary, for sponsors fear the controversy that often goes with religion. Children's television, aside from that on Sunday mornings, knows absolutely nothing of religious symbolization. What remains, then, is the boxed-in clientele of the electronic church, a large yet still limited audience that seems content with its present levels of taste but that is hardly representative of the whole spiritual strivings of the human race. Through prejudice, lack of imagination, or loss of zeal, we—the public, the arbiters of television and religion—have successfully screened it off from view and largely kept if off the screen. That leaves the cross among the pink flamingos and in the unavailing prayer over Chi Chi.

QUESTIONS

1. Explain why you think that Marty's beginning—the story about Tammy Faye Bakker, Theologian of the Year—is or is not effective. (Does the beginning establish the tone for the rest of the essay?)

2. Summarize the argument of this essay.

3. To what standards of taste does television religion appeal, according to Marty? What specific examples does he give?

4. What does Marty mean by "plastic culture"?

5. Explain what Marty means by: "That leaves the cross among the pink flamingos. . . ."

6. In your opinion, does TV Christianity belittle its viewers, appealing to the lowest common denominator?

7. What kinds of religious experience do not, according to Marty, translate well onto TV?

8. Were you in agreement or disagreement with Marty as you read, or were you simply indifferent? Why? How did your personal attitudes toward religion influence your response to the article?

C. S. LEWIS
The Law of Human Nature

Clive Staples Lewis (1898–1963) was born in Ireland. By career, he was a fellow and tutor at Magdalen College, Oxford, from 1925 to 1954; from 1954 until his death, he was professor of Medieval and Renaissance English at Cambridge. He was a noted scholar (his most famous work being The Allegory of Love); *author of science fiction and the wonderful collection for children,* The Chronicles of Narnia; *and a popular theologian.*

This selection is a notable argument, starting with a specific example and then building logically, step by step, to the conclusion, which appears inevitable: that all humans know the law of human nature, but break it.

Every one has heard people quarrelling. Sometimes it sounds funny and sometimes it sounds merely unpleasant; but however it sounds, I believe we can learn something very important from listening to the kinds of things they say. They say things like this: "How'd you like it if anyone did the same to you?"—"That's my seat, I was there first"—"Leave him alone, he isn't doing you any harm"—"Why should you shove in first?"—"Give me a bit of your orange, I gave you a bit of mine"—"Come on, you promised." People say things like that every day, educated people as well as uneducated, and children as well as grown-ups.

Now what interests me about all these remarks is that the man who makes them is not merely saying that the other man's behaviour does not happen to please him. He is appealing to some kind of standard of behaviour which he expects the other man to know about. And the other man very seldom replies: "To hell with your standard." Nearly always he tries to make out that what he has been doing does not really go against the standard, or that if it does there is some special excuse. He pretends there is some special reason in this particular case why the person who took the seat first should not keep it, or that things were quite different when he was given the bit of orange, or that something has turned up which lets him off keeping his promise. It looks, in fact, very much as if both parties had in mind some kind of Law or Rule of fair play or decent behaviour or morality or whatever you like to call it, about which they really agreed. And they have. If they had not, they might, of course, fight like animals, but they could not *quarrel* in the human sense of the word. Quarrelling means trying to show that the other man is in the wrong. And there would be no sense in trying to do that unless you and he had some sort of agreement as to what Right and Wrong are; just as there would be no sense in saying that a footballer had committed a foul unless there was some agreement about the rules of football.

Now this Law or Rule about Right and Wrong used to be called the Law of Nature. Nowadays, when we talk of the "laws of nature" we usually mean things like gravitation, or heredity, or the laws of chemistry. But when the older thinkers called the Law of Right and Wrong "the Law of Nature," they really meant the Law of *Human* Nature. The idea was that, just as all bodies are governed by the law of gravitation and organisms by biological laws, so the creature called man also had *his* law—with this great difference, that a body could not choose whether it obeyed the law of gravitation or not, but a man could choose either to obey the Law of Human Nature or to disobey it.

We may put this in another way. Each man is at every moment subjected to several sets of law but there is only one of these which he is free to disobey. As a body, he is subjected to gravitation and cannot disobey it; if you leave him unsupported in mid-air, he has no more choice about falling than a stone has. As an organism, he is subjected to various biological laws which he cannot disobey any more than an animal can. That is, he cannot disobey those laws which he shares with other things; but the law which is peculiar to his human nature, the law he does not share with animals or vegetables or inorganic things, is the one he can disobey if he chooses.

This law was called the Law of Nature because people thought that every one knew it by nature and did not need to be taught it. They did not mean, of course, that you might not find an odd individual here and there who did not know it, just as you find a few people who are colour-blind or have no ear for a tune. But taking the race as a whole, they thought that the human idea of decent behaviour was obvious to every one. And I believe they were right. If they were not, then all the things we said about the war were nonsense. What was the sense in saying the enemy were in the wrong unless Right is a real thing which the Nazis at bottom knew as well as we did and ought to have practiced? If they had no notion of what we mean by right, then, though we might still have had to fight them, we could no more have blamed them for that than for the colour of their hair.

I know that some people say the idea of a Law of Nature or decent behaviour known to all men is unsound, because different civilisations and different ages have had quite different moralities.

But this is not true. There have been differences between their moralities, but these have never amounted to anything like a total difference. If anyone will take the trouble to compare the moral teaching of, say, the ancient Egyptians, Babylonians, Hindus, Chinese, Greeks and Romans, what will really strike him will be how very like they are to each other and to our own. Some of the evidence for this I have put together in the appendix of another book called *The Abolition of Man*; but for our present purpose I need only ask the reader to think what a totally different morality would mean. Think of a country where people were admired for running away in battle, or where a man felt proud of doublecrossing all the people who had been kindest to him. You might just as well try to imagine a country where two and two made five. Men have differed as regards what people you ought to be unselfish to—whether it was only your own family, or your fellow countrymen, or everyone. But they have always agreed that you ought not to put yourself first. Selfishness has never been admired. Men have differed as to whether you should have one wife or four. But they have always agreed that you must not simply have any woman you liked.

But the most remarkable thing is this. Whenever you find a man who says he does not believe in a real Right and Wrong, you will find the same man going back on this a moment later. He may break his promise to you, but if you try breaking one to him he will be complaining "It's not fair" before you can say Jack Robinson. A nation may say treaties do not matter; but then, next minute, they spoil their case by saying that the particular treaty they want to break was an unfair one. But if treaties do not matter, and if there is no such thing as Right and Wrong—in other words, if there is no Law of Nature—what is the difference between a fair treaty and an unfair one? Have they not let the cat out of the bag and shown that, whatever they say, they really know the Law of Nature just like anyone else?

It seems, then, we are forced to believe in a real Right and Wrong. People may be sometimes mistaken about them, just as people sometimes get their sums wrong; but they are not a matter of mere taste and opinion any more than the multiplication table. Now if we are agreed about that, I go on to my next point, which is this. None of us are really keeping the Law of Nature. If there are any exceptions among you, I apologize to them. They had much better read some other work, for nothing I am going to say concerns them. And now, turning to the ordinary human beings who are left:

I hope you will not misunderstand what I am going to say. I am not preaching, and Heaven knows I do not pretend to be better than anyone else. I am only trying to call attention to a fact; the fact that this year, or this month, or, more likely, this very day, we have failed to practice ourselves the kind of behaviour we expect from other people. There may be all sorts of excuses for us. That time you were so unfair to the children was when you were very tired. That slightly shady business about the money—the one you have almost forgotten—came when you were very hard up. And what you promised to do for old So-and-so and have never done—well, you never would have promised if you had known how frightfully busy you were going to be. And as for your behaviour to your wife (or husband) or sister (or brother) if I knew how irritating they could be, I would not wonder at it—and who the dickens am I, anyway? I am just the same. That is to say, I do not succeed in keeping the Law of Nature very well, and the moment anyone tells me I am not keeping it, there starts up in my mind a string of excuses as long as your arm. The question at the moment is not whether they are good excuses. The point is that they are one more proof of how deeply, whether we like it or not, we believe in the Law of Nature. If we do not believe in decent behaviour, why should we be so anxious to make excuses for not having behaved decently? The truth is, we believe in decency so much—we feel the Rule of Law pressing on us so—that we cannot bear to face the fact that we are breaking it, and consequently we try to shift the responsibility. For you notice that it is only for our bad behaviour that we find all these explanations. It is only our bad temper that we put down to being tired or worried or hungry; we put our good temper down to ourselves.

These, then, are the two points I wanted to make. First, that human beings, all over the earth, have this curious idea that they ought to behave in a certain way, and cannot really get rid of it. Secondly, that they do not in fact behave in that way. They know the Law of Nature; they break it. These two facts are the foundation of all clear thinking about ourselves and the universe we live in.

QUESTIONS

1. Briefly summarize Lewis's argument concerning the law of human nature. Explain why you do or do not find it convincing.

2. Now that you have summarized the argument, look at the last paragraph of the essay, in which Lewis gives his own summary. Does yours agree with his? If not, how does it differ?

3. Compare C. S. Lewis's method of arguing with Martin Marty's technique. In what ways are the two same? In what ways do they differ? (Examine, for example, the use of specific examples and the organizations of the arguments.)

4. Suppose you were in a debate with Marty. How would you refute his argument?

D. H. LAWRENCE

From Reflections on the Death of a Porcupine

David Herbert Lawrence (1885–1930) was one of the great modern writers. The son of a Nottingham coal miner, Lawrence graduated from University College, Nottingham, and became a school teacher in a London suburb. However, his career was not to be one of quiet respectability and stability. In 1912, he and Frieda von Richthofen Weekly—wife of one of his former professors and cousin of the German nobleman who was to become world famous as the "Red Baron"—eloped to Europe. From this time on, the couple moved about the world, seldom remaining in one place long enough to establish themselves. In the eighteen years that they were together, they lived in New Mexico, Mexico, Australia, Italy, and Switzerland and in various parts of England.

*Lawrence's novels—*Sons and Lovers*(1913),* The Rainbow *(1915),* Women in Love *(1920), and* Lady Chatterley's Lover *(1928), to name only the most widely known—have always been highly esteemed; his poetry is quite often reprinted in anthologies; but his non-fiction prose has never gained the audience which it deserves.* Sea and Sardinia *(1921),* Mornings in Mexico *(1927), and* Etruscan Places *(1932) are masterpieces in the genre of travel literature, and Lawrence's essays are always vigorous and vivid.*

In "Reflections on the Death of a Porcupine" we see Lawrence at his best as a writer of description.

However, toward its midpoint, the essay shifts from description to argumentation, contending that strict equality is simply not in the scheme of things, a point of view that many find elitist or even fascist.

There are many bare places on the little pine trees, towards the top, where the porcupines have gnawed the bark away and left the white flesh showing. And some trees are dying from the top.

Everyone says porcupines should be killed; the Indians, Mexicans, Americans all say the same.

At full moon a month ago, when I went down the long clearing in the brilliant moonlight, through the poor dry herbage a big porcupine began to waddle away from me, toward the trees and the darkness. The animal had raised all its hairs and bristles, so that by the light of the moon it seemed to have a tall, swaying, moonlit aureole arching its back as it went. That seemed curiously fearsome, as if the animal were emitting itself demon-like on the air.

It waddled very slowly, with its white spiky spoon-tail steering flat, behind the round bear-like mound of its back. It had a lumbering, beetle's, squalid motion, unpleasant. I followed it into the darkness of the timber, and there, squat like a great tick, it began scrapily to creep up a pine-trunk. It was very like a great aureoled tick, a bug, struggling up.

I stood near and watched, disliking the presence of the creature. It is a duty to kill the things. But the dislike of killing him was greater than the dislike of him. So I watched him climb.

And he watched me. When he had got nearly the height of a man, all his long hairs swaying with a bristling gleam like an aureole, he hesitated, and slithered down. Evidently he had decided, either that I was harmless, or else that it was risky to go up any further, when I could knock him off so easily with a pole. So he slithered podgily down again, and waddled away with the same bestial, stupid motion of that white-spiky repulsive spoon-tail. He was as big as a middle-sized pig: or more like a bear.

I let him go. He was repugnant. He made a certain squalor in the moonlight of the Rocky Mountains. As all savagery has a touch of squalor, that makes one a little sick at the stomach. And anyhow, it seemed almost more squalid to pick up a pine-bough and push him over, hit him and kill him.

A few days later, on a hot, motionless morning when the pine-trees put out their bristles in stealthy, hard assertion; and I was not in a good temper, because Black-eyed Susan, the cow, had disappeared into the timber, and I had had to ride hunting her, so it was nearly nine o'clock before she was milked: Madame came in suddenly out of the sunlight saying: "I got such a shock! There are two strange dogs, and one of them has got the most awful beard, all round his nose."

She was frightened, like a child at something unnatural.

"Beard! Porcupine quills, probably! He's been after a porcupine."

"Ah!" she cried in relief. "Very likely! Very likely!"—then with a change of tone; "Poor thing, will they hurt him?"

"They will. I wonder when he came."

"I heard dogs bark in the night."

"Did you? Why didn't you say so? I should have known Susan was hiding—"

The ranch is lonely, there is no sound in the night, save the innumerable noises of the night, that you can't put your finger on; cosmic noises in the far deeps of the sky, and of the earth.

I went out. And in the full blaze of sunlight in the field, stood two dogs, a black-and-white, and a big, bushy, rather handsome sandy-red dog, of the collie type. And sure enough, this latter did look queer and a bit horrifying, his whole muzzle set round with white spines, like some ghastly growth; like an unnatural beard.

The black-and-white dog made off as I went through the fence. But the red dog whimpered and hesitated, and moved on hot bricks. He was fat and in good condition. I thought he might belong to some shepherds herding sheep in the forest ranges, among the mountains.

He waited while I went up to him, wagging his tail and whimpering, and ducking his head, and dancing. He daren't rub his nose with his paws any more: it hurt too much. I patted his head and looked at his nose, and he whimpered loudly.

He must have had thirty quills, or more, sticking out of his nose, all the way round: the white, ugly ends of the quills protruding an inch, sometimes more, sometimes less, from his already swollen, blood-puffed muzzle.

The porcupines here have quills only two or three inches long. But they are devilish; and a dog will die if he does not get them pulled out. Because they work further and further in, and will sometimes emerge through the skin away in some unexpected place.

Then the fun began. I got him in the yard: and he drank up the whole half-gallon of the chickens' sour milk. Then I started pulling out the quills. He was a big, bushy, handsome dog, but his nerve was gone, and every time I got a quill out, he gave a yelp. Some long quills were fairly easy. But the shorter ones, near his lips, were deep in, and hard to get hold of, and hard to pull out when you did get hold of them. And with every one that came out, came a little spurt of blood and another yelp and writhe.

The dog wanted the quills out: but his nerve was gone. Every time he saw my hand coming to his nose, he jerked his head away. I quieted him, and stealthily managed to jerk out another quill, with the blood all over my fingers. But with every one that came out, he grew more tiresome. I tried and tried and tried to get hold of another quill, and he jerked and jerked, and writhed and whimpered, and ran under the porch floor.

It was a curiously unpleasant, nerve-trying job. The day was blazing hot. The dog came out and I struggled with him again for an hour or more. Then we blindfolded him. But either he smelled my hand approaching his nose, or some weird instinct told him. He jerked his head, this way, that way, up, down, sideways, roundwise, and one's fingers came slowly, slowly, to seize a quill.

The quills on his lips and chin were deep in, only about a quarter of an inch of white stub protruding from the swollen, blood-oozed, festering black skin. It was very difficult to jerk them out.

We let him lie for an interval, hidden in the quiet cool place under the porch floor. After half an hour, he crept out again. We got a rope round his nose, behind the bristles, and one held while the other got the stubs with the pliers. But it was too trying. If a quill came out, the dog's yelp startled every nerve. And he was frightened of the pain, it was impossible to hold his head still any longer.

After struggling for two hours, and extracting some twenty quills, I gave up. It was impossible to quiet the creature, and I had had enough. His nose on the top was clear: a punctured, puffy, blood-darkened mess; and his lips were clear. But just on his round little chin, where the few white hairs are, was still a bunch of white quills, eight or nine, deep in.

We let him go, and he dived under the porch, and there he lay invisible: save for the end of his bushy, foxy tail, which moved when we came near. Towards noon he emerged, ate up the chicken-food, and stood with that doggish look of dejection, and fear, and friendliness, and greediness, wagging his tail.

But I had had enough.

"Go home!" I said. "Go home! Go home to your master, and let him finish for you."

He would not go. So I led him across the blazing hot clearing, in the way I thought he should go. He followed a hundred yards, then stood motionless in the blazing sun. He was not going to leave the place.

And I! I simply did not want him.

So I picked up a stone. He dropped his tail, and swerved towards the house. I knew what he was going to do. He was going to dive under the porch, and there stick, haunting the place.

I dropped my stone, and found a good stick under the cedar tree. Already in the heat was that sting-like biting of electricity, the thunder gathering in the sheer sunshine, without a cloud, and making one's whole body feel dislocated.

I could not bear to have that dog around any more. Going quietly to him, I suddenly gave him one hard hit with the stick, crying: "Go home!" He turned quickly, and the end of the stick caught him on his sore nose. With a fierce yelp, he went off like a wolf, downhill, like a flash, gone. And I stood in the field full of pangs of regret, at having hit him, unintentionally, on his sore nose.

But he was gone.

And then the present moon came, and again the night was clear. But in the interval there had been heavy thunder-rains, the ditch was running with bright water across the field, and the night, so fair, had not the terrific, mirror-like brilliancy, touched with terror, so startling bright, of the moon in the last days of June.

We were alone on the ranch. Madame went out into the clear night, just before retiring. The stream ran in a cord of silver across the field, in the straight line where I had taken the irrigation ditch. The pine tree in front of the house threw a black shadow. The mountain slope came down to the fence, wild and alert.

"Come!" said she excitedly. "There is a big porcupine drinking at the ditch. I thought at first it was a bear."

When I got out he had gone. But among the grasses and the coming wild sunflowers, under the moon, I saw his greyish halo, like a pallid living bush, moving over the field, in the distance, in the moonlit *clair-obscur*.

We got through the fence, and following, soon caught him up. There he lumbered, with his white spoon-tail spiked with bristles, steering behind almost as if he were moving backwards, and this was his head. His long, long hairs above the quills quivering with a dim grey gleam, like a bush.

And again I dislike him.

"Should one kill him?"

She hesitated. Then with a sort of disgust:

"Yes!"

I went back to the house, and got the little twenty-two rifle. Now never in my life had I shot at any live thing: I never wanted to. I always felt guns very repugnant: sinister, mean. With difficulty I had fired once or twice at a target: but resented doing even so much. Other people could shoot if they wanted to. Myself, individually, it was repugnant to me even to try.

But something slowly hardens in a man's soul. And I knew now it had hardened in mine. I found the gun, and with rather trembling hands got it loaded. Then I pulled back the trigger and followed the porcupine. It was still lumbering through the grass. Coming near, I aimed.

The trigger stuck. I pressed the little catch with a safety-pin I found in my pocket, and released the trigger. Then we followed the porcupine. He was still lumbering towards the trees. I went sideways on, stood quite near to him, and fired, in the clear-dark of the moonlight.

And as usual I aimed too high. He turned, went scuttling back whence he had come.

I got another shell in place, and followed. This time I fired full into the mound of his round back, below the glistening grey halo. He seemed to stumble on to his hidden nose, and struggled a few strides, ducking his head under like a hedgehog.

"He's not dead yet! Oh, fire again!" cried Madame.

I fired, but the gun was empty.

So I ran quickly, for a cedar pole. the porcupine was lying still, with subsiding halo. He stirred faintly. So I turned him and hit him hard over the nose; or where, in the dark, his nose should have been. And it was done. He was dead.

And in the moonlight, I looked down on the first creature I had ever shot.

"Does it seem mean?" I asked aloud, doubtful.

Again Madame hesitated. Then: "No!" she said resentfully.

And I felt she was right. Things like the porcupine, one must be able to shoot them, if they get in one's way.

One must be able to shoot. I, myself, must be able to shoot, and to kill.

For me, this is a *volta face*. I have always preferred to walk round my porcupine, rather than kill it.

Now, I know it's no good walking round. One must kill.

I buried him in the adobe hole. But some animal dug down and ate him; for two days later there lay the spines and bones spread out, with the long skeletons of the porcupine-hands.

The only nice thing about him—or her, for I believe it was a female, by the dugs on her belly—were the feet. They were like longish, alert black hands, paw-hands. That is why a porcupine's tracks in the snow look almost as if a child had gone by, leaving naked little human footprints, like a little boy.

So, he is gone: or she is gone. But there is another one, bigger and blacker-looking, among the west timber. That too is to be shot. It is part of the business of ranching: even when it's only a little half-abandoned ranch like this one.

Wherever man establishes himself, upon the earth, he has to fight for his place against the lower orders of life. Food, the basis of existence, has to be fought for even by the most idyllic of farmers. You plant, and you protect your growing crop with a gun. Food, food, how strangely it relates man with the animal and vegetable world! How important it is! And how fierce is the fight that goes on around it.

The same when one skins a rabbit, and takes out the inside, one realizes what an enormous part of the animal, comparatively, is intestinal, what a big part of him is just for food-apparatus; for *living on* other organisms.

And when one watches the horses in the big field, their noses to the ground, bite-bite-biting without ever lifting their noses, cropping off the grass, the young shoots of alfalfa, the dandelions, with a blind, relentless, unwearied persistence, one's whole life pauses. One suddenly realizes again how all creatures devour, and *must* devour the lower forms of life.

So Susan, swinging across the field, snatches off the tops of the little wild sunflowers as if she were mowing. And down they go, down her black throat. And when she stands in her cowy oblivion chewing her cud, with her lower jaw swinging peacefully, and I am milking her, suddenly the camomiley smell of her breath, as she glances round with glaring, smoke-blue eyes, makes me realize it is the sunflowers that are her ball of cud. Sunflowers! And they will go to making her glistening black hide, and the thick cream on her milk.

And the chickens, when they see a great black beetle, that the Mexicans call a *toro*, floating past, they are after it in a rush. And if it settles, instantly the brown hen stabs it with her beak. It is a great beetle two or three inches long: but in a second it is in the crop of the chicken. Gone!

And Timsy, the cat, as she spies on the chipmunks, crouches in another sort of oblivion, soft, and still. The chipmunks come to drink the milk from the chickens' bowl. Two of them met at the bowl. They were little squirrely things with stripes down their backs. They sat up in front of one another, lifting their inquisitive little noses and humping their backs.

Then each put its two little hands on the other's shoulders, they reared up, gazing into each other's faces; and finally they put their two little noses together, in a sort of kiss.

But Miss Timsy can't stand this. In a soft, white-and-yellow leap she is after them. They skip, with the darting jerks of chipmunks, to the wood-heap, and with one soft, high-leaping sideways bound Timsy goes through the air. Her snow-flake of a paw comes down on one of the chipmunks. She looks at it for a second. It squirms. Swiftly and triumphantly she puts her two flowery little white paws on it, legs straight out in front of her, back arched, gazing concentratedly yet whimsically. Chipmunk does not stir. She takes it softly in her mouth, where it dangles softly, like a lady's tippet. And with a proud, prancing motion the Timsy sets off towards the house, her white little feet hardly touching the ground.

But she gets shooed away. We refuse to loan her the sitting-room any more, for her gladiatorial displays. If the chippy must be "butchered to make a Timsy holiday," it shall be outside. Disappointed, but still high-stepping, the Timsy sets off towards the clay oven by the shed.

There she lays the chippy gently down, and soft as a little white cloud lays one small paw on its striped back. Chippy does not move. Soft as thistle-down she raises her paw a tiny, tiny bit, to release him.

And all of a sudden, with an elastic jerk, he darts from under the white release of her paw. And instantly, she is up in the air and down she comes on him, with the forward thrusting bolts of her white paws. Both creatures are motionless.

Then she takes him softly in her mouth again, and looks round, to see if she can slip into the house. She cannot. So she trots towards the wood-pile.

It is a game, and it is pretty. Chippy escapes into the wood-pile, and she softy, softly reconnoitres among the faggots.

Of all the animals, there is no denying it, the Timsy is the most pretty, the most fine. It is not her mere *corpus* that is beautiful; it is her bloom of aliveness. Her "infinite variety"; the soft, snow-flakey lightness of her, and at the same time her lean, heavy ferocity. I had never realized the latter, till I was lying in bed one day moving my toe, unconsciously, under the bedclothes. Suddenly a terrific blow struck my foot. The Timsy had sprung out of nowhere, with a hurling, steely force, thud upon the bedclothes where the toe was moving. It was as if someone had aimed a sudden blow, vindictive and unerring.

"Timsy!"

She looked at me with the vacant, feline glare of her hunting eyes. It is not even ferocity. It is the dilation of the strange, vacant arrogance of power. The power is in her.

And so it is. Life moves in circles of power and of vividness, and each circle of life only maintains its orbit upon the subjection of some lower circle. If the lower cycles of life are not *mastered*, there can be no higher cycle.

In nature, one creature devours another, and this is an essential part of all existence and of all being. It is not something to lament over, nor something to try to reform. The Buddhist who refuses to take life is really ridiculous, since if he eats only two grains of rice per day, it is two grains of life. We did not make creation, *we* are not the authors of the universe. And if we see that the whole of creation is established upon the fact that one life devours another life, one cycle of existence can only come into existence through the subjugating of another cycle of existence, then what is the good of trying to pretend that it is not so? The only thing to do is to realize what is higher, and what is lower, in the cycles of existence.

It is nonsense to declare that there *is* no higher and lower. We know full well that the dandelion belongs to a higher cycle of existence than the hartstongue fern, that the ant's is a higher form of existence than the dandelion's, that the thrush is higher than the ant, that Timsy the cat is higher than the thrush, and that I, a man, am higher than Timsy.

What do we mean by higher? Strictly, we mean more alive. More vividly alive. The ant is more vividly alive than the pine-tree. We know it, there is no trying to refute it. It is all very well saying that they are both alive in two different ways, and therefore they are incomparable, incommensurable. This is also true.

But one truth does not displace another. Even apparently contradictory truths do not displace one another. Logic is far too coarse to make the subtle distinctions life demands. . . .

QUESTIONS

1. Explain why you agree or disagree with Lawrence's thesis that "Life moves in circles of power and vividness, and each circle of life only maintains its orbit upon the subjection of some lower circle. If the lower cycles of life are not *mastered*, there can be no higher cycle."

2. How does Lawrence portray the porcupine? As an agreeable of disagreeable creature?

3. In many ways, this essay is strikingly similar to George Orwell's "Shooting an Elephant" (pp. 299–305). After you read "Shooting an Elephant," answer these questions:
    a. In what ways were Lawrence's and Orwell's motives similar? In what ways different?
    b. In what ways are the descriptions of the deaths of the creatures similar?

    c. In what ways were Lawrence's and Orwell's feelings about the killing alike? In what ways different?

4. Why does Lawrence go into such detail about Timsy and the chipmunk? What purpose does the story serve in the essay?

5. Lawrence claims that "Everyone says porcupines should be killed: Indians, Mexicans, Americans all the same." Would that statement and the attitude it portrays be true today?

6. Lawrence's portraits of animals are exceptionally effective. Based on your reading of this essay, how would you say he achieves such vividness?

ERIC HOFFER
The Role of the Undesirables

Eric Hoffer (1902–1983), a self-educated man, worked in box factory in Los Angeles and then became a migratory field worker; for many years he was a longshoreman in San Francisco and held the post of "conversationalist at large" at the University of California, Berkeley. Nearly blind from a fall at five until he was fifteen, he writes, "When my eyesight came back I was seized with an enormous hunger for the printed word." Hoffer's literary reputation began with publication of The True Believer *in 1951.*

Hoffer's prose is lucid and graceful, and his explanation of how he arrived at his insights about the "undesirables" is an excellent example of a good mind thinking about experience and drawing conclusions from it.

In the winter of 1934, I spent several weeks in a federal transient camp in California. These camps were originally established by Governor Rolph in the early days of the Depression to care for single homeless unemployed of the state. In 1934 the federal government took charge of the camps for a time, and it was then that I first heard of them.

How I happened to get into one of the camps is soon told. Like thousands of migrant agricultural workers in California I then followed the crops from one part of the state to the other. Early in 1934 I arrived in the town of El Centro, in the Imperial Valley. I had been given a free ride on a truck from San Diego, and it was midnight when the truck driver dropped me on the outskirts of El Centro. I spread my bedroll by the side of the road and went to sleep. I had hardly dozed off when the rattle of a motorcycle drilled itself into my head and a policeman was bending over me saying, "Roll up, mister." It looked as though I was in for something; it happened now and then that the police got overzealous and rounded up the freight trains. But this time the cop had no such thought. He said, "Better go over to the federal shelter and get yourself a bed and maybe some breakfast." He directed me to the place.

I found a large hall, obviously a former garage, dimly lit, and packed with cots. A concert of heavy breathing shook the thick air. In a small office near the door, I was registered by a middle-aged clerk. He informed me that this was the "receiving shelter" where I would get one night's lodging and breakfast. The meal was served in the camp nearby. Those who wished to stay on, he said, had to enroll in the camp. He then gave me three blankets and excused himself for not having a vacant cot. I spread the blankets on the cement floor and went to sleep.

I awoke with dawn amid a chorus of coughing, throat clearing, the sound of running water, and the intermittent flushing of toilets in the back of the hall. There were about fifty of us, of all colors and ages, all of us more or less ragged and soiled. The clerk handed out tickets for breakfast, and we filed out to the camp located several blocks away, near the railroad tracks.

From the outside the camp looked like a cross between a factory and a prison. A high fence of wire enclosed it, and inside were three large sheds and a huge boiler topped by a pillar of black smoke. Men in blue shirts and dungarees were strolling across the sandy yard. A ship's bell in front of one of the buildings announced breakfast. The regular camp members—there was a long line of them—ate first. Then we filed in through the gate, handing our tickets to the guard.

It was a good, plentiful meal. After breakfast our crowd dispersed. I heard some say that the camps in the northern part of the state were better, that they were going to catch a northbound freight. I decided to try this camp in El Centro.

My motives in enrolling were not crystal clear. I wanted to clean up. There were shower baths in the camp and wash tubs and plenty of soap. Of course I could have bathed and washed my clothes in one of the irrigation ditches, but here in the camp I had a chance to rest, get the wrinkles out of my belly, and clean up at leisure. In short, it was the easiest way out.

A brief interview at the camp office and a physical examination were all the formalities for enrollment. There were some two hundred men in the camp. They were the kind I had worked and traveled with for years. I even saw familiar faces—men I had worked with in orchards and fields. Yet my predominant feeling was one of strangeness. It was my first experience of life in intimate contact with a crowd. For it is one thing to work and travel with a gang, and quite another thing to eat, sleep, and spend the greater part of the day cheek by jowl with two hundred men.

I found myself speculating on a variety of subjects: the reason for their chronic belly-aching and beefing—it was more a ritual than the expression of a grievance; the amazing orderliness of the men; the comic seriousness with which they took their games of cards, checkers, and dominoes; the weird manner of reasoning one overheard now and then. Why, I kept wondering, were these men within the enclosure of a federal transient camp? Were they people temporarily hard up? Would jobs solve all their difficulties? Were we indeed like the people outside?

Up to then I was not aware of being one of a specific species of humanity. I had considered myself simply a human being—not particularly good or bad, and on the whole harmless. The people I worked and traveled with I knew as Americans and Mexicans, Whites and Negroes, Northerners and Southerners, etc. It did not occur to me that we were a group possessed of peculiar traits, and that there was something—innate or acquired—in our make-up which made us adopt a particular mode of existence.

It was a slight thing that started me on a new track.

I got to talking to a mild-looking, elderly fellow. I liked his soft speech and pleasant manner. We swapped trivial experiences. Then he suggested a game of checkers. As we started to arrange the pieces on the board I was startled by the sight of his crippled right hand. I had not noticed it before. Half of it was chopped off lengthwise, so that the horny stump with its three fingers looked like a hen's leg. I was mortified that I had not noticed the hand until he dangled it, so to speak, before my eyes. It was, perhaps, to bolster my shaken confidence in my powers of observation that I now began paying close attention to the hands of the people around me. The result was astounding. It seemed that every other man had been mangled in some way. There was a man with one arm. Some men limped. One young, good-looking fellow had a wooden leg. It was as though the majority of the men had escaped the snapping teeth of a machine and left part of themselves behind.

It was, I knew, an exaggerated impression. But I began counting the cripples as the men lined up in the yard at mealtime. I found thirty (out of two hundred) crippled either in arms or legs. I immediately sensed where the counting would land me. The simile preceded the statistical deduction: we in the camp were a human junk pile.

I began evaluating my fellow tramps as human material, and for the first time in my life I became face-conscious. There were some good faces, particularly among the young. Several of the middle-aged and the old looked healthy and well-preserved. But the damaged and decayed faces were in the majority. I saw faces that were wrinkled, or bloated, or raw as the surface of a peeled plum. Some of the noses were purple and swollen, some broken, some pitted with enlarged pores. There were many toothless mouths (I counted seventy-eight). I noticed eyes that were blurred, faded, opaque, or bloodshot. I was struck by the fact that the old men, even the very old, showed their age mainly in the face. Their bodies were still slender and erect. One little man over sixty years of age looked a mere boy when seen from behind. The shriveled face joined to the boyish body made a startling sight.

My diffidence had now vanished. I was getting to know everybody in the camp. They were a friendly and talkative lot. Before many weeks I knew some essential fact about practically everyone.

And I was continually counting. Of the two hundred men in the camp there were approximately as follows:

Cripples	30
Confirmed drunkards	60
Old men (55 and over)	50
Youths under twenty	10
Men with chronic diseases, heart, asthma, TB	12

Mildly insane 4
Constitutionally lazy 6
Fugitives from justice 4
Apparently normal 70

(The numbers do not tally up to two hundred since some of the men were counted twice or even thrice—as cripples and old, or as old and confirmed drunks, etc.)

In other words: less than half of the camp inmates (seventy normal, plus ten youths) were unemployed workers whose difficulties would be at an end once jobs were available. The rest (60 percent) had handicaps, in addition to unemployment.

I also counted fifty war veterans, and eighty skilled workers representing sixteen trades. All the men (including those with chronic diseases) were able to work. The one-armed man was a wizard with a shovel.

I did not attempt any definite measurement of character and intelligence. But it seemed to me that the intelligence of the men in the camp was certainly not below the average. And as for character, I found much forbearance and genuine good humor. I never came across one instance of real viciousness. Yet, on the whole, one would hardly say that these men were possessed of strong characters. Resistance, whether to one's appetites or to the ways of the world, is a chief factor in the shaping of character; and the average tramp is, more or less, a slave of his few appetites. He generally takes the easiest way out.

The connection between our make-up and our mode of existence as migrant workers presented itself now with some clarity.

The majority of us were incapable of holding onto a steady job. We lacked self-discipline and the ability to endure monotonous, leaden hours. We were probably misfits from the very beginning. Our contact with a steady job was not unlike a collision. Some of us were maimed, some got frightened and ran away, and some took to drink. We inevitably drifted in the direction of least resistance—the open road. The life of a migrant worker is varied and demands only a minimum of self-discipline. We were now in one of the drainage ditches of ordered society. We could not keep a footing in the ranks of respectability and were washed into the slough of our present existence.

Yet, I mused, there must be in this world a task with an appeal so strong that were we to have a taste of it we would hold on and be rid for good of our restlessness.

My stay in the camp lasted about four weeks. Then I found a haying job not far from town, and finally, in April, when the hot winds began blowing, I shouldered my bedroll and took the highway to San Bernardino.

It was the next morning, after I got a lift to Indio by truck, that a new idea began to take hold of me. The highway out of Indio leads through waving date groves, fragrant grapefruit orchards, and lush alfalfa fields; then, abruptly, passes into a desert of white sand. The sharp line between garden and desert is very striking. The turning of white sand into garden seemed to me an act of magic. This, I thought, was a job one would jump at—even the men in the transient camps. They had the skill and the ability of the average American. But their energies, I felt, could be quickened only by a task that was spectacular, that had in it something of the miraculous. The pioneer task of making the desert flower would certainly fill the bill.

Tramps as pioneers? It seemed absurd. Every man and child in California knows that the pioneers had been giants, men of boundless courage and indomitable spirit. However, as I strode on across the white sand, I kept mulling over the idea.

Who were the pioneers? Who were the men who left their homes and went into the wilderness? A man rarely leaves a soft spot and goes deliberately in search of hardship and privation. People become attached to the places they live in; they drive roots. A change of habitat is a painful act of uprooting. A man who has made good and has a standing in his community stays put. The successful businessmen, farmers, and workers usually stayed where they were. Who then left for the wilderness and the unknown? Obviously those who had not made good: men who went broke or never amounted to much; men who though possessed of abilities were too impulsive to stand the daily grind; men who were slaves of their appetites—drunkards, gamblers, and women chasers; outcasts—fugitives from justice and ex-jailbirds. There were no doubt some who went in search of health—men suffering with TB, asthma, heart trouble. Finally there was a sprinkling of young and middle-aged in search of adventure.

All these people craved change, some probably actuated by the naïve belief that a change in place brings with it a change in luck. Many wanted to go to a place where they were not known and there make a new beginning. Certainly they did not go out deliberately in search of hard work and suffering. If in the end they shouldered enormous tasks, endured unspeakable hardships, and accomplished the impossible, it was because they had to. They became men of action on the run. They acquired strength and skill in the inescapable struggle for existence. It was a question of do or die. And once they tasted the joy of achievement, they craved for more.

Clearly the same types of people which now swelled the ranks of migratory workers and tramps had probably in former times made up the bulk of the pioneers. As a group the pioneers were probably as unlike the present-day "native sons"—their descendants—as one could well imagine. Indeed, were there to be today a new influx of typical pioneers, twin brothers of the forty-niners, only in modern garb, the citizens of California would consider it a menace to health, wealth, and morals.

With few exceptions, this seems to be the case in the settlement of all new countries. Ex-convicts were the vanguard in the settling of Australia. Exiles and convicts settled Siberia. In this country, a large portion of our earlier and later settlers were failures, fugitives, and felons. The exceptions seemed to be those who were motivated by religious fervor, such as the Pilgrim Fathers and the Mormons.

Although quite logical, the train of thought seemed to me then a wonderful joke. In my exhilaration I was eating up the road in long strides, and I reached the oasis of Elim in what seemed almost no time. A passing empty truck picked me up just then and we thundered through Banning and Beaumont, all the way to Riverside. From there I walked the seven miles to San Bernardino.

Somehow, this discovery of a family likeness between tramps and pioneers took a firm hold on my mind. For years afterward it kept intertwining itself with a mass of observations which on the face of them had no relation to either tramps or pioneers. And it moved me to speculate on subjects in which, up to then, I had had no real interest, and of which I knew very little.

I talked with several old-timers—one of them over eighty and a native son—in Sacramento, Placerville, Auburn, and Fresno. It was not easy, at first, to obtain the information I was after. I could not make my questions specific enough. "What kind of people were the early settlers and miners?" I asked. They were a hard-working, tough lot, I was told. They drank, fought, gambled, and wenched. They wallowed in luxury, or lived on next to nothing with equal ease. They were the salt of the earth.

Still it was not clear what manner of people they were.

If I asked what they looked like, I was told of whiskers, broad-brimmed hats, high boots, shirts of many colors, sun-tanned faces, horny hands. Finally I asked: "What group of people in present-day California most closely resembles the pioneers?" The answer, usually after some hesitation, was invariably the same: "The Okies and the fruit tramps."

I tried also to evaluate the tramps as potential pioneers by watching them in action. I saw them fell timber, clear firebreaks, build rock walls, put up barracks, build dams and roads, handle steam shovels, bulldozers, tractors, and concrete mixers. I saw them put in a hard day's work after a night of steady drinking. They sweated and growled, but they did the work. I saw tramps elevated to positions of authority as foremen and superintendents. Then I could notice a remarkable physical transformation: a seamed face gradually smoothed out and the skin showed a healthy hue; an indifferent mouth became firm and expressive; dull eyes cleared and brightened; voices actually changed; there was even an apparent increase in stature. In almost no time these promoted tramps looked as if they had been on top all their lives. Yet sooner or later I would meet up with them again in a railroad yard, on some skid row, or in the fields—tramps again.

It was usually the same story: they got drunk or lost their temper and were fired, or they got fed up with the steady job and quit. Usually, when a tramp becomes a foreman he is careful in his treatment of the tramps under him; he knows the day of reckoning is never far off.

In short it was not difficult to visualize the tramps as pioneers. I reflected that if they were to find themselves in a singlehanded life-and-death struggle with nature, they would undoubtedly display persistence. For the pressure of responsibility and the heat of battle steel a character. The inadaptable would perish, and those who survived would be the equal of the successful pioneers.

I also considered the few instances of pioneering engineered from above—that is to say, by settlers possessed of lavish means, who were classed with the best where they came from. In these instances, it seemed to me, the resulting social structure was inevitably precarious. For pioneering de luxe usually results in a plantation society, made up of large landowners and peon labor, either native or imported. Very often there is a racial cleavage between the two. The colonizing activities of the Teutonic barons in the Baltic, the Hungarian nobles in Transylvania, the English in Ireland, the planters in our South, and the present-day plantation societies in Kenya and other British and Dutch colonies are cases in point. Whatever their merits, they are characterized by poor adaptability. They are likely eventually to be broken up either by a peon revolution or by an influx of typical pioneers—who are usually of the same race or nation as the landowners. The adjustment is not necessarily implemented by war. Even our old South, had it not been for the complication of secession, might eventually have attained stability without war: namely, by the activity of its own poor whites or by an influx of the indigent from other states.

There is in us a tendency to judge a race, a nation, or an organization by its least worthy members. The tendency is manifestly perverse and unfair; yet it has some justification. For the quality and destiny of a nation are determined to a considerable extent by the nature and potentialities of its inferior elements. The inert mass of a nation is in its middle section. The industrious, decent, well-to-do, and satisfied middle classes—whether in cities or on the land—are worked upon and shaped by minorities at both extremes: the best and the worst.

The superior individual, whether in politics, business, industry, science, literature, or religion, undoubtedly plays a major role in the shaping of a nation. But so do the individuals at the other extreme: the poor, the outcasts, the misfits, and those who are in the grip of some overpowering passion. The importance of these inferior elements as formative factors lies in the readiness with which they are swayed in any direction. This peculiarity is due to their inclination to take risks ("not giving a damn") and their propensity for united action. They crave to merge their drab, wasted lives into something grand and complete. Thus they are the first and most fervent adherents of new religions, political upheavals, patriotic hysteria, gangs, and mass rushes to new lands.

And the quality of a nation—its innermost worth—is made manifest by its dregs as they rise to the top: by how brave they are, how humane, how orderly, how skilled, how generous, how independent or servile; by the bounds they will not transgress in their dealings with a man's soul, with truth, and with honor.

The average American of today bristles with indignation when he is told that this country was built, largely, by hordes of undesirables from Europe. Yet, far from being derogatory, this statement, if true, should be a cause for rejoicing, should fortify our pride in the stock from which we have sprung.

This vast continent with its towns, farms, factories, dams, aqueducts, docks, railroads, highways, powerhouses, schools, and parks is the handiwork of common folk from the Old World, where for centuries men of their kind had been beasts of burden, the property of their masters—kings, nobles, and priests—and with no will and no aspirations of their own. When on rare occasions one of the lowly had reached the top in Europe he had kept the pattern intact and, if anything, tightened the screws. The stuffy little corporal from Corsica harnessed the lusty forces released by the French Revolution to a gilded state coach, and could think of nothing grander than mixing his blood with that of the Hapsburg masters and establishing a new dynasty. In our day a bricklayer in Italy, a house painter in Germany, and a shoemaker's son in Russia have made themselves masters of their nations; and what they did was to re-establish and reinforce the old pattern.

Only here, in America, were the common folk of the Old World given a chance to show what they could do on their own, without a master to push and order them about. History contrived an earth-shaking joke when it lifted by the nape of the neck lowly peasants, shopkeepers, laborers, paupers, jailbirds, and drunks from the midst of Europe, dumped them on a vast, virgin continent and said: "Go to it; it is yours!"

And the lowly were not awed by the magnitude of the task. A hunger for action, pent up for centuries, found an outlet. They went to it with ax, pick, shovel, plow, and rifle; on foot, on horse, in wagons, and on flatboats. They went to it praying, howling, singing, brawling, drinking, and fighting. Make way for the people! This is how I read the statement that this country was built by hordes of undesirables from the Old World.

Small wonder that we in this country have a deeply ingrained faith in human regeneration. We believe that, given a chance, even the degraded and the apparently worthless are capable of constructive work and great deeds. It is a faith founded on experience, not on some idealistic theory. And no matter what some anthropologists, sociologists, and geneticists may tell us, we shall go on believing that man, unlike other forms of life, is not a captive of his past—of his heredity and habits—but is possessed of infinite plasticity, and his potentialities for good and for evil are never wholly exhausted.

QUESTIONS

1. How does Hoffer's view of human beings square with D. H. Lawrence's? Which do you find most convincing? Why?

2. In what senses could this essay be used as an argument in favor of social programs such as unemployment compensation, government sponsored medical care, and outright grants to the needy?

3. Discuss what Hoffer means when he says, in the last paragraph of the essay, "And no matter what some anthropologists, sociologists, and geneticists may tell us, we shall go on believing that man, unlike other forms of life, is not a captive of his past—of his heredity and habits— but is possessed of infinite plasticity, and his potentialities for good and for evil are never wholly exhausted." What longstanding argument is Hoffer referring to?

4. Now that you have read "The Role of the Undesirables," discuss your reaction to this note about the author:

> Eric Hoffer [who died after this note was written] works three days a week as a longshoreman in San Francisco and spends one day as "research professor" at the University of California in Berkeley.
>
> Of his early life Mr. Hoffer has written: "I had no schooling. I was practically blind up to the age of fifteen. When my eyesight came back I was seized with an enormous hunger for the printed word. I read indiscriminately everything within reach—English and German.
>
> "When my father (a cabinet-maker) died I realized that I would have to fend for myself. I knew several things: One, that I didn't want to work in a factory; two, that I couldn't stand being dependent on the good graces of a boss; three, that I was going to stay poor; four, that I had to get out of New York. Logic told me that California was the poor man's country."

SAMUEL JOHNSON
Freeing a Negro Slave

Samuel Johnson (1709–1784) was a unique man of letters: novelist, essayist, poet, critic, biographer, and compiler of the first comprehensive dictionary of English. Forced by lack of funds to leave Oxford after one year, he earned his living for six years as bookseller and schoolmaster. In 1737, he and his wife settled in London, and he began his literary career, writing for Gentleman's Magazine. *Literary works for which Johnson is known are the biography* Life of Savage *(1744), the long poem "The Vanity of Human Wishes" (1749), periodical essays in* The Rambler *(1750–1752), the "moral romance"* Rasselas *(1759).*

Joseph Knight, a Negro, had been kidnapped as a child and was sold to a Scottish gentleman who paid Knight sixpence a week, which Knight found inadequate once he married; thus, he left his master's service. This is the background of the case for which Johnson wrote the legal brief, to be used by Knight's counsel. The Court of Sessions did free Knight.

In his argument for freeing a Negro slave, Johnson uses compelling logic. As you read the essay, notice how everything follows inexorably from the first sentence.

It must be agreed that in most ages many countries have had part of their inhabitants in a state of slavery; yet it may be doubted whether slavery can ever be supposed the natural condition of man. It is impossible not to conceive that men in their original state were equal; and very difficult to imagine how one would be subjected to another but by violent compulsion. An individual may, indeed, forfeit his liberty by a crime; but he cannot by that crime forfeit the liberty of his children. What is true of a criminal seems true likewise of a captive. A man may accept life from a conquering enemy on condition of perpetual servitude; but it is very doubtful whether he can entail that servitude on his descendants; for no man can stipulate without commission for another. The condition which he himself accepts, his son or grandson perhaps would have rejected. If we should admit, what perhaps may with more reason be denied, that there are certain relations between man and man which may make slavery necessary and just, yet it can never be proved that he who is now suing for his freedom ever stood in any of those relations. He is certainly subject by no law, but that of violence, to his present master; who pretends no claim to his obedience, but that he bought him from a merchant of slaves, whose right to sell him never was examined. It is said that, according to the constitutions of Jamaica, he was legally enslaved; these constitutions are merely positive; and apparently injurious to the right of mankind, because whoever is exposed to sale is condemned to slavery without appeal; by whatever fraud or violence he might have been originally brought into the merchant's power. In our own time Princes have been sold, by wretches to whose care they were entrusted, that they might have an European education; but when once they were brought to a market in the plantations, little would avail either their dignity or their wrongs. The laws of Jamaica afford a Negro no redress. His colour is considered as a sufficient testimony against him. It is to be lamented that moral right should ever give way to political convenience. But if temptations of interest are sometimes too strong for human virtue, let us at least retain a virtue where there is no temptation to quit it. In the present case there is apparent right on one side, and no convenience on the other. Inhabitants of this island can neither gain riches nor power by taking away the liberty of any part of the human species. The sum of the argument is this:—No man is by nature the property of another: The defendant is, therefore, by nature free: The rights of nature must be some way forfeited before they can be justly taken away: That the defendant has by any act forfeited the rights of nature we require to be proved; and if no proof of such forfeiture can be given, we doubt not but the justice of the court will declare him free.

QUESTIONS

1. What is the effect of the first two sentences of the essay? What do you think Johnson wanted them to accomplish with the reader? (Note terms such as "must be agreed," "may be doubted," "impossible not to conceive," and "very difficult to imagine.")

2. According to the distinctions made in the introduction to this chapter, is "Freeing a Negro Slave" argumentation or persuasion? Explain.

3. Both C. S. Lewis and Samuel Johnson refer to natural rights. Do both mean the same thing? Explain.

World Press Review Advertisement

This advertisement originally appeared in the Atlantic.

No one person, publication—or nation—holds a monopoly on it. But you can get *closer* to the truth by examining events and issues from a variety of perspectives. If you look at what's being done, written, and read around the world, you'll have a better grasp of reality.

Where can you find this information? In WORLD PRESS REVIEW—the unique, fast-growing news monthly whose staff reads more than 1,000 foreign newspapers and periodicals and passes the most significant items along to you!

Not paraphrases, but the original texts of articles, features, and editorials, abridged as little as possible, from such renowned journals as *Le Monde* (Paris), *The Economist* (London), *Der Spiegel* (Hamburg), *Ma'ariv* (Tel Aviv), *Asahi Shimbun* (Tokyo),...and yes, *Pravda* (Moscow), and *People's Daily* (Peking). Plus interviews with foreign journalists, writers, and scholars. A world of insight that you haven't been getting from your other news sources! It includes regular departments on politics, business, travel, and culture and hilarious cartoons from around the world.

You'll discover how other nations see themselves, their neighbors, you, and our common problems.

Order today —and discover how reading WORLD PRESS REVIEW gets you closer to the truth!

World Press Review
P.O. Box 915, Farmingdale, N.Y. 11737

Yes! I wish to subscribe to WORLD PRESS REVIEW:

12 issues for just **$17.95**
(In Canada add $2.50; other foreign $7.00)

☐ Payment Enclosed

☐ Charge to: ☐ VISA   ☐ MasterCard

Credit Card No. _____

Expiration Date _____

MasterCard 4-digit Interbank No. ___ ___ ___ ___

Name _____

Address _____

City _____

State _____ Zip _____

QUESTIONS

1. What method does the ad use to get the reader's attention?
2. What action does the ad call for?
3. What claims are advanced by the ad? How do they serve its purpose?
4. What benefits are promised the ad's readers?
5. Explain why you did or did not find the ad persuasive.
6. Judging from the information available, what sort of readers is the ad intended for?

Three on Gun Control

A longstanding issue in American society is gun control. On one side stands the powerful National Rifle Association, and on the other are organizations such as Handgun Control, Inc. These advocates on both sides of the issue use advertisements persuasively to further their points of view. Neither of the ads *argues* on the basis of the logic or data, which is not to say that either one is "wrong" or dishonest.

The essay by Robert Kubey attempts to persuade readers to take a new course of action in regard to violence in society.

ROBERT KUBEY

Instead of Handguns

Robert Kubey is a doctoral candidate in behavioral sciences at the University of Chicago. His essay originally appeared in "My Turn," a regular column in Newsweek and the only part of the magazine which is not staff written.

A young woman I know just bought a rifle and told me, with perverse pleasure, "I wouldn't think twice about blowing the head off anyone who dared take one step inside my house." She's taking a course in the use of firearms.

Another acquaintance of mine is a classical pianist and his wife is a successful writer of children's books. They live in a quiet, progressive college town—as idyllic a community as one could imagine. They, too, have enrolled in the new education of the '80s—they're taking a course which will permit them to legally own and use tear gas. And then there are my other friends who are taking classes in self-defense and martial arts.

My wife and I just took a different sort of course—a class in first aid. In one day we learned the basics of mouth-to-mouth resuscitation, the treatment of cuts, wounds, shock, poisoning and burns; how to aid a person who is choking or has suffered a heart attack or stroke; how to apply bandages, splints and tourniquets; how to handle heat stroke, frostbite, eye injuries and much more. Perhaps we should also have been taught how to aid someone who has been tear-gassed.

At present, our society sorely lacks a sense of mutual responsibility and community—a sense that we are all in this together. As things currently stand, it is more realistic to suspect that a fellow citizen has been trained in the use of a handgun than trained in first aid. But wouldn't it be comforting to know instead that every citizen has been trained to help any other citizen in distress?

DENT

As the quality and frequency of our interactions with neighbors and strangers deteriorate, universal training in first aid might make a small, but appreciable, dent in our national proclivity toward increased alienation, suspicion and privatization.

It is my contention that taking responsibility for others and knowledge of first aid go hand in hand, and it is my firm belief that first aid should be made mandatory in the nation's schools and be taught throughout the years of compulsory education. Many liberal-arts colleges teach a "core curriculum"—a series of courses which every student is required to take and which lay the foundation for subsequent learning. It is understood that every student leaves his or her college knowing certain fundamental things. Other than the three R's, we have no such essential core curriculum in primary or secondary education.

If there is any doubt that there is a need for universal training in first aid, a few statistics may make an impression. In the United States during 1981, almost 10 million injuries resulted in disabilities lasting one day or more. Accidents causing permanent disabilities numbered 350,000, and 99,000 people died accidentally. For youths between 15 and 24, accidents claimed more lives last year than all other causes combined.

For those who wonder how the schools would manage to teach first aid to so many, I have a suggestion. Teenagers taught by adult volunteers could pass their knowledge down to younger children, who would later become instructors themselves. First aid can be taught by young people (the minimum age for a Red Cross instructor's aide is only 13), and in so doing, our youth will gain an increasing sense of responsibility as they grow older. There need be no massive cost to the schools.

First aid also offers children and teen-agers the opportunity to apply what they have learned in other areas of study. Knowing how to stop bleeding or manage a sudden eye injury allows for a practical appreciation and respect for the strengths and fragilities of human anatomy. Such understanding may reduce the likelihood that one would abuse one's own body or that of another. I even believe that a potential young offender, who would otherwise savagely club a defenseless elderly woman while stealing her handbag, might find it more difficult to inflict bodily injury if he had been steeped in first aid over a period of 10 or 12 years of schooling.

MORAL DILEMMAS

For a number of years now, Lawrence Kohlberg, a well-known Harvard psychologist, has been studying whether children's abilities to make moral judgments could be enhanced by classroom discussions of moral dilemmas. His attempts have met with limited success. I would suggest we might improve the moral education of the young by helping children obtain the skills necessary to act morally.

Human beings must acquire a sense of mastery and competence in their early development in order to become healthy, productive adults. What better way to let children know that they are valuable and effective people than to impress upon them at an early age that they could be indispensable in the saving of a life and can teach such essential skills to others?

Give children and adults the skills to act responsibly, and more of them will. And if you're taking a course in karate, guns or tear gas to protect yourself, why not balance your course load with a class that teaches you how to help and heal as well?

Handgun Advertisements

The two advertisements which follow appeared in the September 1982 issue of California *magazine, just before Californians were to vote on gun control legislation.*

DR. ROBERT PIERCE: Husband, Father, Pediatrician and Life Member
of the National Rifle Association.

"I'm a pediatrician and people often ask, 'How can you allow your kids
to shoot guns when you know how dangerous they are?'
Well, I've never treated a child for a gunshot wound, but I've lost count of those
injured by bicycles, kitchen knives, poisons and many household items
that injure children every year by the thousands. The vast majority of gun owners
teach their kids never, never to be reckless with firearms.

"I first joined the NRA when I was in my teens and now my two sons are
members too. I'm teaching them the same respect for guns that my grandfather
taught me so that shooting and hunting
can always be safe activities in our family." **I'm the NRA.**

The NRA sponsors a wide array of shooting programs and activities
for its junior members including basic marksmanship courses and hunter skills seminars.
If you would like to join the NRA and want more information
about our programs and benefits, write Harlon Carter, Executive Vice President.
P.O. Box 37484, Dept. RP-10, Washington, D.C. 20013.

IN 1980, HANDGUNS KILLED
77 PEOPLE IN JAPAN.
8 IN GREAT BRITAIN.
24 IN SWITZERLAND.
8 IN CANADA.
23 IN ISRAEL.
18 IN SWEDEN.
4 IN AUSTRALIA.
11,522 IN THE UNITED STATES.

GOD BLESS AMERICA.

The pen is mightier than the gun.
Write Handgun Control, Inc. Now.
810 18th Street N.W., Washington, D.C. 20006
Or call (202) 638-4723

STOP HANDGUN CRIME BEFORE IT STOPS YOU.

QUESTIONS

1. The National Rifle Association ad shows a man with a gun and identifies him as "Dr. Robert Pierce: Husband, Father, Pediatrician and Life Member of the National Rifle Association." What effect is the ad attempting to achieve by having Dr. Pierce deliver its message?
2. Explain the meaning of the boldface statement "I'm the NRA."
3. Is the NRA ad convincing? Explain. Does the ad appeal mainly to reason or to emotion?
4. Explain the *irony* of the Handgun Control ad.
5. Does the Handgun Control ad appeal mainly to reason or to emotion? Explain.
6. Both advertisements picture guns, but with completely different effects. Explain.
7. If you were to write an essay taking the position of one or the other of the ads, what additional evidence would you include to support that position?
8. How valid is the alternative offered by Kubey in "Instead of Handguns"?
9. What is Kubey's attitude toward self-defense courses?
10. Does Kubey expect people to accept his ideas immediately? What evidence do you have for your answer?
11. In the library, check the "letters to the editor" section of the *Newsweek* magazines that were published shortly after this article appeared. How well did those letter writers understand the claims Kubey made? How did they react to Kubey's point?

DAVID OWEN
Rest in Pieces

"Rest in Pieces," one of the strangest and most weirdly fascinating persuasive essays you are ever likely to read, appeared among the regular columns at the back of Harper's *magazine, among book and film reviews and travel commentary. The section in which the piece appeared was perversely titled "Appetites."*

My wife recently told me she intends to donate her body to science. I found the proposition ghoulish, even though it would relieve me (I intend to survive her) of the expense of disposal. I said that I was determined to have a more traditional send-off: a waterproof, silk-lined, air-conditioned casket priced in the the sports car range, several acres of freshly cut flowers, a procession of aggrieved schoolchildren winding slowly through some public square, a tape-recorded compilation of my final reflections, and, local ordinances permitting, an eternal flame. But after a bit of research, I have come around to her point of view.

Two powerful human emotions—the fear of death and the love of bargains—inexorably conflict in any serious consideration of what to do with an expired loved one, all the more so if the loved one is oneself. Most people secretly believe that thinking about death is the single surest method of shortening life expectancy.

On the other hand, the appeal of the bargain intensifies when a third (though essentially unheard-of) emotion—the desire to do good for its own sake—is injected into the discussion. If, after one is entirely through with it, one's body can be put to some humane or scientific use, enabling life to be preserved or knowledge to be advanced, can one in good conscience refuse? And yet, the mortal coil recoils.

"No freezing in the winter. No scorching in the summer." Such are the advantages of booking space in an aboveground burial condominium, according to a flyer I received not long ago. Printed across the bottom of the page was this disclaimer: *"We sincerely regret if this letter should reach any home where there is illness or sorrow, as this certainly was not intended."* In other words, if this information has arrived at one of the rare moments in your life when it would actually be of immediate use, please ignore it.

That the funeral business is filled with smoothies, crooks, and con men has been well known since at least 1963, when Jessica Mitford published her classic exposé, *The American Way of Death.* Mitford's book is required reading for all mortals, Fit-A-Fut and Ko-Zee, she revealed, were the trade names of two styles of "burial footwear," the latter model described by its manufacturer as having "soft, cushioned soles and warm, luxurious slipper comfort, but true shoe smartness." The same company also sold special postmortem "pantees" and "vestees," enabling funeral directors to gouge a few extra dollars out of any family that could be dissuaded from burying a loved one in her own underwear.

Twenty years later, the death industry is unchanged in almost every particular except cost. Mitford found that the average funeral bill, according to industry figures, was $708. When I visited a local mortuary to price a simple burial for a fictitious ailing aunt, the director rattled off a list of probable charges that added up to more than $5,000, flowers and cemetery plot extra. His estimate included $110 for hauling her body two blocks to his establishment and $80 for carrying it back out to the curb. Pallbearing is a union job in New York City; family members can't lay a hand on a coffin without getting a waiver from the local. ("If they drop the casket, pal," a Teamsters spokesman told me, "you're gonna be in trouble.") Hairdresser, $35. Allowing "Auntie" (as he once referred to her) to repose in his "chapel" for one day—something he told me was mandatory, despite the fact that I said I didn't want a memorial service and that no relatives would be dropping by—would be $400.

The largest single charge we discussed was for the casket. He used the word "minimum" as an adjective to describe virtually any model I expressed an interest in that cost less than $1,500. The single wooden coffin in his showroom was "very" minimum ($1,100). The whole genius of the funeral business is in making you believe you're buying a refrigerator or a sofa or even a car instead of a box that will be lowered into the ground and covered with dirt. Since there are no *real* criteria, other than price, for preferring one such box to another, you end up doing things like sticking your hands inside a few models and choosing the one with the firmest bedsprings. "Women seem to like the color coordination," my Charon said in reference to a 20-gauge steel model (I think it was called the Brittany) with a baby-blue interior. Since the women he was talking about are dead, that word "seem" is positively eerie.

Cremation is becoming a fairly popular choice among people who think of themselves as smart shoppers. The funeral industry has responded to this trend by subtly discouraging its customers from considering cremation and by making sure that cremation is very nearly as expensive as burial in a box. A pamphlet called "Considerations Concerning Cremation," published by the National Funeral Directors Association, Inc., and distributed by morticians, pretends to be evenhanded but is actually intended to horrify its readers. "Operating at an extremely high temperature [a cremation oven] reduces the body to a few pounds of bone fragments and ashes in less than two hours. . . . Most of the cremated remains are then placed in an urn or canister and carefully identified." This last sentence is the funeral director's equivalent of "Most newborn babies are then sent home with their proper mothers." Earth burial, in contrast, is "a gradual process of reduction to basic elements."

If the funeral business dislikes cremation, it positively abhors the donation of bodies to medical schools, because in such cases the opportunities for profiteering are dramatically reduced—though not, to be sure, eliminated. There is virtually nothing you can do, short of being disintegrated by Martians in the middle of the ocean, to keep a funeral director from claiming a piece of the action when you die. Once again, a pamphlet tells the story: ". . . essential to avoid the possibility of disappointment . . . more bodies available than the maximum required . . . rejection *is* permitted by state law . . . you can expect your funeral director to be of assistance. . . ."

One almost wishes one could die tomorrow, the sooner to savor the pleasure of taking one's business elsewhere.

Ernest W. April, associate professor of anatomy at Columbia University's College of Physicians & Surgeons, is the man in charge of superintending Columbia's supply of cadavers. Dr. April shares his office with Rufus, a huge red dog who wandered into his yard one day and doesn't like to be left alone. Also in Dr. April's office are some skulls, an old-fashioned radio, a human skeleton, a spine, a paperback book with a picture of a skull on it, some more skulls, a few microscopes, some big bones on a shelf, and a small plastic bone on the floor (for Rufus).

"Most medical students look forward to receiving their cadaver," Dr. April told me. "Once they have their cadaver they are, from their point of view, in medical school. It's something tangible. There's anticipation, trepidation. In the first laboratory exercise, the students basically come up and meet the cadaver, almost as if it were a patient."

As at all medical schools, Columbia's cadavers are donated. Prospective benefactors eighteen years of age and older fill out anatomical bequeathal forms and return them to the university. Hours, days, weeks, months, or years pass. "When the Time Comes," as one brochure puts it, the donor's survivors call the medical school's department of anatomy. "Within the greater metropolitan area," the brochure says, "arrangements for removal of the body can be made by the medical college. Alternatively, the family may engage a local funeral director to deliver the **unembalmed** body to the medical college at the address on the cover." Medical schools almost always require unembalmed bodies because ordinary cosmetic embalming, the kind sold at the funeral homes, turns skin to the consistency of old shoes and doesn't hold off deterioration for more than a few days. Medical school embalming, on the other hand, is designed for the ages. "We've had some specimens that we've kept for over twenty years," one professor told me. "It's almost like the Egyptians."

Donated cadavers are stored in a refrigerated room until they're needed. Columbia has about 200 students in each class. The ideal student-cadaver ratio is four to one (which means "every two people get one of everything there's two of," a medical student explains). Contrary to what the funeral directors imply, Columbia, like many schools, has fewer bodies than it would like and so must assign five students to each. Ratios as high as eight to one are not unheard of. If the donor consents beforehand, a cadaver bequeathed to one institution may be transferred to another with greater need. New Jersey, for some reason, attracts almost as many cadavers as it does medical students and occasionally ships extras to New York. (That's extra cadavers, not extra medical students.) People who don't like the idea of being dissected by students at all can specify on their bequeathal forms that their bodies are to be used only for research.

"If a person donates his remains for biomedical education and research," Dr. April says, "there's a moral obligation on our part to utilize the body on this premises if at all possible, and only for that purpose. The only exception is that we occasionally do make material that has been dissected available to art students because, going back to the time of Leonardo da Vinci, Raphael, Titian, and Michelangelo, artists have had a real need to know and understand anatomy." Subscribers to public television, among others, should find this prospect irresistible: a chance to benefit science *and* the arts.

When Columbia's anatomy courses end, the cadavers are individually cremated and buried in a cemetery plot the university owns. All of this is done at the university's expense. (In comparison with funeral home rates, the cost of picking up, embalming, storing, cremating, and burying each cadaver is estimated by medical school officials at about $400.) If the family desires, the uncremated remains can be returned at the end of the course, as long as the family asks beforehand and agrees to cover any extra costs.

Nearly all medical schools operate donation programs much like Columbia's. All you have to do is call up the anatomy department at the nearest medical school and ask what the procedure is. A group called the Associated Medical Schools of New York, based at Manhattan's Bellevue Hospital, oversees donations to a dozen or so institutions around the state, including the New York College of Podiatric Medicine and the New York University School of Dentistry. You might think that a podiatry school and a dental school could happily share cadavers, but no school will take less than a whole body.

I sent away for donation information from dozens of medical schools and state anatomical boards. Studying the resulting avalanche of brochures has given me more than a week of intense reading pleasure, making me

DO NOT READ THIS!

Inscribed on a wall at the Office of the Chief Medical Examiner of New York, better known as the morgue, are the words TACEANT COLLOQUIA EFFUGIAT RISUS HIC LOCUS EST UBI MORS GAUDET SUCCERERE VITA. I make this out as, "If you have any sense at all, you won't go downstairs and look at the bodies." But my Latin is weak and my curiosity is strong and I went down anyway. I peered into an autopsy room through a tiny window in the door and came to the conclusion that death is a condition suffered by many young black men, a few old white men, and no women at all. After I had seen much more than enough, my guide took me upstairs to the true object of my visit: Room 601, the morgue museum. In planning the disposal of your body, don't overlook this little-known option.

The morgue museum is not one of New York's better-known attractions. Indeed, it is usually open only to medical students, police academy cadets, and other aspirants to professions that require a solid grounding in morbidity. I was just a humble tourist, but they let me in anyway.

The morgue museum is the Helmsley Palace of final resting places, an elite repository of the bizarre whose requirements for admission are strict but exactly opposite to those of the anatomical donation programs. If you leave a pretty corpse, you don't stand a chance of ending up here. But if you play your cards right—or wrong, I suppose—some extremely interesting part of you could conceivably be immortalized in an institution that, though it isn't the Louvre, is at any rate the most creative waste of taxpayers' money I've ever encountered. The museum's collection is not quite up to date, modern life being what it is, and families being hesitant to put their loved ones on display. But there is still plenty to look at, including:

A scorched bathtub in which a great many people were incinerated by someone; empty cans of inflammable liquids; a helpful display identifying several hundred charred bone fragments belonging to the victims.

The blocked esophagus of a young boy who defeated his brother in a contest to see which of them could swallow the largest unchewed piece of meat.

A number of broken safety harnesses worn by window washers who fell to their deaths.

The fetus of a cyclops with six fingers on each hand and six toes on each foot.

Part of the skull of someone who committed suicide by stabbing himself in the head with a pair of scissors; the entry wound is clearly visible along with evidence of several half-hearted attempts; the scissors.

Some tattoos, in a jar.

The private portions of sex-crime victims.

A pillow through which bullets were fired in the murder of someone.

A barbell that fell from an eighth-floor apartment window onto a pedestrian's head, killing him.

A photograph of a man who died after sitting on a broken drinking glass; the glass he sat on, still stained with blood.

A bra and girdle worn by a transvestite suicide at the time of his death.

An eight-pound heart that belonged to a man who used to complain of chest pains.

A scalp.

The false eyelashes of a dead transvestite; the curling iron used to groom them.

A postcard-sized color photograph of a fifty-eight-year-old Filipino man who had an enormous, deformed, parasitic human fetus growing out of his back; he refused an operation to remove it.

Various mummified infants.

An incomprehensible but apparently ribald cartoon about the autopsy of a beautiful young woman.

The silicone inserts of a dead transsexual.

The face of an air-crash victim, literally blown off in the explosion.

A book belonging to an air-crash victim, with the victim's nose bone embedded in it.

A piece of skin with shark bites on it.

A sign (not an exhibit) promoting the sale of a book called *Where Death Delights* ($12.50).

Some charred fingertips.

A window gate attached to a 700-volt transformer, used by an apartment dweller to protect his domain; the shoe of a burglar who tried to enter the window, was electrocuted, and hung upside down in the building's air shaft for several hours until he was discovered; photographs from his autopsy.

A large photograph of a dead man slumped on a bed with a bullet wound in his head. On a windowsill above the bed is a sign that says, "STOP WORRYING You'll Never Get Out of This World Alive."   D.O.

---

feel at times like a young girl poring over brides' magazines in hopes of discovering the perfect honeymoon. Comparison-shopping for a place to send one's corpse, like all consumer activities, quickly becomes a joy independent of its actual object. There are many factors to consider.

For example, I knew an elderly man who pledged his body to Harvard. When he died last year, his wife contacted a local funeral home to make the arrangements and was told that it would cost about $1,000 above and beyond the standard fee paid by Harvard. When the widow properly balked (all they had to do was drive the corpse fifty miles), the mortician supplied an eight-page letter justifying his charge. Among other problems, he wrote, was "the possibility that a body may be rejected by the Medical School." This conjures up unwanted images of admissions committees, and obliquely suggests that if my friend had aimed a little lower in the first place, the problem might never have arisen.

Medical schools do reserve the right not to honor pledges. All schools turn down bodies that have been severely burned, for obvious reasons. Other requirements vary. Pennsylvania rejects bodies that are "recently operated on, autopsied, decomposed, obese, emaciated, amputated, infectious, mutilated or otherwise unfit." Contagious diseases are particularly worrisome; anatomists keep a careful watch for Jakob-Creutzfeldt disease, a slow-acting virus that kills not only the occasional medical student but also cannibals who dine on the brains of their victims. All schools, as far as I can tell, accept bodies from which the eyes and thin strips of skin have been removed for transplantation. Removal of major organs, however, is almost always unacceptable, which means that organ donors (see below) generally can't also be cadaver donors. The state of Pennsylvania is more lenient in this regard. Most other schools want their cadavers intact, although the University of Kansas will accept bodies from which no more than "one extremity has been amputated."

Stanford's brochure is full of high sentence and King Jamesian resonances, the sort of prose selective colleges use to dishearten the hoi polloi. One section lists five grounds for rejection, each beginning with the phrase " The Division of Human Anatomy will not accept . . ." One thing the Division of Human Anatomy will not stand for is "the body of a person who died during major surgery," which sounds like the medical equivalent of refusing to cross a picket line. The section concludes, *"In summary, the Division of Human Anatomy reserves the right to refuse any body which is, in the opinion of the Division, unfit for its use."*

"Chances are, you have a long and healthy life to live. But a lot of other people don't. . . ." This strangely comforting thought comes from a pamphlet called "The Gift of Life," published by a Cleveland outfit called Organ Recovery, Inc. Since there's usually no way to tell whether your organs or your whole body will be more useful until When the Time Comes, the wisest course is to promise everything to everyone and leave it to the experts to sort things out later.

Organ donation has been given a lot of publicity in recent years. Drivers' licenses in most states now have tiny organ-pledge forms on the back. These forms don't have much legal meaning. At New York's Columbia Presbyterian Hospital, for instance, no one will remove an organ (or cart away a cadaver to a medical school) unless the next of kin give their consent. You could die with an organ-donor card in every pocket, and another one pasted on your forehead, and still no one would touch you if your current or separated but not divorced spouse, son or daughter twenty-one years of age or older, parent, brother or sister twenty-one years of age or older, said no. Prince Charles carries a donor card; but if he dropped dead (God save the King) at Presbyterian, someone would have to get permission from Lady Di before removing anything. If you want to be an organ donor, carrying a card is much less important than making sure your relatives know your wishes.

No matter how thorough you are about clearing the way, however, the chances are slim that your heart, liver, kidneys, or lungs will ever be transplanted into somebody else. Only about one percent of all the people who die are potential kidney donors, for instance, and kidneys are actually removed from only one in five of these. The reason is that a suitable organ donor is that rarest of individuals, a person in marvelous health who is also, somehow, dead. Major organs for transplantation have to be removed while the donors' hearts are still beating, which means that all major-organ donors are brain-dead hospital patients on artificial respiration. The ideal donor is a young man who has played a game of basketball, run a few miles, and then had a safe dropped on his head.

John M. Kiernan, organ recovery coordinator at Columbia Presbyterian, explains that Karen Ann Quinlan is not a potential organ donor, because she is not dead. She is breathing by herself and there is activity in her brain. Every organ donor must be pronounced utterly and irretrievably deceased by two separate physicians who will not be involved in the ultimate transplantation. They are not goners; they are gone. This requirement is meant to reassure people who fear that signing organ-donor cards is the rough equivalent of putting out Mafia contracts on their own lives. I used to share these fears; now they strike me as silly.

The bookshelves in Kiernan's office hold volumes with titles like *Brain Death: A New Concept or New Criteria?* Nearby are a few test tubes filled with darkish blood. Behind his door is a big blue-and-white picnic cooler that he uses to carry transplantable organs from donors to recipients. Big blue-and-white picnic coolers seem to be the industry standard for moving organs, whether across town or across the country. In a cover story on liver transplants last year, *Life* magazine published a picture of a man hoisting a cooler called a Playmate Plus into the back of a station wagon. The cooler contained a liver packed in ice.

If your major organs don't make it (because, say, you've lived a long time and faded away slowly in the comfort of your own bed), there's still hope for lesser service. Almost anyone can give skin, eyes, bone, often without hurting one's chances of getting into medical school. Small strips of skin (whose removal does not disfigure a cadaver) are used to make dressing for burn victims. These dressings help keep many people alive who might die without them. Several parts of the eye can be transplanted. There are perhaps 50,000 people now blind who would be able to see if enough of us followed the example of Henry Fonda and Arthur Godfrey and donated our corneas. Bone transplants eliminate the need for amputation in many cancer cases. The National Temporal Bone Banks Program of the Deafness Research Foundation collects tiny inner-ear bones and uses them in medical research.

None of these programs will save you burial costs the way donating your whole body will. Nor can you receive money for giving all or part of yourself away. Paying for bodies is widely held to be unseemly and is, in fact, against the law. On the other hand, physicians do not to my knowledge refuse payment for performing transplant operations. Maybe the law ought to be rewritten to include a little sweetener for the people who make the operation possible. On still another hand, the last thing Washington needs right now is a lobby for dead people, who only vote in Texas and Chicago as it is.

To find out more about these programs you can either ask your doctor or write to an organization called The Living Bank, P.O. Box 6725, Houston, Texas 77265. The Living Bank is a clearinghouse for organ and whole-body donation, coordinating anatomical gifts all over the country.

Making intelligent consumer choices usually entails trying out the merchandise. In this case, a test drive is out of the question. But since I had never so much as clapped eyes on an actual dead person before, I asked Columbia's Ernest April if he would give me a tour of his anatomy classroom. He agreed somewhat reluctantly, then led me down precisely the sort of stairway you would expect to be led down on your way to a room full of bodies. The classroom, by contrast, was cool and airy and had a high-priced view of the Hudson River. Blue walls, green floor, bright lights, a big blackboard, a lighted panel for displaying X rays, videotape monitors hanging from the ceiling, lots of enormous sinks for washing up.

Also, of course, the bodies. There seemed to be about thirty of them, each one lying on a metal table and covered with a bright yellow plastic sheet. The only noticeable odor in the room was the odor of new plastic, familiar to anyone who has smelled a beach ball. Since the course was drawing to an end, the shapes beneath the sheets were disconcertingly smaller than expected: as dissection progresses, students tag the parts they're finished with and store them elsewhere. To demonstrate, Dr. April pulled back the yellow sheet on the table nearest us, causing a momentary cessation of my heartbeat and revealing the top of a skull, a set of dentures, a long striated purplish thing, some other things, I'm not sure what else. But no arm, the object of his search. Far across the room, a few students were huddled over a dark form that suggested nothing so much as the week after Thanksgiving. My initial queasiness subsided and, with a sort of overcompensating enthusiasm, I asked if I could bound across the room for a closer look. Dr. April gently persuaded me to stay put. "This is late in the course," he said softly. "It's not particularly pleasant."

Unpleasant, yes; but is it disgusting or unbearable? Many people say they can't stand the thought of being dissected; much better, they say, to be fussed over by a funeral director and eased into a concrete vault, there to slumber intact until awakened by choirs of angels. But death is death, and every body, whether lying on a dissection table, baking in a crematorium, or "reposing" in a $10,000 casket, undergoes a transformation that doesn't lend itself to happy contemplation. In terms of sheer physical preservation, a medical school cadaver is vastly more enduring than the recipient of even the costliest ministrations of a funeral director. No casket ever prevented anyone from following the road that Robert Graves described in *Goodbye to All That*: "The colour of the faces changed from white to yellow-grey, to red, to purple, to green, to black, to slimy." The transformation takes hours, days.

Morticians sew corpses' lips together, bringing the needle out through a nostril. Lips are pinned to gums. Eyes are covered with plastic patches, then cemented shut. Orifices are plugged. To prevent loved ones from belching, howling, or worse as the accumulating gases of deterioration escape through any and all available exits, funeral home employees press hard on the abdomen immediately before and after family "viewings." Makeup is slathered on. Abdomens are drained. Leaks are patched. Unsightly lumps and bulges are trimmed away.

The trouble with death is that *all* the alternatives are bleak. It isn't really *dissection* that appalls; it's mortality. It may be gross to be dissected, but it's no less gross to be burned or buried. There just isn't anything you can do to make being dead seem pleasant and appealing. And barring some great medical breakthrough involving interferon, every single one of us is going to die. We should all swallow hard and face the facts and do what's best for the people who will follow us.

Which is why you would think that doctors, who spend their entire lives swallowing hard and facing facts, would be the eagerest anatomical donors of all. But they are not. Of all the people I interviewed for this article—including several heads of anatomical donation programs, a number of medical students, physicians, even the chief medical examiner of New York—only *one* of them, Ernest W. April, had pledged any part of his body to scientific study or transplantation. And April is a Ph.D., not an M.D. "I don't know of any medical student who is going to give his body," a medical student told me.

Do doctors know something? Does it, maybe, *hurt* ? Of course not. Every profession lives in secret horror of its own methods. Most reporters I know can't stand the idea of being interviewed. But society would crumble if we weren't occasionally better than those who believe themselves to be our betters.

Morbid humor at their expense is one thing future cadavers worry about. Medical schools are aware of this and take great pains to keep jokes to a minimum. Still, a certain amount of horsing around is inevitable. Michael Meyers, the man who played Ali McGraw's brother in *Goodbye, Columbus* and went on to become a physician, described some dissection hijinks in a book called *Goodbye Columbus, Hello Medicine.* "By the second week of gross anatomy," Meyers wrote, "it was interesting to notice which members of the class really rolled up their sleeves and dug in (no pun intended—although one group of students did nickname their cadaver 'Ernest,' so they could always say they were 'digging in Ernest') . . ." and so on and so on. This is a level of comedy that I do not, to be perfectly frank, find intimidating. And a cadaver donor who wanted to have the last laugh could arrange to have an obscene or hilarious message ("Socialized Medicine?") tattooed across his chest. Beat them to the punchline. Humorous tattoos don't seem to be grounds for rejection, even at Stanford.

As for dissection itself, it's about what you would expect. "You work through the text," says a young woman just beginning her residency, "and by Halloween you've gotten to the hands. Well, we had a girl in our group who wanted to be a surgeon, and she did the most amazing thing. She dissected off the skin *in one piece.* It was like a golve. It was beautiful. And then there was mine. It looked like someone had been cracking walnuts. Little flecks, you know? And then this graduate student comes up and says, 'Have you found the recurrent branch of the medial nerve?' And I start looking through my pile . . ."

A first dissection, like a sexual initiation, is likely to be a botched job: long on theory and good intentions, short on practical knowhow. Results improve with practice, but early impressions linger. No wonder medical students don't like the idea of being dissected. For many of them, anatomy class is their first real experience of death. Maybe it's a good thing if physicians develop, right from the beginning, an overpowering abhorrence of cadavers. We are all better served if our physicians devote their energies to keeping us from turning into the things they hated to dissect in medical school. Anatomy classes, in a sense, trick grade-grubbing premeds into developing something like a reverence for human life.

Donating one's body is an act of courage, but it's not a martyrdom. Medical students may not immediately comprehend the magnitude of the gift, but so what? I confess I sort of like the idea of one day inhabiting the nightmares of some as yet (I hope) unborn medical student. And if my contribution means that my neighborhood mortician will go to bed hungry, shuffling off to his drafty garret in the Fit-A-Fut coffin shoes I decided not to buy, then so much the better. Dying well is the best revenge.

QUESTIONS

1. At what sort of audience is the essay apparently aimed? How do you know?

2. The ads on pages 344, 349, and 350 have single purposes, but "Rest in Pieces" seems to have several: to persuade readers to a course of action, to inform them about a subject, and to argue against something. Persuade to do what? Inform about what? Argue against what?

3. In what ways does the essay attempt to change readers' attitudes?

4. Is Owens' use of lurid details effective? Explain.

5. Evaluate the essay. Is it convincing? Does the author provide enough backing? Does the author rely largely on an appeal to the emotions?

6. Why would *Harper's*, the magazine in which this essay first appeared, have published it?

MARTIN LUTHER KING, JR.
Letter from Birmingham Jail

Martin Luther King, Jr. (1929–1968), the charismatic Black leader and martyr to an assassin's bullet, was jailed in Birmingham for his activism on behalf of civil rights; while incarcerated, he wrote the letter that follows. Dr. King was founder of the Southern Christian Leadership Conference. He was awarded the Nobel Peace Prize in 1964.

The letter from Birmingham jail has become an American classic, along with such statements about American democracy as Thoreau's "Civil Disobedience" and Lincoln's "Gettysburg Address."

April 16, 1963

MY DEAR FELLOW CLERGYMEN:

While confined here in the Birmingham city jail, I came across your recent statement calling my present activitites "unwise and untimely." Seldom do I pause to answer criticism of my work and ideas. If I sought to answer all the criticisms that cross my desk, my secretaries would have little time for anything other than such correspondence in the course of the day, and I would have no time for constructive work. But since I feel that you are men of genuine good will and that your criticisms are sincerely set forth, I want to try to answer your statement in what I hope will be patient and reasonable terms.

I think I should indicate why I am here in Birmingham, since you have been influenced by the view which argues against "outsiders coming in." I have the honor of serving as president of the Southern Christian Leadership Conference, an organization operating in every southern state, with headquarters in Atlanta, Georgia. We have some eighty-five affiliated organizations across the South, and one of them is the Alabama Christian Movement for Human Rights. Frequently we share staff, educational and financial resources with our affiliates. Several months ago the affiliate here in Birmingham asked us to be on call to engage in a nonviolent direct-action program if such were deemed necessary. We readily consented, and

---

This response to a published statement by eight fellow clergymen from Alabama (Bishop C. C. J. Carpenter, Bishop Joseph A. Durick, Rabbi Hilton L. Grafman, Bishop Paul Hardin, Bishop Holan B. Harmon, the Reverend George M. Murray, the Reverend Edward V. Ramage and the Reverend Earl Stallings) was composed under somewhat constricting circumstances. Begun on the margins of the newspaper in which the statement appeared while I was in jail, the letter was continued on scraps of writing paper supplied by a friendly Negro trusty, and concluded on a pad my attorneys were eventually permitted to leave me. Although the text remains in substance unaltered, I have indulged in the author's prerogative of polishing it for publication. [MLK, Jr.]

when the hour came we lived up to our promise. So I, along with several members of my staff, am here because I was invited here. I am here because I have organizational ties here.

But more basically, I am in Birmingham because injustice is here. Just as the prophets of the eighth century B.C. left their villages and carried their "thus saith the Lord" far beyond the boundaries of their home towns, and just as the Apostle Paul left his village of Tarsus and carried the gospel of Jesus Christ to the far corners of the Greco-Roman world, so am I compelled to carry the gospel of freedom beyond my own home town. Like Paul, I must constantly respond to the Macedonian call for aid.

Moreover, I am cognizant of the interrelatedness of all communities and states. I cannot sit idly by in Atlanta and not be concerned about what happens in Birmingham. Injustice anywhere is a threat to justice everywhere. We are caught in an inescapable network of mutuality, tied in a single garment of destiny. Whatever affects one directly, affects all indirectly. Never again can we afford to live with the narrow, provincial "outside agitator" idea. Anyone who lives inside the United States can never be considered an outsider anywhere within its bounds.

You deplore the demonstrations taking place in Birmingham. But your statement, I am sorry to say, fails to express a similar concern for the conditions that brought about the demonstrations. I am sure that none of you would want to rest content with the superficial kind of social analysis that deals merely with effects and does not grapple with underlying causes. It is unfortunate that demonstrations are taking place in Birmingham, but it is even more unfortunate that the city's white power structure left the Negro community no alternative.

In any nonviolent campaign there are four basic steps: collection of the facts to determine whether injustices exist; negotiation; self-purification; and direct action. We have gone through all these steps in Birmingham. There can be no gainsaying the fact that racial injustice engulfs this community. Birmingham is probably the most thoroughly segregated city in the United States. Its ugly record of brutality is widely known. Negroes have experienced grossly unjust treatment in the courts. There have been more unsolved bombings of Negro homes and churches in Birmingham than in any other city in the nation. These are the hard, brutal facts of the case. On the basis of these conditions, Negro leaders sought to negotiate with the city fathers. But the latter consistently refused to engage in good-faith negotiation.

Then, last September, came the opportunity to talk with leaders of Birmingham's economic community. In the course of the negotiations, certain promises were made by the merchants—for example, to remove the stores' humiliating racial signs. On the basis of these promises, the Reverend Fred Shuttlesworth and the leaders of the Alabama Christian Movement for Human Rights agreed to a moratorium on all demonstrations. As the weeks and months went by, we realized that we were the victims of a broken promise. A few signs, briefly removed, returned; the others remained.

As in so many past experiences, our hopes had been blasted, and the shadow of deep disappointment settled upon us. We had no alternative except to prepare for direct action, whereby we would present our very bodies as a means of laying our case before the conscience of the local and the national community. Mindful of the difficulties involved, we decided to undertake a process of self-purification. We began a series of workshops on nonviolence, and we repeatedly asked ourselves: "Are you able to accept blows without retaliating?" "Are you able to endure the ordeal of jail?" We decided to schedule our direct-action program for the Easter season, realizing that except for Christmas, this is the main shopping period of the year. Knowing that a strong economic-withdrawal program would be the by-product of direct action, we felt that this would be the best time to bring pressure to bear on the merchants for the needed change.

Then it occurred to us that Birmingham's mayoralty election was coming up in March, and we speedily decided to postpone action until after election day. When we discovered that the Commissioner of Public Safety, Eugene "Bull" Connor, had piled up enough votes to be in the run-off, we decided again to postpone action until the day after the run-off so that the demonstrations could not be used to cloud the issues. Like many others, we waited to see Mr. Connor defeated, and to this end we endured postponement after postponement. Having aided in this community need, we felt that our direct-action program could be delayed no longer.

You may well ask: "Why direct action? Why sit-ins, marches and so forth? Isn't negotiation a better path?" You are quite right in calling for negotiation. Indeed, this is the very purpose of direct action. Nonviolent direct action seeks to create such a crisis and foster such a tension that a community which has constantly refused to negotiate is forced to confront the issue. It seeks so to dramatize the issue that it can no longer be ignored. My citing the creation of tension as part of the work of the nonviolent-resister may sound rather shocking. But I must confess that I am not afraid of the word "tension." I have earnestly opposed violent tension, but there is a type of constructive, nonviolent tension which is necessary for growth. Just as Socrates[1] felt that it was necessary to create a tension in the mind so that individuals could rise from the bondage of myths and half-truths to the unfettered realm of creative analysis and objective appraisal, so must we see the need for nonviolent gadflies to create the kind of tension in society

---

[1]The classical Greek philosopher (470?–399 B.C.).

that will help men rise from the dark depths of prejudice and racism to the majestic heights of understanding and brotherhood.

The purpose of our direct-action program is to create a situation so crisis-packed that it will inevitably open the door to negotiation. I therefore concur with you in your call for negotiation. Too long has our beloved Southland been bogged down in a tragic effort to live in monologue rather than dialogue.

One of the basic points in your statement is that the action that I and my associates have taken in Birmingham is untimely. Some have asked: "Why didn't you give the new city administration time to act?" The only answer that I can give to this query is that the new Birmingham administration must be prodded about as much as the outgoing one, before it will act. We are sadly mistaken if we feel that the election of Albert Boutwell as mayor will bring the millennium to Birmingham. While Mr. Boutwell is a much more gentle person than Mr. Connor, they are both segregationists, dedicated to maintenance of the status quo. I have hope that Mr. Boutwell will be reasonable enough to see the futility of massive resistance to desegregation. But he will not see this without pressure from devotees of civil rights. My friends, I must say to you that we have not made a single gain in civil rights without determined legal and nonviolent pressure. Lamentably, it is an historical fact that privileged groups seldom give up their privileges voluntarily. Individuals may see the moral light and voluntarily give up their unjust posture; but, as Reinhold Niebuhr[2] has reminded us, groups tend to be more immoral than individuals.

We know through painful experience that freedom is never voluntarily given by the oppressor; it must be demanded by the oppressed. Frankly, I have yet to engage in a direct-action campaign that was "well timed" in the view of those who have not suffered unduly from the disease of segregation. For years now I have heard the word "Wait!" It rings in the ear of every Negro with piercing familiarity. This "Wait" has almost always meant "Never." We must come to see, with one of our distinguished jurists, that "justice too long delayed is justice denied."

We have waited for more than 340 years for our constitutional and God-given rights. The nations of Asia and Africa are moving with jetlike speed toward gaining political independence, but we still creep at horse-and-buggy pace toward gaining a cup of coffee at a lunch counter. Perhaps it is easy for those who have never felt the stinging darts of segregation to say, "Wait." But when you have seen vicious mobs lynch your mothers and fathers at will and drown your sisters and brothers at whim; when you have seen hate-filled policemen curse, kick and even kill your black brothers

---

[2] American theologian (1892–1971).

and sisters; when you see the vast majority of your twenty million Negro brothers smothering in an airtight cage of poverty in the midst of an affluent society; when you suddenly find your tongue twisted and your speech stammering as you seek to explain to your six-year-old daughter why she can't go to the public amusement park that has just been advertised on television, and see tears welling up in her eyes when she is told that Funtown is closed to colored children, and see ominous clouds of inferiority beginning to form in her little mental sky, and see her beginning to distort her personality by developing an unconscious bitterness toward white people; when you have to concoct an answer for a five-year-old son who is asking: "Daddy, why do white people treat colored people so mean?"; when you take a cross-country drive and find it necessary to sleep night after night in the uncomfortable corners of your automobile because no motel will accept you; when you are humiliated day in and day out by nagging signs reading "white" and "colored"; when your first name becomes "nigger," your middle name becomes "boy" (however old you are) and your last name becomes "John," and your wife and mother are never given the respected title "Mrs."; when you are harried by day and haunted by night by the fact that you are a Negro, living constantly at tiptoe stance, never quite knowing what to expect next, and are plagued with inner fears and outer resentments; when you are forever fighting a degenerating sense of "nobodiness"—then you will understand why we find it difficult to wait. There comes a time when the cup of endurance runs over, and men are no longer willing to be plunged into the abyss of despair. I hope, sirs, you can understand our legitimate and unavoidable impatience.

You express a great deal of anxiety over our willingness to break laws. This is certainly a legitimate concern. Since we so diligently urge people to obey the Supreme Court's decision of 1954 outlawing segregation in the public schools, at first glance it may seem rather paradoxical for us consciously to break laws. One may well ask: "How can you advocate breaking some laws and obeying others?" The answer lies in the fact that there are two types of laws: just and unjust. I would be the first to advocate obeying just laws. One has not only a legal but a moral responsibility to obey just laws. Conversely, one has a moral responsibility to disobey unjust laws. I would agree with St. Augustine[3] that "an unjust law is no law at all."

Now, what is the difference between the two? How does one determine whether a law is just or unjust? A just law is a man-made code that squares with the moral law or the law of God. An unjust law is a code that is out of harmony with the moral law. To put it in the terms of St. Thomas Aquinas:[4] An unjust law is a human law that is not rooted in eternal and

---

[3]Saint Augustine (354–430), church father, theologian, author of *The City of God*.
[4]St. Thomas Aquinas (1225–1274), Italian theologian, author of *Summa Theologica*.

natural law. Any law that uplifts human personality is just. Any law that degrades human personality is unjust. All segregation statutes are unjust because segregation distorts the soul and damages the personality. It gives the segregator a false sense of superiority and the segregated a false sense of inferiority. Segregation, to use the terminology of the Jewish philosopher Martin Buber,[5] substitutes an "I—it" relationship for an "I—thou" relationship and ends up relegating persons to the status of things. Hence segregation is not only politically, economically and sociologically unsound, it is morally wrong and sinful. Paul Tillich[6] has said that sin is separation. Is not segregation an existential expression of man's tragic separation, his awful estrangement, his terrible sinfulness? Thus it is that I can urge men to obey the 1954 decision of the Supreme Court, for it is morally right; and I can urge them to disobey segregation ordinaces, for they are morally wrong.

Let us consider a more concrete example of just and unjust laws. An unjust law is a code that a numerical or power majority group compels a minority group to obey but does not make binding on itself. This is *difference* made legal. By the same token, a just law is a code that a majority compels a minority to follow and that it is willing to follow itself. This is *sameness* made legal.

Let me give another explanation. A law is unjust if it is inflicted on a minority that, as a result of being denied the right to vote, had no part in enacting or devising the law. Who can say that the legislature of Alabama which set up that state's segregation laws was democratically elected? Throughout Alabama all sorts of devious methods are used to prevent Negroes from becoming registered voters, and there are some counties in which, even though Negroes constitute a majority of the population, not a single Negro is registered. Can any law enacted under such circumstances be considered democratically structured?

Sometimes a law is just on its face and unjust in its application. For instance, I have been arrested on a charge of parading without a permit. Now, there is nothing wrong in having an ordinance which requires a permit for a parade. But such an ordinance becomes unjust when it is used to maintain segregation and to deny citizens the First-Amendment privilege of peaceful assembly and protest.

I hope you are able to see the distinction I am trying to point out. In no sense do I advocate evading or defying the law, as would the rabid segregationist. That would lead to anarchy. One who breaks an unjust law must do so openly, lovingly, and with willingness to accept the penalty. I submit that an individual who breaks a law that conscience tells him is

---

[5]Martin Buber (1878–1965), Jewish theologian.
[6]Paul Tillich (1886–1965), German-born American theologian.

unjust, and who willingly accepts the penalty of imprisonment in order to arouse the conscience of the community over its injustice, is in reality expressing the highest respect for law.

Of course, there is nothing new about this kind of civil disobedience. It was evidenced sublimely in the refusal of Shadrach, Meshach and Abednego to obey the laws of Nebuchadnezzar, on the ground that a higher moral law was at stake. It was practiced superbly by the early Christians, who were willing to face hungry lions and the excruciating pain of chopping blocks rather than submit to certain unjust laws of the Roman Empire. To a degree, academic freedom is a reality today because Socrates practiced civil disobedience. In our own nation, the Boston Tea Party represented a massive act of civil disobedience.

We should never forget that everything Adolf Hitler did in Germany was "legal" and everything the Hungarian freedom fighters did in Hungary was "illegal." It was "illegal" to aid and comfort a Jew in Hitler's Germany. Even so, I am sure that, had I lived in Germany at the time, I would have aided and comforted my Jewish brothers. If today I lived in a communist country where certain principles dear to the Christian faith are suppressed, I would openly advocate disobeying that country's antireligious laws.

I must make two honest confessions to you, my Christian and Jewish brothers. First, I must confess that over the past few years I have been gravely disappointed with the white moderate. I have almost reached the regettable conclusion that the Negro's great stumbling block in his stride toward freedom is not the White Citizen's Counciler or the Ku Klux Klanner, but the white moderate, who is more devoted to "order" than to justice; who prefers a negative peace which is the absence of tension to a positive peace which is the presence of justice; who constantly says: "I agree with you in the goal you seek, but I cannot agree with your methods of direct action"; who paternalistically believes he can set the timetable for another man's freedom; who lives by a mythical concept of time and who constantly advises the Negro to wait for a "more convenient season." Shallow understanding from people of good will is more frustrating than absolute misunderstanding from people of ill will. Lukewarm acceptance is much more bewildering than outright rejection.

I had hoped that the white moderate would understand that law and order exist for the purpose of establishing justice and that when they fail in this purpose they become the dangerously structured dams that block the flow of social progress. I had hoped that the white moderate would understand that the present tension in the South is a necessary phase of the transition from an obnoxious negative peace, in which the Negro passively accepted his unjust plight, to a substantive and positive peace, in which all men will respect the dignity and worth of human personality. Actually, we who engage in nonviolent direct action are not the creators of tension. We merely bring to the surface the hidden tension that is already alive. We bring it out in the open, where it can be seen and dealt with. Like a boil that can never be cured so long as it is covered up but must be opened with all its ugliness to the natural medicines of air and light, injustice must be exposed, with all the tension its exposure creates, to the light of human conscience and the air of national opinion before it can be cured.

In your statement you assert that our actions, even though peaceful, must be condemned because they precipitate violence. But is this a logical assertion? Isn't this like condemning a robbed man because his possession of money precipitated the evil act of robbery? Isn't this like condemning Socrates because his unswerving commitment to truth and his philosophical inquiries precipitated the act by the misguided populace in which they made him drink hemlock?[7] Isn't this like condemning Jesus because his unique God-consciousness and never-ceasing devotion to God's will precipitated the evil act of crucifixion? We must come to see that, as the federal courts have consistently affirmed, it is wrong to urge an individual to cease his efforts to gain his basic constitutional rights because the quest may precipitate violence. Society must protect the robbed and punish the robber.

I had also hoped that the white moderate would reject the myth concerning time in relation to the struggle for freedom. I have just received a letter from a white brother in Texas. He writes: "All Christians know that the colored people will receive equal rights eventually, but it is possible that you are in too great a religious hurry. It has taken Christianity almost two thousand years to accomplish what it has. The teachings of Christ take time to come to earth." Such an attitude stems from a tragic misconception of time, from the strangely irrational notion that there is something in the very flow of time that will inevitably cure all ills. Actually, time itself is neutral; it can be used either destructively or constructively. More and more I feel that the people of ill will have used time much more effectively than have the people of good will. We will have to repent in this generation not merely for the hateful words and actions of the bad people but for the appalling silence of the good people. Human progress never rolls in on wheels of inevitability; it comes through the tireless efforts of men willing to be co-workers with God, and without this hard work, time itself becomes an ally of the forces of social stagnation. We must use time creatively, in the knowledge that the time is always ripe to do right. Now is the time to make real the promise of democracy and transform our pending national elegy into a creative psalm of brotherhood. Now is the time to lift our national policy from the quicksand of racial injustice to the solid rock of human dignity.

---

[7]Socrates was brought to trial for corrupting youth and for religious heresies, but apparently these charges were simply coverups for political motives. Found guilty, Socrates was condemned to drink hemlock, a poison.

You speak of our activity in Birmingham as extreme. At first I was rather disappointed that fellow clergymen would see my nonviolent efforts as those of an extremist. I began thinking about the fact that I stand in the middle of two opposing forces in the Negro community. One is a force of complacency, made up in part of Negroes who, as a result of long years of oppression, are so drained of self-respect and a sense of "somebodiness" that they have adjusted to segregation; and in part of a few middle-class Negroes who, because of a degree of academic and economic security and because in some ways they profit by segregation, have become insensitive to the problems of the masses. The other force is one of bitterness and hatred, and it comes perilously close to advocating violence. It is expressed in the various black nationalist groups that are springing up across the nation, the largest and best-known being Elijah Muhammad's Muslim movement. Nourished by the Negro's frustration over the continued existence of racial discrimination, this movement is made up of people who have lost faith in America, who have absolutely repudiated Christianity, and who have concluded that the white man is an incorrigible "devil."

I have tried to stand between these two forces, saying that we need emulate neither the "do-nothingism" of the complacent nor the hatred and despair of the black nationalist. For there is the more excellent way of love and nonviolent protest. I am grateful to God that, through the influence of the Negro church, the way of nonviolence became an integral part of our struggle.

If this philosophy had not emerged, by now many streets of the South would, I am convinced, be flowing with blood. And I am further convinced that if our white brothers dismiss as "rabble-rousers" and "outside agitators" those of us who employ nonviolent direct action, and if they refuse to support our nonviolent efforts, millions of Negroes will, out of frustration and despair, seek solace and security in black-nationalist ideologies—a development that would inevitably lead to a frightening racial nightmare.

Oppressed people cannot remain oppressed forever. The yearning for freedom eventually manifests itself, and that is what has happened to the American Negro. Something within has reminded him of his birthright of freedom, and something without has reminded him that it can be gained. Consciously or unconsciously, he has been caught up by the *Zeitgeist*,[8] and with his black brothers of Africa and his brown and yellow brothers of Asia, South America and the Caribbean, the United States Negro is moving with a sense of great urgency toward the promised land of racial justice. If one recognizes this vital urge that has engulfed the Negro

---

[8]*Zeitgeist*: spirit of the time

community, one should readily understand why public demonstrations are taking place. The Negro has many pent-up resentments and latent frustrations, and he must release them. So let him march; let him make prayer pilgrimages to the city hall; let him go on freedom rides—and try to understand why he must do so. If his repressed emotions are not released in nonviolent ways, they will seek expression through violence; this is not a threat but a fact of history. So I have not said to my people: "Get rid of your discontent." Rather, I have tried to say that this normal and healthy discontent can be channeled into the creative outlet of nonviolent direct action. And now this approach is being termed extremist.

But though I was initially disappointed at being categorized as an extremist, as I continued to think about the matter I gradually gained a measure of satisfaction from the label. Was not Jesus an extremist for love; "Love your enemies, bless them that curse you, do good to them that hate you, and pray for them which despitefully use you, and persecute you." Was not Amos an extremist for justice: "Let justice roll down like waters and righteousness like an ever-flowing stream." Was not Paul an extremist for the Christian gospel: "I bear in my body the marks of the Lord Jesus." Was not Martin Luther an extremist: "Here I stand; I cannot do otherwise, so help me God." And John Bunyan: "I will stay in jail to the end of my days before I make a butchery of my conscience." And Abraham Lincoln: "This nation cannot survive half slave and half free." And Thomas Jefferson: "We hold these truths to be self-evident, that all men are created equal . . ." So the question is not whether we will be extremists, but what kind of extremists we will be. Will we be extremists for hate or for love? Will we be extremists for the preservation of injustice or for the extension of justice? In that dramatic scene on Calvary's hill three men were crucified. We must never forget that all three were crucified for the same crime—the crime of extremism. Two were extremists for immorality, and thus fell below their environment. The other, Jesus Christ, was an extremist for love, truth and goodness, and thereby rose above his environment. Perhaps the South, the nation and the world are in dire need of creative extremists.

I had hoped that the white moderate would see this need. Perhaps I was too optimistic; perhaps I expected too much. I suppose I should have realized that few members of the oppressor race can understand the deep groans and passionate yearnings of the oppressed race, and still fewer have the vision to see that injustice must be rooted out by strong, persistent and determined action. I am thankful, however, that some of our white brothers in the South have grasped the meaning of this social revolution and committed themselves to it. They are still all too few in quantity, but they are big in quality. Some—such as Ralph McGill, Lillian Smith, Harry Golden, James McBride Dabbs, Ann Braden and Sarah Patton Boyle—have written about our struggle in eloquent and prophetic terms.

Others have marched with us down nameless streets of the South. They have languished in filthy, roach-infested jails, suffering the abuse and brutality of policemen who view them as "dirty nigger-lovers." Unlike so many of their moderate brothers and sisters, they have recognized the urgency of the moment and sensed the need for powerful "action" antidotes to combat the disease of segregation.

Let me take note of my other major disappointment. I have been so greatly disappointed with the white church and its leadership. Of course, there are some notable exceptions. I am not unmindful of the fact that each of you has taken some significant stands on this issue. I commend you, Reverend Stallings, for your Christian stand on this past Sunday, in welcoming Negroes to your worship service on a nonsegregated basis. I commend the Catholic leaders of this state for integrating Spring Hill College several years ago.

But despite these notable exceptions, I must honestly reiterate that I have been disappointed with the church. I do not say this as one of those negative critics who can always find something wrong with the church. I say this as a minister of the gospel, who loves the church; who was nurtured in its bosom; who has been sustained by its spiritual blessings and who will remain true to it as long as the cord of life shall lengthen.

When I was suddenly catapulted into the leadership of the bus protest in Montgomery, Alabama, a few years ago, I felt we would be supported by the white church. I felt that the white ministers, priests and rabbis of the South would be among our strongest allies. Instead, some have been outright opponents, refusing to understand the freedom movement and misrepresenting its leaders; all too many others have been more cautious than courageous and have remained silent behind the anesthetizing security of stained-glass windows.

In spite of my shattered dreams, I came to Birmingham with the hope that the white religious leadership of this community would see the justice of our cause and, with deep moral concern, would serve as the channel through which our just grievances could reach the power structure. I had hoped that each of you would understand. But again I have been disappointed.

I have heard numerous southern religious leaders admonish their worshipers to comply with a desegregation decision because it is the law, but I have longed to hear white ministers declare: "Follow this decree because integration is morally right and because the Negro is your brother." In the midst of blatant injustices inflicted upon the Negro, I have watched white churchmen stand on the sideline and mouth pious irrelevancies and sanctimonious trivialities. In the midst of a mighty struggle to rid our nation of racial and economic injustice, I have heard many ministers say: "Those are social issues, with which the gospel has no real concern." And I have watched many churches commit themselves to a completely other-worldly religion which makes a strange, un-Biblical distinction between body and soul, between the sacred and the secular.

I have traveled the length and breadth of Alabama, Mississippi and all the other southern states. On sweltering summer days and crisp autumn mornings I have looked at the South's beautiful churches with their lofty spires pointing heavenward. I have beheld the impressive outlines of her massive religious-education buildings. Over and over I have found myself asking: "What kind of people worship here? Who is their God? Where were their voices when the lips of Governor Barnett dripped with words of interposition and nullification? Where were they when Governor Wallace gave a clarion call for defiance and hatred? Where were their voices of support when bruised and weary Negro men and women decided to rise from the dark dungeons of complacency to the bright hills of creative protest?

Yes, these questions are still in my mind. In deep disappointment I have wept over the laxity of the church. But be assured that my tears have been tears of love. There can be no deep disappointment where there is not deep love. Yes, I love the church. How could I do otherwise? I am in the rather unique position of being the son, the grandson and the great-grandson of preachers. Yes, I see the church as the body of Christ. But, oh! How we have blemished and scarred that body through social neglect and through fear of being nonconformists.

There was a time when the church was very powerful—in the time when the early Christians rejoiced at being deemed worthy to suffer for what they believed. In those days the church was not merely a thermometer that recorded the ideas and principles of popular opinion; it was a thermostat that transformed the mores of society. Whenever the early Christians entered a town, the people in power became disturbed and immediately sought to convict the Christians for being "disturbers of the peace" and "outside agitators." But the Christians pressed on, in the conviction that they were "a colony of heaven," called to obey God rather than man. Small in number, they were big in commitment. They were too God-intoxicated to be "astronomically intimidated." By their effort and example they brought an end to such ancient evils as infanticide and gladiatorial contests.

Things are different now. So often the contemporary church is a weak, ineffectual voice with an uncertain sound. So often it is an archdefender of the status quo. Far from being disturbed by the presence of the church, the power structure of the average community is consoled by the church's silent—and often even vocal—sanction of things as they are.

But the judgment of God is upon the church as never before. If today's church does not recapture the sacrificial spirit of the early church, it will lose its authenticity, forfeit the loyalty of millions, and be dismissed as an irrelevant social club with no meaning for the twentieth century. Every day I meet young people whose disappointment with the church has turned into outright disgust.

Perhaps I have once again been too optimistic. Is organized religion too inextricably bound to the status quo to save our nation and the world? Perhaps I must turn my faith to the inner spiritual church, the church within the church, as the true *ekklesia* and the hope of the world. But again I am thankful to God that some noble souls from the ranks of organized religion have broken loose from the paralyzing chains of conformity and joined us as active partners in the struggle for freedom. They have left their secure congregations and walked the streets of Albany, Georgia, with us. They have gone down the highways of the South on tortuous rides for freedom. Yes, they have gone to jail with us. Some have been dismissed from their churches, have lost the support of their bishops and fellow ministers. But they have acted in the faith that right defeated is stronger than evil triumphant. Their witness has been the spiritual salt that has preserved the true meaning of the gospel in these troubled times. They have carved a tunnel of hope through the dark mountain of disappointment.

I hope the church as a whole will meet the challenge of this decisive hour. But even if the church does not come to the aid of justice, I have no despair about the future. I have no fear about the outcome of our struggle in Birmingham, even if our motives are at present misunderstood. We will reach the goal of freedom in Birmingham and all over the nation, because the goal of America is freedom. Abused and scorned though we may be, our destiny is tied up with America's destiny. Before the pilgrims landed at Plymouth, we were here. Before the pen of Jefferson etched the majestic words of the Declaration of Independence across the pages of history, we were here. For more than two centuries our forebears labored in this country without wages; they made cotton king; they built the homes of their masters while suffering gross injustice and shameful humiliation—and yet out of a bottomless vitality they continued to thrive and develop. If the inexpressible cruelties of slavery could not stop us, the opposition we now face will surely fail. We will win our freedom because the sacred heritage of our nation and the eternal will of God are embodied in our echoing demands.

Before closing I feel impelled to mention one other point in your statement that has troubled me profoundly. You warmly commended the Birmingham police force for keeping "order" and "preventing violence." I doubt that you would have so warmly commended the police force if you had seen its dogs sinking their teeth into unarmed, nonviolent Negroes. I doubt that you would so quickly commend the policemen if you were to observe their ugly and inhumane treatment of Negroes here in the city jail;

if you were to watch them push and curse old Negro women and young Negro girls; if you were to see them slap and kick old Negro men and young boys; if you were to observe them, as they did on two occasions, refuse to give us food because we wanted to sing our grace together. I cannot join you in your praise of the Birmingham police department.

It is true that the police have exercised a degree of discipline in handling the demonstrators. In this sense they have conducted themselves rather "nonviolently" in public. But for what purpose? To preserve the evil system of segregation. Over the past few years I have consistently preached that nonviolence demands that the means we use must be as pure as the ends we seek. I have tried to make clear that it is wrong to use immoral means to attain moral ends. But now I must affirm that it is just as wrong, or perhaps even more so, to use moral means to preserve immoral ends. Perhaps Mr. Connor and his policemen have been rather nonviolent in public, as was Chief Pritchett in Albany, Georgia, but they have used the moral means of nonviolence to maintain the immoral end of racial injustice. As T. S. Eliot has said: "The last temptation is the greatest treason: To do the right deed for the wrong reason."

I wish you had commended the Negro sit-inners and demonstrators of Birmingham for their sublime courage, their willingness to suffer and their amazing discipline in the midst of great provocation. One day the South will recognize its real heroes. They will be the James Merediths, with the noble sense of purpose that enables them to face jeering and hostile mobs, and with the agonizing loneliness that characterizes the life of the pioneer. They will be old, oppressed, battered Negro women, symbolized in a seventy-two-year-old woman in Montgomery, Alabama, who rose up with a sense of dignity and with her people decided not to ride segregated buses, and who responded with ungrammatical profundity to one who inquired about her weariness: "My feets is tired, but my soul is at rest." They will be the young high school and college students, the young ministers of the gospel and a host of their elders, courageously and nonviolently sitting in at lunch counters and willingly going to jail for conscience' sake. One day the South will know that when these disinherited children of God sat down at lunch counters, they were in reality standing up for what is best in the American dream and for the most sacred values in our Judaeo-Christian heritage, thereby bringing our nation back to those great wells of democracy which were dug deep by the founding fathers in their formulation of the Constitution and the Declaration of Independence.

Never before have I written so long a letter. I'm afraid it is much too long to take your precious time. I can assure you that it would have been much shorter if I had been writing from a comfortable desk, but what else can one do when he is alone in a narrow jail cell, other than write long letters, think long thoughts and pray long prayers?

If I have said anything in this letter that overstates the truth and indicates an unreasonable impatience, I beg you to fogive me. If I have said anything that understates the truth and indicates my having patience that allows me to settle for anything less than brotherhood, I beg God to forgive me.

I hope this letter finds you strong in the faith. I also hope that circumstances will soon make it possible for me to meet each of you, not as an integrationist or a civil-rights leader but as a fellow clergyman and a Christian brother. Let us all hope that the dark clouds of racial prejudice will soon pass away and the deep fog of misunderstanding will be lifted from our fear-drenched communities, and in some not too distant tomorrow the radiant stars of love and brotherhood will shine over our great nation with all their scintillating beauty.

Yours for the cause of Peace and Brotherhood,
MARTIN LUTHER KING, JR.

QUESTIONS

1. In the paragraph that begins "We have waited for more than 340 years for our Constitutional and God-given rights," King uses very long sentences. Why do you you think he does so when he uses shorter sentences in much of the rest of the piece?

2. Explain King's attitude toward and opinions about the "white moderates."

3. Is King's argument now irrelevant, or does it still apply to the American situation? Explain.

4. Explain King's distinction between just and unjust laws.

5. What was King urging his readers to *do*?

6. Several writers in this collection deal with aspects of the Black experience in America: Eldridge Cleaver (pp. 29–37), Roger Wilkins (pp. 103–08), Claude Brown (pp. 109–17), and Langston Hughes (p. 227). What attitudes and opinions do these writers share?

SUGGESTIONS FOR WRITING

1. Choose an ad that tries to persuade readers to buy a product—anything from candy bars to Cadillacs—and analyze the means that the ad uses. What sort of reader is the ad aimed at? How do you know? Does the ad use data? If so, what kind? How about visual appeal? What kind does it have? What is the basis of the ad's appeal? Does it make promises, bribes, or threats? Does the ad use emotion or logic to persuade its readers? Describe the kind of appeal the ad makes.

2. Find an editorial or column that attempts to persuade readers to take action—for instance, to vote for a certain candidate, to support a bond issue, or to attend a rally. Analyze the argument of the editorial or column. Is the argument based on fact? If so, what kinds of facts, and how are they presented (e.g., as statistical data or as human interest stories)?

3. Choose an issue about which you feel strongly and write an essay aimed at convincing your classmates to take some action.

4. Choose an issue about which you feel strongly, and write an essay aimed at convincing your classmates *not* to take some action.

CHAPTER FIVE

Focus on Style

W*ebster's New Collegiate Dictio-nary* tells us that "style" is the "mode of expressing thought in language: *esp.*: a manner of expression characteristic of an individual, period, school, or nation." And if style is the "mode" (fashion or way) of expressing meaning, then it must have identifiable features. In fact, when we try to characterize a writer's style, we "point to" *syntax (sentence structure), diction (word choice), figurative language (such as metaphor), imagery,* and *voice.* Each of these stylistic concerns will be dealt with in the sections to follow.

From this section, you will undoubtedly gain valuable knowledge about how others write—the syntactic patterns that Hemingway and Faulkner chose, Mark Twain's use of imagery, the irony that characterizes the prose of H. L. Mencken. More important, however, you should learn from your readings ways to make your own writing more effective. Once you understand a device of style, you can employ it in your own writing, thus increasing your own ability to give thought to the nuances and shades that make the difference between expressing *exactly* what you mean and *approximately* what you mean.

Syntax

When you read a sentence such as *Walter eats pasta*, you get one "idea," but you get two "ideas" from the following sentence: *Craving food, Walter eats pasta.* The two "ideas" are something like this: *Walter craves food. Walter eats pasta.* This is to say that in "Craving food, Walter eats pasta," we know who craves food and who eats pasta (Walter, in both cases); thus, we have two ideas in one complete sentence. The syntax of language enables us to combine two or more ideas in one sentence.

By manipulating syntax, we can also create special effects in writing. For example, Abraham Lincoln often used *balanced* sentence structures to emphasize his points:

> Both parties [the North and the South] deprecated war;
>   but one of them would *make* war rather than let the
>   nation survive;
>   and the other would *accept* war rather than let it
>   perish.
>
> *—"Second Inaugural Address"*

The two clauses are almost identical in structure and thus are *balanced*.

Writers also use syntax to change sentence emphasis. For example, in the first sentence *George Burns* receives heavy emphasis, but in the second the emphasis is on *Gracie Allen*.

George Burns—the perfect foil for him was Gracie Allen.

Gracie Allen—she was the perfect foil for George Burns.

In this section of the present chapter, you will gain practice in creating a versatile style: the ability to pack sentences with meaning and to vary sentence arrangement for emphasis.

If the only tool you have is a hammer, you must treat everything as a nail. If your syntactic options are limited, you are forced to pound your ideas out of shape.

TOM WOLFE
From *The Electric Kool-Aid Acid Test*

Tom Wolfe's style in the selection that follows is as unconventional as the people he is writing about. To achieve his effects, Wolfe violates many of the "rules" of punctuation and grammar, but always for a purpose.

As you read the selection, be alert to the unconventional, the kind of syntax that is not used in most writing.

[1] That's good thinking there, Cool Breeze. [2] Cool Breeze is a kid with three or four days' beard sitting next to me on the stamped metal bottom of the open back part of a pickup truck. Bouncing along. Dipping and rising and rolling on these rotten springs like a boat. [3] Out of the back of the truck the city of San Francisco is bouncing down the hill, all those endless staggers of bay windows, slums with a view, bouncing and streaming down the hill. One after another, electric signs with neon martini glasses lit up on them, the San Francisco symbol of "bar"—thousands of neon-magenta martini glasses bouncing and streaming down the hill, and beneath them, hundreds, thousands of people wheeling around to look at this freaking, crazy truck we're in, their white faces erupting from their lapels like marshmallows—streaming and bouncing down the hill—[4] and God knows they've got plenty to look at.

[5] That's why it strikes me as funny when Cool Breeze says very seriously over the whole roar of the thing, "I don't know—when Kesey gets out I don't know if I can come around the Warehouse."

[6] "Why not?"

[7] "Well, like the cops are going to be coming around like all feisty, [8] and I'm on probation, [9] so I don't know."

[10] Well, that's good thinking there, Cool Breeze. [11] Don't rouse the bastids. [12] Lie low—like right now. [13] Right now Cool Breeze is so terrified of the law he is sitting up in plain view of thousands of already startled citizens wearing some kind of Seven Dwarfs Black Forest gnome's hat covered in feathers and fluorescent colors. [14] Kneeling in the truck, facing us, also in plain view, is a half-Ottawa Indian girl named Lois Jennings, with her head thrown back and a radiant look on her face. Also a blazing silver disk in the middle of her forehead alternately exploding with light when the sun hits it or sending off rainbows from the defraction of lines in it. [15] And, oh yeah, there's a long-barreled Colt .45 revolver in her hand, only nobody in the street can tell it's a cap pistol as she pegs away, kheew, kheew, at the erupting marshmallow faces like Debra Paget in . . . in . . .

[16]—Kesey's coming out of jail!

[17] Two more things they are looking at out there are a sign on the rear bumper reading "Custer Died for Your Sins" and, at the wheel, Lois's enamorado Stewart Brand, a thin blond guy with a blazing disk on his forehead too, and a whole necktie made of Indian beads. No shirt, however, just an Indian bead necktie on bare skin and white butcher's coat with medals from the King of Sweden on it.

[18] Here comes a beautiful one, attaché case and all, the day-is-done resentful look [19] and the . . . shoes—how they shine!—[20] and what the hell are those beatnik ninnies—[21] and Lois plugs him in the old marshmallow [22] and he goes streaming and bouncing down the hill . . .

[23] And the truck heaves and billows, blazing silver red and Day-Glo, [24] and I doubt seriously, Cool Breeze, that there is a single cop in all of San Francisco today who does not know that this crazed vehicle is a guerrilla patrol from the dread LSD.

QUESTIONS

1. Unit *1* is a conventional sentence and is punctuated as such. Unit 2 is also just one sentence, but it is punctuated as if it consisted of three sentences. (It would normally be punctuated thus: "Cool Breeze is a kid with three or four days' beard sitting next to me on the stamped metal bottom of the open back part of a pickup truck, bouncing along, dipping and rising and rolling on those rotten springs like a boat.")
   a. Point out other places in the selection where Wolfe uses unconventional punctuation.
   b. What effect does he achieve with this unconventional use of punctuation?
   c. Would it be wise or appropriate for a student writing a paper for a history course to use such idiosyncratic punctuation? Why or why not?
2. Rewrite unit *1* so that punctuation is conventional. What do you gain by the rewrite? What do you lose?
3. Wolfe uses much repetition in our excerpt. Point out where he does this. Why is this stylistic device, in your opinion, effective or ineffective?
4. The following rewrite contains all of the "ideas" that are in unit *14*:

   A half-Ottawa Indian girl named Lois Jennings is kneeling in the truck. She is facing us. She is also in plain view. Her head is thrown back. She has a radiant look on her face. She also has a blazing silver disk in the middle of her forehead. It alternately explodes with light when the sun hits it, or it sends off rainbows from the defraction of lines in it.

Compare the original and the rewrite, and then discuss the following questions:
- a. Which version is easier to read?
- b. Which, in your opinion, is more effective? Why?
- c. Do you think that Wolfe's style, as represented in the original, has anything to do with his success and popularity as a writer? Explain.

5. Wolfe uses many "–ing" phrases: "bouncing and streaming down the hill," "dipping and rising and rolling," "people wheeling around to look," "their white faces erupting from their lapels," and so on. Discuss the effect and usefulness of these phrases.

6. In your own style, rewrite unit 17, but in the process, don't lose any of the ideas.

7. Try to imitate Wolfe's style. Using your own content, write about an incident in the way that Wolfe might.

ERNEST HEMINGWAY

From *A Moveable Feast*

Born in Oak Park, Illinois, in 1899, Ernest Hemingway became one of the great American writers, receiving the Nobel Prize in literature in 1954. Among his memorable works are A Farewell to Arms *(1929),* Death in the Afternoon *(1932),* For Whom the Bell Tolls *(1940), and* The Old Man and the Sea *(1952). His memoir,* A Moveable Feast, *was published in 1964, three years after his death.*

Hemingway is known for his "lean," "economical" prose.

The selection by Tom Wolfe in the chapter is as gaudy and assertive as rock-'n'-roll, but Hemingway's is easy and understated.

Then there was the bad weather. It would come in one day when the fall was over. We would have to shut the windows in the night against the rain and the cold wind would strip the leaves from the trees in the Place Contrescarpe. The leaves lay sodden in the rain and the wind drove the rain against the big green autobus at the terminal and the Café des Amateurs was crowded and the windows misted over from the heat and the smoke inside. It was a sad, evilly run café where the drunkards of the quarter crowded together and I kept away from it because of the smell of dirty bodies and the sour smell of drunkenness. The men and women who frequented the Amateurs stayed drunk all of the time, or all of the time they could afford it, mostly on wine which they bought by the half-liter or liter. Many strangely named apéritifs were advertised, but few people could afford them except as a foundation to build their wine drunks on. The women drunkards were called *poivrottes* which meant female rummies.

The Café des Amateurs was the cesspool of the rue Mouffetard, that wonderful narrow crowded market street which led into the Place Contrescarpe. The squat toilets of the old apartment houses, one by the side of the stairs on each floor with the two cleated cement shoe-shaped elevations on each side of the aperture so a *locataire* would not slip, emptied into cesspools which were emptied by pumping into horse-drawn tank wagons at night. In the summer time, with all windows open, we would hear the pumping and the odor was very strong. The tank wagons were painted brown and saffron color and in the moonlight when they worked the rue Cardinal Lemoine their wheeled, horse-drawn cylinders looked like Braque paintings. No one emptied the Café des Amateurs though, and its yellowed poster stating the terms and penalties of the law against public drunkenness was as flyblown and disregarded as its clients were constant and ill-smelling.

All of the sadness of the city came suddenly with the first cold rains of winter, and there were no more tops to the high white houses as you walked but only the wet blackness of the street and the closed doors of the small shops, the herb sellers, the stationery and the newspaper shops, the midwife—second class—and the hotel where Verlaine had died where I had a room on the top floor where I worked.

It was either six or eight flights up to the top floor and it was very cold and I knew how much it would cost for a bundle of small twigs, three wire-wrapped packets of short, half-pencil length pieces of split pine to catch fire that would warm the room. So I went to the far side of the street to look up at the roof in the rain and see if any chimneys were going, and how the smoke blew. There was no smoke and I thought about how the chimney would be cold and might not draw and of the room possibly filling with smoke, and the fuel wasted, and the money gone with it, and I walked on in the rain. I walked down past the Lycée Henri Quatre and the ancient church of St.-Étienne-du-Mont and the windswept Place du Panthéon and cut in for shelter to the right and finally came out on the lee side of the Boulevard St.-Michel and worked on down it past the Cluny and the Boulevard St.-Germain until I came to a good café that I knew on the Place St.-Michel.

It was a pleasant café, warm and clean and friendly, and I hung up my old waterproof on the coat rack to dry and put my worn and weathered felt hat on the rack above the bench and ordered a *café au lait*. The waiter brought it and I took out a notebook from the pocket of the coat and a pencil and started to write. I was writing about up in Michigan and since it was a wild, cold, blowing day it was that sort of day in the story. I had already seen the end of fall come through boyhood, youth and young manhood, and in one place you could write about it better than in another. That was called transplanting yourself, I thought, and it could be as necessary with people as with other sorts of growing things. But in the story the boys were drinking and this made me thirsty and I ordered a rum St. James. This tasted wonderful on the cold day and I kept on writing, feeling very well and feeling the good Martinique rum warm me all through my body and my spirit.

A girl came in the café and sat by herself at a table near the window. She was very pretty with a face fresh as a newly minted coin if they minted coins in smooth flesh with rain-freshened skin, and her hair was black as a crow's wing and cut sharply and diagonally across her cheek.

I looked at her and she disturbed me and made me very excited. I wished I could put her in the story, or anywhere, but she had placed herself so she could watch the street and the entry and I knew she was waiting for someone. So I went on writing.

The story was writing itself and I was having a hard time keeping up with it. I ordered another rum St. James and I watched the girl whenever I looked up, or when I sharpened the pencil with a pencil sharpener with the shavings curling into the saucer under my drink.

I've seen you, beauty, and you belong to me now, whoever you are waiting for and if I never see you again, I thought. You belong to me and all Paris belongs to me and I belong to this notebook and this pencil.

Then I went back to writing and I entered far into the story and was lost in it. I was writing it now and it was not writing itself and I did not look up nor know anything about the time nor think where I was nor order any more rum St. James. I was tired of rum St. James without thinking about it. Then the story was finished and I was very tired. I read the last paragraph and then I looked up and looked for the girl and she had gone. I hope she's gone with a good man, I thought. But I felt sad.

I closed up the story in the notebook and put it in my inside pocket and I asked the waiter for a dozen *portugaises* and a half-carafe of the dry white wine they had there. After writing a story I was always empty and both sad and happy, as though I had made love, and I was sure this was a very good story although I would not know truly how good until I read it over the next day.

As I ate the oysters with their strong taste of the sea and their faint metallic taste that the cold white wine washed away, leaving only the sea taste and the succulent texture, and as I drank their cold liquid from each shell and washed it down with the crisp taste of the wine, I lost the empty feeling and began to be happy and to make plans.

Now that the bad weather had come, we could leave Paris for a while for a place where this rain would be snow coming down through the pines and covering the road and the high hillsides and at an altitude where we would hear it creak as we walked home at night. Below Les Avants there was a chalet where the pension was wonderful and where we would be together and have our books and at night be warm in bed together with the windows open and the stars bright. That was where we could go. Traveling third class on the train was not expensive. The pension cost very little more than we spent in Paris.

I would give up the room in the hotel where I wrote and there was only the rent of 74 rue Cardinal Lemoine which was nominal. I had written journalism for Toronto and the checks for that were due. I could write that anywhere under any circumstances and we had money to make the trip.

Maybe away from Paris I could write about Paris as in Paris I could write about Michigan. I did not know it was too early for that because I did not know Paris well enough. But that was how it worked out eventually. Anyway we would go if my wife wanted to, and I finished the oysters and the wine and paid my score in the café and made it the shortest way back up the Montagne Ste. Geneviève through the rain, that was now only local weather and not something that changed your life, to the flat at the top of the hill.

"I think it would be wonderful, Tatie," my wife said. She had a gently modeled face and her eyes and her smile lighted up at decisions as though they were rich presents. "When should we leave?"

"Whenever you want."

"Oh, I want to right away. Didn't you know?"

"Maybe it will be fine and clear when we come back. It can be very fine when it is clear and cold."

"I'm sure it will be," she said. "Weren't you good to think of going, too."

QUESTIONS

1. Compare the following rewrite of lines 1 through 7 with the original:

   Then there was the bad weather, which would come in one day when the fall was over, making us shut the windows in the night against the rain, the cold wind stripping the leaves from the trees in the Place Contrescarpe, the leaves lying sodden in the rain and the wind driving the rain against the big green autobus at the terminal.

   Now answer the following questions:
   a. Is the original or the rewrite more effective? Explain.
   b. In what ways is the style of the rewrite similar to Wolfe's style?

2. Choose one of the shorter paragraphs in the selection, and rewrite it in the style of Tom Wolfe. (See pp. 383–85.)

3. Note how many *coordinating conjunctions* ("and," "but," "for," "so," "or") Hemingway uses. It might be said that his style is characterized by *coordination*. What is the effect of his continual use of this device?

4. What device of style do you find in lines 75–77? What is the effect of this device?

5. What is the effect of the very short sentence, line 84, "But I felt sad"? What does this tell you about variety in sentence length?

6. What interests you about the style of the paragraph starting on line 29 and ending on line 34? (Of course, there can be many answers to this question.)

7. Write a "sketch" of one of your own experiences, attempting to imitate the style of Ernest Hemingway.

WILLIAM FAULKNER

From On Privacy

William Faulkner (1897–1962) stands with Ernest Hemingway—who was almost exactly his contemporary—as one of the great American writers. Faulkner's novels are a chronicle of Southern history as seen through the eyes of a great imaginative artist. Among his major works are The Bear, The Sound and the Fury, Light in August, *and* As I Lay Dying. *In 1950, Faulkner was awarded the Nobel prize.*

Faulkner is known for his long sentences and complex syntax. Here is a typical Faulkner sentence from The Bear:

> The dogs were there first, ten of them huddled back under the kitchen, himself and Sam squatting to peer back into the obscurity where they crouched, quiet, the eyes rolling and luminous, vanishing, and no sound, only that effluvium which the boy could not quite place yet, of something more than dog, stronger than dog and not just animal, not just beast even.

Hemingway and Faulkner, then, contrast as stylists, one easy and "natural," the other more elaborately structured and even ornate. However, to characterize them is not to judge them. One is not better than the other; both use the style necessary to achieve the effects they want.

This was the American Dream: a sanctuary on the earth for individual man: a condition in which he could be free not only of the old established closed-corporation hierarchies of arbitrary power which had oppressed him as a mass, but free of that mass into which the hierarchies of church and state had compressed and held him individually thralled and individually impotent.

A dream simultaneous among the separate individuals of men so asunder and scattered as to have no contact to match dreams and hopes among the old nations of the Old World which existed as nations not on citizenship but subjectship, which endured only on the premise of size and docility of the subject mass; the individual men and women who said as with one simultaneous voice: 'We will establish a new land where man can assume that every individual man—not the mass of men but individual men—has inalienable right to individual dignity and freedom within a fabric of individual courage and honorable work and mutual responsibility.'

Not just an idea, but a condition: a living human condition designed to be coeval with the birth of America itself, engendered created and

---

[*Harper's*, July 1955; the text printed here has been taken from Faulkner's typescript.]

simultaneous with the very air and word America, which at that one stroke, one instant, should cover the whole earth with one simultaneous suspiration like air or light. And it was, it did: radiating outward to cover even the old weary repudiated still-thralled nations, until individual men everywhere, who had no more than heard the name, let alone knew where America was, could respond to it, lifting up not only their hearts but the hopes too which until now they did not know—or anyway dared not remember—that they possessed.

A condition in which every man would not only not be a king, he wouldn't even want to be one. He wouldn't even need to bother to need to be the equal of kings because now he was free of kings and all their similar congeries; free not only of the symbols but of the old arbitrary hierarchies themselves which the puppet-symbols represented—courts and cabinets and churches and schools—to which he had been valuable not as an individual but only as that integer, his value compounded in that immutable ratio to his sheer mindless numbers, that animal increase of his will-less and docile mass.

The dream, the hope, the condition which our forefathers did not bequeath to us, their heirs and assigns, but rather bequeathed us, their successors, to the dream and the hope. We were not even given the chance then to accept or decline the dream, for the reason that the dream already owned and possessed us at birth. It was not our heritage because we were its, we ourselves heired in our successive generations to the dream by the idea of the dream. And not only we, their sons born and bred in America, but men born and bred in the old alien repudiated lands, also felt that breath, that air, heard that promise, that proffer that there was such a thing as hope for individual man. And the old nations themselves, so old and so long-fixed in the old concepts of man as to have thought themselves beyond all hope of change, making oblation to that new dream of the new concept of man by gifts of monuments and devices to mark the portals of that inalienable right and hope: 'There is room for you here from about the earth, for all ye individually homeless, individually oppressed, individually unindividualised.'

QUESTIONS

1. The first sentence in the essay might be "diagrammed" thus:

This was the American dream:
    a sanctuary on the earth for individual man:
    a condition in which he could be free
        not only of the old established closed-
        corporation hierarchies of arbitrary power
            which had oppressed him as a mass,

but free of that mass
into which the hierarchies of church and
state had compressed and held him
individually thralled and impotent.

On the basis of this diagram, what can you say about the structure and effect of the sentence?

2. Here is a difficult but suggestive question: How does the following help you understand the structure of our entire excerpt?

This was the American dream . . . A dream simultaneous among the separate individuals of men so asunder and scattered as to have no contact to match dreams and hopes among the old nations of the Old World . . . Not just an idea, but a condition . . . A condition in which every man would not only not be a king, he wouldn't even want to be one.

3. What prominent stylistic feature do you find in this passage from paragraph 5?

The dream, the hope, the condition which our forefathers did not bequeath to us, their heirs and assigns, but rather bequeathed us, their successors, to the dream and the hope.

4. What stylistic devices do Wolfe, Hemingway and Faulkner have in common?

5. What is the effect on the reader of Faulkner's elaborate syntax?

6. Explain why the elaborate syntax does or does not fit the purpose of Faulkner's essay. In other words, is Faulkner's style appropriate to his message?

7. In a "Faulknerian" style, explain one of your beliefs—about religion, government, family, art, sports, or any other topic that has special significance for you.

Diction

All of the following sentences convey approximately the same information, but they are quite different in their effects:

1. We didn't chow down at seven.   COLLOQUIAL
2. We didn't eat at seven.   INFORMAL SPOKEN AND WRITTEN
3. We didn't dine at seven.   INFORMAL WRITTEN
4. We did not dine at seven.   FORMAL WRITTEN

Even though these examples, out of context, are artificial, they do illustrate the point about diction: word choice, much like choice in wardrobe, has social consequences.

The first sentence would normally appear in writing only as dialogue, for colloquial language is characteristically spoken, not written. The second sentence could well appear either in speech or in writing: the contraction "didn't" is one mark of informality, and the verb "eat" is a common usage. Probably the third sentence would occur in speech, but in somewhat formal situations. For most of us, the verb "dine" is not common usage. The fourth sentence is typical of formal written usage, with its avoidance of the contraction and its use of the somewhat "snooty" verb "dine."

Jargon is another important aspect of diction. Every trade and profession has its specialized vocabulary, with which the "insiders" are completely familiar, but which often sounds like a foreign language to "outsiders." Thus, linguists speak of "suprasegmental phonemes," "extraposition transformations," and "deep structures"; plumbers know about P-traps, ells, and T's; and, as everyone knows, computers involve a whole dictionary of jargon, from a specialized meaning of "menu" through "software" and "hardware."

To be sure, there are other ways to cut the pie of usage, but the point here is simply this: diction (or word choice) is an important element of style. For example, Abraham Lincoln wrote:

Four score and seven years ago our fathers brought forth on this continent a new nation, conceived in liberty, and dedicated to the proposition that all men are created equal.

He *did not* write:

> Eighty-seven years ago our ancestors established on this continent a new country, thought up in liberty and pledged to the idea that all men are made equal.

The words convey approximately the same information, but the effect is quite different.

The following selections will provide you with examples of the stylistic consequences of diction.

FLANNERY O'CONNOR

From *The Habit of Being: Letters of Flannery O'Connor*

Mary Flannery O'Connor (1925–1964) was born in Georgia and educated to the
Women's College of Georgia and the State University of Iowa, where she took a
Master of Fine Arts degree. Like Faulkner, O'Connor used the South as both the
setting and the theme of her works, which portray the comedy and the tragedy of the
region. A victim of the disease lupus, she spent the last ten years of her life as an
invalid on her mother's Georgia farm.

As you read this selection, note O'Connor's choice of words and the effect that
her diction has on you as a reader.

To "A."

29 November 56

Sunday morning I read the thing in the paper that said what the play
was about, and I decided that just couldn't be mine and that if it was, I
better not see it. I'm sure it couldn't have been from what you say, because
my contract specifically stated that I was to get story credit. If I don't I can
sue them for a million bucks and buy my mama a jeep with nylon
cushions.

Nobody with any connections at Doubleday or any connection with
the O. Henry has notified me about the O. Henry prize but according to [a
friend] at Davidson's I am going to get it . . . Don't tell me that bird
announced it over that program when I read? It would be mighty funny if it
weren't true and people thought I had spread the word. Well I didn't. But
if I am going to get it, fine and dandy, as I think it is $300 untaxable
dollars . . . The enclosed from Powers on the subject of "Greenleaf." I'll
look up the letters from C.J. and send them to you if I can produce them
out of my purgatorial filing system. Actually, I haven't much idea what
those sonnets mean. I guess you'd have to sit down and read them every
day for a month—but the point is, you probably could sit down and read
them every day for a month—so I conclude they're real poetry . . .

I was honestly able to say that I thought [B.] should keep on writing his
stories and that he should send these two out—which is what he allowed
he wanted to know. I think, as a matter of fact, that he has a natural gift for
presenting a scene without strain. Anybody who talks as much as he does
and as much about trivia could hardly help having a facility for fiction, a
lot of which depends on the ability to mimic the social scene. He didn't tell
me anything about what he meant them to mean so I wasn't troubled with
thinking that dancing one had any deep level—everything in it is quite

well *seen*. If he deludes himself into thinking it is full of symbols, all well and good, but it certainly occurred to me. I liked the one about the funeral better as there was potentially more to it and all the separate scenes were quite good. I wasn't sure it hung together so well but I am afraid to give advice on such things as I am seldom sure. Anyway, I think [he] can achieve a certain gracefulness in writing stories . . .

QUESTIONS

1. Find examples of words and phrases that are, in your opinion, either colloquial or informal.
2. Why do you think O'Connor used colloquial language in her letters to friends?
3. Do you find any evidence of *regionalism* (that is, Southern diction) or *dialect* in this selection?
4. Is it fair to say that Miss O'Connor's diction ranges over several levels, from colloquial to formal? Give examples.
5. What is the overall effect in this letter of O'Connor's diction?
6. In a letter to a friend, use the diction of either a *dialect* that you know or of some *region*.
7. In another letter to a friend, use current *slang*.

JACOB BRONOWSKI
The Hidden Structure

*Jacob Bronowski (1908–1974) was a British mathematician who attempted to
establish a philosophical basis for scientific research. In 1945 he was a member of a
commission sent to Japan to report on the effects of the atomic bombs. Bronowski
was a gifted interpreter of science for laypersons, as his television series "The Ascent
of Man" demonstrated. Among his books and many scientific publications* Science
and Human Values *(1958) perhaps best characterizes its author's concerns.*

*As you read the selection, try to answer this question: for what sort of readers
was Bronowski writing?*

> It is with fire that blacksmiths iron subdue
> Unto fair form, the image of their thought:
> Nor without fire hath any artist wrought
> Gold to its utmost purity of hue.
> Nay, nor the unmatched phoenix lives anew,
> Unless she burn.
>
> Michelangelo, *Sonnet 59*

> What is accomplished by fire is alchemy, whether in the furnace or kitchen stove.
>
> Paracelsus

There is a special mystery and fascination about man's relation to fire,
the only one of the four Greek elements that no animal inhabits (not even
the salamander). Modern physical science is much concerned with the
invisible fine structure of matter, and that is first opened by the sharp
instrument of fire. Although that mode of analysis begins several thousand
years ago in practical processes (the extraction of salt and of metals, for
example) it was surely set going by the air of magic that boils out of the fire:
the alchemical feeling that substances can be changed in unpredictable
ways. This is the numinous quality that seems to make fire a source of life
and a living thing to carry us into a hidden underworld within the material
world. Many ancient recipes express it.

> Now the substance of cinnabar is such that the more it is heated, the more
> exquisite are its sublimations. Cinnabar will become mercury, and passing
> through a series of other sublimations, it is again turned into cinnabar, and
> thus it enables man to enjoy eternal life.

This is the classic experiment with which the alchemists in the Middle
Ages inspired awe in those who watched them, all the way from China to

Spain. They took the red pigment, cinnabar, which is a sulphide of mercury, and heated it. The heat drives off the sulphur and leaves behind an exquisite pearl of the mysterious silvery liquid metal mercury, to astonish and strike awe into the patron. When the mercury is heated in air it is oxidised and becomes, not (as the recipe thought) cinnabar again, but an oxide of mercury that is also red. Yet the recipe was not quite mistaken; the oxide can be turned into mercury again, red to silver, and the mercury to its oxide, silver to red, all by the action of heat.

It is not an experiment of any importance in itself, although it happens that sulphur and mercury are the two elements of which the alchemist before AD 1500 thought the universe was composed. But it does show one important thing, that fire has always been regarded not as the destroying element but as the transforming element. That has been the magic of fire.

I remember Aldous Huxley talking to me through a long evening, his white hands held into the fire, saying, 'This is what transforms. These are the legends that show it. Above all, the legend of the Phoenix that is reborn in the fire, and lives over and over again in generation after generation.' Fire is the image of youth and blood, the symbolic colour in the ruby and cinnabar, and the ochre and haematite with which men painted themselves ceremonially. When Prometheus in Greek mythology brought fire to man, he gave him life and made him into a demigod—that is why the gods punished Prometheus.

QUESTIONS

1. Point out examples of diction that would allow you to characterize this passage as "formal."

2. In the selection, are there any words that you have never encountered before? What are they? What do they mean? How did you determine their meaning, from context or otherwise?

3. What is the Prometheus legend and how does it relate to Bronowski's point?

4. Who is Aldous Huxley? Why does Bronowski assume that his readers will know?

5. On the basis of diction, allusions, and subject matter, what sort of audience do you think Bronowski was aiming at?

Figurative Language

Language can be either figurative or literal. The figurative expression *night's candles* means literally "stars." It might seem, at first glance, that figurative language is nothing but poetic, unnecessary decoration that is stuck onto language by people who really don't want to say what they mean. It turns out, however, that figurativeness is an indispensable property of language; without figures, many ideas would be difficult or even impossible to express, and it is doubtful that some kinds of thought can proceed at all without figurativeness.

The most important kind of figurative language is *metaphor*. Basically, a metaphor is a comparison between two essentially unlike things. Thus, *George is a bull* is a metaphor meaning, among other things, that George is strong and virile. But most metaphors are a good deal more complex and provocative than this one.

A *simile* is a kind of metaphor that makes a comparison through the use of *like* or *as*: Hercules fought *like* a lion in the battle.

Another important figure of speech is *irony*. The ironic effect comes about when the reader realizes that the author intends something other than what she or he actually says. If George is the worst student in the class, and the professor says, "George is certainly gifted in this subject," the professor is undoubtedly being ironic.

There are other figures of speech, hundreds of them in fact, such as *overstatement* and *understatement*. But the purpose here is not to survey all possible figures of speech; it is, rather, to demonstrate how figurative language helps convey meanings and to aid you in using figures effectively.[1]

---

[1]Adapted from *The Contemporary Writer*, First Edition, by W. Ross Winterowd (New York: Harcourt Brace Jovanovich, 1975).

WALLACE STEGNER
From *Beyond the Hundredth Meridian*

Born in Lake Mills, Iowa, in 1909, Wallace Stegner is a man of letters and a teacher. After taking his Ph.D. at the University of Iowa in 1935, he held positions at Augustana College, University of Utah, University of Wisconsin, Harvard, and Stanford.

The subtitle of the book from which the following selection is taken reveals its subject: John Wesley Powell and the Second Opening of the West. *It was Powell who explored the Colorado and navigated the river through what is now called the Grand Canyon.*

Other books by Stegner are The City of the Living *(1956),* A Shooting Star *(1961),* Wolf Willow *(1963), and* The Spectator Bird *(1976).*

The thing that many western boys called their education would have seemed to [Henry] Adams a deprivation, so barren was it of opportunities and so pitiful were its methods and equipment. Considered in any way but in terms of its results in men and women, it *was* a deprivation. But the men it produced over a period of several generations showed such a family resemblance that until immigration drowned them under they constituted a strong regional type, and their virtues as exemplified in a Lincoln or a Mark Twain force the conclusion that this crude society with its vulgar and inadequate culture somehow made noble contributions to mankind. John Wesley Powell, without being a Lincoln or a Mark Twain, was of that persuasion, one of a great company. It is worth looking for a moment at how he was made.

It is easy enough to summarize: he was made by wandering, by hard labor, by the Bible, by an outdoor life in small towns and on farms, by the optimism and practicality and democracy of the frontier, by the occasional man of learning and the occasional books he met, by country schools and the ill-equipped cubs or worn-out misfits who taught them, by the academies and colleges with their lamentable lacks and their industry and their hope, by the Methodism of his father and the prevailing conviction that success came from work and only to the deserving. If there were not many opportunities, if the cultural darkness was considerable, it was also true that in that darkness any little star showed as plainly as a sun.

A homemade education did something to the people who acquired it, and a homemade education was not the exclusive invention of the western settlements. Any rural area, once frontier, retained some of the stamp: the boyhood of a Thurlow Weed[1] or a John Burroughs or a Jay Gould in

---

[1]Thurlow Weed (1797–1882), American journalist and political leader. John Burroughs (1837–1921), American naturalist and author. Jay Gould (1836–1892), American financial speculator.

upstate New York was not greatly different from the boyhood of a Lincoln or a Garfield or a John Muir in the Midwest. But in the Midwest, over immense regions of a peculiar homogeneity in climate, geography, people, and economic status, the homemade education was typical, and it was made more typical by the way in which successive westering waves repeated the whole process in new country. Ohio and Kentucky repeated the backwoods experience of Massachusetts and New York and Pennsylvania; Indiana repeated Ohio; Illinois and Wisconsin and Michigan repeated Indiana; Iowa and Minnesota and Missouri repeated Illinois and Wisconsin; the Dakotas and Nebraska and Kansas repeated, or tried to repeat, Iowa and Minnesota.

QUESTIONS

1. Try to express the ideas in the following sentence without using metaphors:

   But the men it produced over a period of several generations showed such a family resemblance that until immigration drowned them under they constituted a strong regional type, and their virtue as exemplified in a Lincoln or a Mark Twain force the conclusion that this crude society with its vulgar and inadequate culture somehow made noble contributions to mankind.

   a. How difficult was it to eliminate metaphors?
   b. Discuss the losses or gains in the "literal" version.

2. What is the "literal" meaning of the following metaphorical statement: "If there were not many opportunities, if the cultural darkness was considerable, it was also true that in that darkness any little star showed as plainly as the sun"?

3. At first glance, the phrase "homemade education" might not seem metaphorical, but, of course, it is. Explain it.

4. Find other "hidden" metaphors in the passage.

5. Does science use metaphors? Explain.

6. Using metaphors to convey your ideas, write a brief paper about your own education.

Robertson Davies
The Decorums of Stupidity

Robertson Davies was born in 1913 in Thamesville, Ontario, and was educated in Canada and at Oxford. From 1938 to 1940, he was an actor and teacher at the Old Vic theater in London. After returning to Canada, he entered a career as a university teacher and most recently was master of Massey College, University of Toronto. Davies is a prolific writer of fiction, plays and criticism.

As you read the selection, pay careful attention to the methods that Davies uses to make his point clear, and notice also the acid tone of the piece.

Not all rapid reading is to be condemned. Much that is badly written and grossly padded must be read rapidly and nothing is lost thereby. Much of the reading that has to be done in the way of business should be done as fast as it can be understood. The ideal business document is an auditor's report; a good one is finely edited. But the memoranda, the public-relations pieces, the business magazines, need not detain us. Every kind of prose has its own speed, and the experienced reader knows it as a musician knows Adagio from Allegro. All of us have to read a great deal of stuff which gives us no pleasure and little information, but which we cannot wholly neglect; such reading belongs in that department of life which Goldsmith called "the decorums of stupidity." Books as works of art are no part of this duty-reading.

Books as works of art? Certainly; it is thus that their writers intend them. But how are these works of art used?

Suppose you hear of a piece of recorded music which you think you might like. Let us say it is an opera of Benjamin Britten's—*The Turn of the Screw.* You buy it, and after dinner you put it on your record player. The scene is one of bustling domesticity: your wife is writing to her mother, on the typewriter, and from time to time she appeals to you for the spelling of a word; the older children are chattering happily over a game, and the baby is building, and toppling, towers of blocks. The records are long-playing ones, designed for 33 revolutions of the turntable per minute; ah, but you have taken a course in rapid listening, and you pride yourself on the speed with which you can hear, so you adjust your machine to play at 78 revolutions a minute. And when you find your attention wandering from the music, you skip the sound arm rapidly from groove to groove until you come to a bit that appeals to you. But look—it is eight o'clock, and if you are to get to your meeting on time, Britten must be choked off. So you speed him up until a musical pause arrives, and then you stop the machine, marking the place so that you can continue your appreciation of *The Turn of the Screw* when next you can spare a few minutes for it.

Ridiculous? Of course, but can you say that you have never read a book in that fashion?

One of the advantages of reading is that it can be done in short spurts and under imperfect conditions. But how often do we read in conditions which are merely decent, not to speak of perfection? How often do we give a book a fair chance to make its effect with us?

QUESTIONS

1. In the third paragraph, Davies presents an elaborate *analogy*, comparing reading with what? (With analogy, we explain one thing in terms of another.) How does Davies' analogy explain the kind of reading that he is talking about? In your opinion, is the analogy effective?

2. In what sense is the analogy in the third paragraph like a metaphor? Is the analogy actually a metaphor?

3. With an analogy (or extended metaphor, if you prefer that term), describe and analyze some activity with which you are familiar, as Davies uses analogy to describe and analyze the act of reading.

MARK TWAIN
From *The Autobiography*

Samuel Langhorne Clemens (1835–1910), who adopted the pen-name Mark Twain, needs no introduction to readers throughout the world. The following chapter from The Autobiography *is reprinted in its entirety—not merely as an example and teaching device, but as a marvelous piece of writing to be enjoyed for its own sake.*

As you read, notice how vividly Mark Twain captures the details of sound, smell, taste, sight, touch, and also be alert to his gentle, tolerant humor.

The country schoolhouse was three miles from my uncle's farm. It stood in a clearing in the woods and would hold about twenty-five boys and girls. We attended the school with more or less regularity once or twice a week, in summer, walking to it in the cool of the morning by the forest paths and back in the gloaming at the end of the day. All the pupils brought their dinners in baskets—corn dodger, buttermilk and other good things—and sat in the shade of the trees at noon and ate them. It is the part of my education which I look back upon with the most satisfaction. My first visit to the school was when I was seven. A strapping girl of fifteen, in the customary sunbonnet and calico dress, asked me if I "used tobacco"—meaning did I chew it. I said no. It roused her scorn. She reported me to all the crowd and said:

"Here is a boy seven years old who can't chaw tobacco."

By the looks and comments which this produced I realized that I was a degraded object; I was cruelly ashamed of myself. I determined to reform. But I only made myself sick; I was not able to learn to chew tobacco. I learned to smoke fairly well but that did not conciliate anybody and I remained a poor thing and characterless. I longed to be respected but I never was able to rise. Children have but little charity for one another's defects.

As I have said, I spent some part of every year at the farm until I was twelve or thirteen years old. The life which I led there with my cousins was full of charm, and so is the memory of it yet. I can call back the solemn twilight and mystery of the deep woods, the earthy smells, the faint odors of the wild flowers, the sheen of rain-washed foliage, the rattling clatter of drops when the wind shook the trees, the far-off hammering of woodpeckers and the muffled drumming of wood pheasants in the remoteness of the forest, the snapshot glimpses of disturbed wild creatures scurrying through the grass—I can call it all back and make it as real as it ever was, and as blessed. I can call back the prairie, and its loneliness and peace, and a vast hawk hanging motionless in the sky, with his wings spread wide and the blue of the vault showing through the fringe of their end feathers. I can see the woods in their autumn dress, the oaks purple, the hickories washed with gold, the maples and the sumachs luminous with crimson fires, and I can hear the rustle made by the fallen leaves as we plowed through them. I can see the blue clusters of wild grapes hanging among the foliage of the saplings, and I remember the taste of them and the smell. I know how the wild blackberries looked, and how they tasted, and the same with the paw-paws, the hazelnuts, and the persimmons; and I can feel the thumping rain, upon my head, of hickory nuts and walnuts when we were out in the frosty dawn to scramble for them with the pigs, and the gusts of wind loosed them and sent them down. I know the stain of blackberries, and how pretty it is, and I know the stain of walnut hulls, and how little it minds soap and water, also what grudged experience it had of either of them. I know the taste of maple sap, and when to gather it, and how to arrange the troughs and the delivery tubes, and how to boil down the juice, and how to hook the sugar after it is made, also how much better hooked sugar tastes than any that is honestly come by, let bigots say what they will. I know how a prize watermelon looks when it is sunning its fat rotundity among pumpkin vines and "simblins"; I know how to tell when it is ripe without "plugging" it; I know how inviting it looks when it is cooling itself in a tub of water under the bed, waiting; I know how it looks when it lies on the table in the sheltered great floor space between house and kitchen, and the children gathered for the sacrifice and their mouths watering; I know the crackling sound it makes when the carving knife enters its end, and I can see the split fly along in front of the blade as the knife cleaves its way to the other end; I can see its halves fall apart and display the rich red meat and the black seeds, and the heart standing up, a luxury fit for the elect; I know how a boy looks behind a yard-long slice of that melon, and I know how he feels; for I have been there. I know the taste of the watermelon which has been honestly come by, and I know the taste of the watermelon which has been acquired by art. Both taste good, but the experienced know which tastes best. I know the look of green apples and peaches and pears on the trees, and I know how entertaining they are when they are inside of a person. I know how ripe ones look when they are piled in pyramids under the trees, and how pretty they are and how vivid their colors. I know how a frozen apple looks, in a barrel down cellar in the wintertime, and how hard it is to bite, and how the frost makes the teeth ache, and yet how good it is, notwithstanding. I know the disposition of elderly people to select the speckled apples for the children, and I once knew ways to beat the game. I know the look of an apple that is roasting and sizzling on a hearth on a winter's evening, and I know the comfort that comes of eating it hot, along with some sugar and a drench of cream. I know the delicate art and mystery of so cracking hickory nuts and walnuts on a flatiron with a hammer that the kernels will be delivered whole, and I know how the nuts, taken in conjunction with winter apples, cider, and doughnuts, make old people's old tales and old jokes sound fresh and crisp and enchanting, and juggle an evening away before you know what went with the time. I know the look of Uncle Dan'l's kitchen as it was on the privileged nights, when I was a child, and I can see the white and black children grouped on the hearth, with the firelight playing on their faces and the shadows flickering upon the walls, clear back toward the cavernous gloom of the rear, and I can hear Uncle Dan'l telling the immortal tales which Uncle Remus Harris was to gather into his books and charm the world with, by and by; and I can feel again the creepy joy which quivered through me when the time for the ghost story of the "Golden Arm" was reached—and the sense of regret, too, which came over me, for it was always the last story of the evening and there was nothing between it and the unwelcome bed.

I can remember the bare wooden stairway in my uncle's house, and the turn to the left above the landing, and the rafters and the slanting roof over my bed, and the squares of moonlight on the floor, and the white cold world of snow outside, seen through the curtainless window. I can remember the howling of the wind and the quaking of the house on stormy nights, and how snug and cozy one felt, under the blankets, listening; and how the powdery snow used to sift in, around the sashes, and lie in little ridges on the floor and make the place look chilly in the morning and curb the wild desire to get up—in case there was any. I can remember how very dark that room was, in the dark of the moon, and how packed it was with ghostly stillness when one woke up by accident away in the night, and forgotten sins came flocking out of the secret chambers of the memory and wanted a hearing; and how ill chosen the time seemed for this kind of business; and how dismal was the hoo-hooing of the owl and the wailing of the wolf, sent mourning by on the night wind.

I remember the raging of the rain on that roof, summer nights, and how pleasant it was to lie and listen to it, and enjoy the white splendor of the lightning and the majestic booming and crashing of the thunder. It was a very satisfactory room, and there was a lightning rod which was reachable from the window, an adorable and skittish thing to climb up and down, summer nights, when there were duties on hand of a sort to make privacy desirable.

I remember the 'coon and 'possum hunts, nights, with the negroes, and the long marches through the black gloom of the woods, and the excitement which fired everybody when the distant bay of an experienced dog announced that the game was treed; then the wild scramblings and stumblings through briers and bushes and over roots to get to the spot; then the lighting of a fire and the felling of the tree, the joyful frenzy of the dogs and the negroes, and the weird picture it all made in the red glare—I remember it all well, and the delight that everyone got out of it, except the 'coon.

I remember the pigeon seasons, when the birds would come in millions and cover the trees and by their weight break down the branches. They were clubbed to death with sticks; guns were not necessary and were not used. I remember the squirrel hunts, and prairie-chicken hunts, and wild-turkey hunts, and all that; and how we turned out, mornings, while it was still dark, to go on these expeditions, and how chilly and dismal it was, and how often I regretted that I was well enough to go. A toot on a tin horn brought twice as many dogs as were needed, and in their happiness they raced and scampered about, and knocked small people down, and made no end of unnecessary noise. At the word, they vanished away toward the woods, and we drifted silently after them in the melancholy gloom. But presently the gray dawn stole over the world, the birds piped up, then the sun rose and poured light and comfort all around, everything was fresh and dewy and fragrant, and life was a boon again. After three hours of tramping we arrived back wholesomely tired, overladen with game, very hungry, and just in time for breakfast.

QUESTIONS

1. This selection illustrates the power of concrete detail in writing. Point out instances of sense details: sight, touch, smell, hearing, taste.

2. Concrete details create *images*. What are some of the major images in this excerpt?

3. In your opinion, why are sense details often so important?

4. In paragraph three, Mark Twain gives a direct quote: "Here is a boy seven years old who can't chaw tobacco." Suppose he presented the quote indirectly, like this: "The girl reported to the crowd that I was a boy of seven who couldn't chew tobacco." What is lost?

5. Discuss the humor that you find in the chapter from the *Autobiography.*

6. What common and prominent device of style do you find throughout the long fourth paragraph?

7. What is your reaction to Mark Twain's unique diction, as in the following examples?
   a. I know the stain of blackberries, and how pretty it is, and I know the stain of walnut hulls, and how little it *minds* soap and water, also what *grudged experience* it had of either of them.
   b. I know the look of green apples and peaches and pears on the trees, and I know how *entertaining* they are when they are inside of a person.
   Find other examples of Mark Twain's wonderfully inventive use of language.

8. Using imagery to present your impressions, describe and discuss a place with which you are familiar. (Don't hesitate to use Mark Twain as a model for imitation.)

LEWIS THOMAS
From *Note from a Universe Watcher*

Lewis Thomas (born 1913) is president of the Memorial Sloan Kettering Cancer Center and is the author of notable books and articles, including Lives of a Cell: Notes of a Biology Watcher *(1974) and* The Medusa and the Snail: More Notes of a Biology Watcher *(1979).*

Thomas received his M.D. degree at Harvard in 1937 and has been on the medical faculties at Johns Hopkins, Tulane, University of Minnesota, New York University, Yale, and Cornell.

Somewhere, on some remote planet set at precisely the right distance   1
from a star of just the right magnitude and right temperature, on the other side of our galaxy, there is at this moment a committee nearing the end of a year-long study of our own tiny, provincial solar system. The intelligent beings of that place are putting their signatures (numbers of some sort, no doubt) to a paper which asserts, with finality, that life is out of the question here and the place is not worth an expedition. Their instruments have detected the presence of that most lethal of all gases, oxygen, and that is the end of that. They had planned to come, bringing along mobile factories for manufacturing life-giving ammonia, but what's the use of risking strangulation.

The only part of this scenario that I really believe in is that committee.   2
I take it as an article of faith that this is the most fundamental aspect of nature that we know about. If you are going to go looking for evidences of life on other celestial bodies, you need special instruments with delicate sensors for detecting the presence of committees. If there is life there, you will find consortia, collaborating groups, working parties, all over the place.

QUESTIONS

1. *Webster's New Collegiate Dictionary* defines irony thus:

> a pretense of ignorance and of willingness to learn from another assumed in order to make the other's false conceptions conspicuous by adroit questioning . . . the use of words to express something other than and esp. the opposite of the literal meaning. . . .

In light of this definition, explain how you know that Lewis Thomas is being ironic.

2. Perhaps the most famous ironic writing in the Anglo-American tradition is "A Modest Proposal," by Jonathan Swift. If you have not read that great esssay, you should do so. In any case, explain Swift's irony, and compare it with Lewis Thomas's.

3. In a brief piece of writing, present one of your opinions ironically.

H. L. MENCKEN

From *Libido for the Ugly*

Henry Lewis Mencken (1880–1956) is best known for his great study The American Language *(1919), but he was a practicing journalist in Baltimore for most of his life, and he was one of the founders of a popular magazine, now defunct,* The American Mercury.

As the following selection indicates, Mencken was a trenchant social critic with a biting wit, but he saved most of his venom for the American middle class, which he called the "booboisie."

As you read the selection, note Mencken's iconoclastic wit and his critical attitude toward American society.

On a Winter day, not long ago, coming out of Pittsburgh on one of the swift, luxurious expresses of the eminent Pennsylvania Railroad, I rolled eastward for an hour through the coal and steel towns of Westmoreland county. It was familiar ground; boy and man, I had been through it often before. But somehow I had never quite sensed its appalling desolation. Here was the very heart of industrial America, the center of its most lucrative and characteristic activity, the boast and pride of the richest and grandest nation ever seen on earth—and here was a scene so dreadfully hideous, so intolerably bleak and forlorn that it reduced the whole aspiration of man to a macabre and depressing joke. Here was wealth beyond computation, almost beyond imagination—and here were human habitations so abominable that they would have disgraced a race of alley cats.

I am not speaking of mere filth. One expects steel towns to be dirty. What I allude to is the unbroken and agonizing ugliness, the sheer revolting monstrousness, of every house in sight. From East Liberty to Greensburg, a distance of twenty-five miles, there was not one in sight from the train that did not insult and lacerate the eye. Some were so bad, and they were among the most pretentious—churches, stores, warehouses, and the like—that they were downright startling: one blinked before them as one blinks before a man with his face shot away. It was as if all the more advanced Expressionist architects of Berlin had been got drunk on *Schnapps*, and put to matching aberrations. A few masterpieces linger in memory, horrible even there: a crazy little church just west of Jeannette, set like a dormer-window on the side of a bare, leprous hill; the headquarters of the Veterans of Foreign Wars at Irwin; a steel stadium like a huge rat-trap somewhere further down the line. But most of all I recall the general effect—of hideousness without a break. There was not a single decent house within eye-range from the Pittsburgh suburbs to the Greensburg yards. There was not one that was not misshapen, and there was not one that was not shabby.

The country itself is not uncomely, despite the grime of the endless mills. It is, in form, a narrow river valley, with deep gullies running up into the hills. It is thickly settled, but not noticeably overcrowded. There is still plenty of room for building, even in the larger towns, and there are very few solid blocks. Nearly every house, big and little, has space on all four sides. Obviously, if there were architects of any professional sense or dignity in the region, they would have perfected a châlet to hug the hillsides—a châlet with a high-pitched roof, to throw off the heavy Winter snows, but still essentially a low and clinging building, wider than it was tall. But what have they done? They have taken as their model a brick set on end. This they have converted into a thing of dingy clapboards, with a narrow, low-pitched roof. And the whole they have set upon thin, preposterous brick piers. What could be more appalling? By the hundreds and thousands these abominable houses cover the bare hillsides, like gravestones in some gigantic and decaying cemetery. On their deep sides they are three, four and even five stories high; on their low sides they bury themselves swinishly in the mud. Not a fifth of them are perpendicular. They lean this way and that, hanging on to their bases precariously. And one and all they are streaked in grime, with dead and eczematous patches of paint peeping through the streaks.

Now and then there is a house of brick. But what brick! When it is new it is the color of a fried egg. When it has taken on the patina of the mills it is the color of an egg long past all hope or caring. Was it necessary to adopt that shocking color? No more than it was necessary to set all of the houses on end. Red brick, even in a steel town, ages with some dignity. Let it become downright black, and it is still sightly, especially if its trimmings are of white stone, with soot in the depths and the high spots washed by the rain. But in Westmoreland they prefer that uremic yellow, and so they have the most loathsome towns and villages ever seen by mortal eye.

I awarded this championship only after laborious research and incessant prayer. I have seen, I believe, all of the most unlovely towns of the world; they are all to be found in the United States. I have seen the mill towns of decomposing New England and the desert towns of Utah, Arizona and Texas. I am familiar with the back streets of Newark, Brooklyn, Chicago and Pittsburgh, and have made bold scientific explorations to Camden, N. J. and Newport News, Va. Safe in a Pullman, I have whirled through the gloomy, Godforsaken villages of Iowa and Kansas, and the malarious tide-water hamlets of Georgia. I have been to Bridgeport, Conn., and to Los Angeles. But nowhere on this earth, at home or abroad, have I seen anything to compare to the villages that huddle along the line of the Pennsylvania from the Pittsburgh yards to Greensburg. They are incomparable in color, and they are incomparable in design. It is as if some titanic and aberrant genius, uncompromisingly inimical to man, had devoted all the ingenuity of Hell to the making of them. They show grotesqueries of ugliness that, in retrospect, become almost diabolical. One cannot imagine mere human beings concocting such dreadful things, and one can scarcely imagine human beings bearing life in them.

Are they so frightful because the valley is full of foreigners—dull, insensate brutes, with no love of beauty in them? Then why didn't these foreigners set up similar abominations in the countries that they came from? You will, in fact, find nothing of the sort in Europe—save perhaps in a few putrefying parts of England. There is scarcely an ugly village on the whole Continent. The peasants, however poor, somehow manage to make themselves graceful and charming habitations, even in Italy and Spain. But in the American village and small town the pull is always toward ugliness, and in that Westmoreland valley it has been yielded to with an eagerness bordering upon passion. It is incredible that mere ignorance should have achieved such masterpieces of horror. There is a voluptuous quality in them—the same quality that one finds in a Methodist sermon or an editorial in the New York *Herald-Tribune*. They look deliberate.

On certain levels of the human race, indeed, there seems to be a positive libido for the ugly, as on other and less Christian levels there is a libido for the beautiful. It is impossible to put down the wallpaper that defaces the average American home of the lower middle class to mere inadvertence, or to the obscene humor of the manufacturers. Such ghastly designs, it must be obvious, give a genuine delight to a certain type of mind. They meet, in some unfathomable way, its obscure and unintelligible demands. They caress it as "The Palms" caresses it, or the art of Landseer, or the ecclesiastical architecture of the United Brethren. The taste for them is as enigmatical and yet as common as the taste for vaudeville, dogmatic theology, sentimental movies, and the poetry of Edgar A. Guest. Or for the metaphysical speculations of Arthur Brisbane. Thus I suspect (though confessedly without knowing) that the vast majority of the honest folk of Westmoreland county, and especially the 100% Americans among them, actually admire the houses they live in, and are proud of them. For the same money they could get vastly better ones, but they prefer what they have got. Certainly there was no pressure upon the Veterans of Foreign Wars at Irwin to choose the dreadful edifice that bears their banner, for there are plenty of vacant buildings along the trackside, and some of them are appreciably better. They might, indeed, have built a better one of their own. But they chose that clapboarded horror with their eyes open, and having chosen it, they let it mellow into its present shocking depravity. They like it as it is: beside it, the Parthenon would no doubt offend them. In precisely the same way the authors of the rat-trap stadium that I have mentioned made a deliberate choice. After painfully designing and erecting it, they made it perfect in their own sight by putting a completely impossible pent-house, painted a staring yellow, on top of it. The effect is truly appalling. It is that of a fat woman with a black eye. It is that of a Presbyterian grinning. But they like it.

Here is something that the psychologists have so far neglected: the love of ugliness for its own sake, the lust to make the world intolerable. Its habitat is the United States. Out of the melting pot emerges a race which hates beauty as it hates truth. The etiology of this madness deserves a great deal more study than it has got. There must be causes behind it; it arises and flourishes in obedience to biological laws, and not as a mere act of God. What, precisely, are the terms of those laws? And why do they run stronger in America than elsewhere? Let some honest *Privat Dozent* apply himself to the problem.

QUESTIONS

1. In your own words, characterize the "voice" of the author of this selection.

2. If satire is, according to *Webster's New Collegiate Dictionary,* "a literary work holding up human vices or follies to ridicule and scorn," in what sense is this selection a satire?

3. How does Mencken feel about the material used to build the houses in the coal and steel towns? What images and words does he use to convey his feelings?

4. What is Mencken's final judgment about the United States? Do you think that he is overstating his case (using the figure of speech called hyperbole) to make his point, or do you think that he literally believes that Americans love ugliness for its own sake?

5. Using Mencken as a model, write a satire on some place, person, or institution that you think needs reforming.

Glossary of Rhetorical Terms

abstraction   An abstract idea is one such as "democracy," "truth," or "love." In effective writing, abstract ideas are usually developed through concrete examples or instances. For example, a writer might explain "democracy" by describing a town meeting, convey his idea of "truth" by relating an instance when someone told the whole truth at great personal cost when a bit of fibbing would have saved that person, or show the meaning of "love" by referring to the example of Jesus.

allusion   A reference to a historical or literary figure or event. In "The Love Song of J. Alfred Prufrock," T. S. Eliot has his narrator say, "I am not Prince Hamlet, nor was meant to be"—an allusion to Shakespeare's *Hamlet*. If the reader knows that work, the allusion carries a great deal of meaning. Allusion, then, is a way of packing a few words with meaning.

analogy   Comparing two items that are alike in certain ways. The object of analogy is to use the familiar to explain the unfamiliar. For example, drawing an analogy between a computer and the human brain might help a reader who knows about computers understand something about the brain.

argument   A line of reasoning and evidence to establish a point and thus change a reader's mind. Well-known arguments are Thoreau's "Civil Disobedience" and Martin Luther King, Jr.'s "Letter from Birmingham Jail."

autobiography   The story of one's life, or part of one's life, written by him- or herself. Examples of autobiography from world literature are those by St. Augustine, Benvenuto Cellini, Benjamin Franklin, and Henry Adams.

balance   Elements of sentences are obviously equivalent, balancing one another grammatically, as in the following examples:

> There is no sense in hoping
>   for that which already exists
>   or
>   for that which cannot be.
> > —*Erich Fromm*

> We go
>   wherever the wind blows,
> we take
>   whatever we find.
> > —*Danilo Dolci*

biography A life history, an account of a life, written by someone other than the subject, in contrast with *autobiography*, which is written by the subject. Carl Sandburg's biography of Lincoln is an example.

colloquial language Language that might be used in conversation but that would seem out of place in formal writing. For instance, "I haven't got any money" is colloquial. In formal usage, the idea would be expressed as "I have no money."

composing process The methods, techniques, and procedures one uses in writing. Sometimes, for the sake of discussion, the composing process is broken down into *prewriting* (gathering material, getting ideas, planning), *writing* (the actual composition of the piece), and *postwriting* (revising to improve the development, structure, and style of the paper and proofreading to eliminate mechanical errors).

dialogue In its most common meaning, the conversation among two or more characters in a story, novel, narrative poem, or play. Dialogue, then, is what the characters say directly to one another. Dialogue can also mean "conversation" in a wider sense: reasoning together about some topic.

diary A day-by-day record of events, usually not intended to be read by others. Diaries are often so personal their writers do not wish to share them. Journals are less personal and are often intended for publication.

diction Word-choice. Diction can be slangy ("The *bubble-gummers* from the high school crowded the arcade"), formal, uneducated ("Them guys ain't here yet"), and so on.

essay A discussion in writing of a limited topic. The *informal* essay is marked by the personality of the writer, who reveals personal experiences and opinions; the *formal* essay is less personal. Typically, the essay deals with a topic of interest to a broad audience among the educated.

exploratory essay An essay in which the writer comes to no conclusion, but reveals many facets of his or her topic. The purpose of the exploratory essay is to open up subjects for consideration and discussion.

exposition Writing (usually prose) that *explains*, *explores*, or *argues*. In explanation, the writer gives *reasons for* (an opinion, an idea, or an action) or tells *how to* do something. In argument, the writer establishes a point through the use of logic and evidence. (See "argument.")

expository writing See "exposition."

figurative language A special use of language for effect. Such *figures of speech* as *alliteration* (repetition of initial word sounds) rely on the structure or sound of language. In the following example, note the alliterative repetition of "b" and "f":

The fair *breeze blew*, the white *foam flew*,
The *furrow followed free*.

But such figures of speech as metaphor rely on language meaning for their effect. We know that the following example is a *metaphor* because what it literally says does not square with reality:

> All the world's a stage
> And all the men and women merely players.
> —*William Shakespeare*

Figurative language, then, might be divided into figures of structure and figures of meaning.

form   The reader's over-all sense of the structure of a piece of writing. If writing is formless, the reader cannot determine which points go where or what is the main point.

formal usage   See "diction."

hyperbole   A figure of speech in which *overstatement* is used for effect. For example,

> He [a lion] roared so loud, and looked so wonderous grim,
> His very shadow durst not follow him.
> —*Alexander Pope*

image   In writing, an image is a passage that gives the reader a sense impression: the sounds of a busy street corner, the sight of a secluded valley in the country, the smell of a delicatessen. Writers often define their *abstractions* through imagery.

informal usage   The kind of language that one finds in personal letters and in some informal essays, characterized by use of contractions (for example, "isn't" rather than "is not"), everyday vocabulary as opposed to specialized word use (for example, "daily" rather than "quotidian," "doctor" rather than "physician"). Informal usage in writing is similar to the conversational style of educated people.

irony   A conflict between what the speaker or writer says literally and what he or she actually means. For example, in a great ironic essay, "A Modest Proposal," Jonathan Swift "recommended" that children be slaughtered and used for food as a way of alleviating poverty in eighteenth-century Ireland. His actual purpose, however, was to draw attention to the desperate economic situation that left people in the direst poverty.

journal   A daily record of one's thoughts, impressions, and activities. Writers often compose journals with the intention of publishing them later; thus, the journal is less personal and intimate than the *diary*. Writers also use their journals as sources of ideas for writing.

memoir   A form of writing in which people reflect on and report events from their past lives. Prominent statesmen and generals often write memoirs after they have retired.

metaphor   A stated or implied equation of one item with another. In metaphor, the equation is not literal, but figurative. For example, "An automobile is a vehicle" is not a metaphorical statement, because an automobile literally is a vehicle. However, "An automobile is a sub-urban steed" is a metaphor, because an auto is not literally a horse. The purpose of metaphor is to reveal emotional or allusive meanings. For example, in calling an automobile a "suburban steed," one evokes the fiery mounts that knights rode into battle. Metaphors are not always of the form "X is Y." "The candles of the night" is a metaphor meaning "stars," and can be "translated" as "stars are the candles of the night."

meter   The rhythmic patterns in poetry. The four meters used in English verse are *iambic* (one unstressed and one stressed syllable)

Had WE but WORLD eNOUGH and TIME

trochaic (a stressed syllable followed by an unstressed syllable)

DOUble, DOUble, TOIL and TROUble

anapestic (two unstressed syllables followed by a stressed syllable)

Like a CHILD from the WOMB, like a GHOST from the TOMB

dactylic (rarely used)   (a stressed syllable followed by two unstressed syllables, as in the word "manikin": MAN i kin).

narrative   An account of a sequence of events; a story, either factual or fictional.

overstatement   A figure of speech which uses exaggeration for effect. The technical term is "hyperbole." For example, to express the monstrous-ness of her act in murdering the king, Lady Macbeth says that she will never be able to wash his blood from her hand and that the spot will make all the seas red:

. . . this my hand will rather
The multitudinous seas incarnadine,
Making the green one red.

parallelism   Grammatical equivalence. For example, when a sentence has a compound subject, grammatically equivalent elements fill the subject slots. Thus, the following sentence is not parallel:

To ski, hiking, and *movies* are George's favorite ways of relaxing.

"To ski" is an infinitive, "hiking" is a present participle, and "movies" is a noun. The following revision makes the sentence parallel:

Skiing, hiking, and *going* to movies are George's favorite ways of relaxing.

personal essay   An essay in which the personality of the writer is prominent. Often the personal essay has autobiographical and anecdotal content. It is more intimate and often less tightly structured than the formal essay. See "essay."

personal writing   Writing in which the focus of interest is largely on the writer. We read personal writing, such as autobiographies and journals, not so much to learn about the world "out there" as to learn about and get to know the writer.

persuasion   Writing or speech that is intended to bring about some action. It is like *argument* in that it attempts to establish the validity of its claims and points of view, but it goes beyond argument in that it urges some course of action on the reader.

revision   Improving a piece of writing by adding necessary material, cutting out unnecessary material, rearranging for better effect, and substituting more effective material for less effective. Revision should not be confused with *proofreading*, in which the writer "cleans up" mechanical errors such as misspellings and improper punctuation.

rhetoric   According to Aristotle, the art of finding the available means of persuasion in regard to any subject whatever. Modern definitions of rhetoric, however, stress its function in fostering understanding among people. To study rhetoric is to study what makes language work in society; thus, rhetoric might be viewed as the global field which deals with language in use.

rhyme   Similarity or identity of sounds in verse. Rhyme usually occurs at the ends of lines:

She was a phantom of *delight*
When first she gleamed upon my *sight*

satire   A blending of a critical attitude with humor and wit. The "take-offs" on political figures that are typical of Monty Python are satire.

sentence structure See "syntax."

simile A figure of speech that, like *metaphor*, equates two items, but, unlike metaphor, uses either "like" or "as" to express the equation. Simile is actually a variation or form of metaphor.

> The inflated style is itself a kind of euphemism. A mass of Latin words falls upon the facts *like* soft snow, blurring the outlines and covering up all details.
>
> —*George Orwell*

slang Terms used to produce an effect such as humor, hipness, or cynicism. Slang is out of place in formal usage. Slang terms are usually short-lived, entering the language for a short period and then expiring. Examples of slang terms that have been used in past years are "Tin Lizzy" for Model-T Ford, "scratch" for money, "hooch" for alcoholic beverages, and "gat" for gun. Slang terms that seem to have established themselves in extremely informal usage are "beat it" and "scram" (for leave) "dough" (for money), "Coke" (for Coca Cola), "con" (for convict).

style The characteristic manner in which a writer expresses his or her ideas. Writers use preferred kinds of syntax or sentence structure, vocabulary that is theirs alone, and unique figures of speech. Just as a person's handwriting has an individual style, so does his or her writing in the broader sense.

syntax Sentence structure. In analyzing syntax, one looks at phrases and clauses. For example, the following sentence consists of one clause (Judith analyzes syntax) modified by a prepositional phrase (With tremendous concentration):

> With tremendous concentration, Judith analyzes syntax.

The main clause consists of a subject (Judith) and a predicate (analyzes syntax). The predicate consists of a verb (analyzes) and its object (syntax). The prepositional phrase consists of a preposition (with), its object (concentration), and an adjective modifying that object (tremendous).

theme 1) a practice writing exercise, usually assigned in a composition class; 2) the central idea in a work. Thus, you can write a *theme* about the *theme* of guilt in *The Scarlet Letter*.

tone The attitude of the author toward his or her subject; the "voice" that comes through in a piece of writing. Thus, the tone can be humorous or cynical, bored or excited, sophisticated or naive.

understatement Most commonly, saying the direct reverse of what one intends and thereby stressing a point. For example, if I say, "God is not unmindful of the plight of his children," I mean that God is extremely aware of that plight. If I say that Reggie Jackson is "a pretty fair hitter," I mean that he is a superb hitter.

vignette   A sketch or essay characterized by vividness and brevity.

voice   The sense that the reader has of the "speaker" in a piece of writing. See "tone."

writing   As distinguished from "handwriting" or "penmanship," the process of projecting meanings through *structures* to an *audience* in a *scene*. Writing and thinking are not separable, and writing is an important instrument of thought. Without writing, there could be no modern technology, no philosophy in the Western sense, and probably no higher mathematics.

Copyrights and Acknowledgments

A 5
B 6
C 7
D 8
E 9
F 0
G 1
H 2
I 3
J 4